Federalism and Internal Conflicts

Series Editors
Soeren Keil
School of Psychology, Politics and Sociology
Canterbury Christ Church University
Canterbury, UK

Eva Maria Belser
University of Freiburg
Freiburg, Switzerland

This series engages in the discussions on federalism as a tool of internal conflict resolution. Building on a growing body of literature on the use of federalism and territorial autonomy to solve ethnic, cultural, linguistic and identity conflicts, both in the West and in non-Western countries, this global series assesses to what extent different forms of federalism and territorial autonomy are being used as tools of conflict resolution and how successful these approaches are.

We welcome proposals on theoretical debates, single case studies and short comparative pieces covering topics such as:

- Federalism and peace-making in contemporary intra-state conflicts
- The link between federalism and democratization in countries facing intra-state conflict
- Secessionism, separatism, self-determination and power-sharing
- Inter-group violence and the potential of federalism to transform conflicts
- Successes and failures of federalism and other forms of territorial autonomy in post-conflict countries
- Federalism, decentralisation and resource conflicts
- Peace treaties, interim constitutions and permanent power sharing arrangements
- The role of international actors in the promotion of federalism (and other forms of territorial autonomy) as tools of internal conflict resolution
- Federalism and state-building
- Federalism, democracy and minority protection

For further information on the series and to submit a proposal for consideration, please get in touch with Ambra Finotello ambra.finotello@palgrave.com, or series editors Soeren Keil soeren.keil@canterbury.ac.uk and Eva Maria Belser evamaria.belser@unifr.ch

More information about this series at
http://www.palgrave.com/gp/series/15730

Martin Belov
Editor

Territorial Politics and Secession

Constitutional and International Law Dimensions

palgrave
macmillan

Editor
Martin Belov
University of Sofia 'St. Kliment Ohridski'
Sofia, Bulgaria

Federalism and Internal Conflicts
ISBN 978-3-030-64401-7   ISBN 978-3-030-64402-4 (eBook)
https://doi.org/10.1007/978-3-030-64402-4

Cover illustration: Westend61 / Getty Images

This Palgrave Macmillan imprint is published by the registered company Springer Nature Switzerland AG.
The registered company address is: Gewerbestrasse 11, 6330 Cham, Switzerland

Praise for *Territorial Politics and Secession*

"The book offers a kaleidoscope of perspectives on a burning topic, which is gradually moving from the rule of force to the rule of law. For this reason, territorial politics and secession are now key aspects in several disciplines. This volume casts light on the most significant debate in legal, political, philosophical and geographical studies and explores some ongoing disputes. A must-read book."

—Francesco Palermo, *University of Verona and Eurac Research, Italy*

"This is a terrific collection of essays on the socio-legal dimensions of territoriality, territorial politics, and secession in comparative constitutional law and international law. The book's strong thematic organisation allows the concerns and contributions of the several disciplines to 'speak to each other' in a rigorous scholarly conversation. The country studies provide fresh analyses of even the most widely discussed cases. The way the book brings doctrinal, theoretical, and empirical analysis of territoriality and secession together is methodologically state-of-the art. It is a major contribution to both research and teaching."

—Asanga Welikala, *University of Edinburgh, UK*

"A collection of scholars from three continents tackle the vital question why, despite the ongoing processes of globalisation and digitalisation, territorial politics including the making of new borders, in particular through secessionist movements, have not simply withered away but gain more and more prominence. This book, due to its multifaceted approach combining (comparative) constitutional law and international law with international relations and conflict management perspectives, offers fresh insight not only from its range of case studies regarding the challenges of secession, humanitarian intervention, ethnofederalism, regionalism or devolution, but also a critical analysis of the underlying key concepts and legal principles and rules of territorial politics such as sovereignty, territorial integrity, non-intervention, or the internal and external self-determination of peoples. This volume is thus a source book for researchers and practicioners alike."

—Joseph Marko, *University of Graz, Austria; former international judge of the Constitutional Court of Bosnia and Herzegovina*

Contents

Notes on Contributors

Punsara Amarasinghe is a PhD candidate in law at Institute of Law, Politics and Development in Sant Anna School for Advanced Studies in Pisa, Italy. He was a visiting researcher at Global Legal Studies Center at University of Wisconsin Madison and held one-year research fellowship at the Faculty of Law at Higher School of Economics in Moscow. He holds LL.M in public international law from South Asian University, New Delhi, India.

Zemelak A. Ayele is an associate professor at the Addis Ababa University, where he is also the Director of the Center for Federal Studies. He received LL.B from Addis Ababa University, Advanced Diploma in Federalism from the Institute of Federalism, Fribourg University, and LL.M and LL.D from the UWC. He has widely written in the area of decentralisation and federalism in Ethiopia and Africa, including a book on 'Local Government in Ethiopia: Advancing development and accommodating ethnic minorities' (Baden-Baden-Nomos Verlagsges). He was a National Research Foundation (NRF) Post-doctoral research fellow under the South African Research Chair in (SARCHi) Multilevel Government, Law and Policy, at the Dullah Omar Institute for Constitutional Law, Governance and Human Rights of the University of the Western Cape (UWC), South Africa. He was also a visiting researcher at the Institute of Federalism, Fribourg University, and the Catholic University of Leuven.

Martin Belov is Professor in Constitutional and Comparative Constitutional Law at the University of Sofia 'St. Kliment Ohridski'. He is

Vice Dean of the University of Sofia 'St. Kliment Ohridski', Faculty of Law responsible for the international relations and digitalization. Martin Belov has been visiting professor at University Paris II Pantheon-Assas (2019), University Roma Tre, Rome, Italy (2019), Goethe-University Frankfurt am Main, Germany (2019), University of Girona, Spain (2019), University 'Pompeu Fabra', Barcelona, Spain (2019), Europa-University Viadrina, Frankfurt/Oder, Germany (2017 and 2018), University of Bari, Italy (2018), European Law and Governance School, Athens (2017–2018), University of Södertorn, Stockholm, Sweden (2017), Scuolla Superiore Sant'Anna, Pisa, Italy (2016), University of Warsaw, Poland (2015), University of Lisbon, Portugal (2012), State University of Milan, Italy (2011), University of Cologne, Germany (2007–2009), and so on. Martin Belov has been project researcher at the Max-Planck Institute for European Legal History, Frankfurt am Main, Germany (2010–2012) and visiting researcher at the Institute for Federalism, Fribourg, Switzerland (2014). He has specialized at the University of Oxford (UK) (2017), Max-Planck Institute for Comparative Public Law and International Law, Heidelberg, Germany (2009), and many other academic institutions. Martin Belov is member of the European Group of Public Law, International Association of Legislation, the Advisory Board of the Central and Eastern European Forum of Young Legal, Political and Social Theorists and other scientific and academic organizations. Martin Belov is member of the scientific boards of many academic journals. He has published 19 books and more than 90 scientific papers.

Emanuel Castellarin is a professor at the University of Strasbourg since 2016. He also teaches at several other universities (Sorbonne Law School – Université Paris 1, Université Paris 2 – Panthéon-Assas, Sciences Po Paris). His publications include a monograph on the participation of the European Union in international economic institutions (2017), a co-edited volume on the Treaty of Versailles (2020) and several articles and book chapters in international economic law, general international law and EU external relations law.

Yonatan T. Fessha is Professor of Law at the University of the Western Cape in South Africa. His teaching and research focuses on examining the relevance of constitutional design in dealing with the challenges of divided societies. He has written widely on matters pertaining to but not limited to federalism, constitutional design, autonomy and politicized ethnicity. His publications include books on "Ethnic diversity and federalism: Constitution making in South Africa and Ethiopia (Ashgate, 2010)" and 'Federalism and courts in Africa: Design and impact in comparative perspective' (co-edited, Routledge, 2020). He has contributed to constitution-building projects, including in Sudan, South Sudan and Yemen. He was a Michigan Grotius Research Scholar at the University of Michigan. He was also a recipient of the Andrew Mellon postdoctoral fellowship. He is a Marie-Curie fellow at the Institute for Comparative Federalism at Eurac Research (Italy).

Mira Kaneva is Assistant Professor in International Law and International Relations at the Faculty of Law, University of Sofia "St. Kliment Ohridski". She is a research associate with the Institute for Security and International Studies and a member of the managing board of Sofia Security Forum. Her research interests encompass international relations theory, international law and ethics, global governance, diplomacy and negotiations, foreign policy analysis and international security.

Costanza Margiotta is Associate Professor of Philosophy and Theory of Law, University of Padua, Italy. She holds a PhD in Legal Theory from the European University Institute, Florence. Her research focuses on secession in international law, European citizenship, codification and interpretation of international law, and on slavery, race and law. She has written widely on these and related areas.

Giuseppe Martinico is Full Professor of Comparative Public Law at the Scuola Superiore Sant'Anna, Pisa. In Pisa he also serves as STALS (Sant'Anna Legal Studies) Editor.
Prior to joining the Scuola Sant'Anna, he was García Pelayo Fellow at the Centro de Estudios Políticos y Constitucionales (CEPC), Madrid, and Max Weber Fellow at the European University Institute, Florence. His research interests cover both comparative and European constitutional law, fields in which he published extensively in international peer-reviewed journals in three languages (English, Italian and Spanish).

Jorge E. Núñez started his academic career teaching Introduction to Law in 1997 in his native Argentina (Universidad Nacional de La Plata). He moved to the United Kingdom where he was awarded his PhD in Law (Manchester). After teaching Jurisprudence in the School of Law, the University of Manchester, he joined Manchester Metropolitan

University as Lecturer in Law in 2013. He has also taught Law in Beijing, China-EU School of Law, in their Double Master Programme. His research interests are varied but he is particularly keen on issues related to legal and political theory and public international law and relations. In one of his books entitled *Sovereignty Conflicts and International Law and Politics* (2017), he combines these interests in a unique form. He offers a solution to sovereignty conflicts such as Gibraltar, Falklands Islands and Kashmir applying the international institution of shared sovereignty as viewed through the lenses of distributive justice principles. His latest book is *Territorial Disputes and State Sovereignty*. International Law and Politics (2020).

Sabrina Ragone is Associate Professor of Comparative Public Law at the University of Bologna and a senior research affiliate of the Max Planck Institute for Comparative Public Law and International Law in Heidelberg (MPIL). She was previously a research fellow at the MPIL and at the Centre for Political and Constitutional Studies in Madrid. She has held research and visiting professor positions in several academic institutions in Europe, as well as in Latin America and the US (Harvard University, Boston College, Texas A&M, among others). Her extensive publications address comparative law methodology and substance proposing innovative perspectives on constitutional adjudication and territorial decentralization. Among her recent books, “Desafíos de la función judicial: un acercamiento desde el derecho público comparado”, Ediciones Olejnik, 2018; “Managing the Euro Crisis: National EU policy coordination in the debtor countries” (edited), Routledge, 2018; “Parlamentarismos y crisis económica: afectación de los encajes constitucionales en Italia y España”, Bosch, 2020.

Maja Sahadžić is a research fellow and guest professor at the University of Antwerp. Her work experience includes earlier academic positions at the universities in Bosnia and Herzegovina, Croatia and the United States of America. She has also worked as a lawyer, consultant, advisor and journalist. So far, she has authored books, book chapters and papers within the field of comparative constitutional law, asymmetrical federalism, multilevel governance, multinational societies, alternative conflict solutions, extreme constitutionalism, diplomacy, and terrorism and security.

Nikos Skoutaris is Associate Professor in EU Law at the University of East Anglia. His research interests lie in the intersection between EU law, comparative constitutional law and conflict resolution theory. He has written extensively on Brexit and its effect on the UK territorial constitution.

Joan Solanes Mullor is Lecturer of Constitutional Law at Pompeu Fabra University, Barcelona, Spain. He was a postdoctoral researcher at the Faculty of Law of Trento University (2015), and he was appointed a visiting scholar at KU Leuven (2013) and a visiting researcher at Harvard Law School (2009). He received his PhD in law from Pompeu Fabra University (2014) and holds an LLM from Harvard Law School (2009). His research areas include institutional design, separation of powers, public regulation and territorial organization of power.

Arenca Trashani specializes in human rights and international law at home and abroad. She is finishing her PhD in international law at Tirana University. From 1995 to 2005 she lectured at the University of Shkodra "Luigj Gurakuqi" international human rights and public international law courses. From 2005 to 2013, she was a member of the Albanian Parliament. She was Member of the Legal Affairs Committee and EU Integration Committee and Head of the Sub-committee on Human Rights. From 2005 to 2007, she was Minister of European Integration. She works as a lecturer of international law and international organisations at the University of "Luigj Gurakuqi", Law Faculty in Shkodra. At the same time she works as an independent expert on various programs on women's rights with UNDP and NDI, as well as on the problems of law and its approximation with European law and European integration issues as an external expert with EU Delegation in Tirana. She has several publications in the field of international law, human rights and European law.

CHAPTER 1

Introduction

Martin Belov

Territory is the ultimate playground of constitutionalism and international relations. Thus, it is of existential relevance also for constitutional and international law. Territory is a fundamental precondition for policy-making. It is simultaneously a strategic political resource, basic framework, furthest limit, and decisive framework of policy-making, polity, and politics. Law is setting the rules of the game, while territory is objectively predetermining their aim, efficiency, and feasibility. Thus, territory is an object of special interest for public law in general and for constitutional and international law in particular.

This book aims at exploring fundamental issues of territorial politics—the politics related to territory and territoriality—which are having huge constitutional and international law relevance. It is multidiscoursive collective enterprise of scholars coming from different fields of public law. The prevailing viewpoints in the book are related to theory of constitutionalism, constitutional and international law, and international relations.

M. Belov (✉)
University of Sofia 'St. Kliment Ohridski', Sofia, Bulgaria
e-mail: mbelov@uni-sofia.bg

M. Belov (ed.), *Territorial Politics and Secession*, Federalism and Internal Conflicts, https://doi.org/10.1007/978-3-030-64402-4_1

Thus, the constitutionalist and public international law discourses are framing the whole approach of the book towards territoriality, territorial politics, and secession. This fact safeguards the conceptual and methodological cohesion of the book structured around important themes of constitutional law, public international law, and theory of international relations.

Another important common denominator for all the chapters in this edited volume is the socio-legal approach used for the accomplishment of the analysis. All contributions offer important insights of the legal foundations of territorial politics. They explore the legal basis of the issues under research looking for answers in constitutional and international law.

Nevertheless, the analysis provided by the contributions to this volume is not limited to the normative or institutional foundations of the issues at stake. They go beyond valid law and explore the 'law in action', the application of law in its socio-legal and political context. They also take into account the theoretical and intellectual-imaginary implications of the legal phenomena under scrutiny. Thus, the book is generally marked by the decisive socio-legal approach to the problems of territorial politics and secession. To sum up, the conceptual and methodological framework of the analysis is based on constitutional and international law discourse founded on socio-legal approach.

The book is thematically focused on the topical problems of territorial politics. One of these issues is of special importance. This is the secession. Consequently, secession as a key problem of constitutional and international territorial politics is well exposed and driven to the front of the range of conceptual issues under research. This is due to the fact that secession is one of the most intriguing contemporary problems of territorial politics producing challenging questions for constitutional and international law theory and cracks and uncertainties for the legal orders that need thorough research and urgent explanation, preferably in comparative and interdisciplinary perspective.

Secession is rather a volatile phenomenon with diverse legal and socio-legal implications. It produces increasing trembling of the constitutional and international law terrain and attracts the attention of public law scholars and political scientists. This is the main reason why the current edited volume is structured around these two key issues—territorial politics as a general, fundamental and framing concept and secession as one of its most visible manifestations requiring urgent conceptual answers that take into account both the requirements of the valid law and the de facto imperatives of the socio-legal context.

Nevertheless, the aim of the book is definitely not limited to secession. It goes well beyond secession offering original analysis of multitude of other forms of territorial politics. Devolution, balancing between integration and disintegration within the conceptual model of regionalism, territorial dispute resolution, humanitarian intervention, and forms of sub-national territorial politics are also discussed in this volume together with self-determination, revolution, referenda for independence, and secession.

The book is based on the following logic. It provides theoretical conceptualisation of territory and territorial politics. Then, it offers critical assessment of territorial politics with a view to important and topical issues such as secession, territorial dispute resolution, and self-determination and with a view to the key constitutional principles—sovereignty, democracy, rule of law, and the protection of human rights.

The book offers novel account on politics of exiting and remaining with a view to national and sub-national secession, direct democratic self-determination, and politics of regionalism. It provides original studies of sub-national constitutionalism with particular attention to ethnocentric nationalism and its impact on territorial politics. The book combines theoretical contributions with comparative research and important case studies. Thus, it offers new theoretical suggestions, provides for comparative schemes promoting better understanding of territorial politics and secession, and contains essential case studies.

It must be mentioned that the case studies are not only informative but also containing key insights for the theory of territorial politics and secession and their comparative legal and socio-legal research. Moreover, the case studies are wide-ranging and not limited to Europe. The book provides insightful analysis of some cases which are already a must for such scientific research, for example, Brexit, the UK devolution (with emphasis on Scotland and Ireland), Catalonia, and the centripetal forces in Northern Italy. It also contains important contributions to the literature devoted to sub-national constitutionalism and ethnocentric models of federalism. Apart from the European case of Bosnia and Herzegovina, there are also chapters devoted to Ethiopia and Sri Lanka. The research of Canadian federalism and the secessionist claims and processes in Quebec completes the comparative picture based on case studies. Hence, the book provides for a balanced approach to the case studies including four European and three non-European (North American, Asian, and African) case studies.

Part I opens the discussion with critical assessment of several issues of paradigmatic and conceptual importance which are then explored in more detail in the subsequent chapters. These are the phenomena of territory, territoriality, and territorial politics, the key issue of secession with its multifaceted nature as both revolutionary and conservative device, and the problems of revolution and devolution in contemporary European territoriality triggering debates on the territorial politics of exiting.

In Chap. 2, some of the key concepts underlying the whole book are critically and reflexively defined. These are the concepts of territory, territoriality, and territorial politics. The chapter offers critical assessment of the conceptualisation of territoriality under the framing paradigms of Westphalian, post-Westphalian, and neo-Westphalian constitutionalism.

Special attention is devoted not only to the crisis of territoriality experienced in recent decades but also to the re-emergence of territoriality during the trend towards re-nationalisation which became visible in the context of the COVID-19 pandemic. The chapter provides an account of the constitutional importance of territorial politics in the age of globalisation and digitalisation. It discusses the impact of these phenomena on territoriality of power and its constitutional and international law implications.

Chapter 3 of the book, written by Costanza Margiotta, is related to the problem of theoretical conceptualisation of secession. The author believes that 'the concept of secession has both a conservative and a revolutionary character'. She proves her thesis exploring secession from the perspective of both internal and external sovereignty. Margiotta devotes special attention to the issues of the impact of secession on territorial integrity and the relationship between secession and peoples' right to self-determination and secession and democracy.

In this regard, her chapter is part of the general discussion on the relation between secession, self-determination, and their impact on democracy and rule of law. This issue is one of the conceptual pillars of the book. However, several chapters are especially focused on this problem. These are the chapters of Joan Solanes Mullor, Emanuel Castellarin, and Giuseppe Martinico. Margiotta's interest of territorial politics of decolonisation and state formation relates her contribution to Chap. 7 written by Emanuel Castellarin while her analysis of borders is connected to the problems of territory and territoriality explored in Chap. 2.

In Chap. 4 Mira Kaneva explores devolution and devolutionary territorial politics. In her account 'devolution in territoriality constitutes a new normality in the networks of interdependence'. Kaneva aims at defining the framework for devolutionary and evolutionary territorial politics. She provocatively defines this as a search for the 'practical and moral "red lines" to devolution in the European context'. Starting with an outline of the main trends in European territorial politics of integration the chapter continues with research on the impact of devolution of constitutional and European orders. The chapter concludes with application of Kaneva's theoretical viewpoints on devolution and exiting in the context of Brexit. Thus, the chapter joins the discussion on Brexit provided also in Chap. 9 by Nikos Skoutaris.

Part II of the book continues the debate on territorial politics focusing it on one of its most important dimensions. It explores the relationship between territorial politics and sovereignty. Sovereignty has always been in an ambiguous relation with self-determination and human rights. Self-determination is both a key aspect of sovereignty and a potential latent threat to the sovereignty of the framing community when accomplished by sub-national communities. Preservation of human rights is a key imperative of constitutional and international law. Sovereignty as a key principle of constitutional law and a key factor in international relations has not always been at ease with human rights, especially the rights of members of distinct sub-national communities.

The tension between sovereignty, self-determination, and human rights is conceptualised in Part II through the prism of different forms of territorial politics having fragile legal standing in international law, for example, humanitarian intervention, or being traditionally problematic as the instruments for territorial dispute resolution. Hence, the contributions published in Part II are rooted mainly in international law. They are tackling problematic phenomena with rather fuzzy standing in international law having also constitutional impact.

The uneasy relationship between sovereignty, self-determination, and human rights is discussed from constitutional law perspective also in Part V of the book. On the basis of important and informative case studies, the authors of the chapters framed by Part V explore the impact of ethno-territorial politics on sovereignty, self-determination, and human rights in the context of sub-national politics.

In Chap. 5 of the book Jorge E. Núñez tries to offer an original account of the relationship between territorial disputes and sovereignty believing that their reconciliation is a matter of intellectual and political strategy. The author stipulates that the comprehensive understanding of state sovereignty and territorial disputes as multilayer and multi-contextual phenomena is the appropriate standpoint for the better explanation of their complexity. Núñez defines the concepts of sovereignty and territorial disputes. He emphasises the need to conceptualise sovereignty not as an absolute concept but as a concept with certain important limitations. In his view this is the way for reconciliation between sovereignty and territorial dispute resolution. However, this is possible only in the context of a global constitutional ordering embedding territorial politics within the context of the pluralism of pluralisms paradigm. Moreover, Núñez outlines the need to take into account all agents of territorial disputes and territorial dispute resolution policy, namely, the individual, the community, and the state.

The chapter not only offers thorough analysis but also is very informative providing multiple examples and case studies of territorial disputes all over the world. It is part of an intellectual discussion related to territorial politics in international relations including also the chapters of Mira Kaneva and Arenca Trashani.

In that regard Chap. 6, written by Arenca Trashani, enriches the international law and international relations arm of the book providing research of the rather disputed and important problem of humanitarian intervention as a form of territorial politics. The author explores the impact of humanitarian intervention on state sovereignty and human rights. She is looking for the possible justifications of this rather problematic and contested method of territorial politics. In that regard, Trashani outlines the main aspects of the theory of humanitarian intervention, explores the United Nations (UN) system of humanitarian intervention, and assesses the unilateral and collective humanitarian interventions. The author also offers critical account on the impact of humanitarian intervention on the right to self-determination.

Part III of the book explores the procedural discourse of territorial politics of independence and secession. It raises important questions related to the impact of self-determination, independence referenda, and secession on democracy and rule of law. The two chapters published in Part III have one but important common denominator. This is the procedural discourse on secession and the importance of the procedure for the accomplishment of secession for maintaining democracy and the rule of law. Both chapters explore the use of referenda for the accomplishment of secession, thus focusing on direct democratic territorial politics. This common issue for both contributions is researched from two different perspectives—the use of referenda in international territorial politics for self-determination (Chap. 7) and the constitutionalisation of secession in the case law of the supreme courts and in the practice of secession referenda (Chap. 8).

Chapter 7, written by Emanuel Castellarin, focuses on independence referenda as a tool for constitutional and international territorial politics. It offers broader account on these referenda going beyond post-colonial situations of self-determination and independence through direct democracy. Castellarin explores the use of direct democracy for international territorial politics and its impact on identity, self-determination, and recognition claims. The main thesis of the author is 'that, in spite of their shortcomings, independence referendums can convey a new conception of the international society, which can be translated into a new vision of self-determination and of territorial structures'. He critically assesses the rather peripheral status of independence referenda in international law apart from decolonisation and post-colonial situations. Castellarin believes 'that independence referendums can indeed contribute to the renewal of self-determination and of territorial politics, provided that procedural standards of international law are developed'.

In Chap. 8 Giuseppe Martinico explores the exit-related conditionality, federalism, and secession. The author provides an insightful analysis of 'the role that the referendum can play in the proceduralisation of secession in federal systems'. The research commences with outline of the process of constitutionalisation of secession. It explores the set of techniques developed by the courts—and more precisely by the Canadian Supreme Court—in order to cope with secession. Martinico reconstructs the steps used by this court to constitutionalise secession in the Canadian constitutional order. In the first part of his chapter Martinico explores 'how to proceduralise secession in light of the notion of "exit-related conditionality"'. The second part of the chapter is devoted to outlining the 'reasons for prudence in the use of referendums in contexts of representative democracy'. Although focusing on the Canadian experience the author sets it in a telling and topical comparative perspective drawing also conclusions with huge importance for the comparative constitutional research on secession.

Part IV of the book brings to the front the stretching of territorial politics between integration and disintegration. It includes three chapters devoted to highly visible and topical case studies of constitutional orders where disintegrative forces massively challenge the integrative territorial politics of the state. Chapter 9 offers an account on Brexit and the secessionist challenges in the UK. Chapter 10 outlines the territorial politics of regionalism in Italy between integration and disintegration. Chapter 11 explores the Catalan secessionists' challenge and the attempts at reconciling their quest for independence and constitutionalism.

Chapter 9, written by Nikos Skoutaris, shows 'how the UK's withdrawal from the European Union (EU) and the relevant implementation policies challenge the fragile balance of the UK territorial constitution'. It explores the challenges to the UK integrity and, vice versa, the variants, preconditions, and procedures for eventual secession of Scotland and Northern Ireland from it.

Skoutaris presents the constitutional foundations of the UK territorial politics with special emphasis on the constitutional framework for the integration of Scotland, Northern Ireland, and Wales. He offers informative and topical outline of the UK territorial constitution. The overview of the process of devolution in the UK is followed by two important questions posed by the author. The first one is how does Brexit challenge devolution and what will be its consequences for the British and European future of Scotland and Northern Ireland. Skoutaris explores the Procrustean bed in which Scotland and Northern Ireland are stretched between the UK and the EU. The second and more concrete question is 'which tier will "take back control" of those repatriated powers?' In other words, will Brexit lead to more centralised or more decentralised and devolved UK.

Moreover, Skoutaris explores which would be the eventual path that Scotland and Northern Ireland would have to go along in order to reintegrate in the EU. He comes to the conclusion, based on solid exploration of legal arguments, that the path to independence and re-joining the EU will be legally easier for Northern Ireland than for Scotland. Instead, there are much more de facto impediments for such potential process in Northern Ireland than in Scotland. Skoutaris finalises his analysis with the conclusion that 'the intoxicating cry of "taking back control" ironically seems to destabilise the Union and strengthen the European prospects of those two regions'.

Chapter 10, written by Sabrina Ragone, analyses the territorial politics of regionalism in Italy. It is illustrative of a state stretched between integration and disintegration and coping with moderate secessionist challenges. In contrast to many of the chapters in this edited volume, which explore ethnocentric secessionism resulting in claims for self-determination, autonomy, and independence, Ragone's chapter offers an account of a system, in which the centripetal and secessionist forces are not ethnically grounded. In that regard, her chapter offers an important background for the analysis of secessionism which demonstrates both similarities and differences from the more radical cases based on ethnocentric nationalism or on religious fragmentation of society.

Ragone provides informative outlook of the evolution of Italian regionalism. The historical analysis serves as an important background setting the context for the current debates for reform of the Italian constitutional model for territorial politics and the recent referenda for increased autonomy and even for independence. In that regard, the author clearly demonstrates the different stages of the evolution of Italian regionalism and the driving forces behind them. Ragone is also suggesting possible trends for the development of the Italian constitutional model of regional state.

In Chap. 11 Joan Solanes Mullor provides insightful, provocative, and original analysis of the Catalan secessionism. The originality of the contribution stems from the successful attempt of the author to explore the main arguments of the Catalan secessionist movement from both legal and socio-legal perspectives. Solanes Mullor uses constitutionalist paradigm as a key reference for such evaluation. However, he does not stick to the institutional-normative dimension of the problem, but goes beyond it offering an informative journey in the 'Zeitgeist', the ideological conceptions and the socio-legal practices generated and performed during the recent events in the trend for Catalan secession.

Joan Solanes Mullor systematises the criticism against the Spanish constitutional order used in the secessionist argumentation and tactics in three main groups. These are the critics against the origin of the 1978 Spanish Constitution, the critics against the practice for application of this constitution, and the critics against constitutionalism itself. Moreover, he systematically presents the tools of secessionists used for attacking the constitutional order and shows their allocation within and beyond constitutionalism. Finally, Solanes Mullor outlines also the possible features of a post-independence scenario. The author properly writes that the lessons from the Catalan case might be of high relevance also in comparative perspective having important repercussions to the situation in the UK and Canada—cases that are explored in the current volume as well.

The book concludes with Part V devoted to territorial politics of subnational ethnocentric constitutionalism. Thus, it includes contributions engaged in two important debates. These are the debates on sub-national constitutionalism and sub-national territorial politics and on ethnocentric nationalism and its impact on constitutional integrity, territorial politics, and secession. The case studies are carefully chosen. They offer insights for ethnocentric sub-national constitutionalism on three continents—Europe, Africa, and Asia. They demonstrate how three rather different constitutional orders—Bosnia and Herzegovina, Ethiopia, and Sri Lanka—functioning in non-identical socio-political context are coping with ethnic and religious diversity which is producing aspirations for internal or external secession.

Chapter 12, written by Maja Sahadžić, explores the ethno-territorial politics and sub-national constitutionalism in Bosnia and Herzegovina. The author provides the reader with an outline of the complicated constitutional history of the country setting the current problems in their historical context. She demonstrates the path dependencies of the issues at stake producing turbulences in the asymmetric multilevel constitutional order of the country.

Sahadžić explicitly defines the aim of her chapter: to explore the effects of sub-national constitutionalism on territorial politics. Using Bosnia and Herzegovina as an example she 'investigates the interplay between identity, territory, autonomy claims, and sub-national constitutionalism' offering 'insights about cohesive and divisive qualities of sub-national constitutionalism in Bosnia and Herzegovina'. The author 'explores whether and how wide sub-national constitutional autonomy counteracts autonomy claims in Bosnia and Herzegovina'. This is done through contrasting of ethno-territorial and ethno-nationalist with the more cohesive unitary versions for the constitutional structure of the state. Sahadžić explains why the former have definitely prevailed over the latter.

Special attention is devoted to the development of sub-national constitutionalism in Bosnia and Herzegovina. Sahadžić analyses the scope of sub-national autonomy and the tendencies and trends in its development on the levels of the entities and the cantons. Sahadžić analyses the driving forces behind sub-national constitutionalism. She defines territory and identity as both cohesive and divisive features and explores how 'ethno-territorial balance is maintained through the institutionalisation of conflict'.

In Chap. 13 Yonatan Fessha and Zemelak Ayele analyse the Ethiopian experience with sub-national constitutionalism in the context of ethnocentric federalism. They provide an insightful research on the important problem of internal secession. The chapter is methodologically grounded on socio-legal approach to the problem which is explicitly announced already in the title with the aim of presenting both the law and politics of internal secession. This approach allows the reader to grasp the determinants of the context and the socio-political driving forces of internal conflict triggering internal secession.

The chapter is focused on one particular case of internal secession. This is the process for the establishment of the new Sidama state within the Ethiopian federation through its internal secession from the Southern Nations Nationalities and Peoples state. The authors present the constitutional and political context which stimulates ethnic communities in Ethiopia to demand for the establishment of their own states. They place internal secession in the context of ethnic federalism in Ethiopia. Fessha and Ayele explain the procedural issues for internal secession in Ethiopia and explore the politics of internal secession. Here they focus on the use of referendum and the particularly challenging constitutional amendment issues produced by internal secession.

The final Chap. 14 is written by Punsara Amarasinghe. It explores the impact of ethnic nationalism in Sri Lanka. More precisely, it focuses on the Tamil secessionist movement. Amarasinghe informs us about the ethnic discontents and rivalries in the post-colonial Sri Lanka especially with a view to the civil war between Sinhalese majority and the Tamil ethnic minority. He presents the main stages of unfolding of the ethnic conflict between the two hostile communities in Sri Lanka. This is done on the basis of analysis of the cornerstone events, relevant literature, and the shifts in the socio-political context. Thus, Amarasinghe's chapter further develops the socio-legal approach to territorial politics and secession used not only in the other two chapters included in Part V but also by all contributors to this edited volume. Amarasinghe comes to the conclusion that 'the lack of serious commitment to seek a satisfactory answer for the ethnic discontent under political framework appears to be the biggest problem in post-civil war Sri Lanka'.

In fact, all three chapters of Part V provide visible and comprehensive historical perspective of ethnocentric sub-national territorial politics, thus offering important insights for the comparative study of sub-national constitutionalism in divided societies. The chapters of Sahadžić, Fessha and Ayele, and Amarasinghe demonstrate the fragility of composite societies with internally hostile cultures deeply divided on the basis of ethnos and nationality of religion. Indeed, such issues are behind secessionism and disintegrative territorial politics in general, thus being object of analysis also of many of the other chapters of this edited volume. However, the greatest value of Sahadžić, Fessha and Ayele, and Amarasinghe chapters is that they offer contextual dissection of divided societies providing analysis of both the legal issues and the socio-political context. Taken in conjunction with each other and as a group, these three chapters provide informative comparative perspective spotting and mapping the problems of ethnocentric sub-national constitutionalism in three continents. Thus, they are valuable not only as case studies but also as a comparative sample that is especially useful if read together.

PART I

Territoriality and Territorial Politics in Constitutional and International Law

CHAPTER 2

Territory, Territoriality and Territorial Politics as Public Law Concepts

Martin Belov

1 Introduction

This chapter aims at exploring the role of territory and territoriality in public law with special emphasis on constitutional and to lesser extent on international law. This is necessary in order to give conceptual basis for the subsequent debates on the different forms of territorial politics provided by the other chapters of this book. Hence, this chapter is focusing on territory and territoriality as fundamental paradigms conceptually framing the subsequent discourses on federalism, devolution, secession, direct democratic self-determination, territorial dispute resolution and humanitarian intervention.

The chapter opens with clarification and systematisation of the different aspects of territory and their reflection in the legal order and in the intellectual discourse on public law consisting of the doctrine and the

M. Belov (✉)
University of Sofia 'St. Kliment Ohridski', Sofia, Bulgaria
e-mail: mbelov@uni-sofia.bg

M. Belov (ed.), *Territorial Politics and Secession*, Federalism and Internal Conflicts, https://doi.org/10.1007/978-3-030-64402-4_2

constitutional anthropology of the socio-legal communities. Territory is conceptualised as a phenomenon with three aspects—empirical (factual), normative-institutional and imaginary-conceptual. The third aspect of territory is defined as a separate concept, namely, territoriality. Thus, the analysis takes also into account the semiotic importance of the relationship between territory and territoriality with its implications for understanding or misunderstanding, constructing, deconstructing and reconstructing of constitutional and international territorial politics.

Territoriality is presented as the imprint of territory in the imaginary constitutionalism. It is defined as a signifier of territory as fact and the territory as institution in the intellectual-imaginary discourse. The different features of territoriality as well as its role as a key concept of the imaginary discourse of constitutional and international law are discussed. The different models of territoriality are presented. More precisely, I am offering critical assessment of the conceptualisation of territoriality under the framing paradigms of Westphalian, post-Westphalian and neo-Westphalian constitutionalism.

Special attention is devoted to the crisis of territoriality with its complex manifestations as well as to the re-emergence of territoriality during the trend towards re-nationalisation which became visible during the COVID-19 pandemic. The chapter offers an account of the constitutional importance of territorial politics in the age of globalisation and digitalisation. It discusses the impact of these phenomena on territoriality of power and its constitutional and international law implications.

Furthermore, the chapter presents an outline of the concept of territorial politics. The definition of the phenomenon and the demarcation of its conceptual scope is followed by systematisation of the main tools for territorial policy-making.

2 Territory and Territoriality as Fundamental Concepts with Paradigmatic Importance for Constitutional and International Law

Territory is an element of the natural, physical reality. It is a part of the sphere of the real, empirical and factual. Territory is the most prominent dimension of space as a physical, factual context of social life and relations.[1] This is due to the fact that territory is that part of space which is inhabited by the people. It is the spatial segment which serves as a factual background of key concepts of law such as jurisdiction, sovereignty and state territory, thus having strategic importance for constitutional and international law and for public law in general.

Space and time form the fundamental conceptual framework within which law operates. They are ultimate limits and ultimate empowerments of the legal order. And they are open for conceptual modelling and paradigmatic definition by legal theory—although with respect to their essential minimal characteristics which are objectively predetermined. Later, it will be demonstrated that globalisation, 'time-space compression'[2] and digitalisation are challenging the basic characteristics of territory and space as fundamental frames of territorial politics.

Territory and space are substantially independent with regard to their core characteristics from their legal institutionalisation in constitutional, international and generally in public law and from their conceptualisation by legal, constitutional and international law theory. Hence, territory and space as facts precede their theoretical conceptualisation by constitutional theory, socio-legal studies, political and legal philosophy and theory of international relations and their legal institutionalisation as elements of public law. Nevertheless, territory and space are also objects of modelling by both law and legal theory, thus having imprints and representations in the sphere of ideas.

Ontologically territory and space precede their legal institutionalisation and their constructive, conceptual or imaginary encoding in the text of the constitution, the constitutional, international and public law. Territory and space are existential artefacts with paradigmatic importance for public law. Hence, logically and substantially territory and space are autonomous from human mind, human understanding and the social, political and legal reflections on physical determinants of human socio-political coexistence. They are independent variables in the scheme of power and objective determinants and framing paradigms for public law and public and state power. This allows the teleological deconstruction, construction and reconstruction of territory and space in theory and valid law.

[1] See Paasi (2003) p. 117.
[2] See Eriksen (2014) p. 39 and Brenner (1999) p. 39.

While territory and space are partially independent from human mastering—in theory and in valid law—territoriality and spatiality are signification proxies that serve the function of human conceptualisation of the empirical facts they stand for. Exactly territoriality and spatiality demonstrate the capability of territory and space to be objects of human mastering in valid law as well as in legal theory.[3] Territoriality and spatiality make territory and space prone to human imagination moulding their legal institutionalisation and theoretical conceptualisation.

Territory and space are independent variables of the constitutional and international legal order to the extent that they cannot be immediately and as such reshaped, reordered or institutionalised. They can be legally arranged only through their intellectual conceptualisation via their imaginary imprints—territoriality and spatiality. Territoriality and spatiality are not categories of the valid law but of the imaginary discourse of constitutionalism and international law forming the ideal constitutional model of territory. Hence, 'territory and space as facts' are object of double representation—first, in constitutional imagination in the form of territoriality and spatiality and, then, in the legal order (especially in public law) as 'territory and space in law'.

This double status of the territory and space—as legal institution and as fact—is tricky and may be source of misunderstandings. It may lead to conceptual confusion with practical implications for the proper understanding of the territory as fact, as legal institution and as intellectual representation, conceptualisation and signification of the former.

Exactly due to their existence as 'rough material', as substantial precondition of socio-political reality, territory and space are detached from the possibility of their immediate mastering and representation in law. They are, as such, substantially and existentially independent from the forms and manifestations they achieve through their conceptualisation via human mind and human understanding. Hence, as such, they are objective preconditions for shaping of the institutional dimension of territory and space by social, political and legal theory and by constitutional, administrative, international and European Union (EU) law.

In other words, territory and space as facts must be represented in the institutional-normative order established by law and in the mindset of the members of the socio-legal community. The factual territory and space must be transformed into legal categories with normative-institutional

[3] See also N. Brenner, op. cit., pp. 39–78.

dimension and with projection in human understanding shaping the imaginary-psychological aspect of constitutionalism and the intellectual perception of public law in collective socio-legal imaginaries.

This representation, being both theoretical conceptualisation and legal institutionalisation, is of great importance for territoriality politics. Territorial politics works exactly with the signifiers of the territory and space as facts—the territory and space as legal institution and the territoriality and spatiality as theoretical concepts—and not directly with the 'rough material'. However, it is limited, fostered and generally framed by the dimensions of territory and space provided by the legal order or, more precisely, by a multitude of legal orders. Very frequently, territorial politics is stretched in a field of representations and misrepresentations of territory and space serving as both plans for territorial politics and argumentative strategies for building, launching and justifying it in front of the domestic and the international communities.

Social and political philosophy, theory of state and law and especially theory of constitutional and international law frequently work with representations of territory and space. They conceptualise territory and space as territoriality and spatiality.[4] Territoriality and spatiality are ideal, conceptual models of the territory and space. In that regard, territoriality and spatiality are theoretical constructs which symbolise, represent and stand for territory and space in the legal order and in legal theory.

Hence, while territory and space are elements of the factual reality and are traditionally perceived as objective preconditions of constitutionalism, territoriality and spatiality are phenomena belonging to the theoretical conceptualisation of the territory and space serving as conceptual frameworks and providers of meaning. They are also encoded in the symbolic-imaginary aspects of constitutionalism in their capacity as signifiers of territory and space being structural elements of empirical and normative-institutional dimensions of constitutionalism.

Thus, territoriality and spatiality are important for both pragmatic, symbolic-imaginary and emotional territoriality politics. These aspects of territorial politics mutually limit and at the same time reinforce themselves. This is demonstration of the strategic interdependence between territory as fact, norm and idea, the latter forming the concept of territoriality.

[4] See Vollaard (2009) pp. 687–706, Ruggie (1993) pp. 139–174 and Sack (1983) pp. 55–74.

Territory and space have multiple institutionalisations in public law. They may gain the shape of state or federal territory, territory of a sub-state unit (federal, quasi-federal or administrative territorial) or territory of international organisation. Territory may be defined as autonomous territory, independent or dependent territory, protectorate and so on. Territory may be disputed or undisputed, occupied or legally governed. Territory may be indirectly defined also via state borders. In that regard, the different forms of territory are submerged to different legal regimes. They are object of different instruments for accomplishment of territorial politics and are dependent on various normative ideologies of territoriality as part of the ideal constitution and the imaginary dimension of space in law.

We have to differentiate between territory as element of the factual reality (as physical space) and territory as element of the normative reality of law (as legal institution, as institution of constitutional, international law, etc.). Hence, territory is not represented in law by territoriality. Territoriality represents territory only in the ideal discourse of constitutionalism and constitutional law containing constitutional theory, constitutional imaginaries and the representation of the constitutional facts and constitutional institutions.

Territoriality is a conceptual representation of territory in its double meaning—as empirical and physical phenomenon and as legal institution. Thus, we have composite chain of phenomenological and conceptual representation. Territory as a fact is represented in the legal reality by the territory as an institution of the constitutional, administrative or the international law. However, it may be represented also directly in the sphere of the symbolic-imaginary and thus in symbolic-imaginary constitutionalism as semiotic code, constitutional myth or element of constitutional memories, dreams or normative ideas. Here territory operates as a strategic core for the construction of inspirational and aspirational territory politics.

Territory as fact and as institution may also trigger different constitutional and international narratives on territoriality. Hence, territoriality is not monolithic but rather multidiscoursive concept which is broadly framing various and sometimes competing narratives. The constitutional narratives on territoriality are produced mainly by the theory, the constitutional and ordinary legislator and the courts practice. The international law narratives are result not only of the interference of a plurality of national constitutional narratives, but also of the activity of the international producers of law and legal meaning. Obviously, the last category includes multiple narrators being the most influential stakeholders of international territorial politics, for example, international organisations and their courts and law-making bodies.

Indeed, there are different imaginary perceptions of territory as territoriality in the symbolic-imaginary discourse of constitutionalism with immediate repercussions also for the institutionalisation of territory in valid law. The most prominent and widespread among them is the concept of territory as 'territorial container'[5] adjusted to the conceptual and pragmatic demands of 'closed territorial statehood'. This has been the predominant model of territoriality during Westphalian modernity and its key type of statehood—the territorial nation state. Nevertheless, alternative conceptual models of territoriality, for example, networked territoriality, transversal territoriality, spaces of flows or even aterritoriality, also exist.[6]

Territoriality is usually imagined as a holistic concept, but it may also denominate fragmented space. Examples are the global cities and the transversally bordered spaces.[7] Holistic variants of territoriality, apart from the fixed and container-like territoriality, are the networked territoriality of global trade empires (frequently being a combination between fixed territoriality of the metropolitan territory and networked territoriality of the colonies) and the non-fixed territoriality of regional and continental empires.[8] In addition, territoriality may be determined (the case of fixed territoriality of nation states), non-determined but determinable (the case of the open imperial territoriality) and indeterminable (the different cases of fluid territoriality of the spaces of personal flows).

There are also forms of aterritoriality, post-territoriality and even aterritoriality, for example, the global information and financial capital spaces of flows based on 'time-space compression'.[9] They are conceptually challenging the very territorial paradigm of power, although currently coexisting and making selective and asymmetric benefits from it. In that regard, the forms of aterritoriality and post-territoriality are also challenging the holistic perception and model of territoriality.

[5] Brenner, op. cit., p. 55; Taylor (1994) pp. 151–162 and Taylor (1995) pp. 1–15.

[6] See Belov (2018a).

[7] For the transversally bordered spaces and the global cities see Sassen (2001) pp. 1–480, Sassen (2015) p. 17 and the following and Sassen (2013) p. 23.

[8] See Antonsich (2009) pp. 789–806.

[9] See Eriksen, op. cit.

Furthermore, from a semiotic perspective, territory as legal institution, provided by public law, is both a signifier and signified. It is a signifier of territory as fact. Hence, territory as institution represents territory as fact in the legal order. Territory as institution is also signified. It is an object of representation and signification of elements of the symbolic-imaginary constitutionalism structured around the concept of territoriality.

In other words, the symbolic-imaginary phenomenon of territoriality may simultaneously represent both the territory as fact and the territory as institution. Thus, we can have signification of territory in the sphere of symbolic-imaginary constitutionalism in a twofold way—first, directly since territory as fact may be immediately represented by territoriality and, second, indirectly via intermediate representation of the factual territory by the normative-institutional territory as provided by the valid public law.

This duality of representation of territory via territoriality may open space for multitude of options for speculative signification and misrepresentation. There might be mismatch between territory as political project and the legal and factual status of territory. Territorial disputes, secessionist claims and dreams for territorial unification usually thrive on the basis of such mismatch between the factual, normative and symbolic-imaginary representation of territory in the realm of territoriality. Symbolic-imaginary territoriality project sometimes have 'factual normativity' on the political behaviour of the stakeholders of territoriality politics due to their capability to mobilise political support and 'grasp the minds' of the public.

Each constitution—directly or much more frequently indirectly and implicitly—provides for a model of territoriality of power. This model is based on the territory as factual phenomenon, but might also be detached from factual reality. The territory as fact is just an occasion and starting point for the development of the constitutional—institutional, textual and imaginary—model of territoriality. The constitutional model of the territoriality of power underlines and frames the concept, tools and modes for the accomplishment of territorial politics. Thus, territorial politics is performed within the framework and with the tools related not to the territory as fact but to territory as institution. However, the territorial politics is pragmatically and teleologically dependent also from the territory as a fact.

3 Models of Territoriality Stretched Between Westphalian, Post-Westphalian and Neo-Westphalian Constitutionalism

The traditional and widespread model of territoriality of power conceptualises the state as 'territorial container'.[10] It has been inherited by the territorial state of early Modernity which has been later on upgraded and substantially transformed into a territorial nation state. The constitutional model of territoriality of power offered by the nation state is structured around a complex of fixed territoriality, optimal territorial spread of the nation as personal substrate of the state usually presented as 'national ideal' (typically in ethno-cultural sense) and strive at perfect match between territory, nation and power.

The territoriality model of the state as 'territorial container' matches very well and works together with the 'three element theory' of Georg Jellinek who defines the state as unity of power, people and territory.[11] Both concepts gained the status of official normative ideology of the territorial nation state and worked as a basis for territorial politics in the period from the second half of the nineteenth century until the beginning of the twenty-first century. The state as 'territorial container' has been the core ideology of Westphalian statehood, Westphalian constitutionalism and Westphalian territorial politics.[12]

This constitutional model of territoriality of power, based on fixed territoriality achieved after the accomplishment of aspiringly 'perfect' national unification, is currently challenged in the context of globalisation and its territorial effects. There are two main challenges. The first one is the emergence of aterritorial and post-territorial forms of power related to the IT revolution. The second one is the decapsulation and fracture of the 'territorial container' of the national statehood by multiple fluid phenomena which are not respecting the 'container-like' territoriality of state power. These are the spaces of flows—migration flows, financial capital flows and information flows.[13]

[10] See Brenner, op. cit. and Taylor, op. cit.

[11] Jellinek (2010) pp. 1–835.

[12] For the concept of Westphalian constitutionalism see Belov (2019a), Belov (2019b) and Belov (2019c).

[13] See Belov (2018a).

The IT revolution and the synergy between globalisation and digitalisation of space and power increase the importance not only of aterritorial and post-territorial forms of power. They also trigger new networked forms of topography of power. Thus, the traditional 'geography of power', inherited from Westphalian statehood and framing the world map exclusively on the basis of 'territorial containers' of states, is now asymmetrically enriched with new forms of power geography. They consist of post-Westphalian 'spaces of flows', 'networks', 'dots and spots of aterritoriality' and 'transversally bordered spaces'.[14]

However, since recently, the power geography includes in parallel also, to an extent paradoxically, forms of neo-Westphalian territoriality. These forms are now gaining the shape of regional unions claiming degree of autonomy from the Westphalian realm of nation states, but include also international organisations, traditional claimants for global superpower, for example, USA, China and Russia, and states asserting such status in more recent times, for example, India, Brazil and Turkey. We are witnessing also the rise of neo-imperial territorial politics. The tendency of the emergence of the latter is demonstrated by the annexation of Crimea by Russia and by the territorial disputes fostered by the neo-ottoman policy of Turkey in the Eastern Mediterranean.

Recently, the COVID-19 crisis has demonstrated that there are also other flows which cannot be mastered on the basis of Westphalian type of self-entrench territoriality and, thus, have trans-territorial dimension. These are the disease flows related to epidemics and pandemics. Indeed, diseases, epidemics and pandemics have always endangered the mankind and have paralleled its existence. However, the COVID-19 pandemic is maybe the first one which has drawn the invisible, but rather painfully feasible borders of isolation, quarantine, blockade, special movement regimes and specific targeted free movement corridors in the context of free movement prohibition.

The COVID-19 pandemics exposed the inadequacy of the nationalist approach to territoriality and territorial politics. It clearly demonstrated that global events can be mastered only on the basis of coordinated efforts and are resilient to strictly national or even regional politics framed in the

[14] For the post-Westphalian constitutional geometry see Belov (2018b).

'Procrustean bed' of Westphalian territorial politics based on closed statehood and 'container-like' territoriality. The same is valid for all other global phenomena such as climate change, large ecological disasters, terrorism and migration. Indeed, it seems that COVID-19 pandemic has triggered the re-emergence of Westphalian territorial politics of closed statehood. However, again seemingly paradoxically, it implicitly promoted also neo-Westphalian territorial politics of free movement restrictions drawing the new demarcation lines between strategic opponents, some of which have been until recently close allies.

Moreover, the COVID-19 pandemic has demonstrated that, although temporally, there might be forms of 'emergency territoriality'. The most visible among them are the 'cursed spaces' (the hotspots of disease), the sanitary zones and the special transport corridors. Such temporary 'emergency' and 'pandemic' territoriality might become rather regular phenomenon in the future having in mind the destructive effects of migration flows on free movement in the EU activating nationalist defence territorial politics and reactivating closed statehood. Particularly new threat is the increasing danger of 'emergency government' related to both 'world risk society'[15] and new global and regional risks—health, ecologic, military, terrorist, migration and so on.

The combination of 'emergency territoriality regimes', increasing territorial disputes, for example, in the Middle East, North Africa and Eastern Mediterranean, unilateral secessionism and separatism may produce detrimental effects both to the traditional models of 'fixed and container-like territoriality', based on closed statehood, and to post-Westphalian global and networked territoriality, based on open statehood. It may trigger fragmented territoriality and rather asymmetric geography of power. Thus, territorial politics may shift from jurisdictional management of the 'territorial container' and peaceful international dispute management (Westphalian model) to 'emergency and ad hoc measures for territorial containment of threats and disasters' preventing transition to more open society, and universalised territorial politics of free movement and liberty. Thus, unfortunately, we may be entering a phase of neo-Westphalian regionalism aiming at most at 'controlling and containing the chaos'.

[15] See Beck (1992) pp. 1–272.

4 Crisis of Territoriality or New Territorial Entrapment? The Constitutional Importance of Territorial Politics in the Age of Globalisation and Digitalisation

Territory is a traditional precondition of socio-political life. It is a long-established physical and institutional framework of power, state and society. It is the factual basis for authority, legitimacy and jurisdiction of power. The whole range of constitutional and international law imaginaries is based on the concept of territoriality of power.

Most of the important theories of state and law use territoriality as *conditio sine qua non*. The concepts of independence, autonomy, self-determination and self-governance, the principles of state sovereignty and non-interference in the internal functioning of the states are entrenched in territory as legal institution and in territoriality as conceptual projection of territory. Welfare redistribution and taxation, being direct preconditions for the welfare state, are also typically focused on territory and territoriality.

Territoriality of power influences also less territorially attached concepts such as democracy and the rule of law, which are conceivable also as trans-territorial and post-territorial phenomena. However, the reality shows that they are still to large extent territory dependent and territoriality sensitive. Separation of powers, even when going beyond the state and serving as organising principle of international and supranational orders, is also territory entrenched and territoriality dependent.

Nevertheless, territory and territoriality of power are currently experiencing deep crisis which has important manifestations. We are witnessing the emergence of aterritorial and even post-territorial forms of power.[16] The massive digitalisation of social life produces also digitalisation of power, state and society.[17] There are rising forms of public engagement and even of policy-making which are territorially detached and placed mostly or even exclusively in the virtual reality. The digitalisation of power is paralleled by its physical dematerialisation and by its territorial detachment. It undermines key aspects of public power which are derivatives of its territoriality, for example, jurisdiction, territorial authority and deduction of legitimacy from territorially framed community. The immediate

[16] See Belov (2018a).

[17] See Wagner et al. (2019), Celeste (2018), De Gregorio (2020) and Redeker et al. (2015).

implications are visible in elections and in tendencies in restructuring of the public sphere, media, tax and welfare policies which are increasingly dysfunctional when defined on strictly territorial basis.

Thus, we are currently experiencing deep and increasing tension between traditional territory-based constitutional and international legal conceptualisation of power and the emergent new forms of power which are less territory dependent, daring for reformulation of traditional conceptualisations of territory and requiring public law—constitutional, international and EU law—capable of framing and providing for solid basis for trans-territorial, post-territorial and aterritorial public power phenomena. Territoriality of power is currently coexisting in a rather tense way with the emergence of trans-territoriality, post-territoriality and aterritoriality.[18]

This is a massive challenge also to territorial politics. The core of democratic territorial politics is focused on the provision of coherent, just and efficient model of the territorial structure of power capable of integrating diverse societies on a peaceful manner and within democratic and rule-of-law-based framework. Authoritarian territorial politics is very much dependent on territory and territoriality as well. So far, democracy and authoritarianism are rather territoriality entrenched. This has been the status quo until the beginning of the twenty-first century. All forms of constitutional politics, based on sovereigntist or globalist, on democratic or authoritarian, on procedural or substantive logic, required territory and territoriality. Independence claims, secession, fusion and merger of states, constitutional and administrative reconfiguration of power were grounded on territory and territoriality and on the subsequent distinctions of internal and external, local, regional, national, international and supranational territorial politics.

However, dematerialisation and the territorial detachment of public power, which is paralleled by its digitalisation, make redundant the conceptualisation of spatiality and territoriality of power as holistic phenomena and overall all-encompassing power matrices. The territorial decompression of the state conceived as 'territorial container' is produced by both new forms of territoriality triggered, for example, by space of flows, and by the emergence of post-territorial (virtual, digital and Internet-based) power reality. It is result of the simultaneous unfolding of globalisation, and IT revolution producing glocalisation of power.

[18] For concepts of post-territorial structuring of public power and socio-legal communities see Chandler (2007) pp. 116–119 and Chandler (2012).

Glocalisation of power may mean reinforcement of the global and local dimensions of power to the detriment of the national one. It may denominate the global spread of new forms of power active locally in a dispersed manner. However, glocalisation may also connote the reinforcement of the 'global-local' architecture of power organised on brand new level through the medium and in the sphere of Internet.[19]

In particular, constitutional law is focusing on the territorial structure of the state power, on integration, secession and other forms of expression and on determination of territory-based interests and identities. However, it is not prepared to conceptualise, institutionalise and work with aterritorial forms of state and public power. Digital integration, digital secession and digital determination of interests and group identities are not yet conceived as constitutional phenomena and as issues which should be integrated in the overall constitutional model of public power. This is due to the territorial embeddedness of power and the lack of understanding of the rising importance of the territorial detachment of power which we are witnessing in recent decades in the context of the IT revolution at the beginning of the twenty-first century.

Hence, the constitutional model and conceptualisation of power remain entrenched in physical reality—in space and territory and in spatiality and territoriality as their representation—while there is a whole new power reality—the digital world—which is not just an upgrade of the existing territorial statehood. In fact, it is a profound new reality with deep constitutional implications which are not yet adequately addressed by the current territorial politics. In that regard, one may even dare to suggest that we should go beyond territory and territoriality and start conceptualising a novel post-territorial politics capable of addressing the challenges of a post-territorial and aterritorial world, from legal—constitutional, international and administrative law—perspective.

Consequently, globalisation and the IT revolution may profoundly challenge the very concept of territorial politics. They may rearrange the underlying concept of spatiality of law producing deep crisis on conceptual, normative and factual levels. The 'time-space compression' and the emergence of post-territorial and aterritorial forms of power are just first indicators of such trend.

[19] For the different meanings and uses of glocalisation see Robertson (2012), Swyngedouw (1997) pp. 137–166, Swyngedouw (2004) pp. 25–48 and Khondker (2005) p. 13.

To an extent paradoxically, digitalisation and dematerialisation of space as fundamental precondition and framework for power might be paralleled with some persisting conflictual forms of territorial politics such as territorial disputes, referendums for self-determination (autonomy or independence) and secession. Thus, it is highly likely that the post-territorial realm of power will not replace territory and territoriality but will coexist with them. The result will be split of power geography into two separate domains—territory entrenched and Internet entrenched. This might be the new power reality of the twenty-first century which does not replace the territoriality of power but profoundly changes the perspective challenging the totality and universality of its territorial entrenchment. In that regard, the emergence of aterritorial and post-territorial constitutional and international politics is the real revolution in the sphere of geography of power.

5 The Concept of Territorial Politics

Territorial politics is the special type of public politics that is related to the territorial structure and the territorial implications of public power.[20] It has multiple dimensions—international, constitutional and administrative, which are mutually interrelated. Territorial politics is fundamental for the construction and understanding of statehood and the international community since it is predetermining the basic categories of legal coexistence such as jurisdiction, authority and validity.

Territorial politics is addressing the territory as a key precondition and an element of statehood and as strategic determinant of existence and functioning of public power. Territorial politics is rather visible in the constitutional scheme of composite and complex territorial orders organised as multilevel constitutional schemes. These are the federations and hybrid unitary states with autonomies, regionalism and devolution.

Territorial politics is of special importance also in states with territorial units that possess special status and for states part of which territory is target of secessionist claims or object of territorial dispute. Such cases usually represent special occasions for interference of the territorial politics of the state and of its territorial unit or territory inhabited by population

[20] For the concept and features of territorial politics see the book series 'Comparative Territorial Politics', edited by M. Keating, A. H. Schakel and M. Tatham and published by Palgrave as well as Detterbeck and Hepburn (2018) pp. 1–432.

claiming independence, autonomy or other forms of special territorial treatment. Especially when dealing with territorial disputes, but also in case of autonomy, self-determination or secession, there are also other actors involved in territorial policy-making. These may be other states or international organisations.

Actually, territorial politics is important also in less complex territorial orders such as the unitary states. The very choice of Unitarianism is the result of deliberate territorial politics which must be subsequently further developed and sustained.

Territorial politics is available also to international organisations and to the EU. In the context of the EU, one should distinguish between territorial politics of the international organisation (or the EU) and territorial politics of the member states. The fact that territorial politics may be performed also by the EU and international organisations demonstrates that it is not necessarily and absolutely preconditioned on state sovereignty. Nevertheless, the dysfunctionality of international organisations' territorial politics and its dependence on decisions of the member states are also visible, especially in cases of territorial dispute resolution and humanitarian interventions. International organisations and the EU are also not at ease with referenda for self-determination since they may consist in a challenge to the sovereignty of their member states.

Territorial politics is present in all historic and contemporary political orders. It is a universal power phenomenon available in all power schemes. The ever presence of territorial politics is the result of the territorial entrenchment of public power which became weakened only recently in the context of virtualisation, digitalisation and globalisation of power.

Territorial politics was existent in Antiquity and Middle Ages. But it has become even more important in Modernity with the emergence of constitutionalism and the subsequent constitutionalisation of territorial politics during the 'long nineteenth century'[21] and its internationalisation in the course of the twentieth century and the beginning of the twenty-first century.

[21] See Hobsbawm (1995) and (1996a, b).

6 Typology of Territorial Politics

Here I am providing a concise outline of the types of territorial politics. I am focusing mainly on the constitutional territorial politics and, thus, on the constitutional foundations, constitutional toolkit and the constitutional manifestations of territorial politics. Special emphasis is added to the constitutional forms and instruments for territorial policy-making in composite and complex states, especially in federations, and in multicultural and pluralist societies loaded with deep centrifugal forces and socio-political tensions with constitutional relevance. This will not preclude the outlining also of the shapes and main issues related to other forms of constitutional politics different from the constitutional one (e.g. administrative and international law territorial politics). Nor it will prevent the exposure of constitutional politics outside of the realm of federalism, for example, in unitary states.

Territorial politics is not only a top-down exercise stemming from the will of the state. It is also result of the activity, policy and engagement of the power units and the constitutional actors allocated on all levels of the territorial structure of statehood. Indeed, it is the state which has the final say about the ultimate rules—especially the constitutional rules—of territorial politics. However, the sub-state units have also multiple tools for shaping the national territorial politics and for engagement not only in the application, but also in the forming of the territorial politics of the state. Moreover, the sub-state units are not only granted tools for implementation of the territorial politics as defined by the state. In many cases they have also competences for engagement in the formulation of the national territorial politics. These tools will be just outlined in the remaining part of this chapter. They are explored in more detail and on the basis of comparative research and case studies in the rest of the chapters published in this volume.

Territorial politics is mainly performed by the state. And there are four main dimensions of the state territorial politics—first, external and directed towards the international relations; second, internal and directed towards the sub-state units of public power and to the administrative territorial units for local governance and self-governance; third, internal and horizontal, where the formation of national territorial politics is performed. In the member states of the EU there is also one additional, fourth, vertical quasi-external dimension of the territorial politics. It regulates the territorial politics between the EU as quasi-federal and quasi-constitutional order and its member states.

Moreover, the vertically directed territorial politics may be internal (directed towards the sub-state units) or external, addressing the supranational and international layers of public power. Furthermore, there is an internal horizontal, functional and not structural dimension of national territorial politics as well as horizontal dimension of the international territorial politics stemming out and reflecting the formal equality of the sovereign states in the international community.

The existence of the above-mentioned dimensions of state territorial politics is irrespective of whether the state is nation state or multicultural state, democracy or authoritarian state, unitary state, federation or hybrid system. Of course, the internal vertical dimension of state territorial politics is much more visible in multilevel constitutional orders than in unitary states. In addition, the horizontal national dimension of territorial politics is much more complex in multilevel constitutional orders. This is due to the fact that they provide for multiple actors engaged in territorial politics, for example, second chambers (especially federal councils) and supreme and constitutional courts with enhanced competences for the resolution of vertical conflicts of public power. In addition, in multilevel constitutional orders the national territorial politics have to respect the spheres of legislative, executive, financial, administrative and many other competences of the sub-national, federal units.

Territorial politics may be accomplished also by sub-state units—federated units (states, cantons, lands, etc.) and the regional and local self-government entities (regions, municipalities, etc.) which are also engaged in territorial politics. In other words, they are not only objects of territorial politics of the state, but also active players in territorial politics and in multilevel power games performed within the territorial framework of public power.

Nevertheless, the territorial politics of the sub-state units—the sub-national territorial politics—is framed by the constitutional order and thus by the overall constitutional territorial politics of the state. Hence, the sub-national territorial politics is secondary and to great extent derivative from the state territorial politics. The main exception is revolutionary territorial politics of sub-national units performed either as unilateral secession or as attempts at gaining additional autonomy by virtue of civil disobedience.

Territorial politics may be accomplished also by several states simultaneously addressing common political issues related to territory. This is the case of mutual negotiated exchange of territory, but also of military conflicts related to territory. This means that territorial politics may be performed by legal or illegal means. It may be accomplished in the context of war or peace.

Humanitarian intervention is a peculiar case of territorial politics. It has rather particular nature since it is based on the concept of 'just war',[22] which is rather disputed. Moreover, it is directed mainly at humanitarian and human rights' issues while territorial problems are formally subsumed thereto.

Finally, territorial politics may be accomplished by or within international organisations and supranational regimes, such as the EU. This type of territorial politics is not limited to international territorial dispute resolution. It includes all types of territorial policy-making.

The state may perform territorial politics in different policy domains, with regard to wide range of issues, within or outside of the territorial boundaries of its jurisdiction. Thus, the state may accomplish international or national territorial politics. The territorial politics of the state may concern the national level or may be accomplished on the different subnational levels of public power—regional, local and so on. It may concern constitutional or administrative issues. Finally, the territorial politics may be based on pure facts or it may have legal background. The premodern territorial politics has been grounded on facts or on durable legal conventions. The modern territorial politics is norm-based. It always has or is at least supposed to have direct or indirect, explicit or implicit constitutional foundations from which it derives its authority and legitimacy.

We can distinguish between constitutional territorial politics and administrative territorial politics. Constitutional territorial politics is enshrined in the constitution of the state. If the state is federation, the constitutional territorial politics is composite phenomenon contained and provided by constitutions on two levels—the federal and the sub-federal (sub-national).

One can differentiate between two concepts of multilevel constitutional territorial politics. In a broader sense, all constitutional territorial politics is actually multilevel one. This is due to the fact that the territorial

[22] For the very recent on the concept of 'just war' see the publications of the just war symposium in Philosophia, Volume 48, Issue 4, September 2020 and especially Cebula (2020).

structure of the state is hierarchically organised, usually following the shape of symmetric or asymmetric power pyramid. Hence, even in case of unitary states, where there is only one constitution on the national level, serving as container and ultimate source of the constitutional territorial politics, this politics is still multilevel following the hierarchical and pyramid-like structure of the state power. This phenomenon can be defined as multilevel constitutional territorial politics in a wider sense. It is present in all forms of state independently from the fact whether the state is unitary, federation or a hybrid.

There is also a second option. This is the multilevel constitutional territorial politics in a narrower sense. It is characteristic for the multilevel constitutional orders—typical or atypical cases of federalism. In this case, multilevel constitutional territorial politics is not only projection of the constitutional model of territorial politics enshrined in the national constitution. It is contained and stems from at least two layers of constitutionalism—the federal (national) and the sub-federal (sub-national). This true or narrow version of multilevel constitutional territorial politics raises series of additional questions related to the coordination of the politics enshrined in this multitude of constitutional orders and applied on multiple levels of not just ordinary, but constitutional policy-making. Hence, multilevel constitutional territorial politics in federations and federal-like unitary states (e.g. the states with regionalism, autonomies and devolution) is much more complicated raising problems of policy coordination, joint decision-making and competing and concurring policy-making.

Administrative territorial politics formally differs from constitutional territorial politics on the basis of two main criteria. First, while constitutional territorial politics is enshrined in the constitution and has explicit or implicit constitutional dimension, the administrative territorial politics in not. It is provided by other sources of law—parliamentary legislation, acts of the institutions of the executive power and so on. Second, constitutional territorial politics concerns the fundamental issues with huge importance and typically high added political value, whereas the administrative territorial politics encompasses policies of lesser political relevance which serve the implementation of more technical and concrete details of territorial policy-making.

Nevertheless, this distinction should not be taken either for granted or as absolute. It can be only relative one. This is due to the fact that administrative territorial politics must be in compliance with the constitution. Thus, it must have a constitutional background and foundation. In that regard, administrative territorial politics looks like second grade, more technical, constitutional territorial politics being its implementation and further development.

Furthermore, apart from the purely formal distinction based on the criterion whether the territorial politics is explicitly and formally provided by the constitution, there are many cases where the distinction between constitutional and administrative territorial politics is a matter of grade and not so much of substance. This means that there are some obvious cases in which clear distinction between constitutional (politically important, related to fundamental institutional design and human rights) and administrative (less political and related to expert and technocratic issues) territorial politics can be made. However, there is a wide range of cases where such distinction is less possible or indeed impossible.

Last but not least, one should also make distinction between internal and external territorial politics. The internal territorial politics can be either constitutional or administrative (or a combination of both of them) as just has been explained. External territorial politics can also be divided into two main groups. However, this distinction follows different criterion. Thus, we can distinguish between external territorial politics of the state (which is usually at the same time also constitutional) and external territorial politics of the EU and international organisations. The latter is grounded on international and supranational law, having also constitutional foundations in the constitutions of the member states.

Territorial politics has never been entirely domestic phenomenon. Determination of the state borders, resolution of territorial disputes as well as the finding of solutions to trans-border and cross-border issues has always been the element of the external policy of the states. This was also the case in Antiquity, the Middle Ages and the early Modernity. Good examples are the territorial plebiscites which were held to determine the belongingness of border territories to one of several neighbouring states. However, with the emergence of international law with the advancement of the twentieth century and with the rise of international and supranational regimes with administrative and even with constitutional character this external dimension of the territorial politics grew in importance, got 'thicker' in terms of content and size and has acquired also administrative and, in the context of the EU, even a constitutional dimension. Hence, since the second half of the twentieth century we can talk of international territorial politics.

Further distinctions of territorial politics can be made. They are going beyond the already accomplished differentiation between constitutional, administrative and international law politics and between factual and legally grounded territorial politics. Such is the distinction between integrative and disintegrative territorial politics.

All constitutions aim at providing feasible, effective and legitimate, if possible, scheme for social integration. The maintenance of the territorial integrity of the state is an important element of the overall constitutional scheme for social integration. Integrative territorial politics has many dimensions. It reflects different aspects of the state activity especially in the sphere of administrative, financial, cultural and other policies directed at protecting social-territorial diversity while preserving unity of the state. The establishment of representative bodies safeguarding the regional territorial interests and institutions capable of maintaining the constitutionally enshrined balance of competences related to the vertical separation of powers such as the second chambers and the constitutional and supreme courts are among the key elements of institutional design providing integrative constitutional territorial politics. Instruments for imposition of the will of the state and for safeguarding the general interest of the nation, such as the federal execution and federal intervention, are also part of the arsenal of tools for territorial integration. Nevertheless, such instruments are always 'last resort' since they are usually disproportionate except in the most extreme cases of threat of non-compliance with fundamental principles of state integrity or key structural territorial policies of the state.

The main example of disintegrative territorial politics is unilateral secession. It is actually extra-legal last resort instrument for the achievement of independence of territories with rebellious population which is largely dissatisfied with the overall constitutional order or with its inclusion in the state. Otherwise, secession, if legally provided, may have also integrative function, which is demonstrated also by Costanza Margiotta and Giuseppe Martinico in their chapters published in this book. It may pacify passion for unilateral secession and public discontent, including revolts and public disobedience. It may channel the unpreventable claims for independence while preventing the secession of other territorial entities. Or may be an incentive for independence.

In other words, constitutionally enshrined or constitutionally permitted secession is a chameleonic tool which may pacify territorial independence tensions but also foster and promote territorial disintegration. Thus, secession may be an instrument for both integrative and disintegrative territorial politics depending on the socio-political context.

Another important distinction is between unitarian, federalist and confederal territorial politics. All constitutional models of territoriality target the achievement of a degree of desired unity and integration. However, they achieve it in a different way.

Unitarian territorial politics aims at providing integration, coherence and unification of the territory on the basis of a simple constitutional model of territoriality which is not emphasising socio-cultural distinctions structured on territorial basis. Federalist model of territorial politics prefers the accommodation of territorially reflected socio-cultural differences via complex structure of the territorial distribution of power. Such structure should allow higher degree of autonomy of the territorial units and enhanced constitutional and administrative toolkit for safeguarding both the territorial integrity of the federal state and the identities and interests of the composite subgroups which compose its society. Finally, the confederal territorial politics is using integrity only in an instrumental way and allows it only insofar as it is efficient and functional for the satisfaction of the interests of the confederated units.

Hence, there is large variation between the values of Unitarianism, federalism and confederalism which is accomplished on the basis of different constitutional models of the territorial structure of the state and via diverging constitutionally provided instruments for the achievement of the constitutional goals of territorial integration and power allocation.

Further differentiation can be made between representative and direct democratic territorial politics. Territorial politics is usually accomplished through the structures and in the forms of representative democracy. It is the parliaments—national or sub-national—which adopt the legislative and approve the financial framework of territorial politics. They have the final say also for the international territorial politics performed by the state. The second chambers serve integrative and representative functions in multilevel constitutional orders safeguarding the vertical separation of powers. It is the governments and the other institutions of the executive power which implement the territorial politics of the state. And it is the courts that safeguard the constitutional model for the distribution of competences in the territorial structure of power and thus serve as ultimate protectors of the constitutional framework of territorial politics.

Hence, constitutional territorial politics is accomplished on the basis of representation, integration, authority and legitimacy building by the institutions of the representative democracy. That is why representative territorial politics prevails. Another issue is whether the representation and integration are sufficiently efficient, legitimate and authoritative.

Nevertheless, there are also important occasions of direct democratic constitutional politics. Sometimes they supplement, upgrade and further develop the overall representative model of territorial politics. This is the case of British devolution referenda which have been held in Scotland and Wales in 1979 and 1997, in Greater London in 1998, in North-East England in 2004 and again in Wales in 2011. The same is true for the referendum on the "Good Friday" agreement which has been held in Northern Ireland in 1998. Cases of direct democratic addendum to the overall representative territorial politics are the internal territorial plebiscites which are held for the accomplishment of administrative territorial reforms on the level of the lands (in Germany), the regions (in Italy) or the municipalities (in Bulgaria).

There are however also cases of discontent, conflict or even confrontation with this model expressed via direct democratic means. The most visible example is the referendum for independence which has been held in 2017 in Catalonia and in Iraqi Kurdistan. An intermediate status have the independence referendums held in 2014 in Scotland and in 2018 in New Caledonia since they have been negotiated between the national and regional authorities and have been approved by the national government. Thus, they have been a form of negotiated policy-making containing both representative and direct democratic decision-making.

Finally, one can differentiate between evolutionary-integrative, devolutionary and revolutionary territorial politics. The evolutionary-integrative territorial politics is the mainstream and predominant version of territorial politics. It is the territorial politics performed in most states. It is forming the large portion of territorial politics even in states with devolutionary territorial politics and with occurrences of revolutionary territorial politics. Evolutionary-integrative territorial politics is based on constitutionally enshrined model of territorial distribution of power aiming at preservation of the territorial integrity of the state and providing for the legal tools for the accomplishment of territorial politics.

Devolutionary territorial politics is performed in states with devolution. Typical example is the UK, but devolutionary processes may be found out also in Spain, Canada and to lesser extent also in Italy. Devolutionary territorial politics may get the shape of functional quasi-federalism in one of its versions such as state with devolution, state with autonomies and states with regionalism. Devolutionary territorial politics exists also in federations such as Belgium or Canada. Finally, the granting of territorial autonomy is also a form of devolutionary territorial politics.

Furthermore, definition of the concept of revolutionary territorial politics is also necessary. It should also include an outline of the populist territorial politics as a variant of revolutionary territorial politics.

The concept of revolution in constitutional law is extremely diverse.[23] Revolution may be conceptualised as a factual event leading to radical change of the established constitutional, political and/or social order. Revolution may also be conceived as radical rupture of the legal continuity, as massive 'unconstitutional constitutional amendment'[24] without necessarily having radical impact on the socio-political field. Revolution may be denomination of radical leap forward in the technological development with recourses to the legal, political and social order.[25]

Hence, revolution may be purely legal, purely factual or mixed phenomenon. It may concern the legal order, the political order, the social order, the stage of intellectual or technological development, some or all of them. Moreover, revolution may be used as a semiotic code enshrined in the constitution which signifies revolutionary constitutional memories, revolutionary constitutional project for radical reform of state and society, revolutionary founding myths and radical democratic tradition. In the last case, the revolutionary constitutional tradition is increasingly defined in theory as radical, populist or revolutionary constitutionalism.[26]

Here I am adhering to the following conceptualisation of revolutionary territorial politics. Revolutionary territorial politics is usually illegal and unconstitutional. It takes the shape of unsolicited unilateral secession or civil disobedience triggered by discontent with territorial politics which de facto serves as radical escape from it.

Revolutionary territorial politics is the performance of the authority of sub-state territorial unit or the regionally allocated population which is challenging the territorial authority of the state and disrupting the territorial equilibrium. Thus, revolutionary territorial politics encompasses all forms that challenge the territorial integrity of a constitutional order.

[23] See, for example, Jacobsohn and Roznai (2020) pp. 1–384, Albert (2020) p. 424 and Belov and Abat i Ninet (2020).

[24] Roznai (2017) pp. 1–368.

[25] See Kuhn (1996) pp. 1–212.

[26] See Albert, op. cit. and Blokker (2019) pp. 536–553, https://doi.org/10.1093/icon/moz028

Revolutionary territorial politics is a provocation to the holistic nature of the territorial order of statehood with its repercussions and implications in the constitutional order. The challenges imposed by revolutionary territorial politics might concern the scope and the structure of the territory, the validity of the constitutional law on parts of the territory, the monopoly of the state power for determining the key parameters of societal coexistence, the imposition of foreign views regarding the human rights regimes applicable on the territory and so on. The most important forms of radical policy-making challenge the concepts of territorial jurisdiction, territorial identity and territorial belongingness.

7 Conclusion

Territory is one of the pillars of constitutionalism. It is both fundamental precondition and inevitable framework for unfolding of constitutionalism. It is limit, opportunity and independent variable. Territory has multiple projections in constitutional law, constitutional theory and constitutional imagination. Directly or through the concept of territoriality it underlines key concepts of rational, emotional and imaginary-visual constitutionalism.

Territoriality allows for conceptual mastering of territory. It is the intellectual tool for construction, deconstruction and reconstruction of different regimes of territory in valid law and of various conceptual models of territoriality in legal theory and in the imaginary discourse of constitutionalism. Thus, territory and territoriality have huge pragmatic importance for legal practice and for the legal order—especially for its constitutional and international law dimensions. However, they are also key analytical and constructive paradigms of legal theory. Some of their manifestations are also reflected or even entrenched in constitutional anthropology of different socio-legal communities having durable impact on constitutional civilisation.

Territorial politics is the public politics related to issues of territory and territoriality. It is accomplished through a set of instruments for mastering of the socio-legal and political implications of territory and territoriality. Territorial politics is accomplished mostly by means provided by constitutional and international law. The most important of them are discussed in the subsequent chapters of this book.

References

Albert, R. (Ed.). (2020). *Revolutionary Constitutionalism. Law, Legitimacy, Power*. Oxford: Hart.

Antonsich, M. (2009). On Territory, the Nation-State and the Crisis of the Hyphen. *Dialogues in Human Geography, 33*(6), 789–806.

Beck, U. (1992). *Risk Society: Towards a New Modernity*. Thousand Oaks: SAGE.

Belov, M. (2018a). Rule of Law in Space of Flows. In M. Belov (Ed.), *Rule of Law at the Beginning of the Twenty-First Century*. The Hague: Eleven publ.

Belov, M. (2018b). The Challenges to Westphalian Constitutional Geometry in the Age of Supranational Constitutionalism, Global Governance and Information Revolution. In M. Belov (Ed.), *Global Constitutionalism and Its Challenges to Westphalian Constitutional Law*. Oxford: Hart.

Belov, M. (2019a). Judicial Dialogue – Westphalian or Post-Westphalian Constitutional Phenomenon? In M. Belov (Ed.), *Judicial Dialogue*. The Hague: Eleven.

Belov, M. (2019b). Global Rule of Law instead of Global Democracy? Legitimacy of Global Judicial Empire on the Edge Between Westphalian and Post-Westphalian Constitutionalism. In M. Belov (Ed.), *The Role of Courts in Contemporary Legal Orders*. The Hague: Eleven.

Belov, M. (2019c). *Revolution, Contestation and Transition: Towards a New Global Constitutional Order?* The Global blog of the Graduate Institute of Geneva. Available at: https://theglobal.blog/2019/01/14/revolution-contestation-and-transition-towards-a-new-global-constitutional-order/

Belov, M., & Abat i Ninet, A. (Eds.). (2020). *Revolution, Transition, Memory, and Oblivion. Reflections on Constitutional Change*. Cheltenham: Edward Elgar.

Blokker, P. (2019). Populism as a Constitutional Project. *International Journal of Constitutional Law, 17*(2), 536–553.

Brenner, N. (1999). Beyond State-Centrism? Space, Territoriality and Geographical Scale in Globalization Studies. *Theory and Society, 28*(1), 39–78.

Cebula, A. (2020). Just War Theory Symposium: Introduction. *Philosophia, 48*. https://doi.org/10.1007/s11406-020-00249-8.

Celeste, E. (2018). *Digital Constitutionalism: Mapping the Constitutional Response to Digital Technology's Challenges* (HIIG Discussion Paper Series 2).

Chandler, D. (2007). The Possibilities of Post-Territorial Political Community. *Area, 39*(1), 116–119.

Chandler, D. (2012). The Limits of Post-Territorial Political Community. In L. Beckman & E. Erman (Eds.), *Territories of Citizenship. Palgrave Studies in Citizenship*. London: Palgrave Macmillan. https://doi.org/10.1057/9781137031709_6.

De Gregorio, G. (2020). The Rise of Digital Constitutionalism in the European Union. *International Journal of Constitutional Law* (forthcoming).

Detterbeck, K., & Hepburn, E. (Eds.). (2018). *Handbook of Territorial Politics*. Cheltenham: Edward Elgar.

Eriksen, T. (2014). *Globalization. Key Concepts*. London: Bloomsbury.

Hobsbawm, E. (1995). *The Age of Extremes: The Short Twentieth Century, 1914-1991*. London: Abacus.

Hobsbawm, E. (1996a). *The Age of Revolution: 1789–1848*. New York: First Vintage Books.

Hobsbawm, E. (1996b). *The Age of Capital: 1848–1875*. New York: First Vintage Books.

Jacobsohn, G., & Roznai, Y. (2020). *Constitutional Revolution*. London: Yale University Press.

Jellinek, G. (2010). *Allgemeine Staatslehre*. Paris: Nabu Press.

Khondker, H. (2005). Globalisation to Glocalisation: A Conceptual Exploration. *Intellectual Discourse, 13*(2), 181–199.

Kuhn, T. (1996). *The Structure of Scientific Revolutions*. Chicago: University of Chicago Press.

Paasi, A. (2003). Territory. In J. Agnew et al. (Eds.), *A Companion to Political Geography*. Malden: Blackwell.

Redeker, D., Gill, L., & Gasser, U. (2015). *Towards Digital Constitutionalism? Mapping Attempts to Craft an Internet Bill of Rights* (Berkman Center Research Publication 15).

Robertson, R. (2012). Globalisation or Glocalisation? *The Journal of International Communication, 18*(2), 208–191.

Roznai, Y. (2017). *Unconstitutional Constitutional Amendments: The Limits of Amendment Powers*. Oxford: Oxford University Press.

Ruggie, J. G. (1993). Territoriality and Beyond. *International Organization, 47*(1), 139–174.

Sack, R. (1983). Human Territoriality: A Theory. *Annals of the Association of American Geographers, 73*(1), 55–74.

Sassen, S. (2001). *The Global City, New York, London, Tokyo*. Princeton: Princeton University Press.

Sassen, S. (2013). When Territory Deborders Territoriality. *Territory, Politics, Governance, 1*(1), 21–45.

Sassen, S. (2015). From National Borders to Embedded Borderings: One Angle into the Question of Territory and Space in a Global Age. In W. de Been, P. Arora, & M. Hildebrandt (Eds.), *Crossroads in New Media, Identity and Law*. London: Palgrave Macmillan.

Swyngedouw, E. (1997). Neither Global nor Local: 'Glocalization' and the Politics of Scale. In K. Cox (Ed.), *Spaces of Globalization, Reasserting the Power of the Local*. New York/London: The Guilford Press.

Swyngedouw, E. (2004). Globalisation or 'Glocalisation'? Networks, Territories and Rescaling. *Cambridge Review of International Affairs, 17*(1), 25–48.

Taylor, P. J. (1994). The State as Container: Territoriality in the Modern World-System. *Progress in Human Geography, 18*(2), 151–162.

Taylor, P. J. (1995). Beyond Containers: Internationality, Interstateness, Interterritoriality. *Progress in Human Geography, 19*(1), 1–15.

Vollaard, H. (2009). The Logic of Political Territoriality. *Geopolitics, 14*(4), 687–706.

Wagner, B., Kettemann, M., & Vieth, K. (2019). *Research Handbook on Human Rights and Digital Technology: Global Politics, Law and International Relations.* Cheltenham: Edward Elgar.

CHAPTER 3

Secession in Law: A Revolutionary or a Conservative Concept?

Costanza Margiotta

1 Introduction

From a legal-philosophical perspective, the concept of secession has both a *conservative* and a *revolutionary* character, which explains many of the problematic interactions between law and secession and between democracy and secession[1] and the difficulties in identifying which of the existing legal orders (i.e. constitutional, international, or European) should govern secession.[2] The *revolutionary* character of secession emerges in the inter-

[1] Many are the problems of the (difficult) relationship between secession and democracy: between them the value of the majority rule (Closa 2019) and of the referendum in the secessionist process. When referring to the definition of new external borders, majority rule and referendum can be considered respectful of the accepted democratic principles. On these issues see Margiotta (2019).

[2] Among the most recent books on secession: Norman (2006); Pavković, Radan (2007); Pavković, Radan (2011); Cabestan, Pavković (eds.) (2013); Walter, Ungern-Sternberg, Abushov (2014); Sterio (2018).

C. Margiotta (✉)
University of Padua, Padua, Italy
e-mail: costanza.margiotta@unipd.it

M. Belov (ed.), *Territorial Politics and Secession*, Federalism and Internal Conflicts, https://doi.org/10.1007/978-3-030-64402-4_3

national context: secession is deplored by the international community, as the exercise of such a right would put in danger the territorial integrity of those same States that create international law. That same character emerges also assuming a *purely* democratic approach to secession, while the conservative character emerges if one looks at secession only with a state-centred perspective. In this chapter I shall try to explain this double nature of secession also in its relation with the right of self-determination: most particularly the chapter aims to deal with the following issues: (1) how secession weakens the status of the principle of territorial integrity as an absolute principle or as one of the super-norms of international law; (2) the relationship between secession and peoples' right to self-determination, too often incorrectly associated; and (3) the problematic interactions between democracy and secession, outlining how from a *purely* democratic point of view the inherent *revolutionary* character of secession should emerge.

2 Secession and Territorial Integrity

Addressing the issue of territorial choice entails addressing the concept of borders. One way to look at both issues is from the point of view of secessionist movements or, better still, from the concept and the right of secession. The current specificity of secession is that it constitutes a crisis of every consolidated arrangement of borders and a symptom of the tension in the 'border's element': secession leads, and, since 1989 in particular, has been leading, to a process of a general displacement of borders. Secessions are expressions of an order crisis in the international community and international law. In my opinion, the capacity to neutralise this crisis and its potentially destabilising elements—keeping alive the systemic structure of the international legal order—still has to be demonstrated, since law somehow always needs to follow the facts, and that facts are the over 200 demands of secession around the world.

Globally, as the decolonisation era has ended and there are no *terrae nullius* left on the planet, secession has proved to be one of the main causes of state proliferation and of borders shifting. On the other side, and simultaneously, secession does not entail a change in the concepts of state and border. The creation of states is still the goal of secessionist movements. Such movements do not envision any new or atypical forms of political organisation, they are not against the idea of the state, they just want to create a *new* one. Secessionist claims are demands to draw new borders, proving that borders are still relevant on a global scale. In fact, from the viewpoint of internal sovereignty or of sovereign states, secession appears to be a conservative rather than a revolutionary concept, as it does not force us to rethink the traditional understandings concerning the nature and structure of the state as political space, around which modernity has developed. In other words, secession is still politics *within* the state and not *beyond* it.

On the other hand, from the point of view of external sovereignty, a cornerstone of the international order, secession exhibits all of its destabilising potential. It represents the most dangerous threat to the stability and conservation (including of borders) on which the international community is based. It highlights the most conservative aspect of that community: the strenuous defence of the prerogatives of external sovereignty, which entail the absence of a right of secession in the international legal system. Afraid of the erosion of external sovereignty, the community of States has adopted a critical stance against the shifting of borders and state proliferation.

At the global level, the possibility that external sovereignty may be put under stress by the formation of new States (following secession) leads to the question of whether the ban on secession hides fears that such formation, beyond a certain number, may put at risk the survival of the State system itself—that is, of the systemic structure of international law that gives secession its meaning. On one hand, secession has to be analysed from an international perspective, since it represents a confirmation of the state system and has a meaning because of that system. On the other hand, in systemic terms, secession has both an internal and an external function: it demands recognition from the system as something admitted by that system, if not as part of that system, that is, as a legal right recognised by the international legal system. At the same time, it appears to be the ultimate benefit that can be taken from a system that has been left behind and whose existence is at risk.

Frightened by the erosion of external sovereignty, the international community of states has mostly adopted a critical stance against state proliferation and the shifting of borders.[3] Though if international law explicitly aspires to critically determine the very *raison d'être* of states promoting and sanctioning their own disintegration through recognition of the right

[3] On secession and international law, see Sterio (2018); Kohen (ed) (2006); Walter, von Ungern-Sternberg, Abushov (eds.) (2014); Dahlitz (2003); Copp (1998).

to secede, it could turn law into a revolutionary instrument, different from and contrary to what tends to be expected from law, namely, stability and conservation. Secession has to be deplored by the international community, as the exercise of such a right would put in danger the territorial integrity of those same states that create international law.

Secession weakens the status of the principle of territorial integrity as an absolute principle or as one of the super-norms of international law. Secession takes the 'sacredness' out of the idea that borders are fixed, even though the fact that borders are still relevant is confirmed. Secession makes territorial choice an issue and attracts attention to the issue of borders and the immobility that impedes the rise of new legal instruments capable of overcoming the fixity of borders themselves.[4] Secession brings a dynamic element with itself, as it entails that the borders of a territorial unity may be changed through specific procedures by a territorially clustered group, independently from the geopolitical original unity and against the principle of conservation of territorial integrity.

The *revolutionary* character of secession—which paradoxically would legitimise its *conservative* dimension (the state building within the context of a new sovereign entity)—emerges in the international context. Rather than an arbitrary interpretation of *exit*, secession is a complex problem inherent in the relationship between legal and political systems and has its roots in the very nature of the right of secession, being both uncertain and largely destructive. Among contemporary rights, this right seems external to the legal system, though it claims to be conceivable by that same system, if not really to be part of it, and to be a legal title in the international framework. Its function is both external and internal to the dynamics of the system of states: secession closes the curtain on an old equilibrium and opens on a new perspective.

If secession aspires to present itself as a 'right', it can be conceived, in systemic terms, only as the 'ultimate right', the ultimate advantage that can be taken from a system that has been left behind and is at risk. When secession aspires to become a real right, it turns into an uncertain and destructive right, a legal source of instability.[5] Secession stands against the

[4] Irti (2001).

[5] It is no coincidence that the majority of the States with a constitutional provision on secession have ended in dissolution, on this issue see Margiotta (2017a, 2017b, 2019).

traditional notion of perpetuity of state constitutions (as the constituent power) and of indivisibility of sovereignty.[6]

3 Secession and Peoples' Right to Self-Determination

From an international perspective, the close connection between secession and borders—the former necessarily entails a claim to the latter—constitutes one of the main differences between secession and self-determination, which are often incorrectly associated.[7] Self-determination, as a concept and as a principle of international law, as well as a right, has always been in line with the idea of territorial integrity and has never meant territorial choice.[8] Generally, its exercise has not entailed new borders. Peoples' right to self-determination is often used as an easy legitimation at the international level for secession, by placing the former as the legal foundation of the latter. However, the principle of self-determination has always been applied in a way that does not include secession.[9]

The right of self-determination, already recognised by the United Nations (UN) Charter, has been accompanied by the rules of border intangibility and territorial integrity. In the decolonisation process, people who are recognised as having the right to self-determination have the corresponding duty not to modify borders as they stood after colonialism ended.[10] Thus, borders and territory identify and limit groups entitled to the right of self-determination. In other words, people have been defined by international law on the basis of their geographic location.[11]

[6] Calhoun, *February 15–16, 1833* (1992), at 433–434: 'The sovereignty is in the several States, and that our system is a union of twenty-four sovereign powers, under a constitutional compact, and not of a divided sovereignty between the States severally and the United States. In spite of all that has been said, I maintain that sovereignty is in its nature indivisible. It is the supreme power in a State, and we might just as well speak of half a square, or half of a triangle, as of half a sovereignty' (1851; 1853); on this see Margiotta (2007), at VII.

[7] This incorrect association was reaffirmed, for example, by Klabbers (2006).

[8] On this see Margiotta (2005): ch. VI; Hannum (1993); Knop (2002); Guarino (1984).

[9] As emerged from the opinion of the Canadian Supreme Court with regard to secession in Quebec: *Referente re Secession of Québec*, 20 agosto 1998. See, among others, Martinico (2019).

[10] This is why I do not think it is possible to think self-determination in a post-colonial age.

[11] The UN General Assembly in Resolution 1514 (XV) deems any effort aimed at the partial or total destruction of the political unity and the territorial integrity of a State definitively incompatible with the UN Charter. See Knop (2002) which criticises the way the

Self-determination concerns the content of political action rather than its 'container', with political action developing within existing borders without concerning these borders. Unlike secession, the object of self-determination is not to draw new borders, but to 'choose by whom to be governed and not to have an alien government in a given territory'. 'People' refers to the people located within the borders established by colonial powers, as it was the territory set by colonial forces that identified the people who are now entitled to the right of self-determination. People are therefore identified with the entire population that settled in a pre-existing geopolitical unity, with the people's destiny being decided by territory rather than the territory being decided by the people.[12] Not surprisingly, the territory that was mapped by colonial powers was not subject to relevant changes when colonised people exercised their right for self-determination, allowing the international community to absorb, in accordance with international law, the crisis caused by anti-colonial forces. Self-determination, as a legal foundation of the decolonisation process, was therefore able to reduce disorder in the international community, even though self-determination had political consequences inside the colonial system.

Through an analysis of decolonisation, it is possible, among other things, to identify the elements of which the principle of self-determination is composed. First, by means of such an analysis, it is possible to state that the unity of the collective entity exercising the right of self-determination is the precondition, rather than the result, of the political emancipation, so much so that it requires the concrete definition of the criteria for belonging to that collective entity.[13] Second, it is possible to observe that self-determination, state (nation) and people (and nation) are concepts that appear to be difficult to separate.

Furthermore, the principle of self-determination seems to have the state as a necessary outcome of its exercise. The simple status of people

principle of self-determination has been applied by the UN and the Organisation of African Unity in connection to decolonisation.

[12] See *Western Sahara*, Advisory Opinion, ICJ Reports, 122 (Separate Opinion of Judge Dillard): 'It is for the people to determine the destiny of the territory, and not the territory the destiny of the people'.

[13] Criteria have been defined as follows during the decolonisation period: 'being part of a resident (*permanent*) people at the time of the political independence, of a separate and distinct colony from the "metropolis", territorially defined along the same borders as the colonial power'.

ended up as a transitory condition in the decolonisation process, since people did not appear to have any other right than to become a state, and then to be absorbed by such entities.[14] However, a gap remains between a state and its people that makes it impossible for the two concepts to be regarded as one. The gap is between people, as a project moved by a desire for freedom, and nation, as a community ascriptively defined. It is secession that has caused the crisis of, and unveiled, what was assumed and established by the law—that is the stability, unity, and homogeneity of the subject that exercises, for anti-colonial purposes, its right of self-determination, and the presumed coincidence between people and state.[15] Between a state and its people there is always a space that remains empty and that impedes their reciprocal identities from being fully established. It is in this space of non-coincidence that secession becomes meaningful or that the many demands of separation, which emerged at the end of the decolonisation process, find their meaning. The potentialities of secession are to look at the limits of the idea that state and people-nation are whole identities. The attempt, inherent in secession, to break the unity of people-nation highlights what is given for granted in self-determination: the identification, within a given territory, of nation, people, and state. Secession, thus, reveals the biggest mistake made by those who consider state and people as a single unity and takes the issue of who exercises self-determination and its identity to centre stage.

4 Secession and Democracy

However, the possibilities provided by secession to look at the limits of self-determination, which has always enjoyed a good reputation among political and legal commentators, are accompanied, as already noted, by its close link to the state, with borders and traditional systems of belonging. Today requests for secession do not anymore appear as requests of recognition of the right to 'choose with whom to live' in the territory on which the exercise of sovereignty is claimed, as it has been since the end of the 80s of last century. In fact, for long secession[16] has shown the crisis and

[14] Senese (1992), 89 ff.

[15] The State has been the necessary outcome of the exercise of the right to self-determination. The mere *status* of people is a transitory situation, since people do not seem to have any other right than to become a State and to then be absorbed by this entity.

[16] See Margiotta (2005), Chap. VIII, on secession theories.

breaking up of the State, as traditionally understood as an artificial entity, in favour of an organicist view of it, with the connected need for an exclusive space and a revival of a natural qualification of the political order.[17] Theories of secession were aimed at the need for a reciprocal identity between nation and state—reciprocity that, as mentioned above, would not be guaranteed by self-determination. The desire to 'choose with whom to live' has for long belonged to the phenomenon of secessionist movements, whose demands for sovereignty corresponded to the desire to decide whom to exclude or with whom not to live. Unsurprisingly, the major theories of this view on secession,[18] the self-determination theories of secession, which raised the issue of territorial choice as a value without looking at aporias that may be present, and which, even though not explicitly, supported claims for the recognition of a right to 'choose with whom to live', in the end used to increase the value of the State and its borders as the only and best political form to express national culture. According to these theories, it is the state that grants the national group with the possibility to normatively govern the belonging (and thus the citizenship) of their own members; a guarantee that a group 'trapped' within states, where nation and state do not coincide, would not have.

Today, on the contrary, the major theories tend to value the connection between democracy and secession, instead of the relation between secession and nationalism, and the *democratic theories of secession* are more suitable for understanding the current stage of secessionist phenomenon. The democratic framework seems to be the most attractive for these new movements, particularly against the anti-liberal stigma that was often attributed to separatist movements, their leaders, and scholars of ethnic nationalism. The new leaders tend to value the right to vote and freedom of the members of a territorially concentrated group. And secessionist movements tend no longer to use the *honourable* language of the principle of self-determination and have begun to use the *demonized* concept of secession.

The recent rejection of the language of self-determination by secessionist leaders in Europe shows that when there is a question of breaking the

[17] Galli (2001), 67.

[18] Three theoretical approaches to secession stand out among the existing ones: *national self-determination theories of secession*, which justify all form of secession in terms of self-determination of peoples-nation; *choice theories of secession*, which apply the principle of democracy and the right of association to the choice of borders; and *just-cause theories of secession*, which regard secession as a right compensating for certain injustices.

territorial integrity of existing states, the exact terms to use are those of secession and not of self-determination, even though there is no international legal coverage to legitimise the separation. More importantly, the democratic appeal for this 'secessionism of a new type' is strategic because the consequences of declaring independence, including recognition by the international community, depend on the way in which the new state was born. The respect for majority rule, in the final analysis, does not affect the final outcome of the secessionist attempt, but it does guarantee that the factual situation, if it manages to produce the requirements of statehood, will not encounter obstacles in the international realm concerning the extension of all sovereign prerogatives and duties to the new subjects. The purpose of this new type of secessionism is to correct the form of the existing state through democratic means. What I call a 'secessionism of a new type', like the ones attempted by Catalonia and Scotland,[19] clearly refers to the *democratic theories of secession*[20] rather than turning to *self-determination theories of secession*.

As a scholar of the right to secede and of the history of secession, I think it is important that secessionist movements have move towards the democratic framework for secession. But this does not mean that international law confers any entity within a state with the right to declare its independence unilaterally, even though achieved democratically. The legal and political consequences of the declaration itself, including recognition by the international community, depend on the way in which the new state was born. Certainly, recent practice seems to reveal that respect for the democratic principle is *necessary*, but *not sufficient*, for the international community to absorb the secessionist process.

In any case, as a general rule, the creation of a state cannot be in contrast with the aspirations of the people and the consensus of the population involved. Internal consent is a necessary condition if the movement for independence wants to self-legitimise in front of the international community, but, contrary to the assumptions of the democratic theories

[19] Kraus, Gifra (2017), at 20: 'The most characteristic feature of this new secessionism is the goal of "correcting" the shape of a given state unit by democratic means. In this respect, Catalonia has obvious commonalities with Quebec and Scotland. We do not argue that [ethno-nationalist] motives are completely absent in Catalonia today, but we want to highlight that they clearly play a secondary role in comparison with the *civic* demands to find a democratic solution to the Catalan question'.

[20] See Beran (1998); Wellman (2005); Philpott (1995); McGee (1992).

of secession, it is not sufficient to give someone else a moral obligation to recognise independence.

If following the democratic rules provides more opportunities for the secessionist movement to enter into a negotiation process with the central state and to have the support of the international community, declaring unilateral secession is still illegitimate even when the democratic procedures have been followed by the separatist group. According to the Canadian Supreme Court, 'a failure of the duty to undertake negotiations and pursue them according to constitutional principles may undermine that government's claim to legitimacy which is generally a precondition for recognition by the international community'.[21] In other words, alongside the traditional elements of statehood (people, territory, and government) there is also the legitimacy of the process of state formation. The legitimacy of the process of state formation must counterbalance that of effectiveness, by virtue of which an act of secession, even unilateral and unconstitutional, should be recognised by the international system, if successful.

The question of the legitimacy of the process of state formation overlaps with the justification of secession *exclusively* in democratic terms. One of the problems is if secession can be justified entirely on the basis of democracy or if it needs to refer to pre-democratic elements in order to find its full justification.

For me it seems impossible to justify secession *exclusively* in democratic terms, since democratic theories always find it necessary to refer to the pre-democratic definition of the criteria for belonging to secessionist groups. Secession is always reinforced by other pre-democratic elements. Groups that are traditionally settled in a specific territory and that express a will to secede are, in the overwhelming majority of cases, national (ethnic or cultural) minorities. In this respect, *choice theories of secession*[22] reproduce,[23] at least in part, the weaknesses of *national self-determination theories*.

[21] Canadian Supreme Court, Reference Re Secession of Quebec [1998] 2 S.C.R. 217, para. 103.

[22] Bengoetxea (2019): 'When it comes to the normative, practical philosophical debate, claim of sovereign right and the democratic will of the people is the most recurrent argument for secession'. The most important justification for secession relies on the democratic principle, especially when based on a general consensus.

[23] See Beran (1998); Wellman (2005); Philpott (1995); McGee (1992).

In order to secede democratically, a group must express its will in a referendum or plebiscite. Accordingly, in order to democratically address a secessionist dispute, the first step would be to determine who would be given the right to vote. Although theorists of democratic secession tend to argue that the expression of a desire to secede by a territorial group through a referendum or plebiscite is sufficient to legitimise it, it is clear that they need to determine in advance which group can claim a given territory. Appeal to historical tradition, which would link the group to the territory, and a common attachment to the territory itself, appears to precede any democratic consensus. Territory and voters must, in some way, be determined before deciding anything.

In practice, the right to secede is granted primarily on the basis of nationality, as is demonstrated by the fact that *choice theories of secession* affirm that the right to secede should not be granted to groups that are not in a position to give birth to viable states and do not satisfy certain conditions.[24] As a consequence, from the democratic point of view, the overall practicability of secession prevents many territorially concentrated groups from enjoying the democratic right to secede. But from a *purely* democratic point of view, if one accepts the secession of a territorial group from a state, one must also accept the secession of another territorial group within the seceding state, and so on, accepting the recursive nature of secession[25]: accepting, in other words, the inherent *revolutionary* character of secession. Otherwise it is unclear what the *democratic theory of secession* would add to the *national self-determination theories* of secession, for which the collective autonomy of the group justifies the right to secessionist self-determination. This new type of secessionism, whose purpose is to correct the form of the existing state through democratic means, risks reflecting itself in the old nationalistic secessionism.

Not risking this effect would mean accepting as a consequence the necessary recognition of the right for all groups, if not all individuals, to secede, bringing secession as the 'ultimate right' to its extreme consequence and obliging us to rethink the only form of political organisation invented since modernity, the state.

[24] Wellman (2005).

[25] Margiotta (2005), ch. VIII Para 3 and Bauböck (2019).

References

Bauböck, R. (2019). A Multilevel Theory of Democratic Secession. *Ethnopolitics, 18*(3), 227–246.

Bengoetxea, J. (2019). Secession v Forceful Union. A Provisional Enquiry into the Right to Decide to Secede and the Obligation to Belong. In C. Closa, C. Margiotta, & G. Martinico (Eds.), *Between Democracy and Law: The Amorality of Secession*. London: Routledge.

Beran, H. (1998). A Democratic Theory of Political Self-Determination for a New World Order. In P. B. Lehning (Ed.), *Theories of Secession* (p. 32). London: Routledge.

Cabestan, J. P., & Pavković, A. (Eds.). (2013). *Secessionism and Separatism in Europe and Asia: To Have a State of One's Own*. Abingdon: Routledge.

Closa, C. (2019). A Critique of the Theory of Democratic Secession. In C. Closa, C. Margiotta, & G. Martinico (Eds.), *Between Democracy and Law: The Amorality of Secession*. London: Routledge.

Copp, D. (1998). International Law and Morality in the Theory of Secession. *The Journal of Ethics, 2*(3), 219.

Dahlitz, J. (2003). *Secession and International Law: Conflict Avoidance—Regional Appraisals*. The Hague: Asser.

Galli, C. (2001). *Spazi politici. L'età moderna e l'età globale*. Bologna: Il Mulino.

Guarino, G. (1984). *Autodeterminazione dei popoli e diritto internazionale*. Jovene.

Hannum, H. (1993). Rethinking Self-Determination. *Virginia Journal of International Law, 34*, 1.

Irti, N. (2001). *Norma e luoghi. Problemi di geo-diritto*. Roma-Bari: Laterza.

Klabbers, J. (2006). The Right to Be Taken Seriously: Self-Determination in International Law. *Human Rights Quarterly, 28*(1), 186.

Knop, K. (2002). *Diversity and Self-Determination in International Law*. Cambridge: Cambridge University Press.

Kohen, M. G. (2006). *Secession: International Law Perspectives*. Cambridge: CUP.

Kraus, P. A., & Vergés Gifra, J. (2017). Introduction. In P. A. Kraus & J. Vergés Gifra (Eds.), *The Catalan Process: Sovereignty, Self-Determination and Democracy in the 21st Century* (p. 195). Barcelona: Institut d'Estudis de l'Autogovern.

Margiotta, C. (2005). *L'ultimo diritto. Profili storici e teorici della secessione*. Bologna: Il Mulino.

Margiotta, C. (2007). Introduzione, in John C. Calhoun. *Secessione e libertà*, edited by Costanza Margiotta Torino: La Rosa.

Margiotta, C. (2017a). Perchè la secessione fa paura? Un aggiornamento su «l'ultimo diritto». *Governare la paura, 3*, 37.

Margiotta, C. (2017b). Sulla (im)possibilità della secessione. Per una legalità «liminale». *Ordines, 2*, 43.

Margiotta, C. (2019). An Update on Secession as the "Ultimate Right". For a Liminal Legality. In C. Closa, C. Margiotta, & G. Martinico (Eds.), *Between Democracy and Law: The Amorality of Secession*. London: Routledge.

Martinico, G. (2019). 'A Message of Hope': A Legal Perspective on the Reference. In G. Delledonne & G. Martinico (Eds.), *The Canadian Contribution to a Comparative Constitutional Law of Secession: Legacies of the Quebec Secession Reference* (pp. 249–263). Basingstoke: Palgrave.

McGee, R. W. (1992). A Third liberal Theory of Secession. *The Liverpool Law Review, 14*(1), 45.

Norman, W. (2006). *Negotiating Nationalism: Nation-Building, Federalism, and Secession in the Multinational State*. Oxford: Oxford University Press.

Pavković, A., & Radan, P. (2007). *Creating New States: Theory and Practice of Secession*. Burlington: Ashgate.

Pavković, A., & Radan, P. (2011) *The Ashgate Research Companion to Secession*. Aldershot: Ashgate.

Philpott, D. (1995). In Defense of Self-Determination. *Ethics, 105*, 352.

Senese, S. (1992). *Oltre il diritto di farsi Stato*, in AA.VV., *Radici e nazioni*. Roma: Manifestolibri, 89 ff.

Sterio, M. (2018). *Secession in International Law. A New Framework*. Cheltenham: Edward Elgar.

Walter, C., von Ungern-Sternberg, A., & Abushov, K. (Eds.). (2014). *Self-Determination and Secession in International Law*. Oxford: OUP.

Wellman, C. H. (2005). *A Theory of Secession. The Case for Political Self-Determination*. Cambridge: CUP.

CHAPTER 4

Revolution and Devolution in Contemporary European Territoriality: Political Orders and Moral Borders in *Exit*-ing

Mira Kaneva

1 Introduction

In a reverse manner to a Kafkaesque universe, McEwan's *Cockroach* (from the 2019 eponymous novella) transmutes into the British prime minister only to be implicated in the farcical insect-brained universe of Reversalism, in which the flow of money is reversed. Parallels with the "counterclockwise" political, social, and economic effects from Brexit are inevitable, and this impact is approximating to grim atomizing tendencies in the European system.

This chapter argues that devolutionary processes such as deepening autonomy and enlarging transfer of power to different levels are a normal tendency in the complex networks of interdependence that sustain European integration. Still, throughout the last decade, a certain peak in devolution has become visible. It consists in the ever growing aspirations

M. Kaneva (✉)
University of Sofia, Sofia, Bulgaria

M. Belov (ed.), *Territorial Politics and Secession*, Federalism and Internal Conflicts, https://doi.org/10.1007/978-3-030-64402-4_4

for independence within the integrative community or even for emancipation from the community (the so-called *Exit*-ing discourse and practices), starting from the Brexit precedent.

The main theoretical and, therefore, pragmatic concern runs as follows: are there any limits to devolution? If so, how should they be set so that they do not become contagious? Some 55 years ago Karl Deutsch's doubts sounded like "*European integration [...] has stopped or reached a plateau...*" (Deutsch 1966, p. 355)—very much echoing the current virile pandemics lingo. The chapter tries to disperse the panicky presumptions that devolutionary trends are an imminent threat to European integrity. What poses certain risks, instead, is the abuse of revolutionary rhetoric in the clichés about regaining control, the defense of sovereignty, the rise of extreme nationalism. More or less, these speech acts stir insecurity and instability for they rely heavily on calls for emergency and mobilization against enemies. A certain paradox comes as a consequence—the devolutionary discourse tries to revolutionize high politics by demands for abrupt and irreversible change in the course of the integrative progress, but at the same time, it cannot produce sustainable results besides populist narrative. The tentative conclusion is that these revolutionizing ambitions about reconfiguration of the European territorial and legal unity are to no avail because, practically speaking, they confront simple hackneyed solutions with the social complexity. From an ethical viewpoint, they do not prove to be legit, as they try to advance the moral geography of othering and exclusion—something completely incompatible with the European values of solidarity.

The structure of the chapter runs as follows. The first section is focused on the theoretical post-functionalist assumptions about the development of regional integration and disintegration made by communitarians and the dictum about the interdependence between the spatial and the temporal domains in international relations studies. Then it advances the main critical argument about the normalcy of devolution and its quasi-revolutionary deviation in political rhetoric and social mobilization. The third section, the case study, concentrates on the Brexit conundrum, as it readily illustrates the volatility of revolutionary territorial politics and its failure to be an incorruptible alternative to the existing legal and political order.

2 About Some Theorizing

The European Integration Process as a Symptomatic Transmission of Benefits and Non-Benefits. Why Flatten the Curve?

It is not the tension between universalism and particularism that is the recurrent topic in European political thought on territoriality; it is more about the spillover between different models of community—from the radically pluralist Westphalian state-centric system, through solidarist projects such as integration communities or federation, to even more encompassing global community visions. This spillover may follow any random order—there is no predetermined logic of the development of territoriality except for the accidental logic of major events in history. These are actually the intricacies of the interdependence of spatiality and time, the so-called spatio-temporalities that mark the uneven and complex development, especially with the deterritorialization of the state in digital space (a study on spatio-temporalities by Harvey 2005 in Gieseking 2014, 12–16; a more specific research on digital networks as the new spatial order in Sassen 2008). For example, the pre-Westphalian European system is based on the universalistic dynastic principle which in the mid-seventeenth century was succeeded by the anarchic state-centric organizing principle, but there was, especially a century ago, further moves toward universalistic projects, such as the utopian Wilsonian harmony of interests and the Leninist classless dogma.

On a strictly theoretical note, there exists a transition in the scope of political loyalty, whether on a micro-level (nationality), on a meso-level (belonging to a regional community), or on a macro-level (cosmopolitanism). In practical terms, these levels co-exist because social and political relations stagger between the two poles of inclusivity and exclusivity according to the context. There are multiple competing logics in each sphere of global affairs, for example, border politics may be exclusive when imposing control in times of refugee flows or inclusive in economic boom years when migrant workers' influx would further wealth; these opposing considerations determine the decision-making process. Our conceptual analysis tries to evaluate critically the predominant narrative by connecting "*normative, empirical, and practical dimensions of moral inclusion and exclusion*" (Linklater 1990, p. 151).[1] Thus, we rely on a relatively more systematic and comprehensive approach to the problem, employed by critical theorists of international relations.

As the attributive "critical" suggests, the critical approach is about demystification of the existing order and resistance to regressive ideologies. It is, therefore, seen as a more prescriptive approach than the utterly descriptive and empirically based Realist school. It claims to be advancing an emancipatory project of humanity. In our particular case of territoriality, critical theorists try to debunk the sanctity of Westphalian sovereignty as an integrative constituent of the progress of contemporary nation-states. In the recent few (four to five) years, though, nation-states have increasingly been implicated in power politics, so it seems that we are revisiting the déjà vu of raison d'état. As *R. B. Walker* admits, conventional wisdom about classical geopolitical interests turns out to "*offer a more appropriate interpretation of contemporary trajectories than wild claims about innovation and transformation*" (Walker 1998, p. 131).[2] As mundane as it sounds, the catchphrase about constant, rapid, and unpredictable transformations has been indicative of the continuity and inevitability of change.

So, on a horizontal scale, ever since the possibility of a progressive history during the Enlightenment, evolution is a steadfast marker of socio-political order, despite some deviations toward revolution and counter-revolution (restoration). However, contemporary accelerative tendencies of globalization challenge the established categories about this linear development. That is why, critical theorists assert, the principle of sovereign identity (state-centric territoriality) should not be taken as an unquestioned assumption. Evolution seems to have abandoned the predictable linear form of development and is more appropriately characterized by patterns of intricate connections. In these interactions, non-state actors revolutionize the concept of sovereignty. It is not about whether states remain obstinate or become obsolete, but it is about the non-linear evolution of global affairs. The Westphalian state-system narrative, based on European exceptionalism (Kayaoglu 2010),[3] is no longer feasible; it

[1] Critical theorists insist on "*widening the circle of community to include those who are currently excluded by separate states*" through the much contested prism of cosmopolitan ethics.

[2] Rob Walker's work takes a turn in a post-Marxist direction.

[3] A theoretical critique of the English school and constructivist IR scholarship's bias about the prominence of the Westphalian argument.

fails to diagnose the complex "physiology" of pluralism and diversity as opposed to monolithic state-centrism.

These interdependences imply that change is not merely a string of causes and consequences. As *Buzan* summarizes a symposium on The Global Transformation, historical dynamics is not "*something we can isolate, disassemble, and test*"; it is rather "*temporally specific assemblages*" (Buzan and Lawson 2016, p. 505). Thus, events (the concrete piece) can be combined to yield recurrent patterns (the abstract picture); they bring about change, but at the same time they can be theorized as possessing some continuity. Any critical (groundbreaking) event is not a "Big Bang", a change out of the blue; it is a sudden manifestation of a gradual transformation. In the same way, Brexit is a cluster of relatively clear causes that have culminated in a popular vote with unclear consequences on European territoriality; it shouldn't be interpreted as an abrupt stroke to the integrative processes, but as a symptom of some systemic dysfunctions.

The term "order" in this sense means a persistent pattern and does not necessarily imply stability or explicit arrangement—it is an analytical tool that principally seeks to represent the actual configuration of social forces (Gill 1997, pp. 5–24). The political structure is therefore reproduced through the discourse and actions of the agents involved (the so-called intersubjective meanings from a constructivist point of view); from a critical standpoint, it is about some conflicting forces that necessitate the dialectic of transformation (the status quo as the thesis, the change as the anti-thesis). In a similar pattern, theorizing is inherently dialectical—on the one hand, there is some traditional theorizing according to established paradigms; on the other hand, there emerges a divergent paradigm that radically challenges the tenets of the preceding one (Lijphart 1974, p. 57).[4] For example, the evolutionary explanation of Brexit would draw upon rational arguments (realist national interests or liberal calculations of gains and losses); the devolutionary reasoning would count on a more critical approach to populist rhetoric and popular attitudes.

On a vertical scale, the meso-level (the communitarian one) is supposed to be the most encompassing of the polarizing trends outlined above. In this chapter we discuss European integration process through the prism of *Karl Deutsch*'s communication theory. *Deutsch* and his colleagues at

[4] A side remark: international relations is not a truly scientific discipline, as *Kuhn* (1970) argues, since it is not self-contained and is open to communication with "an audience larger than its own profession".

Princeton University devoted their efforts to the study of world political institutions in the 1950s and made some findings on the formation of security communities not only as a string of historical events but also as complex sites for social interactions such as imposition of norms and compliance with values. The recurrent patterns of integration, like other relative uniformities in history, raise the problem of the comparability of historical events. They also point to its evolutionary nature in the sense that it perpetuates over time despite crises and critical events.

Territoriality has little say in the formation of integrative communities, since the search is not for a "shallow 'universal state'" (Deutsch 1953, p. 195), but for an enduring unity that is based on social mobilization and economic transactions. Not unlike the way scholars in border studies are wary of the territorial trap, *Deutsch* tries to avoid the "*nation-state trap*". This cognitive trap is a misconception that any kind of polity is just a nation-state writ large (e.g. empires) or a nation-state writ small (e.g. city-states) (Deutsch 1967/1979, p. 310 in Drulák and Druláková 2014, p. 334). The fault with the nation-state is that it may breed nationalism and thus provoke violence because of politics based on exceptionalism or deprivation. Moreover, the nation-state is incapable of guaranteeing survival to its population, either the physical one because of the revolutionizing of military technology or the socio-economic one because of the fluctuations of the economic cycles.

Integration, we may infer, is far from skin-deep. It doesn't suffice to interconnect communication channels because integration isn't subsumed under the economic logic of bargaining—the benefits. Communication is about the "*possession of adequate memories and decoding routines*" (Deutsch 1974, p. 114), so that the nations understand each other—these are, figuratively speaking, non-benefits, such as norms, values, beliefs, practices, and symbolic gestures. In *Deutsch*'s usage, integration is "*the attainment, within a territory, of a 'sense of community' and of institutions and practices strong enough and widespread enough to assure, for a 'long' time, dependable expectations of 'peaceful change' among its population*" (Deutsch 1957, p. 5). An integrative community, therefore, is based on some kind of amalgamation (merging of units) that brings about the dynamics of non-violent co-existence.

The European Union (EU), first of all, has long ago crossed the narrow threshold of such a community by meeting the precondition of the absence of warfare. Next, the EU has broadened the concept of community by developing mutual loyalties and trust, the so-called *we-feeling* (Deutsch

1957, p. 36) of perception and responsiveness to shared vital needs. This sense of community is manifested in the body of common rights and obligations that are binding on all EU members (acquis) and in the functions of EU institutional structure. Thirdly, the sense of community requires practices (habitual behavior) that are invested in social learning, such as common policies in different areas and are highly indicative of the neo-functionalist logic of the spillover.

Social learning may incite disillusionment with the direction of the integrative process and then a more active participation of dissenting groups in the community. If the supranational elites are isolated from the national societies, as in some cases with EU bureaucracy, some nation-states may opt for indifference or resistance (a specific disintegration impulses), even exemption. The fracture in the vertical ties (supranational cohesion) may give an impetus to a break-up in the horizontal ties (intergovernmental cooperation or membership). So the political orders are interrelated by some moral dilemmas of legitimacy, empowerment, transparency, and accountability.

A milestone in the uneven development of EU integration wase the French and Dutch referendums in 2005, rejecting the Treaty establishing the Constitution for Europe. The campaign played a vital role in priming certain attitudes in the public, so the turnout was driven by specific issue concerns, such as the cultural threat from Eastern European immigrants, rather than general dissatisfaction with the European Union. They incited an anxiety about the stagnation of the integrative process and prompted doubts about two sets of questions. The first one concerns the vertical development, the so-called deepening of the integration by federalization, that is, supranational decision-making and ultimate delegation of sovereign competences to a higher order. We are going to address it as problems of differentiation of European integration. The second one concerns the horizontal development by excessive or deficient enlargement. We are going to address it as problems of the leaving of EU members, the so-called Exiting, that provokes a specific disorder and obsession with state-centrism and homogenous territoriality.

The Contagious Effect of the Devolution of Orders

The pace and scope of developments in the integrative community have in some respect overtaken the traditional theoretical debates between realists, neo-functionalists, and liberal intergovernmentalists. There has been a prominent shift from integration to Europeanization which turns the focus from top-down processes of EU institution-making to the more critical processes from below, such as the changes in boundaries and penetration of national systems of governance. The problem with integration theory is that it takes for granted that the impact of EU legislation is relatively uniform across states. The EU is a complex system that consists of heterogeneous units in a specific hierarchy because of the binding effect of European law, and these units feature strong independent institutional arrangements at the same time. That's why national governments may perceive and pursue common objectives in very different ways.

Andersen and *Sitter* challenge the idea that there is one basic type of European integration. They construct a four-fold typology, following for looser coupling between levels and pressure of decoupling at the national level (Andersen and Sitter 2006, pp. 320–321). Apart from the homogenous integration model of classical theories, in reality there is little convergence in organizational structure and behavior at the national level with the ongoing processes at the supranational level. Outside the scope of homogeneous integration stay aligned, autonomous, and deviant integration; for the purposes of this study we are going to concentrate on deviant integration alone.

Deviant integration is seen as an anomaly that occurs when a state is (formally) committed to strict interpretation of EU norms, but faces strong local resistance to a policy. It is a radical interpretation of the evolutionary integrative process that we perceive as a vertical deviation or devolution from it. Even after an EU law has been transposed into national legislation, there may be enduring and strong pressure from affected actors to circumvent or ignore the norms in order to preserve existing practices, quite often formulated as a defense of national interests. But is it really a defense or a failure to defend the national interests in an integrative community? *Andersen* and *Sitter* recognize the inexperienced Eastern European countries as policy-takers with limited capacities to influence the EU (Andersen and Sitter 2006, p. 326)[5] and therefore laggards in implementing the rule of law.

There are two distinct subtypes of this deviant integration, though. EU law is seen as problematic to the "new" member states as it compromises illegitimate practices perceived as normalcy (such as corruption and dysfunctional legal system) because it cannot reconcile with the limited state

[5] Hereby we infer to the latest members Bulgaria, Romania, and Croatia.

capacity. In other member states, such as Britain and Denmark, EU regulatory regime (esp. enforcement by directives) is seen as illegitimate since it affects internal sovereignty (the autonomy of domestic decisions, e.g. in intellectual property rights, in monetary function, etc.) or national traditions.

The devolution in integration is a specific revolution in the integrative process because it transforms it radically. Of course, the scope of divergence varies. The heterogeneity in the devolutionary effects is often termed generally as differentiated integration (De Neve 2007, p. 517, n. 1).[6] The governance in Europe is not uniform (obviously, it is neither based solely on hierarchy as in the bureaucracy nor on parity as in civil society); it is instead segmented by policy areas and levels of government, even by subgroups of states or regions in states. It seems that the binary approach to European member states has long passed its expiration date and has been substituted by multiple degrees in integration, with the Schengen area and the Eurozone being the most illustrative cases in point.

The dichotomy between the vanguard group and the laggards (the avant-garde and the marginalized) or the core and periphery is no longer valid. We doubt that a differentiated approach allows for a lesser divide among European states and prescribes a legitimate policy solution, but at least it describes the permeability and complexity of the integrative effects that may easily turn into disintegrative ones. Some authors uphold the argument that the centripetal effect of integration has a specific coercive power by maintaining the threat of being excluded and it has served as a negotiation tool for the recalcitrant UK to be brought to the table after a deadlock in the negotiations of the 1985 Single European Act (De Neve 2007, p. 512). Apart from overcoming the risks of opting out, this centripetal effect has the persuasive power of opting in, especially with new member states that are attracted by the material benefits of enlargement such as EU cohesion funds.

Still, the centrifugal effect of integration has proved to be dominant tendency of the behavior of sovereign states in recent years. *Schimmelfennig*

[6] De Neve finds the term sufficiently descriptive, since it encompasses the following terminologies: *flexible integration (e.g. Stubb 2002); asymmetrical integration (Sbragia 1993); multispeed (e.g. Martin & Ottaviano 1995); double speed (Hoffmann 2000); variable-geometry (e.g. Pisani-Ferry 1997); concentric circles (e.g. Usher 1997); à la carte Europe (e.g. Verhofstadt in press); poly-centric Europe (Wind 1998); vanguard nations (Fischer 2000); pioneer group (Chirac 2000, 2006); core Europe (e.g. Hoffmann in de Schoutheete 2000); "hub and spokes" Europe (Miles 2003); and advanced integration (Lenaerts & Van Nuffel in press).*

applies the term "*differentiated disintegration*" to describe the "*the selective reduction of a state's level and scope of integration*" (Schimmelfennig 2018, p. 1). Disintegration varies in its range—from the selective exiting from specific policies (the abovementioned opting out or internal disintegration) to the radical act of leaving the community (external disintegration). The shift in sovereign functions, therefore, can go both ways. The evolutionary direction meets the conditions for a successful integrative process, as *E. Haas* defines "*the process whereby political actors in several distinct national settings are persuaded to shift their loyalties, expectations, and political activities toward a new and larger center, whose institutions possess or demand jurisdiction over the pre-existing national states*" (Haas 1961, pp. 366–367). This is actually a shift in territoriality for both the Union and the nation-state, as far as it has a unifying impact of being included in a community with both supranational and intergovernmental competences, and results in the (ultimate) dissolution of internal border control. The devolutionary effect has also its impact on territoriality because it consists in the withdrawal from further integrative efforts and the ensuing of reinstated sovereign rule, including border control.

What are the factors that facilitate disintegration? There are two discernible reasons—the first one is based on the logic of intergovernmental bargaining and the calculation of gains and profits; the second one is based on neo-functionalism and the logic of spillover. First, in material terms, there are findings that wealthier member states are more likely to gain opt-outs from treaty revisions. The reason why is that they are more reluctant to integrate deeply for fear of redistribution or out of concern that deep integration with poorer countries might undermine their governance capacity and efficiency (Schimmelfennig 2016). Second, in ideational terms, disintegration is a frequent phenomenon among member states with widespread exclusive national identities that increase the salience of sovereignty transfers (Hooghe and Marks 2005). If spillover effects do occur, there exists a probability of politicization of the integrative process and a populist Eurosceptic backlash.

Therefore, using theoretical frameworks such as *Hirschman*'s on exit, voice, and loyalty, we can have insights how nation-states react and try to protect their resilient sovereignty functions in international institutions. When a development in the integrative process is not consistent either with their national interests (from political Realism perspective) or their identity (from a social constructivist perspective), they may demonstrate their discontent by vetoing policy change or opting out altogether

(Hirschman 1970 in Jensen and Slapin 2012, p. 782). The blocking of change may be preferable to the creation of a multispeed union where laggards are left behind on certain contentious issues. Still, this provision is not working under the pressure of public opinion and domestic bargaining.

At the same time, certain devolution (in the meaning of delegation) of power to democratic institutions within some states such as the UK takes place. The systems of regional and federal government established on the continent have not proved static, so devolution to regional authorities is in process. The devolution reforms were instituted through a series of Acts of the Westminster Parliament—Scotland Act 1998; Government of Wales Act 1998; Northern Ireland Act 1998 (Hopkins 2002, p. 167). Thus there are two types of devolutions—first in sovereignty and territoriality at the national level and, next, at the community level where centrifugal forces might give a halt to integrative policies.

The autonomy afforded by the devolutionary process in a growing number of nation-states is a result of the complex set of networks and agreements. Autonomy normally encompasses measures of self-rule, where constituent units contain elected governments that have meaningful measures of authority over local matters, in decision and execution (Agranoff 2004, p. 26). This means that autonomy is developed through devolution or the transfer of power vertically to political authorities at local levels in unitary states and horizontally to autonomous units in federative states and unions.

Apart from the normative and institutional dimensions of territorial devolution in nation-states, there is an undergoing process of rhetorical contention over European integration. Resistances can be defined as manifestations of hostility toward one or several aspects of European integration perceived as a threat with respect to one's values (Crespy and Verschueren 2009, p. 382). Interestingly, the historical ascent of Euroscepticism dates back to Great Britain in the late 1980s when the term was coined by the press as part of anti-narrative of the "anti-marketeers" in the European Economic Community (EEC). It then diffused during the debate over the ratification of the Maastricht treaty. Then, in the late 1990s and the 2000s it created the false dichotomy between regulation, on the one hand, and liberalization, on the other (between the statist and globalist discourse). Such a critical perspective focuses on the discursive aspect and encompasses actors beyond and below the political elites and their policies, as well as it relocates Europe in the wider realm of conflict and contention.

Whenever there is some constitutional issue that concerns basic sovereignty principles such as power, territoriality, rights, or other issues enlarging or deepening the integrative process, it is transferred to the popular vote. Still, as *Hooghe* notes, referendums are "*élite-initiated events which can have élite-defying consequences. They are used for immediate effect, but their institutional impact has a considerable half-life*" (Hooghe and Marks 2009, p. 20). We would rather argue that instead of shifting the initiative to citizens and single-issue groups, and disarming party elites, referendums pass the buck from political élites to the citizens. They legitimize anti-elitist parties and their polarizing agenda. Through this civil mobilization we can observe further devolution of the vertical political order in decision-making which raises subsequent moral dilemmas.

Empiricism: Case Study of Exiting. The Brexit "Popular Coup"—The False Moral Dilemmas and Pragmatic Implications of Populist "Distancing"

Britain's leaving the European Union seems like an entry into a terra incognita of unknown variables. Paradoxically, although Brexit was expected to restore the state's sovereignty in decision-making, it has so far narrowed its discretionary powers in key areas that necessitate complicated choices, such as the freedom of movement and the common market. The 2016 referendum was supposed to legitimize a renegotiation UK-EU relations as drafted in "The new settlement for the United Kingdom in a Reformed European Union'" (GOV.UK 2015). Britain reclaims its sovereignty in four areas:

- opting out from the economic governance;
- dismissal of the bureaucratic burden in competitiveness;
- sovereignty (in the broadest sense of discretion when implementing EU law);
- waiving of free movement (Council of the European Union 2016).[7]

In practice, even before the referendum, Britain made advantage of its differentiated integration—opting out from the Eurozone and the

[7] *Conclusions: The United Kingdom and the European Union*. European Council, 18 and 19 February 2016 http://www.consilium.europa.eu/en/meetings/european-council/2016/02/18-19/

Schengen information system; reservations as to the cooperation on justice and home affairs, as well as the Charter of fundamental rights, and concessions in budget installments. The binary formulation of the two options (Bremain/Brexit) didn't propose any adequate exit from the critical situation and turned the referendum question into a false moral dilemma instead.

The 2011 European Union Act was an effort not only to put brakes to any further transfer of loyalties to the integrative community, but also to legally reaffirm that UK sovereignty (and especially legislative powers) had been revoked during the membership. The so-called sovereignty clause, though not articulating the word "sovereignty" itself, unambiguously uncovered the impossibility to find a legal formula to a constitutional term. The issue recurred in Cameron's draft for Sovereignty law which never saw the light of day. Still sovereignty became part and parcel of the pre-referendum discourse—Brexit is proclaimed as the panacea for independence. The contention of ideas between the systemic and the anti-systemic discourse actually presents a false dichotomy—both offer dysfunctional clichés.

When we refer to the abovementioned reasons for disintegration, we can assert that both are available. First, from the material point of view, Brexiters claim to have advanced their decision on solely pragmatic grounds. They reject the Brussels bureaucratic machinery (the institutional criticism) and over-regulation (the normative criticism) as a generic medication to social and economic problems. Next, from the ideational point of view, Brexit is explained as a manifestation of the insular positioning of a former empire that identifies itself more readily with former colonies and dependent territories than with the Continent.

When discussing the devolutionary trends, we should broaden our analysis with the populist discourse. Populism, despite being conspicuously critical to the status quo, doesn't persist over long periods of time as it polarizes the public sphere by its nihilism. The most delegitimizing trait of Exiting populists is that they finally accommodate themselves with the criticized power structures, such as the radical conservative circles. Populist leaders, apart from being quasi-rational (by the use of generalizations and provoking extreme sentiments), endorse reactionary feelings, nostalgia, and suspicion toward progress. They maintain anti-immigrant feelings by exploiting mass primal fears and drawing moral boundaries to separate nationals from aliens. The hysterical discourse of othering and exclusion that manipulates public opinion marks the transition of EU integration to disintegration or the devolution of the elitist project or "elite conspiracy" (Inglehart 1977, p. 322) to public concern and even diffuse threat. The UK Independence Party (UKIP) combined its traditional Europhobia with "*strident opposition to mass immigration and the free movement of EU nationals*" (Clarke et al. 2017, p. 88); this is how several "anti"-messages with no substantiality whatsoever communicated referendum results.

Brexit in fact legitimized the ongoing process of bordering, that is, the construction of restrictions through discourses (political rhetoric), practices (border control procedures), and structure (institutional impediments). This bordering might be even on an everyday basis (Forkert in Guderjan et al. 2020, p. 134)—while usually perceived as legal mechanism for inclusion or exclusion, they are also cultural (based on conceptions, beliefs, values, etc.). They become instrumental for the management of public feelings and the framing of political agenda.

Objective factors such as positive pay-offs overcome subjectively created endogenous tensions. *Schmitter* argues, in this regard, that there is "*a 'hypothesis of natural entropy' which suggests that all integration processes will tend toward a state of rest or stagnation – unless disturbed by exceptional (i.e., unpredictable) or exogenous conditions not present in the original convergence or in the institutions themselves*" (Schmitter 1970, p. 847). The disintegrative dynamics seems to have been detained within the European intricate institutional architecture (for four years now) and to relatively easily bring devolution back to normalcy.

A similar showcase for disintegrative populism is the ensuing "referendum" democracy in Catalonia which further implicated the territoriality question by secessionist attempts. Secessionist doubts in Scotland and Ireland follow suit and thus constitute a sui generis devolution in this specific aspect of sovereignty. On a horizontal scale, viewing the electoral map (detailed polling date on The Electoral Commission GOV.UK 2016), there is a distinct split in territorial preferences as voting patterns delineate tensions in the "set of connected spaces" (Cochrane in Guderjan et al. 2020, pp. 109–130). Scotland and Northern Ireland voice their autonomous choice to remain in the EU, whereas Wales shares Brexit attitudes with England. Typically, fringe, or non-mainstream, parties are theoretically and empirically seen as Eurosceptic, but as far as regionalist parties are concerned, such as the Scottish National party, they tend to be more Europhile (Jolly 2007, p. 271). This deviation in the populist attitudes might be explained with the pursuit of further legitimation of their other devolutionary causes related to their emancipation from the state.

Since there is no clear-cut legal mechanism that allows for the remaining of Scotland in the EU, the reverse logic might be applicable—Scotland leaving the UK before Brexit. However, a preceding secessionism (*#indyref2*) is unattainable due to three factors: improbability of vast popular support, lack of constitutional grounds for a binding effect, and further complications with a second membership candidacy. Some resemblance in the disintegrative precedent may be drawn with Greenland and Denmark in the 1973 referendum for EC membership. Greenland's negative vote accelerated its demand for home rule. However, this was accompanied by more complex processes—first, urbanization and modernization that carried with it feelings of alienation and loss of ethnic identity; second, the formation of a political consciousness. Moreover, this aspiration must not be confused with the nationalistic claim for secession (Johansen and Sørensen 1983); it is more about "*a post-Danish sovereign nation state in the making*" (Gad 2014). In a similar pattern, Scotland doesn't insist on its secessionist claims but rather counts on its leverage like veto power in Brexit negotiations.

Wales, on the one hand, is less divided as a society—which may explain the lower support for Brexit, compared with England and with what one might expect, given the socio-economic characteristics of Wales; moreover, there is no relationship between national identification and voting in the referendum (Mackay in Guderjan et al. 2020, pp. 175–187).

With Ireland, on the other hand, Bremain serves as a guarantee for its sovereignty in terms of territorial integrity and independence. Not until Brexit has the Western border to Ireland been visible and now it might shatter the fragile grounds for peace between the Unionists-Catholics (the supporters for unification) and the Unionists-Protestants (the champions of the status quo). *Wright* reasons polemically that it is "*in the context of Northern Ireland more than anywhere else that the interlinkages and tensions between UK domestic politics and its Brexit aspirations are thrown into sharpest relief*" (Wright in Martill and Staiger 2018, pp. 112–113). Utilizing Northern Ireland's moral imperative for a peace process as a bargaining chip in the talks on the special arrangement for the UK in its future trading relationship with the EU would confront the EU with a Gordian knot to untie.

3 The Reversalism of a Conclusion?

In a nutshell, in this study we have tried to transfer the communicative theorists' assumptions to the different levels of integration on both a horizontal and a vertical scale. When discussing the horizontal scale in terms of development, it has been asserted that stagnation incites evolutionary change. When discussing the vertical scale in terms of orders and delegation of powers, it has been contended that devolution is a progress itself because traditionalist (positivist) views on sovereignty and territoriality, especially in the EU, have changed. It is, namely, the post-positivist critical approach of analysis of the Brexit-related narrative and acts that unveils several false moral dilemmas. Paradoxically, Brexit as a rhetorical gesture reverses against itself—it seems and sounds revolutionary with its calls for devolution from the center (the overarching Brussels bureaucracy), but, in the end, it collaborates with the establishment and capitulates to great power politics, economic cycles, pandemic waves, and the like.

References

Agranoff, R. (2004). Autonomy, Devolution and Intergovernmental Relations. *Regional & Federal Studies, 14*(1), 26–65.

Andersen, S. S., & Sitter, N. (2006). Differentiated Integration: What Is It and How Much Can the EU Accommodate? *Journal of European Integration, 28*(4), 313–330.

Buzan, B., & Lawson, G. (2016). Theory, History, and the Global Transformation. *International Theory, 8*(3), Cambridge University Press, 502–522.

Clarke, H., Goodwin, M., & Whiteley, P. (2017). Brexit. Why Britain Voted to Leave the European Union. In M. Guderjan et al. (Eds.), *Contested Britain. Brexit, Austerity and Agency* (pp. 117–130). Cambridge: Cambridge University Press.

Cochrane, A. (2020). From Brexit to the Break-Up of … England? Thinking In and Beyond the Nation. In M. Guderjan et al. (Eds.), *Contested Britain. Brexit, Austerity and Agency* (pp. 161–173). Bristol: Bristol University Press.

Crespy, A., & Verschueren, N. (2009). From Euroscepticism to Resistance to European Integration: An Interdisciplinary Perspective. *Perspectives on European Politics and Society, 10*(3), 377–393.

De Neve, J.-E. (2007). The European Onion? How Differentiated Integration Is Reshaping the EU. *European Integration, 29*(4), 503–521.

Deutsch, K. W. (1953). The Growth of Nations: Some Recurrent Patterns of Political and Social Integration. *World Politics, 5*, 168–195.

Deutsch, K. W. (1957). *Political Community and the North Atlantic Area. International Organization in the Light of Historical Experience*. Princeton: Princeton University Press.

Deutsch, K. W. (1966). Integration and Arms Control in the European Political Environment: A Summary Report. *The American Political Science Review, 60*(2), 354–365.

Deutsch, K. W. (1974). Between Sovereignty and Integration: Conclusion. *Government and Opposition, 9*(1, Winter), 113–119.

Deutsch, K. W. (1967/1979). Nation and World. In *Tides Among Nations*. New York: The Free Press, Cit. in: Drulák, P., & Drulákova, R. (2014). The Richness of the Liberal Tradition in International Relations: Karl Deutsch on Political Community and the European Integration. *International Relations, 28*(3), 333–349.

EU Council. (2016). *Conclusions: The United Kingdom and the European Union*. European Council. http://www.consilium.europa.eu/en/meetings/european-council/2016/02/18-19/. Accessed 27 Jul 2020.

Forkert, K. (2020). 'Not an International Health Service': Xenophobia, Brexit and the Restoration of National Sovereignty. In M. Guderjan et al. (Eds.), *Contested Britain. Brexit, Austerity and Agency* (pp. 131–144). Bristol: Bristol University Press.

Gad, U. P. (2014). Greenland: A Post-Danish Sovereign Nation State in the Making. *Cooperation and Conflict, 49*(1), Special Issue: Postimperial Sovereignty Games in Norden (March), 98–118.

Gill, S. (1997). Transformation and Innovation in the Study of World Order. In S. Gill & J. H. Mittelmann (Eds.), *Innovation and Transformation in International Studies* (pp. 5–24). Cambridge: Cambridge University Press.

GOV.UK. (2015). *A New Settlement for the United Kingdom in a Reformed European Union*. https://www.gov.uk/government/uploads/system/uploads/attachment_data/file/475679/Donald_Tusk_letter.pdf. Accessed 27 Jul 2020.

GOV.UK. (2016). *How Britain Voted*. https://yougov.co.uk/news/2016/06/27/how-britain-voted/. Accessed 27 Jul 2020.

GOV.UK: The Electoral Commission. (2016). *EU referendum Results*. https://www.electoralcommission.org.uk/find-information-by-subject/elections-and-referendums/past-elections-and-referendums/eu-referendum/electorate-and-count-information. Accessed 27 July 2020.

Haas, E. B. (1961). International Integration: The European and the Universal Process. *International Organization, 15*(3), 366–392.

Harvey, D. (2005). Spacetime and the World. In J. J. Gieseking et al. (Eds.), 2014. *The People, Place, and Space Reader* (pp. 12–16). New York/London: Routledge.

Hirschman, A. O. (1970). *Exit, Voice, and Loyalty*. Cambridge, MA: Harvard University Press.
Hooghe, L., & Marks, G. (2005). Calculation, Community and Cues: Public Opinion on European Integration. *European Union Politics, 6*(4), 419–443.
Hooghe, L., & Marks, G. (2009). A Postfunctionalist Theory of European Integration: From Permissive Consensus to Constraining Dissensus. *British Journal of Political Science, 39*, 1–23.
Hopkins, W. J. (2002). *Devolution in Context: Regional, Federal & Devolved Government in the Member States of the European Union*. London: Cavendish Publishing Limited.
Inglehart, R. (1977). Parochialism, Nationalism, and Supra-Nationalism. In *The Silent Revolution. Changing Values and Political Styles Among Western Publics*. Princeton: Princeton University Press.
Jensen, C. B., & Slapin, J. B. (2012). Institutional Hokeypokey: The Politics of Multispeed Integration in the European Union. *Journal of European Public Policy, 19*(6), 779–795.
Johansen, O., & Sørensen, C. L. (1983). Greenland's Way Out of the European Community. *The World Today, 39*(7/8), 270–277.
Jolly, S. K. (2007). The Europhile Fringe? Regionalist Party Support for European Integration. *European Union Politics, 8*(1), 109–130.
Kayaoglu, T. (2010). Westphalian Eurocentrism in International Relations Theory. *International Studies Review, 12*(2), 193–217.
Lijphart, A. (1974). The Structure of the Theoretical Revolution in International Relations. *International Studies Quarterly, 18*(1), 41–74.
Linklater, A. (1990). The Problem of Community in International Relations. *Alternatives: Global, Local, Political, 15*(2, Spring), 135–153.
Mackay, H. (2020). Understanding Brexit in Wales: Austerity, Elites and National Identity. In M. Guderjan et al. (Eds.), *Contested Britain. Brexit, Austerity and Agency* (pp. 175–187). Bristol: Bristol University Press.
Sassen, S. (2008). Assembling mixed spatial and temporal orders: Elements for a Theorization. In *Territory, Authority, Rights. From Medieval to Global Assemblages* (pp. 378–398). Princeton: Princeton University Press.
Schimmelfennig, F. (2016). Good Governance and Differentiated Integration. Graded Membership in the European Union. *European Journal of Political Research, 55*(4), 789–810.
Schimmelfennig, F. (2018). Brexit: Differentiated Disintegration in the European Union. *Journal of European Public Policy*. Informa UK (Taylor & Francis). https://doi.org/10.1080/13501763.2018.1467954.
Schmitter, P. C. (1970). A Revised Theory of Regional Integration. *International Organization, 24*(4, Autumn), 836–868.

Walker, R. B. J. (1998). International Relations as Political Theory. In S. Sim (Ed.), *Post-Marxism. A Reader* (pp. 130–142). Edinburgh: Edinburgh University Press.

Wright, N. (2018). Brexit and Ireland: Collateral Damage? In B. Martill & U. Staiger (Eds.), *Brexit and Beyond. Rethinking the Futures of Europe* (pp. 105–113). London: UCL Press.

PART II

Territorial Politics and Sovereignty

CHAPTER 5

Territorial Disputes and State Sovereignty Reconciled

Jorge E. Núñez

1 Introduction

The world is a puzzle of different and intricate relations at local, regional and international levels. This pluralism of pluralisms includes different peoples, beliefs and assumptions that translate into a myriad of factual inter-relations, rules and policies. Despite the many conflict resolution rules and procedures, realpolitik shows that affinities are rare and that differences exacerbate the distance between local, regional and international agents. One kind of such differences, territorial disputes, gives a clear example of the zero-sum game that the claimed and claiming agent play because they feed their differences rather than recognizing their affinities.

Current conceptualizations and characterizations in legal and political sciences fail to acknowledge the intricacy sovereignty and territorial disputes have. These disciplines and others cut through sovereignty and territorial disputes as natural sciences dissect a living being. The contrast between natural sciences and law and political science is evident. The

J. E. Núñez (✉)
University of Manchester, Manchester, UK
e-mail: J.Nunez@mmu.ac.uk

M. Belov (ed.), *Territorial Politics and Secession*, Federalism and Internal Conflicts, https://doi.org/10.1007/978-3-030-64402-4_5

former understands the sample as part of a larger and more complex entity, while legal and political sciences define and characterize sovereignty and territorial disputes by reference only to a limited perspective. Thereafter, any application of these concepts and characterizations to real-life situations such as the many territorial disputes around the world (e.g. Jerusalem, Gibraltar, Falkland/Malvinas Islands) will be limited by the *a priori* frame of reference. Indeed, these frames of reference act as *a fortiri* bias.

So far, sovereignty and territorial disputes have been at odds. But they do not need to. On the one hand, sovereignty, both at the level of the individual and at the level of the state, seems to be binary. On the other hand, territorial disputes assume a plurality of agents. The challenge remains to reimagine a notion of sovereignty that can enable a pluralism of pluralisms where individuals in civil societies and states in the regional and international arenas leave aside their differences and recognize their affinities.

Sovereignty at the level of the individual seems to be absolute and, therefore, binary. Ideas such as self-ownership, "otherhood" and gender-defined roles clearly indicate a binary understanding of sovereignty biased by *a fortiori* assumptions. Pre-conceived notions, like "You are Y because I am X" or "I am X because you are Y" whether the point of reference is the interpreter or the subject referred to, show the dichotomy between self-identification and otherhood.[1] Sovereignty at the level of the state has been absolute since its birth. With Bodin and Hobbes articulating the modern and current understanding of state sovereignty, any given population and/or government will be sovereign over a territory if and only if they are the sole law-maker.

At the crux of both these understandings of absolute, exclusive, binary sovereignty (at the level of the individual and at the level of the state) there is a self-evident question. Because every individual is unique (arguably, the same is true of states as well) the binary, absolute, exclusive understanding of sovereignty results in differentiating that who I am (or my state is) from any other individual (or any other state).

[1] These partial interpretations fail to recognize other elements important to any hermeneutics such as cultural, stylistic and disciplinary differences. Linked to this, there is a case for a variety of interpretations or "unlimited semiosis." See Stella Bullo, *Evaluation in Advertising Reception: A Socio-Cognitive and Linguistic Perspective* (Springer, 2014); Hans-Georg Gadamer, *Philosophical Hermeneutics* (Berkeley: University of California Press, 1976); Hans Jauss, *Toward and Aesthetic of Reception* (University of Minnesota Press, 1982); Martyn P. Thompson, "Reception Theory and the Interpretation of Historical Meaning," *History and Theory* 32 (1993): 248–272; and others.

If such a sketch were correct, individuals (and states) of different kinds would have some options in their inter-relations: neutrality, friendship or cooperation, and enmity. Logically and intuitively, an absolute understanding of sovereignty could only accept neutrality or enmity. In the case of neutrality, both agents would remain completely absolute because each of them would have exclusivity over their sphere of influence. In the case of enmity, the addition is the will any or both of the agents may have to dominate or annihilate the other.

Friendship or cooperation, in turn, begs further exploration. Because if any agent enters into any kind of relation with any other agent (in fact or in theory), there would be an acknowledgment of the existence of the others and an interaction between the two. The degree of interaction may vary from a simple acknowledgment of their reciprocal existence to joint ventures of any kind. The simple, basic acknowledgment may remain as neutrality, in which case, both agents too remain absolute. However, in the event these agents start interacting and that interaction evolves into reciprocal or unilateral concessions, the absoluteness disappears.

The key in solving the puzzle has to do with accepting that an absolute understanding of sovereignty is one of several choices, a conception of the concept and not the concept itself. Normatively and factually, sovereignty always includes limitations. It is the historically conditioned conception of sovereignty as absolute brought from the Middle Ages into contemporary times that disables more appropriate approaches to current realities. Absolute sovereignty served a purpose at the time there was social, political, legal, financial chaos in Europe. Territorial disputes and the plurality of pluralisms implicit within require an updated, more inclusive conception of sovereignty that can deal with the inter-play of different agents at different levels, either the level of the individual or the level of the state, and on different contexts, the domestic, the regional and the international platforms.

The first and second parts of the chapter will introduce the two main paradigms at play: sovereignty and territorial disputes. The former shows three aspects: a normative or theoretical side, a factual side and an axiological side. The later implies different issues, agents and contexts.

Sovereignty includes a normative or theoretical side as defined, for example, by law; a factual side as defined, for example, by political science; and an axiological side that enables to choose between an exclusive or an inclusive view. Both on the theoretical side and on the factual side, sovereignty includes limitations. Whether these limitations allow for domination or cooperation is, simply put, an axiological choice.

Territorial disputes as a pluralism of pluralisms imply leaving behind binary understandings in theory and fact about the world around us. The pre-conception of the world divided between "I" and "You" or "Us" and "Others" or any other such as gender-based classifications are not sufficient to capture the complexity that operates in our civil and international societies. To gain a more complete understanding of territorial disputes it is imperative to distinguish between claims, issues at stake and contexts. Both the challenger and challenged parties in a territorial dispute will refer to the legality and legitimacy of their respective claims as well as the illegality and illegitimacy of those of their counterpart in the difference. The nature of these claims is as broad as conceivable and ranges from referring to law, history and religion to natural resources, national honor and minorities. Although claims and issues at stake are related, they each have their place in a territorial dispute. For example, a territorial dispute may commence because of a historical claim but it may include several other issues at stake such as bordering minorities, leader's prestige and interference of external agents. In addition to claims and issues at stake, they may each have local, regional and international relevance.

The chapter argues that territorial disputes are complex, multi-subjective, multi-contextual and multi-faceted and aims to sketch a global and inter-disciplinary brief view of state sovereignty and territorial disputes. It is in the comprehensive understanding as multilayer and multi-contextual nature of state sovereignty and territorial disputes that a path toward a better explanation of their complexity can be built.

2 Sovereignty

Concept and Conceptions

There are several conceptions of sovereignty.[2] Unsurprisingly, the conventional norms of sovereignty are constantly challenged.[3] How to define and characterize sovereignty is of utmost importance for territorial dis-

[2] For an extensive analysis on different views, conceptions and historical evaluations of "sovereignty" see Christian Volk, "The Problem of Sovereignty in Globalized Times," in *Law, Culture and the Humanities* (February 2019); Neil Walker, ed., *Relocating Sovereignty* (London and New York: Routledge, 2018); Kirby Brown, "Sovereignty," in *Western American Literature* 53, no. 1 (2018): 81–89; G. Picker, *Sovereignty Beyond the State: Exception and Informality in a Western European City* (Int. J. Urban Reg. Res, 2019); and others.

[3] Stephen D. Krasner, "Sovereignty, Think Again," *Foreign Policy*, January/February (2001).

putes. While an absolute, exclusive and closed conception of sovereignty can only guarantee *status quo* and potential escalation into conflict, the acknowledgment of a limited, inclusive and open account of the same term can enable cooperation and peaceful and permanent ways out. To be more precise, it is not that because of the necessity to resolve territorial disputes amicably and endurably sovereignty must change. Sovereignty already offers what is required to move from zero-sum games between challenger and challenged agents in territorial disputes toward beneficial solutions to all parties. It is simply because the ongoing questions about sovereignty miss the mark by either centering the attention on purely tangential points or their lack of scientific integration that scientific disciplines should collaborate in bringing in line their understandings about it. In brief, some of the ongoing questions about sovereignty are:

> Why are we constantly "questioning sovereignty"? Why are we inclined to accuse sovereignty of "hypocrisy" or to reduce it to a "game"? Why are we concerned to "relocate" sovereignty or to search for its "fragments"? Why do we consider sovereignty to be "in transition", perhaps even "in crisis"?[4]

To offer a simple answer to all the previous questions, from a purely theoretical understanding, sovereignty has four uses[5]: (a) domestic sovereignty refers to the organization of public authority within a state and the level of effective control exercised by those holding authority; (b) interdependence sovereignty has to do with the ability of public authorities to control trans-border movements; (c) international legal sovereignty centers on the recognition of states or other entities and (d) Westphalian sovereignty and the exclusion of external actors from domestic authority configurations.

All the aforementioned uses in law and politics have a common root. They are informed by Bodin and Hobbes. To illustrate the crossover between the classical and more contemporary views in sovereignty, two quotations follow:

[4] Neil Walker, "Sovereignty Frames and Sovereignty Claims," University of Edinburgh, School of Law, Working Papers (2013), p. 1.

[5] Stephen D. Krasner, *Sovereignty: Organized Hypocrisy* (New Jersey, Princeton: Princeton University Press, 1999).

> Aieltie or Sovereignty is the most high, absolute, and perpetual power over the citizens and subjects in a Commonwealth.[6]

> A Supreme authority in a state. In any state sovereignty is vested in the institution, person, or body having the ultimate authority to impose law on everyone else in the state and the power to alter any pre-existing law…In international law, it is an essential aspect of sovereignty that all states should have supreme control over their internal affairs.[7]

Any use and conception of sovereignty include the notions of the highest, supreme, absolute authority in a territory and over a population. It is a concept that has always referred to the concentration of power. Yet, the concentration of power when sovereignty was introduced in law and politics was due to historical reasons. In any case, sovereignty has always included limitations of different natures.[8]

Historically, sovereignty appeared between the fifteenth and sixteenth centuries. At the time, power had to be monistic.[9] Therefore, sovereignty as characterized by Bodin and Hobbes was conditioned by the context. The absolute nature of sovereignty was a historically determined axiological choice. *Les Six Livres de la République* and Leviathan are not a historical coincidence. Both these works and the so-claimed absoluteness were time-bound. In that sense, sovereignty is a product of social construct.[10] All accounts of sovereignty including realists such as Morgenthau, Carr and Waltz, interdependence and dependence writers, conceptual analyses like the ones from Hinsley, James and Jackson, and social constructions theories accept conceptual, historical, domestic and international limitations.[11]

The subtle differences between the many accounts of sovereignty do not alter its limitations. Conceptions about sovereignty differ on the surface because of their assumed starting point. For example, depending on

[6] Jean Bodin, *The Six Bookes of Commonweale* (Impenfis G. Bishop 1903), 84.

[7] Elizabeth A. Martin and Jonathan Law, *A Dictionary of Law* (Oxford University Press 2006).

[8] Quentin Skinner, "A Genealogy of the State," *Rivista di Storia delle Idee* 2:1 (2013): 46–61, in particular p. 60, fn. 115.

[9] Dora Kostakopoulou, "Floating Sovereignty: A Pathology or a Necessary Means of a State Evolution?" *Oxford Journal of Legal Studies* 22 (2002): 135–156, 135.

[10] Thomas J. Biersteker and Cynthia Weber, eds., *State Sovereignty as Social Construct* (Cambridge: Cambridge University Press, 1996), pp. 1–21.

[11] *Ibid.* See also Cynthia Weber, "Writing Sovereign Identities: Wilson Administration Intervention in the Mexican Revolution," *Alternatives: Global, Local, Political* 17 (1992): 313–337, in particular p. 334, fns. 1 and 2.

the legal or political perspective, "sovereignty" may mean power or imply authority. Similarly, sovereignty can be viewed as internal or external, as purely normative and conceptual or factual and substantive, in a vertical or horizontal way, and as an attribute of a person, a body, a state or a supranational entity. This is because conceptions of sovereignty base their construction centered on norms, facts or values. From there, it is possible to identify factual sovereignty, normative sovereignty and axiological sovereignty.

For example, the statement: "Russians take over Crimea" may refer to a group of people from Russian ascent moving to another land called Crimea (factual realm) as well as the Russian Federation's "population" and/or "government" invaded or claimed back "territory" under, arguably, their jurisdiction (legal realm). Whether the Russian Federation illegally "invaded" or rightly "claimed back" the "territory" in question will depend on the axiological assessment of the facts in light of the relevant applicable law.

Consider too a legal and political concept such as "self-determination." Legal science will rely on public international law documents like article 1 (2) of the UN, UN General Assembly Resolution 1514 article 2, UN General Assembly Resolution 2649 article 1 and UN General Assembly Resolution 2625 Article e. It may appear the legal concept of "self-determination" is clearly defined because it has been included in legal documents. However, this so-called simple concept brings several hermeneutical problems, and questions about the meaning of its legal characterization (i.e. dismemberment of territory, the right to determine political status and the concept of "people") bring interpretative disagreements in law and politics.

Absolute Sovereignty and Limitations

The acknowledgment of limitations is important to solve territorial disputes. Conversely, an absolute understanding implies the continuation of the *status quo* and potential escalation into conflict. Absolute sovereignty translates into a mutually exclusive and collectively exhaustive result in territorial disputes: challenger and challenged agents take the stand that "victory for us is to see you suffer."[12] In other words, because an absolute

[12] Philip C. Winslow, *Victory for Us Is To See You Suffer: In the West Bank with the Palestinians and the Israelis* (Beacon Press: 2007).

understanding of sovereignty means that a territory under question can be granted to only one of the claiming agents, a solution implying non-binary is not possible (i.e. you or I can win but never both of us). On the contrary, limitations in sovereignty allow for cooperation between opposed agents because they accept in law and in fact the possibility to have interrelations between states without diminishing their respective spheres of influence.

The author has previously dealt with conceptual and substantial limitations in sovereignty as well as why in every case, factually, normatively and axiologically, sovereignty accepts imitations. *Brevitatis cuasa*, sovereignty is not absolute. Sovereignty has conceptual and substantive limitations. Thus, sovereignty exists in different realms. Broadly, factual sovereignty or sovereignty *de facto* refers to the actual control people or their representatives have over a territory.[13] In turn, sovereignty *de jure* implies, internally, the existence of a set of authorities (government) that is the exclusive law-maker and law-interpreter, and, externally, the recognition by peers of their legal existence as sole law-maker and law-interpreter in a determined territory.

These limitations to sovereignty do not curtail what states may do in law and in fact. On the contrary, it is because these limitations that states can be part in cooperative ventures. As a sovereign entity, states may face several limitations in law and fact such as plural jurisdiction, bilateral and multilateral agreements, and actions or omissions by their peers. If a population, large or small, chooses to have one ruler and that ruler distinguishes inhabitants between, for example, free and slaves according to their law, this decision is purely a value judgment. For whatever reason, the ruler valued positively to divide legally that population into two different kinds of groups. This same ruler could, instead, choose to follow a more inclusive rule of law and distinguish inhabitants in some other way, for example, by classifying people in adults and minors or legally abled and legally disabled.

[13] For an understanding about the distinction between sovereignty *de facto* and sovereignty *de jure* see Nina Caspersen, "Collective Non-recognition of States," in Gëzim Visoka, John Doyle and Edward Newman, eds., *Routledge Handbook of State Recognition* (Oxon and New York: Routledge 2020); R.K. Pruthi, *The Political Theory* (New Delhi: Sarup and Sons, 2005), 72; Kostas A. Lavdas, Spyridon N. Litsas and Dimitrios V. Skiadas, *Stateness and Sovereign Debt: Greece in the European Conundrum* (Maryland: Lexington Books, 2013), 66–70; and many others.

When the situation includes more than one sovereign state and, consequently, more than one population, territory and government, the different realms remain. Different sovereign states will have their own people, territory and government and it will be their axiological choice (value judgment) to decide whether they deal legally and factually with their peers on an equal standing basis or not. This does not mean that law may recognize sovereign equality and that recognition ought to translate into empirical equality. It is a fact that some states are "more equal" than others in realpolitik, despite public international law granting legal sovereign equality.[14]

Sovereignty does not preclude the possibility to have cooperative approaches to conflict and dispute resolution. In fact and in law, sovereignty can be inclusive or exclusive depending only on an axiological choice. Bilateral and multilateral agreements for cooperation are examples of the former, while occupation and blockades are examples of the latter.

The above brief sketch about factual, normative and axiological sovereignty aimed to show that in all cases there is no absoluteness but limitations. Thus, it is by virtue of these limitations that sovereign states are able to enter in bi- and multilateral relationships with their peers. Indeed, these bi- and multilateral relationships may take the form of cooperation or domination. Yet, in any case it is because sovereignty has factual, normative and axiological limitations that these inter-relations are possible.

Vertical and Horizontal Views

Another way to assess sovereignty and capture its limitedness has to do with two different views: vertical and horizontal. A vertical view of sovereignty acknowledges internally, regionally and internationally one lawmaker per population and territory. Vertically, sovereignty is concentrated and centralized. In turn, a horizontal view of sovereignty may see different arrangements. For example, a system of check and balances and division of powers such as in federal states or a mixture of supranational and intergovernmental institutions and law such as in the European Union. Therein, horizontally, power or authority can be dispersed and des-centralized.

[14] Hans Kelsen, "The Principle of Sovereign Equality of States as a Basis for International Organization," *Yale Law Journal* 53:2 (1944): 207–220; R. P. Anand, "Sovereign Equality of States in International Law," *International Studies*, 8:3 (1966): 213–224; Ronnie Hjnorth, "Equality in the Theory of International Society: Kelsen, Rawls and the English School," *Review of International Studies* 37:5 (2011): 2585–2602; and many others.

The vertical view may limit the existence in law to singularities. It is the horizontal view that enables to cut through the singularity and helps find common ground for potential cooperation and consensus. For example, at the level of the individual, a vertical view may accept self-ownership and, taken to the extreme, a will overriding the others (extreme examples such as cannibalism and slavery illustrate this). At the level of the state, a vertical view allows for domination where a state acts in an arbitrary and discretionary manner in relation to its peers (examples such as colonialism can be compared to cannibalism or intra-species predator and pseudo-, quasi- or failed states can be compared to slavery). By recognizing the horizontal view of sovereignty in the context of territorial disputes, it is possible to enable individuals in civil societies and states in the international arena to co-create or cooperate in law and in fact. The horizontal view accepts what is self-evident in law and in fact for both sovereignty and territorial disputes: a plurality of pluralisms.

Consider the cases of Kashmir, the Israel-Palestine difference and the border between Mexico and the United States. A vertical view of these examples shows separate sovereign entities territorially defined: for Kashmir, China, India and Pakistan; for the Israel-Palestine difference, at least Israel and the *de facto* State of Palestine (other Middle Eastern states may be included); and for the border between Mexico and the United States, at least these two (other Latin American stated may be included). What in principle, because of the vertical view, may seem very different disputes have horizontally several points in common. All three examples assessed horizontally show: bordering minorities, sociological issues such as culture, ethnicity, language and religion, natural resources and their consequent exploration and exploitation, governmental components such as applicable law (local, regional and international), leaders' prestige and corruption, the direct or indirect presence of regional and international organizations such as United Nations, OTAN, OEA and OAS, and many more.

3 Pluralism of Pluralisms

Globally, there is a pluralism of pluralisms. Each individual sovereign state includes communities and individuals of different kinds. Assuming the state as a single legal entity, the limitations to sovereignty may be unilateral, bilateral, multilateral or, even, imposed by the pre-existent context. Unilateral limitations have to do with those solely present in or created by the state of reference. Bi- and multilateral limitations refer to those that exist because any state part of the global network will have inter-relations with its peers. These inter-relations in the form of, for example, international agreements may curtail or enhance their sovereignty. Finally, those limitations imposed by the context include the ones imposed by public international law and customs. Consider the case of a newly formed and recognized sovereign state. This new state will have to comply with, for example, United Nations pre-existing rules should their representatives wanted to join the international organization. Uni-, bi- and multilateral and contextual limitations may be internal or external, normative or factual and may result in domination or cooperation.

Whether inwardly or outwardly considered, as purely normative and conceptual or factual and substantive, centered on a vertical or horizontal view, sovereignty is always limited. The many conceptions have to do with factors beyond sovereignty itself. Either because of the discipline of reference, the methodology these disciplines use or the part of the object under study (i.e. sovereignty) they take into consideration or give preeminence to, these many conceptions are the result. It is in the acknowledgment of these conceptions of sovereignty (based on facts, norms, values, views, etc.) where there is room for the inter-play between states. Because of these conceptions accept one way or another the limitedness of sovereignty it is possible to have bi- and multilateral international agreements. It is for the same reason that state may enter into cooperative joint ventures when faced with a difference such as territorial dispute.

Certainly, *status quo* and escalation into conflict are alternatives. However, this is true as well as for peaceful and permanent solutions. Sovereignty is not the cause of these (and any other) differences. Sovereignty may be a subterfuge for territorial disputes but not their reason. Since it is possible to make use of the limitations in sovereignty in order to enable cooperative arrangements, it is feasible to use these arrangements to come to an understanding in any territorial dispute. The fact most of these differences have been ongoing for so long has to do with a political and purely axiological choice (value judgment) by the respective leaders or governments rather than by sovereignty itself. Sovereignty does not imply a mutually exclusive and collectively exhaustive way out for territorial disputes. This is an over-simplification and a biased wrong assumption. Sovereignty, because of its limitations, allows to accommodate a plurality of pluralities.

The next section will introduce another key concept "territorial disputes" and show similarly true. Territorial disputes may be characterized by reference to the exclusive sovereignty of a certain territory but it does not need to. Territorial disputes are more complex than a simplistic binary difference and, because of this complexity, it is possible to solve them. In the same vein as sovereignty, territorial disputes can accommodate a plurality of pluralisms. Because any territorial dispute will present at least two agents, namely, the challenged and challenger, the plurality is evident. However, to assume each agent as an individuality, and therein, territorial disputes as binary, is a mistake. Each individual agent in a territorial dispute brings pluralism within. Hence, territorial disputes imply a pluralism of pluralisms and limited sovereignty offers the necessary normative, factual and axiological tools to accommodate this complexity.

4 Territorial Disputes

A territorial dispute is a conflict of interests[15] where there is a disagreement between states about the sovereignty over territory (land, water outer or cyber-space). Territorial disputes are highly complex and non-binary. They imply a pluralism of pluralism. A binary understanding where challenged and challenger agents are solely identified as the only relevant elements is to have a mistaken assumption. Any territorial dispute has to do with different agents (e.g. individuals, communities and states) that play a role in several contexts (local, regional and international). The different claims by the challenger and the challenged agent and the issues at stake add to the intricacy. Territorial disputes are multi-subjective, multi-contextual and multi-faceted.

Territorial disputes are complex because of the many variables at play such as agents involved, claims issues at stake and contexts. A simplistic view may assume, for example, that territorial issues like Crimea, Falkland/Malvinas Islands and Kashmir may have to do with public international law, natural resources and the domestic contexts and only two or eventually three main agents (i.e. for Crimea, the Russian Federation and Ukraine;

[15] For the notions of identity and conflict of interest, the author follows Rawls: "there is an identity of interests since social cooperation makes possible a better life for all than any would have if each were to live solely by his own efforts. There is conflict of interests since persons are not indifferent as to how the greater benefits produced by their collaboration are distributed, for in order to pursue their ends they each prefer a larger to a lesser share." See John Rawls, *A Theory of Justice*, Revised Edition (Oxford: Oxford University Press, 1999), 4.

for the Falkland/Malvinas Islands, Argentina and the United Kingdom; for Kashmir, China, India and Pakistan). However, each of the aforementioned examples include a myriad of agents, a variety of claims and issues at stake and a combination of domestic, regional and international contexts. The sub-sections below will briefly present agents, claims, issues at stake and contexts to characterize, at least broadly, territorial disputes and provide evidence of their complexity.

5 Agents: The Individual, the Community and the State

To define and characterize the agents in a civil and global society it is necessary to agree on the frame of reference when dealing with territorial disputes and who may be considered as a legitimate agent. For the purpose of this chapter, the frame of reference has to do with state sovereignty and territorial disputes.

Ergo, in any territorial disputes there are different kinds of subjects. In basic terms, it is simple to identify at least the individual, the community and the state. Any subject at the level of the individual or at the level of the state requires a set of conditions to be a player in the civil or global societies. In other words, each unit of concern has to fulfill defined criteria determined by the discipline of reference (e.g. law, political science, morality) to be acknowledged domestically and internationally as an agent. Depending on the quality of that acknowledgment, the consequent rights and obligations can be part of a territorial dispute or not. Consider, for example, the case of the Israel-Palestine difference where, on the surface, it is self-evident to identify Israelis and Palestinians but a more thorough analysis should include people living in Israel (a *de jure* and *de facto* sovereign state); people living in Palestine (a *de facto* state); diaspora; refugees and settlers in contested lands.

On the one hand, each sovereign state is internationally an autonomous and independent legal order. Internationally (external sovereignty), it is simple to identify a state as a potential legitimate agent in a territorial dispute. However, the way in which every sovereign state may define internally in law what to be an "individual" or a "community" or how to represent these individuals or communities may mean may be similar but it does not need to. For example, in very simple terms, in a sovereign state A there may be legally able nationals (1), legally unable nationals (2) and legally third country nationals (3). In this example, (1), (2) and (3) may have same basic rights in common. Assuming a democratic legal regime, the basic rights may be political and non-political and the government would represent the will of the represented in a territorial dispute. However, (1), (2) and (3) will have as well different rights and obligations. For instance, while (1) may vote and stand for national elections, (2) and (3) may not be able. In that sense, with regard to political right to vote and stand for elections, (1) is a person legally defined and empowered while (2) and (3) are not.[16] In turn, if the assumption had to be with a non-democratic legal regime, there would be a different set of rules and, consequently, different definitions and characterizations about who may be an "individual" or a "community," what their rights and obligations may be and how these individuals and communities (and their interests) would be represented in a territorial dispute. For example, morally, it may be possible to argue that all individuals part of community should be entitled to the same opportunities regardless of their nationality, ethnicity, gender, religion and so on when a negotiation about a territorial dispute takes place. Legally, however, the situation may differ. It is only the legal concept of a citizen (or national) that may be characterized as having legal rights and obligations according to relevant national rules and, therefore, these citizens (or nationals) may be taken into account in the event of negotiations.

6 Claims

Although related, claims and issues at stake are not synonyms. A claim has to do with the reason a challenger or a challenged agent may use to argue over the sovereignty of the territory in question. The claim may be based on legal or non-legal elements.[17] Several examples of the former come

[16] This is the extreme formal and logical view in legal theory where a person is a pure legal concept and any human being can be classified as person if and only if rules refer to themselves, their actions and omissions or their legal status. See Hans Kelsen, *General Theory of Norms* (Oxford: Oxford University Press, 1991) and Hans Kelsen, *Introduction to the Problems of Legal Theory* (Oxford: Oxford University Press, 1992).

[17] Norman Hill, *Claims to Territory in International Law and Relations* (London, New York and Toronto: Oxford University Press, 1945); Norman John Greville Pounds, *Political Geography* (New York: McGraw-Hill, 1972); Robert Strausz-Hupé and S. T. Possony, *International Relations in the Age of the Conflict Between Democracy and Dictatorship* (New York: McGraw-Hill, 1954).

from public international law such as occupation, prescription, cession, accretion and conquest. The latter can include culture, history religion, ethnicity, ideology and so on. The concept of "colorable claim"[18] acknowledges both legal and non-legal kinds of claims. In that sense, a challenger or a challenged agent in a territorial dispute may have a colorable claim if they bring a reason plausible enough to prove the feasibility be sovereign over the territory in question.

Consider, for example, cases like Crimea, the Kashmir and Cyprus. Crimea includes the Russian Federation basing their claim on the historical title, while Ukraine argues illegality based on public international law. Kashmir finds India and Pakistan using legal and non-legal claims. Cyprus presents a society sociologically and geographically divided according to factual and legal claims that include religion, history and regional international law (i.e. European Union Law).

Note the colorable claim refers only to admissibility and does not acknowledge or guarantee the challenger or challenged agents are sovereign over the territory in question. The colorable claim refers to the legitimacy a claiming agent may have to bring a claim about the sovereignty of a territory based on feasible evidence (e.g. historical, legal, sociological). The final decision about the sovereignty of the territory in question has to be dealt by the procedure of choice such as negotiation, enquiry, mediation, conciliation, arbitration, judicial settlement, resort to regional agencies or arrangements or any other peaceful means the challenger and challenged agents choose.

7 Issues at Stake

While a claim has to do with the reason a challenger or a challenged agent in a territorial dispute may have to claim sovereignty over the same territory, issues at stake refer to any other matter that results because of the dispute itself. Consider, for example, cases such as the San Andres archipelago dispute between Colombia and Nicaragua or the South China Sea situation with Brunei, Indonesia, Malaysia, the Philippines, Taiwan and Vietnam in addition to China. On the surface, challenged and challenger may claim based on public international law and The Law of the Sea

[18] A colorable claim is an expression used in law to refer to a claim strong enough to have a reasonable chance of winning but does not assert that the claim is certain or even likely to win.

Convention. The case of San Andres is settled. However, there are several ongoing issues at stake. First, arguments between Nicaragua and Colombia about their borders are common.[19] Second, the regional impact on peace, security and natural resources is clear.[20] Third, the socio-legal and political way in which the Raizal community is addressed.[21] In turn, the South China Sea has issues at stake in the contexts. With $3.37 trillion total trade in 2016 and 40% of the global liquefied natural gas trade transited through the area in 2017,[22] the area has domestic, regional and international issues at stake.

In general terms, issues at stake are related to at least one of the elements that form a sovereign state: population, territory and government. Unsurprisingly, issues at stake sociologically defined include, for example, bordering minorities and shared background (such as religion, language and ethnicity); territorially centered issues at stake involve geostrategic location, natural resources and so on and governmental-based influences compromise leaders' prestige, forms of government and so on. Although in theory these and other issues at stake are simple to identify and characterize in their individuality, in actual territorial disputes they appear closely interlinked as the San Andres and South China Sea example show.

8 Contexts: The Local, the Regional and the International

Related to the previous sub-sections, any agents (individual, community, state), claim and issue at stake may have three reference backgrounds in relation to sovereignty and territorial disputes: the local, regional and international contexts. Morally, sociologically, financially local and regional contexts may have different interpretations. Expressions such as nationalism, national identity and tribe may be as flexible as fluid. However, legally,

[19] Mariano V. Ospina, "'Nicaragua v. Colombia' A Stalemate in the Caribbean," in *Global Security Studies* 4:4 (2013): 31–40.

[20] Maria Otero, "Problems in the Caribbean: The Absence of Finality to the Territorial Dispute in Nicaragua V. Colombia Will Have Negative Impacts in the Region," in *The University of Toledo Law Review* 46:3 (2015): 617–646.

[21] James Ross, "Routes for Roots: Entering the 21st Century in San Andrés Island, Colombia," in *Caribbean Studies* 35:1 (2007): 3–36.

[22] Global Conflict Tracker by Council of Foreign Relations https://www.cfr.org/interactives/global-conflict-tracker#!/conflict/territorial-disputes-in-the-south-china-sea accessed 29/07/2019.

the domestic context is strict. As a result, the regional and international contexts are *a priori* defined by how the national legal order establishes the domestic dimension. For example, in terms of territorial disputes, if the challenger and the challenged agents decided to leave the stalemate produced by the *status quo* and went into negotiations to find a permanent and peaceful solution, the outcome would result in determining the extension of the territory in dispute, its borders and so on. In the example, by the agreement about the borders, a domestic situation would result in changes in the regional and international areas. A legal change in or acknowledgment about a border might have several consequences including use of natural resources, applicable financial system, the inclusion or exclusion of human rights.

How each context and a territorial dispute shape reciprocally their nature and characteristics is unique. In theory, there are clearly identifiable features in the international context (balance of military forces, prior gain of territory, common alliance and previous settlement), the regional context (common past, geographical location, development and natural resources) and the domestic context (prior unresolved disputes, prior loss of territory and the aftermath of decolonization). Realpolitik, however, shows these contexts and their respective salient characteristics combine in different ways depending on the territorial dispute, time and space.

Arguably, in some territorial disputes, there is evidence suggesting that the domestic context is the most relevant (e.g. San Andres between Nicaragua and Colombia). However, in most cases, the regional and international contexts have a decisive part to play. The Israel-Palestine difference includes regional agents in the Middle East as well as international interested parties (at least, clearly, the United States and the United Kingdom). Similarly, in Kashmir where India and Pakistan appear as obvious opponents. However, to leave aside the assessment external agents like China, Russia and the United States would be naïve.

9 Vertical and Horizontal Views

Similar to sovereignty, territorial disputes may offer a vertical and horizontal view. A vertical view of territorial disputes can only acknowledge a plurality of agents locally, regionally and internationally. Challenger and challenged agents are singularities and each of them present their own population, territory and government regardless of how they are defined and characterized (e.g. by reference to legal, sociological or political features). Conversely, a horizontal view of territorial disputes may accept regularities in the different agents vertically defined. Challenger and challenged agents may have commonalities in terms of, for example, the claims and issues at stake that cut across the vertical singularities. Consequently, states individually considered are completely sovereign regionally and globally for a vertical view. For a horizontal view, however, they may share common elements such as the ethnicity of their populations, language and culture. In fact, these horizontal commonalities may have to do with any of the elements that characterize the state vertically. In terms of territory, states may share the use of common natural resources such as a river running through internationally and legally defined borders.

Consider the situations in Kashmir, Gibraltar and the border between the United States and Mexico. In all these cases, it is effortless to identify vertically the singular agents. Horizontally, each of them include several commonalities between the involved agents. Kashmir includes natural resource as well as bordering minorities. Sociological and political components such as religious and cultural elements together with political unification are present in India and Pakistan. In Gibraltar, sociologically and economically, La Línea provides clear evidence of the horizontal interlinks with Spain. Politically, the European Union, Brexit and North Atlantic Treaty Organization (NATO) force shifts in the international and regional agendas of Spain and the United Kingdom.[23] In turn, the Americas include several resolved and ongoing territorial disputes that clearly show horizontal coincidences rooted in European colonialism. Despite the resolution in law, Mexico-United States border has domestic, regional and international relevance because of migration issues, nationalism and actions intended to boost political prestige.

The previous sub-sections include brief references to different agents, claims, issues at stake, contexts and views. With only a glimpse of territorial disputes it should be self-evident any study about them needs careful thought. More importantly, any attempt to settle them peacefully and permanently requires a comprehensive understanding of their intricacy. The many cases around the world such as the Israel-Palestine difference, the South China Sea, Kashmir, the Falkland/Malvinas Islands and Crimea show clearly the need to reimagine the way in which these and similar

[23] Uğur Burç Yildiz and Anil Çamyamaç, "Explaining the European Union's Changing Position towards the Gibraltar Question after the Brexit Referendum," *Mediterranean Journal of Social Sciences* 8:4 (2017): 21–30.

disputes are assessed both in law and politics, conceptually and substantively. Unless scholars accept the complexity in these highly controversial territorial disputes and adopt a shift in their studies, a potential for peaceful and permanent resolution will remain elusive.

10 Conclusion

Territorial disputes and sovereignty may be at odds but they do not need to. Both territorial disputes and sovereignty are complex. It is in that complexity that territorial disputes may find in sovereignty a way out toward a peaceful and permanent settlement. In that vein, this chapter is an attempt to sketch how the limitations in sovereignty may enable cooperation between challenged and challenger agents in a territorial dispute.

The first part of the chapter showed that it is plausible to have another account on sovereignty. Traditionally assumed to be absolute and, therefore, not shareable, sovereignty accepts limitations of different kinds. The modern account of sovereignty (Bodin, Hobbes and their predecessors) seems to an obstacle for cooperation. However, this chapter challenged the narrow view by locating the conception historically. Indeed, the so-called absoluteness in sovereignty is a historically determined axiological choice. Factually and normatively, sovereignty accepts limitations. This factual, normative and axiological limitations may induce domination or cooperation. In the former case, any agent in a territorial conflict may do as they wish with their counterpart and cement the volatile legal and political situation a stalemate brings. In the latter, the same agents may opt to cooperate with each other by entering into negotiations about the sovereignty of the territory in question. These negotiations do not mean a by-default solution. Yet, they are a promising move from a *status quo.*

The second part of the chapter concentrated the attention on territorial disputes. Being multi-subjective, multi-level and multi-contextual, the importance about differentiating between agents, claims, issues at state and contexts should be evident. In order to have a better and more informed understanding of territorial disputes, these should be evaluated in their whole intricacy. The high complexity in territorial disputes should not be a deterrent for their peaceful and permanent solution. It is in that complexity where the way out is. To understand territorial disputes only defined by a particular discipline or by reference to one of the many elements (e.g. territory) is to guarantee an over-simplistic analysis. Therefore, any understanding based on this analysis will be biased by its *a priori* narrow departing assumptions and conceptions.

Both sovereignty and territorial disputes may be assessed vertically and, therefore, as singularities. Consequently, an absolute understanding of sovereignty results in territorial disputes being collectively exhaustive and mutually exclusive: the sovereignty of the claimed territory can be acknowledged to only one of the claiming agents. Alternatively, a horizontal view allows for cooperation by recognizing the limitedness in sovereignty and, therein, the ability challenged and challenger agents in a territorial dispute have to find solutions beneficial to all.

The Israel-Palestine difference, Kashmir, Gibraltar, the Falkland/Malvinas Islands and many others need resolving. Despite the many rules and procedures in law and politics available to assess and potentially solve these differences, their pervasiveness is obvious. Unsurprisingly, there is an urgency given by social, political, financial, legal and other realities around the world to solve them peacefully and permanently. Because of the scarce usefulness of these rules and procedures and the urgency volatile territorial disputes present, it is both prudent and advisable to reimagine ways in which the problematic situations can be evaluated.

These pages are a brief theoretical exercise to bring evidence about the need to agree on a minimum inter-disciplinary set of conceptual elements related to territorial disputes. Moreover, it underlines the need of a multi-disciplinary and multi-dimensional evaluation. The former has to do with recognizing the importance of legal and political sciences as well as others not traditionally related to the study of territorial disputes. The latter refers to the notion that territorial disputes and sovereignty may be territorially defined and characterized but to have a comprehensive evaluation, other elements such as population and government should also be considered. By identifying in theory the elements territorial disputes may have in common it may be possible to generate hypothesis and conclusions to address them in a different, more comprehensive way. The hope remains in establishing some guidelines for policymaking in dispute settlement and conflict resolution that could be theoretically feasible and pragmatically applicable.

References

Anand, R. P. (1966). Sovereign Equality of States in International Law. *International Studies, 8*(3), 213–224.

Biersteker, T. J., & Weber, C. (Eds.). (1996). *State Sovereignty as Social Construct*. Cambridge: Cambridge University Press.

Bodin, J. (1903). *The Six Bookes of Commonweale*. Impenfis G. Bishop.

Brown, K. (2018). Sovereignty. *Western American Literature, 53*(1), 81–89.

Bullo, S. (2014). *Evaluation in Advertising Reception: A Socio-Cognitive and Linguistic Perspective*. Basingstoke: Palgrave Macmillan.

Caspersen, N. (2020). Collective Non-Recognition of States. In G. Visoka, J. Doyle, & E. Newman (Eds.), *Routledge Handbook of State Recognition*. Oxon/New York: Routledge.

Gadamer, H.-G. (1976). *Philosophical Hermeneutics*. Berkeley: University of California Press.

Greville Pounds, N. J. (1972). *Political Geography*. New York: McGraw-Hill.

Hill, N. (1945). *Claims to Territory in International Law and Relations*. London/New York/Toronto: Oxford University Press.

Hjnorth, R. (2011). Equality in the Theory of International Society: Kelsen, Rawls and the English School. *Review of International Studies, 37*(5), 2585–2602.

Huth, P. K. (2001). *Standing Your Ground: Territorial Disputes and International Conflict*. Ann Arbor: University of Michigan Press.

Jauss, H. (1982). *Toward and Aesthetic of Reception*. Minneapolis: University of Minnesota Press.

Kelsen, H. (1944). The Principle of Sovereign Equality of States as a Basis for International Organization. *Yale Law Journal, 53*(2), 207–220.

Kelsen, H. (1991). *General Theory of Norms*. Oxford: Oxford University Press.

Kelsen, H. (1992). *Introduction to the Problems of Legal Theory*. Oxford: Oxford University Press.

Kostakopoulou, D. (2002). Floating Sovereignty: A Pathology or a Necessary Means of a State Evolution? *Oxford Journal of Legal Studies, 22*, 135–156.

Krasner, S. D. (1999). *Sovereignty: Organized Hypocrisy*. Princeton: Princeton University Press.

Krasner, S. D. (2001, January/February). Sovereignty, Think Again. *Foreign Policy*.

Lavdas, K. A., Litsas, S. N., & Skiadas, D. V. (2013). *Stateness and Sovereign Debt: Greece in the European Conundrum*. Maryland: Lexington Books.

Martin Elizabeth, A., & Law, J. (2006). *A Dictionary of Law*. Oxford: Oxford University Press.

Ospina, M. V. (2013). "Nicaragua v. Colombia" a Stalemate in the Caribbean. *Global Security Studies, 4*(4), 31–40.

Otero, M. (2015). Problems in the Caribbean: The Absence of Finality to the Territorial Dispute in Nicaragua V. Colombia Will Have Negative Impacts in the Region. *The University of Toledo Law Review, 46*(3), 617–646.

Picker, G. (2019). Sovereignty Beyond the State: Exception and Informality in a Western European City. *International Journal of Urban and Regional Research, 43*(3), 576–581.

Pruthi, R. K. (2005). *The Political Theory.* New Delhi: Sarup and Sons.

Rawls, J. (1999). *A Theory of Justice* (Rev. ed.). Oxford: Oxford University Press.

Ross, J. (2007). Routes for Roots: Entering the 21st Century in San Andrés Island, Colombia. *Caribbean Studies, 35*(1), 3–36.

Skinner, Q. (2013). A Genealogy of the State. *Rivista di Storia delle Idee, 2*(1), 46–61.

Strausz-Hupé, R., & Possony, S. T. (1954). *International Relations in the Age of the Conflict Between Democracy and Dictatorship.* New York: McGraw-Hill.

Thompson, M. P. (1993). Reception Theory and the Interpretation of Historical Meaning. *History and Theory, 32*, 248–272.

Volk, C. (2019, February). The Problem of Sovereignty in Globalized Times. *Law, Culture and the Humanities.* https://doi.org/10.1177/1743872119828010.

Walker, N. (2013). *Sovereignty Frames and Sovereignty Claims* (Working Papers). Edinburgh: University of Edinburgh, School of Law

Walker, N. (Ed.). (2018). *Relocating Sovereignty.* London/New York: Routledge.

Weber, C. (1992). Writing Sovereign Identities: Wilson Administration Intervention in the Mexican Revolution. *Alternatives: Global, Local, Political, 17*, 313–337.

CHAPTER 6

Humanitarian Intervention and Its Impact on State Sovereignty and Human Rights

Arenca Trashani

1 Introduction

The developments of the new world order are also reflected in the evolution of humanitarian intervention theory making it one of the leading institutes of the international law at the end of the twentieth century and the beginning of the twenty-first century. There is an emerging debate as to how applying specific criteria for humanitarian intervention might help to increase the chances of success and secure support for such interventions (CSS Strategic Briefing Papers 2000:1).

Humanitarian intervention has done its long way since the adoption of the United Nations (UN) Charter as a kind of just war, but at the same time, one of the most controversial concepts in world politics. The system inaugurated in 1945 was revolutionary indeed because it postulated that in future states ought to endeavour to settle their disputes peacefully and never use force, subject to the exception of self-defence and that an

A. Trashani (✉)
University of "Luigj Gurakuqi", Law Faculty, Shkodër, Albania
e-mail: arenca.trashani@unishk.edu.al

M. Belov (ed.), *Territorial Politics and Secession*, Federalism and Internal Conflicts, https://doi.org/10.1007/978-3-030-64402-4_6

international authority, the UN, would act as a world policing and enforcement agency (Cassese 2005:323).

One of the essential principles of international law is the principle of non-intervention, and at the same time, this is "violated" by the concept of humanitarian intervention. One of the key elements of the post-cold war order was the concept and belief that humanitarianism was married to interventionism, something that would eventually become a reality for the international society (Domagala 2003:4).

The North Atlantic Treaty Organization's "humanitarian war" in Kosovo in 1999 has once again brought to the fore the long-standing legal, political and moral debate surrounding the doctrine of humanitarian intervention and in particular, the right of states to intervene militarily in another state, without Security Council (SC) authorization, to prevent gross violations of fundamental human rights and international humanitarian law (Simons 2000:1). It was the first time that military intervention was taken without the consent of the SC.

Consequently, unlike in the early 1990s, the debate at the end of the decade focused not on the question of whether humanitarian considerations could be characterized as "threats to international peace and security" and justify intervention in the domestic affairs of states, but rather whether such interventions needed the authorization of UN Security Council (De Jounge Oudratt 2000:1).

After Kosovo intervention, the international community had been trying to respond to the disasters and gross violations of human rights with the concept that states have the responsibility to prevent and to protect human rights and that international community have the responsibility to do this when states fail to protect their own citizens' rights. This produced the new concept of the Responsibility to Protect (RtP). The modern concept of RtP is broader than the old doctrine of humanitarian intervention, because it comprises the duty to prevent, to stop and to remedy; it is clear that the former includes the latter, at least in the form of *ultima ratio* intervention to stop the atrocities (Francioni and Baker 2013:2). But more than 20 years after North Atlantic Treaty Organization (NATO) intervention in the former Yugoslavia to protect Albanian people from ethnic cleansing, and the new doctrine of RtP, still the issue of humanitarian intervention continues to divide scholars, researchers and policymakers on the topic of humanitarian intervention.

In this chapter, firstly, we will see how the theory of humanitarian intervention developed after the Second World War under the auspices of the UN and how on the way of its development it plays its role on the evolution and protection of human rights and by no means its impact on the state sovereignty. We will try to tackle and examine the tensions that humanitarian intervention raises between state sovereignty and the protection of human rights. Then, we will analyse how the humanitarian intervention plays its role and have its impact on the evolution and protection of human rights and more specifically on the application of the right to self-determination.

2 Theory of Humanitarian Intervention

The theory of humanitarian intervention is based on the assumption that states in their relationships with their nationals have the international obligation to guarantee to them certain basic or fundamental rights which are considered necessary for their existence and all the maintenance of friendly relations among nations (Abiew 1999:30). These fundamental rights are, no need to say, of great universal importance known by all the most important documents of international human rights law and as a result of all Contracting Parts of the international community.

The most well-known definition of humanitarian intervention has to do with the use of force by a state towards another one to protect the liberty of the nationals of the latter which was unable or unwilling to do so by itself. Humanitarian intervention is the threat or use of force across state borders by a state (or group of states) aimed at preventing or ending widespread and grave violations of the fundamental human rights of individuals other than its citizens without the permission of the state within whose territory force is applied (Holzgrefe 2003:18).

The use of force for humanitarian purposes, in the context of the definition, follows the human rights violations, that is, it does not happen because of the harm of states or cosmopolitan society (Domagala 2003:9). The humanitarian crisis has always dominated the international agenda. Usually, the civil conflict exists when a state is experiencing domestic unrest (Arend and Beck 1993:81). And in the case of internal conflict, the intervention becomes almost necessary and at the same time more difficult because this internal armed conflict can become a threat to the peace and security outside the borders of this country and also because of the way the state in an armed conflict maltreated its citizen severely and systematically, committing gross and massive violations of human rights towards its citizens. This intervention in an internal conflict becomes difficult also because of the principle of non-intervention in the internal affairs of a state.

In a world order in which recourse to war was not legally regulated and in which the relevant decision was, therefore, part of sovereign powers of every single state, a customary rule allowing interventions for humanitarian reasons was not needed nor could it develop under such conditions (Hilpold 2001:441).

That is why, humanitarian intervention cannot be a well-established practice of states since it deals mostly with world politics and at the same time it has to constitute the so-called just war.

Just war will be justified on the cases of violations of human rights at the stage of shocking the conscience of humanity. Thus, the legal community remains divided as to the legality of humanitarian intervention, even though for almost all the cases the legitimacy of the intervention was accepted, but when it comes to the legality this is where states remain sceptic. It is important to note the use of the word legitimacy, as legitimacy does not imply legality (Wing Commander J.E. Linter MA RAF 2005:273). Although it may be morally accepted that the law should provide an answer to Kofi Annan's point that "if humanitarian intervention is, indeed, an unacceptable assault on sovereignty, how should we respond to a Rwanda, to a Sebrenica – to gross and systematic violations of human rights that affect every precept of our community?" (Annan 2000:48).

3 The UN System of Humanitarian Intervention

The Charter of the UN protects a state from the threat or use of force and also from the unlawful interference in its domestic jurisdiction or internal affairs. Article 2(4) of the UN Charter states: "*All Members shall refrain in their international relations from the threat or use of force against the territorial integrity or political independence of any state, or any other manner inconsistent with the Purposes of the United States*" (UN Charter 1945). This is one of the main principles and a kind of milestone in the whole history of the more than 70 years of the UN. At the basis of this principle stays the principle of state sovereignty and that of territorial integrity together with the principle of reciprocity. All these principles together have made the obligation for the international community not to interfere in the domestic affairs of an independent state.

Since 1945, more and more states have been claiming the right to use force to promote various "just causes", even though such uses of force may transgress the territorial integrity or political independence of states (Arend and Beck 1993:85). This has created a debate in the field of humanitarian intervention because often by many states the humanitarian intervention is seen as a justification for the intervention of the weak states by the most powerful states. The International Court of Justice has confirmed this general prohibition on the use of force in the *Corfu Channel Case* (1949) and the *Case Concerning Military and Paramilitary Activities In and Against Nicaragua* (1986) and is considered to be a rule of *jus cogens*—that is, a peremptory norm of international law from which no subject of international law may derogate (O'Connell 2000:58).

The only way to intervene was, and still remains, to show that the intervention is compatible with the Article 2(4) of the Charter. Article 2(4) does not include an absolute right for the prohibition of force. Instead, the force can be used in a manner that does not threaten the territorial integrity or political independence of a State. In essence Article 2(4) does not cover territorial inviolability so that a state's territorial integrity may be preserved even though there is a limited armed foray into that state's territory (D'Amato 1987:37). Since the humanitarian intervention does not seek to challenge attributes of sovereignty, territorial integrity or political independence of a state, it will not fall within the scope of the Article 2(4) prohibition of force norm (Abiew 1999:95).

The parody of sovereignty allows governments to do—or refrain from—pretty well what they please without let or hindrance from any external power (Griffiths et al. 1995:34). Despite the absence of any declared international consensus on the limits to sovereignty, there is nevertheless a consistent trend emerging from the crises of recent years (Griffiths et al. 1995:34). It must be said that the responsibilities of states towards their citizens mean that human rights protection must be seen as part of the definition of sovereignty (Abiew 1999:23).

Two arguments made a humanitarian intervention compatible with Article 2(4) of the Charter. Humanitarian intervention must not be seen as a use of force against the territorial integrity or political independence of the target state and it should not be inconsistent with the purposes of the UN (Chesterman 2001:48–53). In a more detailed way, we can say that this has to do with some other provisions of the Charter, with Article 51 which foreseen the right of a state to use force in self-defence or collective self-defence and Article 42 which authorize the use of force to restore international peace and security. Arguments for humanitarian intervention often assume that, once a threshold is reached, a right to use force arises automatically (Vendirame 2013:1).

Almost all the cases of armed intervention after the Second World War have been associated during the act of intervention or in the aftermath with humanitarian motives. Cases of humanitarian intervention during the period 1945–1990 to make some examples are Belgian Congo intervention of 1964, the US intervention in the Dominican Republic of 1965, Indian intervention in East Pakistan (Bangladesh) of 1971, Tanzanian intervention in Uganda of 1979, Vietnam's intervention in Cambodia (Kampuchea) of 1978 and the US interventions in Grenada in 1983 and Panama in 1989 and 1990. In all these cases it can't be denied that the intervention provided some humanitarian relief.

The most debated interventions have been those beyond the decolonization period with the primary purpose for the restoration of democracy. After the Cold War, there was a need to reformulate some clear principles on the guide of the action of the UN to govern humanitarian intervention in defence of the well-being of individuals.

4 Sovereignty and Human Rights

Since the creation of the UN, the doctrine of humanitarian intervention has passed through the difficulties to surpass the essential principle of the existence of a state as an independent subject of international law. The sovereignty of states is a fundamental principle in international relations and is enshrined in the UN Charter in its Article 2/7. Article 2(7) provides that "*nothing in the present Charter shall authorize the United Nations to intervene in matters which are essentially within the domestic jurisdiction of any state or shall require the Members to submit such matters to settlement under the present Charter*". Independent states are vested with their state sovereignty which permits them to fight for their domestic affairs and the non-intervention of other subjects of international law in their domestic affairs. The principle of non-intervention was primarily constructed to help states in their sovereignty and remains a cornerstone of modern international law. State sovereignty as we mentioned above remains one of the essential elements for the existence of an independent state.

With the development of international relations and the importance of individuals as subjects of international law equal as states and international organization, the importance of state sovereignty has always been in the decrease. Even within their territory, states have long been limited by international law in a manner which makes an argument in favour of "absolute" sovereignty difficult to maintain (Hannum 1996:19). Reisman has argued that traditional concepts of "sovereignty" have been replaced by that of "popular sovereignty" vested in the individual citizen of a state (Reisman 1990:866). Lauterpacht and McCourdale have also stated that human rights are superior than those of sovereign states (Lauterpacht 1950:67–72; McCorquodale 2014:301).

One of the essential conditions of the existence of a state is the respect for human rights and the respect for the right of people to self-determination. The protection of human rights has been assigned such overwhelming importance that state sovereignty should no more stand in the way to prevent gross violations of these rights (Hilpold 2001:301). During all the existence of the UN system, the armed intervention in an independent country has been done for humanitarian motives. What underlies the humanitarian debate is the perceived tension between the values of ensuring respect for fundamental human rights and the primacy of the norms of sovereignty, non-intervention and self-determination which are considered essential factors in the maintenance of peace and international security (Danish Institute of International Affairs 1999:14–15). The principle of sovereignty might inhibit the realization of universal human rights. According to this, the Independent Commission of International Humanitarian Issues stated that "*sovereignty need not conflict with humanitarian concerns if States can be brought to define their interests beyond the short term ...The interests of common humanity which transcend national boundaries are not a menace to the vital interests of States*".

According to the doctrine in the law of state responsibility, the obligation on states to respect and protect the fundamental human rights of all human persons is the concern of all states, that is, they are owed *erga omnes* (Simma 1999:2). During the armed conflicts over all the history, civilians have always been the primary target and the primary victims of these armed conflicts even though they were and still are the less protected and innocent category of people in an armed conflict situation.

The primary purpose of the UN after the Second World War was the maintenance of peace and security. Overall the world during these more than 70 years there has been a lot of armed conflict situation which needed the interference of the international community to protect, especially the civilians involved in an armed conflict. Grounds for resorting to war—a component of the just war (*bellium justum*) doctrine—or, as modern international lawyers would put it, as a justification for humanitarian intervention (Meron 1991:110).

When a state's conduct towards its subjects is such that it leads to massacres, brutality, religious or racial persecution, and when these acts are of such nature that they shock the conscience of mankind, the international community has the right to intervene to restore some semblance of civilized conduct (Abiew 1999:44). In this sense, the sovereignty, especially after the end of the Cold War, as an absolute one was no longer defended as before. Also, the Security Council (Article 39) as the organ who can authorize the use of force has modified the meaning of threat to peace and security with the primary aim to include in this meaning the grave humanitarian crisis. This exclusive right of the SC to authorize the use of force is to prevent or to stop widespread deprivations of internationally recognized human rights. In short, practice in UN organs has now clarified that there exists an affirmative legal obligation on the part of governments and authorities to admit humanitarian aid (Griffiths et al. 1995:46).

With the demise of the Eastern bloc Communist systems, the SC seemed to be able to give new life to the concept of humanitarian intervention, this time in a collective form and therefore *prima facie* consistent with the letter of the UN Charter (Hilpold 2001:445). While in the earlier cases states referred primarily to self-defence to justify their use of force, in the 1990s the acting states emphasized a multitude of factors, prominent among them an "implied authorization" by the UN Security Council (Kirsch 2002:327). Another important fact is the so-called internationalization of human rights as the primary factor on the development of humanitarian intervention theory and also in another way of interpreting the rules of international law concerning non-intervention.

The UN Secretary General Perez de Cuellar in his Final Report to the General Assembly in September 1991 stated that:

> *It is now increasingly felt that the principle of non-interference with the essential domestic jurisdiction of States could not be regarded as a protective barrier behind which human rights could be massively or systematically violated with impunity…*
>
> *We need to not impale ourselves on the horns of a dilemma between respect for sovereignty and the protection of human rights… What is involved is not the right of intervention but the collective obligation of States to bring relief and redress in human rights emergencies.* (Report of the SGUN 1991:5)

During the post-Cold War period there was and still is a belief that the state sovereignty implies an obligation for all states as subjects of international law to respect and promote human rights of their citizens. State sovereignty can no longer be used as a shield to perpetrate massive and systematic violations of human rights. The rights of states are no longer assumed to have priority over the rights of individuals (Harris 1995:3).

This evolution for sure came as a result of the development of international human rights law which saw all the subjects of international law promoting and protecting human rights universally. During this evolution, we have the adoption of several significant and elaborated international documents of human rights such as Universal Declaration of Human Rights, UN Covenants on Human Rights of 1966, Genocide Convention and beyond. Also, a regional system of protection of human rights made them of particular importance and also made them prevailing over state sovereignty.

Interventions to protect human rights should thus not be seen as incompatible with state sovereignty but rather affirming it (Abiew 1999:255). These historical documents together with the practice of states have made the protection of innocents becoming a legitimate cause for intervention. When a state respects and promotes the human rights of its citizens it becomes an element to secure its sovereignty also. Going on this line of interpretation after the post-Cold war there was broad support for humanitarian intervention as a mean to protect human rights from massive and gross violations.

On the whole, this development can be regarded as the expression of an increasing willingness by the SC to attribute more importance to internal conflicts if they give rise to an extraordinary humanitarian crisis (Hilpold 2001:447). Due to this there was also a broad interpretation given by the SC to the "threat of peace and security". Internal conflicts where gross human rights occur are no longer matters of internal affairs of an individual state.

The SC has thus considerably enlarged the concept of the threat to the peace laid down in Article 39 of the UN Charter, to include humanitarian crises within one state, which once were deemed to fall primarily within domestic jurisdiction (Cassese 2005:347). For sure humanitarian interventions are always accompanied by the proper interests of the members of the Security Council and especially the interests of the permanent members. Moreover, this is a new challenge that the SC faced during the last decades, the political compromises done by the SC member states especially the permanent members on using their veto on their interest when there was in case a humanitarian intervention. On the other hand, it would be idealistic to assume that the Council's decisions on the topic of the threat to peace and security are entirely objective. The need to halt the horrors of genocide or to address the effects of civil war and internal armed conflict on civilians has been accepted as sufficient justification, even if other motives may be involved (Orford 2003:6).

One of the humanitarian intervention at the end of 1990s was the NATO intervention in Kosovo, which was done without the permission of SC, but based on the gross violations of human rights and genocide applied in the region towards the Albanian people in Kosovo. After that, the International Commission on Intervention and State Sovereignty (ICISS), established by the Canadian government, proposed the notion of responsibility to protect (RtP). RtP is defined as the responsibility of states as well as the international community to protect civilians from human rights violations (Yoshida 2013:1). It is more than obvious that the RtP has the main clue to protect human rights. Even though it is done out of the UN system, the world summit document stressed that

> *138. Each state has the responsibility to protect its population from genocide, war crimes, ethnic cleansing and crimes against humanity. This responsibility entails the prevention of such crimes, including their incitement, through appropriate and necessary means... the international community should as appropriate, encourage and help states to exercise this responsibility and support the United Nations in establishing an early warning capability.*
>
> *139. The international community, through the United Nations, also has the responsibility to use appropriate diplomatic, humanitarian and other peaceful means, following Chapters VI and VIII of the Charter, to help protect populations from genocide, war crimes, ethnic cleansing and crimes against humanity. In this context, we are prepared to take collective action, in a timely and decisive manner, through the Security Council, under the Charter, including Chapter VII, on a case-by-case basis and in cooperation with relevant regional organizations as appropriate, should peaceful means be inadequate and national authorities manifestly fail to protect their populations from genocide, war crimes, ethnic cleansing and crimes against humanity* (UN General Assembly, 60th Session 2005).

The ICISS report argues "*State sovereignty implies a responsibility for the protection of its people*". So we see the shift from the right to intervene to the responsibility to protect, which seems to be the core of the discussion on the humanitarian intervention in our days. This is not just for the states in their own but also very important for the international community when the situation on human rights deters up to the gross violations, genocide, ethnic cleansing and crimes against humanity in a proper state or region.

The ICISS report outlines three important aspects that RtP should include: (1) the responsibility to prevent, (2) the responsibility to react and (3) the responsibility to rebuild. Even though the report argues that it is the SC who is given the authorization for humanitarian intervention, it mentions also the possibility for the General Assembly to act so.

In 2005, the World Summit endorsed the RtP concept, leaving it far more restrictive than those proposed by the ICISS Report (Resolution on the World Summit Outcome 2005). The World Summit has been willing to act according to Chapter VII of the Charter, but it did not recognized "a right" of humanitarian intervention, nor a "duty" to do so within the Charter system (Francioni and Baker 2013:6). Since then RtP is frequently intervened in the scene of humanitarian intervention. The idea that certain wrongful acts constitute a breach of obligations owed to the international community as a whole must represent the fundamental departure from the old structure of international law as a law of mere coexistence and marks the evolution of the international legal order towards a law of independence and moral and intellectual solidarity (Francioni and Baker 2013:15). For sure what is mainly needed is the set of certain criteria from where to start such as (1) imperative necessity, (2) coherence and (3) proportionality. That would help a lot for a legitimate intervention with the main intention to stop gross and systematic human rights violation. States do not have absolute discretion to act within or outside their borders, but the restrictions on either type of sovereignty must not be overstated (O'Meara 2016:21).

The first time the doctrine of RtP was used in Darfur case in 2006 by the SC Resolution expanding the UN mission in Darfur (UN Resolution 1706 2006), followed then by intervention in Libya (UN Resolution 1973 2011). We must say that a long road has been taken indicated by UN Charter and the doctrine of humanitarian intervention and by the elaboration of RtP doctrine but still a progressive reform need to be taken under the international system.

5 Unilateral Interventions

After the Second World War with the adoption of the UN Charter, a general prohibition on the threat or use of force was installed and other than a short-term right of self-defence pending the response of the SC, to which was assigned the exclusive right to use force to respond to "threats to the peace", "breaches of the peace" and "acts of aggression" (Reisman 2000:12–16). The major preoccupation of the UN in 1945 was to identify ways of prohibiting the use of force which in large measure accounted for the significance attached to the principle of non-intervention (Abiew 1999:73).

In the absence of effective action by the UN, unilateral intervention by states was permissible in cases involving gross deprivations of fundamental human rights or trans-border refugee flow. Thus, individual states have undertaken intervention actions to stop humanitarian catastrophes all over the globe. This was based on the UN Charter where individual states may cooperate with the organization or individually or collectively to stop the undergoing of a humanitarian catastrophe. In the name of humanitarian intervention, individual states have undertaken a lot of single interventions towards other states. There was a kind of revival of coercive self-help measures to protect human rights. According to Michael Reisman a "unilateral action" is an act by a formally unauthorized participant which effectively preempts the official decision a legally designated official or agency was supposed to take (Reisman 2000:3).

There were a lot of cases of unilateral intervention in the period after the adoption of the UN Charter, and this reassured the states that the right to unilateral humanitarian intervention is available to them as an option grounded in either the Charter or customary international law. Also, the doctrine helped in this case because many writers in this field suggested that it did not impede using force in the case of the serious violations of human rights. In the period 1945–1989, there has been a considerable number of unilateral humanitarian interventions such as Congo intervention of 1964 by Belgium, the Dominican Republic intervention of 1965 by the USA, the East Pakistani intervention of 1971 by India, the Uganda intervention of 1979 by Tanzania and the Kampuchea intervention of 1978 by Vietnam. All these cases demonstrate that there exists a right to unilateral intervention, even though the use of force from individual states was too much debated that it put an end to the enormous violations of human rights in these states.

For sure there have been many obstacles for these kinds of interventions which Chesterman calls unilateral pro-democratic interventions (Chesterman 2001:120), but the fact remains that there were only a minority of states which do not accept the unilateral intervention. These were states of the socialist camp and also the third world states. Most of the states welcomed the unilateral interventions as a tool to put an end to the gross and massive violations of human rights. It is clear that Cold War tensions and the exercise of the veto were major facts in the United Nation's apparent paralysis: the veto was exercised on 279 occasions, with the result that when the Council did pronounce on that might have attracted its coercive powers, hortatory resolutions were preferred (Chesterman 2001:120). The veto is a crucial factor—though not the only one—in the Council's failure to exercise the authority given to it and the Charter (Schachter 1991:108).

6 Collective Intervention

One of the mechanisms introduced by the international community to handle the humanitarian crisis has been collective interventions. The requirements of multilateral cooperation in dealing with international peace and security have led to a growing recognition among states of the obsolescence of traditional notions of absolute sovereignty (Abiew 1999:138). The supremacy of human rights over the state sovereignty and also the readiness of states as general subjects to intervene in a case of gross violations of human rights have increased especially after the Cold War where there were no more differences between systems of governments between states. Interventions during and after the 1990s had been mainly collective, and few cases could be used to verify whether state-to-state interventions were more or less accepted that had been the case hitherto (Ortega 2001:25).

Even though with the fall of the "iron curtain" was thought that many problems ended that was not true. Now the international community faced other problems such as gross violations of human rights within a single state, intra-states conflicts and also the trans-border refugee flows which made the international community that now was the time to imply new mechanisms to face these new deprivations of human rights. The UN decided to pay more attention to these internal affairs of state in the cases where those affairs caused gross and massive violations of human rights. The most significant change of the role of the UN in armed conflicts was done at the beginning of 1990s firstly with the Resolution 49/182 and then at the beginning of 1992 in a remarkable meeting affirmed their commitment to the UN Charter system and noted the new favourable international circumstances that had enabled the Council to fulfil more effectively its primary responsibility for the maintenance of international peace and security (Chesterman 2001:128). This was a meeting of the Security Council on the level of the Heads of the States and Governments. It was mentioned that this role has changed: "*The absence of war and military conflicts among states does not in itself ensure international peace and security. The non-military sources of instability in the economic, social, humanitarian and ecological fields have become threats to peace and security*" (UNYB 1992).

The history of the UN during the years following the end of the Cold War and the demise of communism knows a lot of collective humanitarian interventions done under the auspices of the UN. Each of these humanitarian interventions was done in the name of the protection of human rights. Taking the view that humanitarian aid should be linked with the development, conflict resolution and social reconstruction, the new humanitarianism shifts the focus from saving lives to supporting social processes and influencing political outcomes (Kernot 2004:5). Normally, the Security Council, as the only official organ to order the use of force under Chapter VII of the Charter, can order the use of force only when there is a threat to peace, breach of the peace or an act of aggression and can permit the member states to use force individually or collectively. The decreasing number of the unilateral intervention especially after the 1990s was also due to the fact that now the SC was able to act at least in almost all the questions for collective intervention. The active presence of the SC as a forum for negotiation, or as a critical factor in deciding the methods for crisis management, along with the convergent stabilizing efforts of regional organizations and states, undercuts the basis for state-to-state intervention (Ortega 2001:16). The decision of the SC remains still one of the main conditions for humanitarian intervention. The Council also came to demonstrate an extraordinarily broad interpretation of its responsibility to maintain international peace and security (Chesterman 2001:121).

The response of the SC to the humanitarian crisis in Bosnia (UNSC Resolution 770 1992), also Somalia (UNSC Resolution 794 1992) and, more recently, Libya (UNSC Resolution 1973 2011), fits the model foreseen by the UN Charter because the Council defined these emergencies as a threat to peace and international security and explicitly authorized the member states under Chapter VII to use "all necessary means" to enforce global humanitarian norms. These actions have ushered in a more vigorous approach to UN conflict management efforts, be it in situations of massive violations of human rights resulting from the collapse of civil wars (Abiew 1999:139). The nature and range of the SC resolutions passed since the Gulf War are almost always interpreted as the Security Council was and still is willing to treat the failure for the guarantee of human rights, democracy and to act against the humanitarian abuses. Moreover, this is the main aim of the collective interventions also, the maintenance of peace and security, and to achieve this, the SC has not hesitated to intervene in the internal affairs of a state. This intervention is always done on the name of the protection of peace and security and against the mass and gross violations of human rights.

The collective response can be made by a group of states or by a regional organization. According to the Article 53 of the Charter, the SC is empowered to utilize regional arrangements for enforcement actions, but this must be done with the authorization of the SC. Also of an extremely helpful was the adoption of the General Assembly Resolution (UNGA Resolution A/Res/46/182 1991) on December 1991 which aimed to strengthen the coordination of the UN's humanitarian assistance in emergencies, as well as to pressure the non-consensual governments to permit aid to people in need during civil wars and other internal conflicts. However, sure the radical change was made at the meeting on 31 January 1992 (UNYB 33 1992) that we have mentioned above. The summit thus sought to strengthen the authority of the UN to negotiate a peaceful resolution of conflicts and to intervene in circumstances that endanger humanity (Abiew 1999:144).

For sure of great help in the last decades was the work of the SC in the field of humanitarian intervention. It seems very difficult to reconcile the practice of the Council during the 1990s with any principle interpretation of its legal mandate. That is why in all the resolutions adopted by the SC during the last three decades, we met certain circumstances, which changed from case to case. In deciding to act against an armed conflict within a state, the SC has its absolute discretion to decide on the topic, a decision which is always influenced and requires for sure the political compromises between the members of the SC.

The collective security system, although put to the test for its defects that could be defined as "structural", continues, however, to stand on a cornerstone that today, as at the time of its establishment, the international community considers indispensable for its survival: the prohibition of the threat and use of force, except in the case of self-defence (Cassese and Gaeta 2008:17).

7 Impact of Humanitarian Intervention on the Right to Self-Determination

With the growing acceptance of self-determination as a legal right, the question as to the legitimacy of the use of force was raised (Shaw 1997:795). The use of force by the outsiders often has to do with the protection of people of the right to self-determination. Being part of the so-called collective rights, the right to self-determination often has also engaged in military intervention. There is a more explicit link between humanitarian intervention and the right to self-determination. Regarding the changing parameters of the principle of non-interference, and also that of self-determination which at the beginning just applied to people living under colonial domination, each state is entitled to help oppressed peoples living in other states to achieve self-determination (Cassese 1995:176).

After 1945 the UN General Assembly attributed a certain degree of legitimacy to the struggle for self-determination carried out by national liberation movements. Although there was no general agreement as to the extent of that legitimacy, some interpreted it to mean that colonized peoples were entitled to act militarily and to receive military support, including legitimate military intervention (Ortega 2001:11). Humanitarian interventions have opened debates on their legality and morality. Claims made about the capacity of international organizations to guarantee values such as order, peace and human rights, democratic governments and self-determination have mirrored the claims made more generally about the capacity of a rational, cosmopolitan international law to tame nationalist passions and local grabs for power (Orford 1999:679). Claims for self-determination became more and more often in the international agenda also requiring the intervention of the international community so that the people within a particular state enjoy their proper right to self-determination.

However, it is difficult to reconcile today with Article 2(4) of the Charter unless one adopts a slightly artificial definition of the territorial integrity criterion to permit temporary violations. Even in the Declaration of Friendly Relations of 1970, we have the obligation of all states to refrain from any forcible action which deprives people of their right to self-determination. The Declaration goes further to say that people struggling for the right to self-determination "are entitled to seek and receive support" from external powers, but such support must be "under the purposes and principles of the UN Charter" (Declaration on Friendly Relation, GA Resolution 2625 1970).

Military intervention in civil wars may have imperialistic or ideological motivations, but the intention may also be to support one of the parties claiming the right to national self-determination (Ortega 2001:6). Since 1965, the General Assembly has moved a step further and started to call upon states to help dependent peoples to achieve self-determination with moral and material assistance (Rigo Sureda 1973:331). During the wars of independence against colonial powers and even more so once the independence was achieved, the foreign military intervention became intimately connected with the ideological divide.

Usually, intervention is prohibited when it coincides with an intervention to the matters which are called matters of exclusive internal affairs of an independent state. The principles of respect for the sovereignty of states and territorial integrity are principles closely allied to the principles of the prohibition of the use of force and non-intervention. Especially when it comes out the principle of territorial integrity, individual states and the whole international community are sensitive to the idea of intervention. The right to self-determination, the external one, includes changes of territorial borders that put the international community in difficulties to act.

The history of humanitarian interventions knows a few cases where a unilateral or collective intervention is undertaken to help specific groups of people to apply their right to self-determination or at least there are few cases where it is explicitly mentioned in the document which allowed the intervention, which means in SC Resolutions, there mostly were merely on a humanitarian basis. This was during the period of decolonization, mostly.

During the last decades, the right to self-determination was little used since in conflicts in which one party claimed this right, such as Croatia, Bosnia, East Timor, Eritrea, Kosovo, Macedonia, Sri Lanka or Western Sahara, external powers have generally exerted a sobering influence in a way that always tried to marginalize this right and to act in a humanitarian intervention purely only on a humanitarian basis. For example, the SC Resolution 688 of 1991 where the SC does not mention at all the right to self-determination of the Kurdish people as a group, as a people or as a minority but just referred to "*the Iraqi population in many parts of Iraq, including most recently in Kurdish – populated areas*" (UNSC Resolution 988 1991). In this case, the right to self-determination of the Kurdish people was not addressed.

No state today would deny the fundamental principle that the people of a nation have the right under international law to decide for themselves what kind of government they want and that this includes the right to revolt and an armed conflict between competing groups (Schachter 1991:158). Usually, the interventions have been done only by humanitarian assistance even when the practice also implies the help for the application of the right of peoples to self-determination.

As we have argued above the humanitarian intervention might be permissible in the cases of extreme humanitarian need. There are formulated a kind of catalogue of criteria to justify humanitarian intervention, and these are:

- fundamental rights must be grossly violated;
- the intervention must be carried out by a group of states;
- the intervention must be regarded only the closer humanitarian concern;
- the principle of proportionality must be respected;
- the Security Council must be informed immediately (Hilpold 2001:450).

Some of these criteria are vaguely formulated, and they have either no clear foundation in international law, or they are formulated in such a general way as to be of no practical value. Humanitarian intervention even though does not have a direct impact on the right to self-determination, especially before the end of the Cold War, if we go further on its practical studies, we see that it is some implication with our right also.

In the period of post-Cold War world that emerged from security, texts is one in which struggle for national identity and self-determination have disintegrated into ethnic, religious and political fragmentation (Weiss 1995:3). A new kind of conflicts emerged at the beginning of the 1990s, internal conflicts rather than international ones, driven by the ethnic hostilities which made people and governments using gross deprivations and violations of human rights to stop people or groups of people to apply their right to self-determination. The need to halt the horrors of genocide or ethnic cleansing, or address the effects of internal armed conflict on civilians, is sufficient justification for military intervention (Orford 1999:691). Also, the internationalization of an internal conflict plays an enormous role in intervening by the international community. Usually, this internationalization of the conflict comes as a result of a severe threat to the peace and security of more than a state of this conflict.

One of these cases is Kosovo, where a totalitarian regime accompanied fighting of the Albanian people in the province for their right to self-determination from Belgrade for almost a decade ending only after the intervention from NATO in the Federal Republic of Yugoslavia. In this case, as we will see, a humanitarian intervention occurred, firstly for stopping the everlasting gross and massive human rights violations in the province and refugee flows in the neighbouring countries but also to help the Albanian people in applying their right to self-determination.

8 Conclusions

A new kind of intervention has emerged during the 1990s, collective ones as a result also of the new kind of conflicts now even in the heart of Europe. Internal conflicts based on the ethnic differences between the different groups living within one state. As a result of these conflicts, many times international community finds itself in front of an armed conflict where a massive violation of human rights, and also an absolute denial of a group of people to apply their legitimate right to self-determination, occurs. The prevention of international and internal armed conflicts or the prompt re-establishment of peace when these conflicts break out, the fight against terrorism, disarmament and a satisfactory regulation of international economic relations conducive to political stability in many countries have remained the principal sore points (Cassese 2005:323).

In theory humanitarian intervention involving the threat or use of armed force and undertaken without the mandate or the authorization of the Security Council will, as a matter of principle, remain in breach of international law (Simma 1999:6). The principle of non-intervention remains a cornerstone of modern international law. In the event of an intervention alleged to be on humanitarian grounds, the better view is that such an intervention is illegal but that the international community may, in extreme circumstances, tolerate the delict (Chesterman 2001: 232). The need to stop the massive and gross violation of human rights through the use of force by the international community needs a new kind of mentality also within the SC as the only and the main body that can authorize the use of force in a specific conflict by a state, group of states or even by a regional organization.

There has been a shift in international law from emphasizing state security to the security of persons and peoples. And this is due to the evolution of human rights protection beyond the borders of their states. The doctrine of humanitarian intervention with all its modification or modernization past through a strict interference in internal affairs of a state to a responsibility to protect human rights with or without their state consent who can't or is not willing to protect. The reservations that emerged in the UN debates and the continuous resistance among states to accept the existence of responsibility, in the sense of legal duty, to protect individuals against massive human rights violations, clearly demonstrates that to date, much uncertainty remains about the legal foundation underlying this new doctrine (Francioni and Baker 2013:6).

References

Abiew, F. K. (1999). *The Evolution of the Doctrine and Practice of Humanitarian Intervention*. The Hague: Kluwer Law International.

Annan, K. (2000). *"We the Peoples"*, *Millennium Report*, para. 217. Available at: https://www.un.org/en/events/pastevents/pdfs/We_The_Peoples.pdf

Arend, A. C., & Beck, R. J. (1993). *International Law and the Use of Force. Beyond the UN Charter Paradigm*. London: Routledge.

Cassese, A. (1995). *Self-Determination of Peoples. A Legal Reappraisal*. Cambridge: Cambridge University Press.

Cassese, A. (2005). *International Law* (2nd ed.). Oxford: Oxford University Press.

Cassese, A., & Gaeta, P. (2008). *Le sfide attuali del diritto internazionale*. Bologna: Il Mulino.

Chesterman, S. (2001). *Just War or Just Peace? Humanitarian Intervention and International Law*. New York: Oxford University Press.

CSS Strategic Briefing Papers. (2000, June). Humanitarian Intervention: Definitions and criteria (Vol. 3, Part 1). Wellington: Victoria University of Wellington. Available: https://www.wgtn.ac.nz/strategic-studies/documents/strategic-briefing-papers/hi.pdf

D'Amato, A. (1987). *International Law: Process and Prospects*. New York: Transnational Publishers.

Danish Institute of International Affairs. (1999). *Humanitarian Intervention. Legal and Political Aspects*. Submitted to the Minister of Foreign Affairs of Denmark.

De Jounge Oudratt, Ch. (2000, August). *Intervention in Internal Conflicts: Legal and Political Conundrums* (Carnegie Endowment for International Peace, Working Paper, No. 15). See: http://www.carnegieendowment.org/files/15oudraat.pdf

Domagala, A. (2003). *Humanitarian Intervention: The Utopia of the Just War? The NATO Intervention in Kosovo and the Restraint of Humanitarian Intervention* (SEI Working Paper No. 76). Sussex European Institute (SEI).

Francioni, F., & Baker, C. (2013). *Responsibility to Protect, Humanitarian Intervention and Human Rights: Lessons from Libya to Mali* (Transworld, Working Paper 15). Available at: http://transworld.iai.it/wp-content/uploads/2013/04/TW_WP_15.pdf

G. A. Res. A/Res/46/182. (1991).

Griffiths, M., Levine, I., & Weller, M. (1995). Sovereignty and Suffering. In J. Harris (Ed.), *The Politics of Humanitarian Intervention*. London: Save the Children, Pinter.

Hannum, H. (1996). *Autonomy, Sovereignty and Self-Determination: The Accommodation of Conflicting Rights*. Philadelphia: University of Pennsylvania Press.

Harris, J. (1995). Introduction: A Time of Troubles – Problems of International Humanitarian Assistance in the 1990s. In J. Harris (Ed.), *The Politics of Humanitarian Intervention*. London: Save the Children, Pinter.

Hilpold, P. (2001). Humanitarian Intervention: Is There a Need for a Legal Reappraisal? *European Journal of International Law (EJIL), 12*(3), 437–435.

Holzgrefe, J. L. (2003). Humanitarian Intervention Debate. In J. L. Holzgrefe & R. O. Keohane (Eds.), *Humanitarian Intervention. Ethical, Legal and Political Dilemmas*. Cambridge: Cambridge University Press.

Kernot, S. (2004). *Humanitarian Intervention: Human Rights Versus Humanitarian Assistance* (School of International Development, Melbourne University Private, Working Paper No. 16). See: http://www.muprivate.edu.au/fileadmin/SID/Working_papers/Working_Paper_16_.pdf

Krisch, N. (2002). Legality, Morality and the Dilemma of Humanitarian Intervention After Kosovo. *EJIL, 13*(1), 323–335.

Lauterpacht, H. (1950). *International Law and Human Rights*. London: Stevens & Sons.

McCorquodale, R. (2014). *International Law*, S. C. Neff in M. D. Evans (4th ed.). Oxford: Oxford University Press.

Meron, Th. (1991). Common Rights of Mankind in Gentilini, Grotius and Suarez. *American Journal of International Law (AJIL), 85*, 116.

O'Connell, M. E. (2000). The UN, NATO, and International Law After Kosovo. *Human Rights Quarterly, 22*, 77.

O'Meara, Ch. (2016). Should International Law Recognize a Right of Humanitarian Intervention to Support and Reflect a Pluralistic Understanding of Sovereignty? *International & Comparative Law Quarterly* 2017. Available at: SSRN: https://ssrn.com/abstract=2876531

Orford, A. (1999). Muscular Humanitarianism: Reading the Narratives of the New Interventionism. *EJIL, 10*(4), 679–711.

Orford, A. (2003). *Reading Humanitarian Intervention. Human Rights and the Use of Force in International Law*. Cambridge: Cambridge University Press.

Ortega, M. (2001), *Military Interventions and the European Union* (Challiot Papers, No. 45). Paris: Institute for Security Studies.

Reisman, M. (1990). Sovereignty and Human Rights in Contemporary International Law. *AJIL, 84*, 866.

Reisman, W. M. (2000). Unilateral Action and the Transformations of the World Constitutive Process: The Special Problem of Humanitarian Intervention. *EJIL, 11*(1), 3–18.

Report of the Secretary-General on the Work of the Organization, UN GAOR, 46th Sess., Supp. No. 1, UN Doc. A/46/1. (1991).

Rigo Sureda, A. (1973). *The Evolution of the Right of Self-Determination, A Study of United Nations Practice*. Leiden: A.W. Sijthoff.

SC Resolution 988. (1991, April 5).

Schachter, O. (1991). *International Law in Theory and Practice*. Dordrecht: Martinus Nijhoff Publishers.

Security Council Summit Statement Concerning the Council's Responsibility in the Maintenance of International Peace and Security, 47 UN SCOR (3046th mtg) Un Doc S/23500. (1992). UNYB 33, 1992.

Shaw, M. (1997). *International Law*. Cambridge: Cambridge University Press.

Simma, B. (1999). NATO, the UN and the Use of Force: Legal Aspects. *EJIL, 10*(1), 1–22.

Simons, P. C. (2000, December). Humanitarian Intervention: A Review of Literature. *The Ploughshares Monitor, 21*(4). Available at: https://ploughshares.ca/pl_publications/humanitarian-intervention-a-review-of-literature-2/#

U.N. (2005). *Resolution on the 2005 World Summit Outcome*, (A/RES/60/1) 24 October 2005. https://undocs.org/A/RES/60/1

U.N. General Assembly, 60th Session. (2005, September 15). Draft Resolution Referred to the High-Level Plenary Meeting of the General Assembly by the General Assembly at its Fifty-Ninth Session (A/60/L.1), accessed December 4, 2012.

United Nations Charter Declaration of Friendly Relations, GA Resolution 2625, 25 UN GAOR Supp. (No. 28) at 121, UN Doc. A/8082 (1970)

UNSC Resolution 1706. (2006) to expand the UN Mission to Darfur (UNMIS).

UNSC Resolution 1973. 2011, March 17, authorising "all necessary measures…to protect civilians", which lead the day after NATO air forces to initiate bombing in Libya.

UNSC Resolution 770. 1992, August 13, through which the SC recognised that the situation in Bosnia & Herzegovina constitutes a threat to peace and security.
UNSC Resolution 794. 1992, December 3, where for the first time in the history of the UN, it was decided to intervene military for strictly humanitarian purposes.
Vendirame, G. (2013). The Law and the Strategy of Humanitarian Intervention. *EJILtalk* 2013. http://www.ejiltalk.org/the-law-and-strategy-of-humanitarian-intervention/
Weiss, Th. G. (1995). On the Brink of a New Era? Humanitarian Interventions, 1991–94. D. C. F. Daniel & B. C. Hayes (Ed.), *Beyond Traditional Peacekeeping*. London: Macmillan.
Wing Commander J. E. Linter MA, RAF. (2005). Humanitarian Intervention: Legitimising the Illegal? *Defence Studies, 5*, 2. https://www.tandfonline.com/doi/full/10.1080/14702430500336459
Yoshida, Y. (2013). *From Kosovo to Libia: Theoretical Assessment of Humanitarian Intervention and the Responsibility to Protect.* New York University. Avaiable at: https://www.e-ir.info/pdf/32316

PART III

The Procedural Discourse of Territorial Politics of Independence and Secession: Democracy and Rule of Law

CHAPTER 7

Territorial Politics Through International Law? Independence Referendums Beyond Post-Colonial Situations

Emanuel Castellarin

1 Introduction

A growing number of independence movements use referendums or referendum demands to support their claims. Yet, after the end of the main waves of decolonisation, the international society ceased to produce new customary norms broadening the scope of the right of peoples to external self-determination (independence), thus implicitly encouraging internal self-determination (different forms of autonomy). Paraphrasing Sieyès' famous pamphlet "Qu'est-ce que le Tiers-État?",[1] it can be observed that

[1] "Qu'est-ce que le Tiers-État? Le plan de cet Écrit est assez simple. Nous avons trois questions à nous faire.1° Qu'est-ce que le Tiers-État? Tout. 2° Qu'a-t-il été jusqu'à présent dans l'ordre politique? Rien. 3° Que. demande-t-il? À y devenir quelque chose" (Sieyès 1789).

This research was supported by the French Fondation des sciences sociales (https://fondation-sciences-sociales.org).

E. Castellarin (✉)
University of Strasbourg, Strasbourg, France

M. Belov (ed.), *Territorial Politics and Secession*, Federalism and Internal Conflicts, https://doi.org/10.1007/978-3-030-64402-4_7

independence referendums are, for some independence movements, everything. So far, independence referendums have been nothing, or almost, under international law applicable outside of post-colonial situations. What do they ask? To be something.

Following this pattern, Sect. 2 formulates the hypothesis that, in spite of their shortcomings, independence referendum can convey a new conception of the international society, which can be translated into a new vision of self-determination and of territorial structures. By contrast, Sect. 3 shows that international law has placed little value in independence referendums so far. Section 4 argues that independence referendums can indeed contribute to the renewal of self-determination and of territorial politics, provided that procedural standards of international law are developed.

2 Independence Referendums and the Identity Crisis of Self-Determination

The expression "independence referendum" encompasses very different phenomena (section "The Diversity of Independence Referendums"). The relatively strong demand for independence referendums beyond post-colonial situations has potential to inspire a liberal-democratic conception of the principle of self-determination (section "Independence Referendums as Vectors of a Potential Liberal-Democratic Renewal of Self-Determination").

The Diversity of Independence Referendums

The creation of new states is considered by some communities, rightly or wrongly, as essential for a full achievement of self-determination. Therefore, accession to independence[2] is the object of several procedures which tend to establish the collective will of relevant communities. This is shown by the enthusiasm for independence referendums, which are votes by which

[2] From the legal point of view, sovereignty and independence are inextricably linked and define the state. However, in political terms sovereignty is increasingly seen "not in the power of making laws - as a legal definition would have it - but in the ability to control outcomes" (Draghi 2019).

the population of a territory decides directly on the proposal to constitute a new state.[3]

In fact, the expression "independence referendum" is used in very different contexts. Referendums, regardless of their purposes, are powerful tools easy to mislead because they offer limited (generally binary) answers to complex problems. Consequently, the object of independence referendums is not always easy to identify, due to the creativity of referendum questions. For example, while the question asked in Scotland in 2014 was very straightforward: "Should Scotland be an independent country?", the one asked in Quebec in 1980 was much more complex.[4] Attempts to overcome a classical vision of self-determination, shaped around the state through the internal/external dichotomy, contribute to the creativity of the referendum questions.

Independence referendums are a very heterogeneous category also from the legal point of view. In some legal systems the term "referendum" only applies to decision-making votes, that is, votes whose legal effect is binding, while other non-binding procedures are simply consultations.[5] However, this distinction is not always easy to draw. For example, the vote of 1 October 2017 in Catalonia was binding under the Catalan Law on the Referendum on Self-determination,[6] but it is more appropriate to define it

[3] Most self-determination referendums are about whether or not to continue as an autonomous entity within the state. Independence referendums are a minority, but their high-profile nature tends to overshadow other self-determination referendums (Suksi 2018). See also Qvortrup (2014) and Sen (2015).

[4] "The Government of Quebec has made public its proposal to negotiate a new agreement with the rest of Canada, based on the equality of nations; this agreement would enable Quebec to acquire the exclusive power to make its laws, levy its taxes and establish relations abroad—in other words, sovereignty—and at the same time to maintain with Canada an economic association including a common currency; any change in political status resulting from these negotiations will only be implemented with popular approval through another referendum; on these terms, do you give the Government of Quebec the mandate to negotiate the proposed agreement between Quebec and Canada?".

[5] For example, French law includes both binding referendums and non-binding consultations. Referendums are framed by Articles 11 (bills on selected issues), 89 (amendments to the Constitution), 72-1 (local decisions) and 88-5 (*accession* of new member states to the European Union) of the Constitution. Consultations are framed by Article L2113-3 of the *Code général des collectivités territoriales* (fusion of *communes*), Articles L123-20–L123-23 of the Code of the Environment (projects that can have an impact on environment), and by specific rules applicable to some territories, such as New-Calendonia.

[6] According to Article 4(3) of Law No. 19 of 6 September 2017, *Ley del referéndum de autodeterminación de Cataluña*, the referendum of 1 October should have had binding

as a consultation, in the light of its constitutionality under Spanish law and of its lack of effectiveness. Similarly, the vote of 18 September 2014 in Scotland was officially referred to as a referendum by the *Scottish Independence Referendum Act* of 2013,[7] but its outcome could have theoretically been reversed by a contrary subsequent law by the British Parliament.[8] Moreover, the legal framework of independence referendums is not always easy to grasp. Some referendums are organised in accordance with domestic law. For example, the organisation of a third independence referendum in Quebec, after those of 1980 and 1995, would be lawful. In some cases, referendums are even organised by mutual agreement between the secessionists and the existing state, like in Montenegro in 2006, in Scotland in 2014, in New Caledonia in 2018[9] and in Bougainville in 2019.[10] This choice does not ensure that all legal questions are solved, but makes it possible to frame the referendum in advance, so as to ensure more legal certainty under domestic law.

Other consultations are organised spontaneously by local authorities, without violating any norm of international law, but *praeter legem* or even *contra legem* under domestic law. Consultations of this kind are often considered without being performed,[11] and in some cases they are prevented through legal procedures.[12] In other cases, they do take place, despite legal and material obstacles, and can fit in a constituent process from the point

effect. In case of a result favourable to independence, the Catalan Parliament would have been required to declare Catalonia's independence no later than ten days after the announcement of the results. Conversely, the consultation of 9 November 2014 would not have had binding effect, according to Catalan Law No. 10 of 26 September 2014, *Ley de consultas populares no referendarias y otras formas de participación ciudadana*.

[7] Scottish Independence Referendum Act 2013, passed by the Scottish Parliament on 14 November 2013; received Royal Assent on 17 December 2013. The Act was based on a political agreement between the devolved Scottish government and the Government of the United Kingdom.

[8] This outcome would have been highly unlikely, as also shown by debates after the Brexit referendum (or, more precisely, consultation), where the only politically available options for the British Parliament were considered to be to perform Brexit or to organise a second referendum, but not to reverse the outcome of the 2016 referendum through a statute.

[9] Turpin (2019).

[10] Underwood (2019).

[11] Independence or autonomist movements, which sometimes envisage an independence referendum, are present in several states. For an analysis of several local situations in Europe, see Turp and Sanjaume-Calvet (2016).

[12] Italian Constitutional Court, No. 118/2015, 29 April 2015, declaring unconstitutional regional law 16 of 19 June 2014 on the organisation of a consultation on the independence

of view of secessionists, like in Catalonia in 2017. Finally, consultations are sometimes organised with the military or paramilitary support of another state, which makes them unlawful under international law. This situation, which can be difficult to identify on a factual level when the activity of the foreign state is combined with the spontaneous mobilisation of the local population, was experienced in some post-Soviet states.[13]

Despite their diversity, independence referendums show the existence of widespread demands in the contemporary international society. Like plebiscites did for the evolution of European borders (especially after 1919) and self-determination referendums did in the context of decolonisation, independence referendums play an important role in the creation of new states in the post-colonial world. Since 1991, independence referendums have been a step in the creation of the vast majority of new states, including the last two states admitted to membership of the United Nations (UN), Montenegro in 2006 and Sudan South in 2011. In recent years, some independence movements used referendums (or referendum demands) to support their claims. The difficulties encountered because of the clear opposition of affected states (or even by other states) radically limited the effectiveness of referendums: despite results allegedly favourable to independence, consultations in Catalonia and Iraqi Kurdistan did not result in the effective establishment of new states. Nonetheless, the spread of the practice of independence referendums could encourage emulation elsewhere and influence the dominant conception of self-determination.

Independence Referendums as Vectors of a Potential Liberal-Democratic Renewal of Self-Determination

One century after Lenin and Wilson, the principle of self-determination of peoples is undergoing an identity crisis. Self-determination is undoubtedly a key factor of territorial politics[14] and its legal implications for post-colonial situations are growingly important.[15] However, whereas the first half

of Veneto; Bundesverfassungsgericht, 2 BvR 349/16, 16 December 2016, declaring unconstitutional the organisation of a consultation aimed at the independence of Bavaria.

[13] Hill and White (2014).

[14] For a recent study, Hilpold (2018).

[15] On the implications of the right to self-determination of the Sahrawi people on two agreements between the European Union and Morocco, CJEU, C-104/16 P, *Front Polisario*, 21 December 2016; C-266/16, *Western Sahara Campaign UK*, 27 February 2018.

of the twentieth century allowed the principle of self-determination to become a norm of customary international law and the second half of the century saw a spectacular burgeoning of its application in decolonisation and immediately after the end of the cold war, at the beginning of the twenty-first century self-determination seems to have lost impetus, at least in its external form and outside of post-colonial situations. The unanimous non-recognition of secessionist processes in Catalonia and in Iraqi Kurdistan clearly demonstrates that the international community refuses to call the legal *status quo* into question.[16] Invoking the right to self-determination even seems to have become inappropriate, or even dangerous in some contexts. In Catalonia, a "right to decide" of constitutional source was presented as a more solid foundation for independence claims, as an alternative to the right to self-determination.[17] Reactions by the international community to the Catalan conundrum also tended to use the lexicon of constitutional law and internal politics.[18] More generally, in a context of reaffirmation of nationalism and sovereignism, self-determination may be associated with inward-looking attitudes and demagoguery.[19] After all, slogans like "Make America great again" and "Take back control" also appeal to the idea of self-determination, and the fact that the principle has been almost exclusively invoked for the benefit of ethnolinguistic communities raises doubt as to its compatibility with an inclusive conception of society. In terms of international stability, self-determination can potentially lead to balkanisation, that is, a high level of fragmentation between uncooperative entities.[20]

To avoid the use of self-determination as a mere expression of the claim of a community against the others, the conceptual basis of self-determination should be renewed. A trend seems to emerge in this direction. Instead of focusing on the outcome, that is, on the right *to* external self-determination, which notoriously exist only within very narrow limits,[21] debates are increasingly shifting towards the right *of*

[16] Hajjami (2017); Sterio (2018); Milano (2018).

[17] *Cappuccio and Corretja* Torrents (2014); Barceló et al. (2015); Cagiao Conde and Ferraiuolo (2016); López (2017), esp. p. 123–128.

[18] For example, Maganza (2017). Like other governments, the Italian government criticised unilateral action and implicitly called upon constitutional dialogue.

[19] Peters (2017).

[20] Cattaruzza (2007).

[21] Among recent works, Dugard (2013), Walter et al. (2013), Lecucq (2017); Christakis and Constantinides (2018).

self-determination, that is, the framing of decision-making processes that allow practicing self-determination. Increased attention to the procedural aspects of self-determination sheds new light both on the perennial problem of defining the holders of the right to self-determination and on external self-determination. All aspects of self-determination have a strong procedural dimension.[22] Theoretically, appropriate procedures allow the emergence, by approximation, of the smallest relevant community to deal with each question that needs collective decisions. Such procedures also allow the definition of relevant communities, for example, by repeated referendums on a progressively reduced territory, which allows the gradual definition of the geographical scope of relevant communities.[23] Similarly, appropriate procedures allow the emergence of the collective will of individuals within a community, which allows its self-organisation and its self-management. Under his conception, self-determination is centred on the individual and can identify, through a bottom-up approach, the collective will of communities at various geographic levels, in a spirit of subsidiarity. The debate on self-determination thus merges with that on the "right to decide" as a claim in constitutional terms,[24] as the principle of self-determination interacts with other liberal-democratic principles and human rights.

In this context, independence referendums can contribute to a renewal of self-determination based on liberal-democratic principles.[25] Although traditionally conceived as a fact which escapes legal analysis,[26] the creation of new states can become a decision governed by legal procedures and based on direct public participation in political affairs. Admittedly, this should not overshadow the strategic use of independence referendums as political instruments: they are often conceived as an option within a broader process, and they can be the object of threats or promises that make it possible to obtain other advantages within the existing states.

[22] Héraud (1975), p. 271–272; Héraud (1994), p. 33–35. The author identifies five dimensions of self-determination: self-assertion (*auto-affirmation*), self-definition, choice of the governing state or right to secede, self-organisation and self-management.

[23] Héraud (1994), p. 35–36. A referendum of this kind ("*plébiscite en cascade*") was organised in 1974–1975 to organise the separation of the Canton of Jura from the Canton of Bern.

[24] Cf. Turp (2017).

[25] On the interplay between democracy and law in secessionist processes and on the distinction between the democratic theory of secession and the theory of democratic secession, see C. Closa et al. (2019).

[26] Jellinek (1922), p. 332.

However, in an international society still centred on interstate relations, independence referendums also manifest the immense ambition of developing new forms of collective expression by individuals about their political future. So far, the framing of independence referendums under international law has not lived up to this ambition.

3 The Limited Role of Independence Referendums Under International Law

International law is not completely indifferent to independence referendums, as it includes norms that apply to them. However, in the absence of a general obligation to organise an independence referendum at the request of a part of the population, international law does not encourage referendum initiatives (section "The Lack of a General Obligation to Organise Independence Referendums"). In addition, independence referendums only have very limited legal effects under international law (section "The Very Limited Legal Effects of Independence Referendums").

The Lack of a General Obligation to Organise Independence Referendums

For any referendum, the modalities of initiatives are crucial. The demand for a "right to decide" in this area partly corresponds to rights recognised under international law both at the universal and at the regional level. Thus, the rights of expression, association and living in a democratic society imply to some extent the right to express views in favour of holding an independence referendum. It has been correctly argued that these rights correspond to an obligation to take into account the demands of the population, including when they are favourable to independence.[27] Furthermore, contrary to what is sometimes suggested, not all questions relating to referendums of independence fall entirely and by nature within the domestic jurisdiction of states. Not all verbal statements are unlawful interferences,[28] which implies that other states may encourage the application or modification of domestic law in order to promote the organisation of an independence referendum, provided that these statements do not put undue pressure on the affected state. As for international organisations

[27] Klabbers (2006); Bell (2016), p. 202.
[28] Combacau and Sur (2019), p. 302.

of which the affected state is a member, it would be excessive to interpret provisions such as Article 2(7) of the UN Charter (domestic jurisdiction of members) or Article 4(2) Treaty on European Union (respect for national identity essential functions of the member states) as prohibiting any action. For example, organs and institutions of the United Nations,[29] of the European Union[30] and of the Council of Europe[31] adopted non-binding legal acts regarding the 2017 consultation in Catalonia. The normative effect of these acts is very weak and their content is particularly cautious on the desirability of the consultation, but the competence of these organisations to adopt non-binding acts in this kind of situation was not questioned.

Nonetheless, international law does not encourage referendum initiatives on questions related to the access to independence. In particular, there is no general obligation to organise an independence referendum upon the request of specific subjects, especially (representing) a part of the population. Several self-determination referendums have taken place within the framework of decolonisation, but even in that case the referendum was not legally necessary for the choice between independence, association with an existing state and integration with an existing state. As long as this choice is free and voluntary, other methods are also legal.[32]

[29] As part of the work of the General Assembly on the implementation of the principle of self-determination, the independent expert Alfred de Zayas "advocated for the United Nations to provide advice and technical assistance to States on viable models of autonomy, federalism and, eventually, referendums" (Report to the Human Rights Council of the Independent Expert on the promotion of a democratic and equitable international order, A/HRC/37/63, 25 January 2018, paras 35 and 51), in particular concerning indigenous peoples (*ibid.*, para. 53).

[30] European Parliament, *Constitution, rule of law and fundamental rights in Spain in the light of the events in Catalonia*, plenary session of 4 October 2017, 2017/2888 (RSP); European Commission, Written response to a question on the repercussions for the European Union should Catalonia become independent, E-005541-17, 5 September 2017; Statement on the events in Catalonia, STATEMENT/17/3626, 2 October 2017.

[31] The Council of Europe Commissioner for Human Rights, without explicitly mentioning the Catalan consultation, expressed concern over the allegations of disproportionate use of force by the Spanish authorities and recommended to the Spain the opening of an investigation (letter of 4 October 2017, www.coe.int).

[32] The choice of association "should be the result of a free and voluntary choice by the peoples of the territory concerned expressed through informed and democratic processes". The choice of integration "should be the result of the freely expressed wishes of the territory's peoples acting with full knowledge of the change in their status, their wishes having been

Given the leeway of the authorities in charge of the transition, the organisation of a referendum does not constitute a subjective right: the authorities are not obliged to hold a referendum upon the request of (a part of) the affected population. *A fortiori*, this also applies to situations where there is no right to external self-determination. States faced with independence movements can freely decide not to hold an independence referendum,[33] even when confronted with strong and continuous demand from the public opinion. This situation is consistent with the overall neutrality of international law with regard to secessionist processes. Indeed, political expediency (and not lawfulness) is the main criterion for analysing the organisation of independence referendums at the international level.

Unilateral secession without acceptance by the affected state is not in itself a violation of international law,[34] but the organisation of an independence referendum without the cooperation of the affected state remains particularly difficult in practical and legal terms. In the absence of contrary international norms, domestic law on secession can set not only the prohibition of consultations on independence, but also the means to ensure the effectiveness of this prohibition, in particular through sanctions.

Ultimately, international law is rather favourable to maintaining the *status quo*: it does not generally prohibit the organisation of independence referendums, but it does not make it possible to overcome the obstacles that domestic law may oppose to them. Under these conditions, the added value of international law over domestic law is very limited regarding the choice to hold a referendum. Thus, especially when domestic law does not encourage the organisation of referendums, negotiating with the affected state is useful or even necessary. This conclusion is also confirmed by the very limited legal effects of independence referendums of independence under international law.

expressed through informed and democratic processes, impartially conducted and based on universal adult suffrage. The United Nations could, when it deems it necessary, supervise these processes" (United Nations General Assembly, Resolution 1541 (XV), Principles which should guide Members in determining whether or not an obligation exists to transmit the information called for under Article 73 e of the Charter, 15 December 1960, Annex, Principles VII and IX). No particular procedure is required for independence (see also Resolution 1514 (XV), 14 December 1960).

[33] Crawford (2006), p. 417.

[34] International Court of Justice, advisory opinion of 22 July 2010, Accordance with international law of the unilateral declaration of independence in respect of Kosovo, paras 79–84.

The Very Limited Legal Effects of Independence Referendums

Far from introducing a radical change in the logic of international law, independence referendums remain one factor among others in the legal framing of territorial politics and more particularly in the process of creating new states. This process remains characterised by the primacy of interstate relations over democracy and by a weak legal framework.

In the 1990s, independence referendums were sometimes regarded as a necessary condition under customary law for the creation of new states. The opinions of the Badinter Commission strengthened this thesis,[35] also defended by some legal scholars with regard to the creation of new states outside of decolonisation.[36] This thesis is attractive, because it is difficult to imagine, in the current state of international law, a secession which would not be unlawful but which would not respect, at least formally, democratic principles. Following this line of reasoning, independence referendums would have a particular meaning outside of decolonisation: they would be necessary to legitimise a situation whose creation does not correspond to a subjective right, but simply to a non-wrongful act.

However, this thesis does not seem to correspond to current customary law. Practice in this area is subject to debate,[37] and it is difficult to assert the existence of an *opinio juris*. The customary nature of the need for an independence referendum for the creation of a new state, persistently contested by some scholars,[38] is now also doubted by former supporters.[39]

Moreover, independence referendums are certainly not a sufficient condition for independence, because they may not have the immediate effect of creating a new state. The legal effects of independence referendums are necessarily more limited. Some consultations are necessarily devoid of any legal effect, as they are organised in the framework of violations of *jus cogens* norms. For example, the controversial consultation of 16 March 2014 on the annexation of Crimea to Russia resulted from threat or use of

[35] Arbitration Commission of the Conference on Yugoslavia, Opinion No. 4 (Bosnia-Herzegovina), 11 January 1992.

[36] Peters (1995); Peters (2014); Tancredi (2006), p. 191; Vidmar (2013).

[37] One may wonder to what extent a referendum is equivalent to the exercise of representative democracy in elections whose electoral campaign is focused on the question of independence, like in Kosovo in 2008. The absence of a referendum during the dissolution of Czechoslovakia also raises the question whether secession is subject to the same regime as state dissolution.

[38] For example, Bílková (2016), p. 212.

[39] Peters (2017).

force against the territorial integrity of Ukraine, as observed by the United Nations General Assembly and by the Venice Commission of the Council of Europe.[40]

Other independence referendums have binding effect, set and limited by domestic law without contravening any international norm. For example, Article 4 of the 2001 Montenegrin statute on referendums, applied to the 2006 independence referendum, established the referendum's binding effect on the Parliament. Sometimes domestic law recognises that a consultation has intermediate legal effects between the total lack of effects and binding effect. For example, in the case of New Caledonia, the consultation has no binding effect, but up to two further consultations may be held if the first consultation rejects the option of full sovereignty, as it happened in 2018.[41] In determining the legal effects of consultations, domestic law can develop original solutions: according to the Supreme Court of Canada, "[a] clear majority vote in Quebec on a clear question in favour of secession would confer democratic legitimacy on the secession initiative which all of the other participants in Confederation would have to recognize" and would necessarily imply negotiations.[42] This solution can inspire other national legal orders,[43] but does not automatically trigger a customary process at the international level.

Legal certainty resulting from the domestic legal framework of independence referendums is never total, but it is high compared to international law. However, the legal effects of several consultations remain uncertain. This is especially true for consultations that are not framed or that are even unlawful under domestic law, but that are organised according to international procedural standards and without contravening

[40] United Nations General Assembly, Resolution 68/262, Territorial integrity of Ukraine, 27 March 2014; European Commission for Democracy through Law (Venice Commission), Opinion 762/2014, Constitutionality of the decision taken by the Supreme Council of the Autonomous Republic of Crimea in Ukraine to organise a referendum, 21 March 2014, para. 22. Independence had been declared on 11 March 2014 by Supreme Council of Crimea and the Sevastopol City Council.

[41] French Organic Law No. 99-209 on New Caledonia, 19 March 1999, Article 217. The second consultation will be held on 6 September 2020.

[42] Supreme Court of Canada, Reference re Secession of Quebec, [1998] 2 SCR 217, 20 August 1998, question 1 and para. 151.

[43] However, transplanting this solution to other legal orders is not always possible. For example, it has been argued that, given the different legal and factual context, the Canadian and British approaches to independence referendums cannot be applied to the Catalan case (Oklopcic (2017)).

international substantive norms. These consultations are undoubtedly endowed with a certain political value, so that their normative effect seems to be weak but not inexistent: arguably, there ensues an obligation to take them into account.

The recommendations of the Council of the League of Nations following the 1920 petition regarding the Åland Islands are an example of this kind of situation. However, the legal effects of these consultations tend to fade before the political effects. Doubts are inevitable on the conduct of voting operations, on results and generally on the effectiveness of applicable norms.

The uncertainty that surrounded the consultation of 2017 in Catalonia[44] corresponds to a situation in which, in several respects, appeal was made more to political than to legal principles.[45] This example shows an inevitable paradox: only an entity that is already very similar to a state can organise an orderly consultation without the support of an existing state.

This paradox is due to the centrality of effectiveness in international law. The state is defined essentially by objective constituent elements: a permanent population, a defined territory, government and the capacity to enter into relations with other states.[46] It is true that the existence of a new state supposes a subjective dimension which is typically manifested by a declaration of independence, to which the independence referendum may be prior.[47] However, the will of the population is not sufficient to constitute a state, which is another way of demonstrating that an independence referendum is not a sufficient condition for independence. Even when a consultation results in the actual constitution of a state, it is still necessary that the constitution of this new state is not made in violation of peremptory norms of international law.

[44] On 7 September 2017, the Spanish Constitutional tribunal suspended the Catalan Law on the Referendum on Self-determination of 6 September. As the result of the consultation was favourable to independence, according to the Catalan authorities (90.2% of favourable votes, with a turnout rate of 43%), a declaration of independence was adopted on 10 October 2017. The declaration was first suspended by the President of the Generalitat of Catalonia, but definitively adopted on 27 October and declared unconstitutional by the Spanish Constitutional tribunal.

[45] Bak McKenna (2017).

[46] Montevideo Convention on the Rights and Duties of States, Article 1, reflecting customary law.

[47] Weller (2017).

The prohibition of the threat and use of force in international relations in a manner inconsistent with the UN Charter[48] constitutes a significant limitation in this regard, as shown by the international non-recognition of Crimea's annexation by Russia. As this is a peremptory norm (*jus cogens*), only the international community of states as a whole can derogate from it.[49] Thus, this norm cannot be derogated from by an interstate agreement, or *a fortiori* by a unilateral act. In other words, an independence referendum is by no means sufficient to make lawful an unlawful process that results in the creation of a state, or the unlawful modification of existing borders. Likewise, the free determination of new borders by an independence referendum is limited by the principle *uti possidetis*, which defines international borders resulting from decolonisation or state dissolution on the basis of former administrative borders.[50] As an ordinary customary norm, the *uti possidetis* principle can be derogated from by an interstate agreement, but a state and *a fortiori* a part of its population cannot derogate from it unilaterally.

Ultimately, independence referendums are not devoid of any effect in international law, but their normative role is limited. Therefore, the next section analyses under what conditions international law can evolve towards a greater promotion of independence referendums and therefore contribute to the procedural renewal of self-determination.

4 Under What Conditions Can Independence Referendums Play a Bigger Role Under International Law?

Enhancing the role of independence referendums under international law is impossible without increased attention to their modalities. The development of procedural standards applicable to independence referendums is necessary to promote freedom, fairness and regularity of the vote (section "The Need to Develop Procedural Standards"). To some extent, the rule of law should also be promoted beyond *Rechtsstaat / Etat de droit*, through the development of international standards autonomous from domestic law (section "The Need to Protect the Rule of Law Beyond *Rechtsstaat / Etat de droit*").

[48] Article 2(4) of the UN Charter.

[49] Article 53 of the Vienna Convention on the Law of Treaties.

[50] Beaudouin (2011); Peters (2013).

The Need to Develop Procedural Standards

An improved international status of independence referendums requires firmer standards regarding their organisation. Such procedural standards make it possible to ensure increased legal certainty without directly touching upon more controversial substantive issues such as the legal effects of referendums, which are closely linked to the basic structures of international law. In terms of legal certainty, the usefulness of these standards is to provide an objective benchmark of the legitimacy of independence referendums, that is, of their abstract aptitude to produce legal effects. A legitimate independence referendum can only be free, fair and regular: more detailed standards would make it possible to clarify these general notions. Especially at the regional level, collections of good practices provide some content, admittedly without binding effect but with some degree of precision, to these procedural standards.

The best established standards are not specifically applicable to independence referendums: as they related to the conduct of electoral campaigns, to the deployment of international observers and so on, they apply to all referendums and even all elections.[51] On issues concerning independence referendums specifically, some standards seem to correspond to a sufficiently unequivocal international practice. For example, independence referendums are normally held within the territorial limits of the region whose independence is proposed, and not throughout the territory of the affected state.[52]

While the existing procedural standards are not negligible, they are far from guaranteeing complete legal certainty as to the conduct of independence referendums. Standards are fuzzy on several critical issues: the existing practice is disparate and multiple solutions are logically acceptable, even on issues of the utmost importance. The conditions of the right to vote (in particular residence or other connections with the affected community) and criteria to set electoral lists are good examples.[53] The practice

[51] Venice Commission, CDL-INF(2001)10-e, Guidelines on the national constitutional referendum, 11 July 2001; Study 371/2006, Code of Good Practice on Referendums, 19 March 2007; Study 190/2002, Code of Good Practice in Electoral Matters: Guidelines and Explanatory Report, 23 May 2003.

[52] Weller (2017).

[53] For example, see the Scottish Independence Referendum (Franchise) Act 2013 and Articles 218–218-3 of French Organic Law No. 99-209 on New Caledonia of 19 March 1999, which create special lists of voters. See also Qvortrup (2017), p. 45–48.

of international organisations sometimes contributes to the inconsistency of standards. For example, the Venice Commission generally discourages setting a minimum turnout or approval rate (*quorum*) for the validity of referendums, because this solution "means that it is in the interests of a proposal's opponents to abstain rather than to vote against it" and could moreover be inconclusive.[54] However, the Commission approved the statute applicable to the referendum in Montenegro in 2006, which provided for a turnout *quorum* of 50%.[55]

The quest for new standards, which is necessary to fill current gaps, questions their legal nature. It can be first assumed that procedural standards are formed in the same way as substantive norms, which are necessarily treaty norms, customary norms or general principles of law.[56] However, assuming that procedural standards have the same source as substantive norms boils down to duplicate inconclusive debates on their allegedly customary nature. The formation of customary norms is hardly compatible with the high technicity of the relevant procedural issues. Practice is scant and, most importantly, *opinio juris* is often impossible to determine: it is unusual that statements of states on independence referendums abroad, when they express legal considerations, relate to detailed procedural issues. In the absence of specifically applicable standards, international law seems to prove of little use in determining the legitimacy of the referendums, so that the same set of facts can be assessed in a radically opposite way. This situation can sometimes satisfy the actors involved, because it tends to make admissible, or even plausible, a vast array of legal qualification of each referendum. However, legal uncertainty is incompatible with the use of the independence referendum as a genuine vector of liberal-democratic principles and thus reduces it to a mere strategic instrument.

It is submitted that some standards of legitimacy of independence referendums are formed differently from substantive standards. Admittedly, like customary standards, procedural standards imply good practices to be followed. However, some procedural standards are principles of pure logic, which are necessary by nature for the free, fair and regular conduct

[54] Venice Commission, Study 371/2006, *cit.* fn 51, paras 50–52.

[55] Venice Commission, Opinion 343/2005, Opinion on the Compatibility of the Existing Legislation in Montenegro concerning the Organisation of Referendums with Applicable International Standards, 19 December 2005, paras 19–28.

[56] Article 38(1) of the Statute of the International Court of Justice.

of the independence referendum. This makes them relatively independent of international practice and even of *opinio juris*. This hypothesis is hardly compatible with a voluntarist conception of international law, which directly or indirectly bases all international norms on state will. However, it reveals a flaw of some of current international procedural standards: the strict adherence to domestic law structures makes these standards useless to determine the legitimacy of independence referendums.

The Need to Protect the Rule of Law Beyond Rechtsstaat / Etat de droit

Procedural standards currently applicable to independence referendums are essentially oriented towards the promotion of the rule of law within the framework of existing states and through domestic law (*Rechtsstat / Etat de droit*). The application of these standards to ordinary votes and elections is free from criticism. However, when applied to independence referendums, some of these standards lead to paradoxical situations.

Procedural standards of international origin are essential when the rule of law within an existing state is put to the test and an independence referendum is held outside or even against the state. It is precisely in this situation that procedural standards focusing on the rule of law within the framework of the state prove to be of little use. To a certain extent, the determination of international standards of legitimacy, that is, whether the referendum is free, fair and regular, must necessarily disregard domestic law. In particular, legality, that is, compliance with constitutional law and domestic laws, is generally considered to be one of the main criteria for the legitimacy of referendums.[57]

However, for independence referendums unlawful under domestic law but not under international law, the vote can only be free and fair if electoral competition guarantees equality of opportunity between the two opposing options of independence and remaining within the existing state.[58] In other words, in these circumstances it by definition is impossible

[57] Venice Commission, CDL-INF(2001)10-e, *cit.* fn 51, para. II.A; Study 371/2006, *cit.* fn 51, para. III.1; Study 190/2002, *cit.* fn 51, para. II.2.A.

[58] Multiple options can be conceived. For example, the plebiscite held on 13 January 1935 in the Saar Basin included three options, as provided by Article 34 of the 1919 Versailles Treaty: (a) maintenance of the League of Nations regime (8.9%), (b) union with France (0.4%) and (c) union with Germany (90.7%). However, options should be conceived so as to allow a free and fair choice between them.

to ensure both the freedom and fairness and the legality of an independence referendum.

As shown by the 2017 consultation in Catalonia, assessing the procedural quality of independence referendums can raise not only factual, but also logical challenges. For example, given the physical restriction of access to polling stations by the police, that vote could not be considered free. At the same time, these restrictions were necessary to guarantee the rule of law through domestic law, which prohibited the consultation. Beyond the freedom of the vote, the issue of its lawfulness also affects his fairness and regularity. For example, the Catalan consultation was certainly irregular, in particular because the independent electoral commission responsible for ensuring the transparency and the objectivity of the referendum procedure did not fulfil its functions due to the collective resignation of its members. At the same time, the resignation sought to avoid the sanctions that members of the committee were subject to under domestic law.[59]

International law is the only way out of the legal, political and logical conundrum of secessionist aspirations and domestic norms. The consolidation of the international status of independence referendums therefore requires international procedural standards that are partly autonomous from domestic law. In this respect, rule of law should also be ensured through international law, which implies moving beyond the mere reference to rule of law through domestic law.

5 Conclusion

The procedural renewal of the right to self-determination seems to have started and is likely to be consolidated in the long run, with a long-standing impact on territorial politics. After helping to structure international society around the state, the principle of self-determination could become the matrix for new forms of collective expression by individuals. Although often imperfect, independence referendums contribute to this long-term trend and express demands linked to the basic structures of the international society. Improving legal certainty of international law applicable to these referendums would be useful. A sudden change in the current legal framework is highly unlikely. However, the future will certainly provide opportunities to test possible progressive developments.

[59] Catalan Law on the Referendum on Self-determination, Article 17; Baquero (2017).

References

Bak McKenna, M. (2017, September 27). The Referendum on Catalan Self-Determination: Long Shots and Legal Flair. *Völkerrechtsblog*. https://voelkerrechtsblog.org

Baquero, C. (2017, September 22). La Sindicatura del referèndum es dissol per evitar les multes del Tribunal Constitucional. *El País*. cat.elpais.com

Barceló, M., et al. (Eds.). (2015). *El derecho a decidir. Teoría y práctica de un nuevo derecho*. Barcelona: Atelier.

Beaudouin, A. (2011). *Uti possidetis et sécession*. Paris: Dalloz.

Bell, C. (2016). International law, the Independence Debate, and Political Settlement in the UK. In A. Mc Harg et al. (Eds.), *The Scottish Independence Referendum. Constitutional and Political Implications* (pp. 197–222). Oxford: Oxford University Press.

Bílková, V. (2016). Territorial (Se)Cession in Light of the Recent Events in Crimea. In M. Nicolini et al. (Eds.), *Law, Territory and Conflict Resolution* (pp. 194–218). Leyden: Brill/Nijhoff.

Cagiao Conde, J., & Ferraiuolo, G. (Eds.). (2016). *El encaje constitucional del derecho a decidir*. Madrid: Catarata.

Cappuccio, L., & Corretja Torrents, M. (Eds.). (2014). *El derecho a decidir*. Barcelona: Un diálogo italo-catalán, Institut d'Estudis Autonomics.

Cattaruzza, A. (2007, December 22). Les référendums d'autodétermination: démocratisation ou balkanisation du monde ? *L'Espace Politique*. http://journals.openedition.org/espacepolitique

Christakis, T., & Constantinides, A. (2018). Territorial Disputes in the Context of Secessionist Conflicts. In M. Kohen & M. Hébié (Eds.), *Research Handbook on Territorial Disputes in International Law* (pp. 343–395). Cheltenham: Elgar.

Closa, C., et al. (Eds.). (2019). *Between Democracy and Law. The Amorality of Secession*. London: Routledge.

Combacau, J., & Sur, S. (2019). *Droit International Public* (13th ed.). Paris: LGDJ.

Crawford, J. (2006). *Creation of States in International Law* (2nd ed.). Oxford: Oxford University Press.

Draghi, M. (2019, February 22). Sovereignty in a globalized world, speech. www.ecb.europa.eu

Dugard, J. (2013). *The Secession of States and Their Recognition in the Wake of Kosovo*. Leyden: Brill/Nijhoff.

Hajjami, N. (2017, October 13). La situation en Catalogne au regard du droit international public. cdi.ulb.ac.be

Héraud, G. (1975). *L'Europe des ethnies* (2nd ed.). Paris/Nice: Presses d'Europe.

Héraud, G. (1994). *Les communautés linguistiques en quête d'un statut*. Nice: Presses d'Europe.

Hill, R. J., & White, S. (2014). Referendums in Russia, the Former Soviet Union and Eastern Europe. In M. Qvortrup (Ed.), *Referendums Around the World. The Continued Growth of Direct Democracy* (pp. 17–42). Basingstoke: Palgrave.

Hilpold, P. (Ed.). (2018). *Autonomy and Self-Determination: Between Legal Assertions and Utopian Aspirations.* Cheltenham: Elgar.

Jellinek, G. (1922). *Allgemeine Staatslehre* (3rd ed., p. 332). Berlin: Springer.

Klabbers, J. (2006). The Right to Be Taken Seriously: Self-Determination in International Law. *Human Rights Quarterly, 28*(1), 186–206.

Lecucq, O. (Ed.). (2017). *Sécession et processus sécessionniste en droit international, européen et constitutionnel.* Paris: Institut Universitaire Varenne.

López, J. (2017). The Right to Decide: a Right of the 21st Century. In P. Kraus & J. Vergés Gifra (Eds.), *The Catalan Process. Sovereignty, Self-Determination and Democracy in the 21st Century* (pp. 121–137). Barcelona: Generalitat de Catalunya.

Maganza, B. (2017, September 29). The Italian Government's Position on the Referendum on the Self-Determination of Catalonia. *Italy's Diplomatic and Parliamentary Practice on International Law.* https://italyspractice.info

Milano, E. (2018). Secession Revisited: General Framework and Lessons from the Referenda in Catalonia and Kurdistan. *Italian Yearbook of International Law, 27*(1), 189–214.

Oklopcic, Z. (2017, September 25). The Referendum on Catalan Self-Determination. Endemic Rhetoric, Interpretive Hypocrisy and Legal Imagination. *Völkerrechtsblog.* https://voelkerrechtsblog.org

Peters, A. (1995). *Das Gebietsreferendum im Völkerrecht: Seine Bedeutung im Licht der Staatenpraxis nach 1989.* Baden-Baden: Nomos.

Peters, A. (2013). The Principle of *Uti Possidetis Juris.* How Relevant Is It for Issues of Secession? In C. Walter et al. (Eds.), *Self-Determination and Secession in International Law* (pp. 95–137). Oxford: Oxford University Press.

Peters, A. (2014, April 16). Sense and Nonsense of Territorial Referendums in Ukraine, and Why the 16 March Referendum in Crimea Does Not Justify Crimea's Alteration of Territorial Status Under International Law. *EJIL: Talk!* www.ejiltalk.org

Peters, A. (2017, October 12). Populist International Law? The Suspended Independence and the Normative Value of the Referendum on Catalonia. *EJIL: Talk!* www.ejiltalk.org

Qvortrup, M. (2014). *Referendums and Ethnic Conflict.* Philadelphia: University of Pennsylvania Press.

Qvortrup, M. (2017). Comparative Analysis of Referendums on Independence and the Proposed Catalan Referendum of October 1, 2017. In D. Turp (Ed.), *Le référendum sur l'indépendance catalane: une évaluation du processus d'autodétermination* (pp. 37–54). Montreal: Institut de recherche sur l'autodétermination des peuples et les indépendances nationales.

Sen, I. G. (2015). *Sovereignty Referendums in International and Constitutional Law*. Berlin: Springer.

Sieyès, E.-J. (1789). *Qu'est-ce que le Tiers-État?* Paris.

Sterio, M. (2018, January 5). Self-Determination and Secession Under International Law: The Cases of Kurdistan and Catalonia. *American Society of International Law Insights*. www.asil.org

Suksi, M. (2018). The Referendum as an Instrument for Decision-Making in Autonomy-Related Situations. In P. Hilpold (Ed.), *Autonomy and Self-Determination: Between Legal Assertions and Utopian Aspirations* (pp. 97–137). Cheltenham: Elgar.

Tancredi, A. (2006). A Normative 'Due Process' in the Creation of States Through Secession. In M. Kohen (Ed.), *Secession: International Law Perspectives* (pp. 171–207). Cambridge: Cambridge University Press.

Turp, D. (2017). Le « droit de decider » de la Catalogne selon le droit international, européen, espagnol, catalan et comparé. In D. Turp (Ed.), *Le référendum sur l'indépendance catalane: une évaluation du processus d'autodéter mination* (pp. 55–72). Montreal: Institut de recherche sur l'autodétermination des peuples et les indépendances nationales.

Turp, D., & Sanjaume-Calvet, M. (Eds.). (2016). *The Emergence of a Democratic Right to Self- Determination in Europe*. Bruxelles: Centre Maurits Coppieters.

Turpin, D. (2019). La consultation relative à l'autodétermination et les élections provinciales en Nouvelle-Calédonie ou le droit constitutionnel revisité. *Revue du droit public, 135*(4), 1013–1045.

Underwood, W. (2019, December 31). The Bougainville Independence Referendum and the 'Duty to Consult'. *EJIL:Talk!*. www.ejiltalk.org

Vidmar, J. (2013). *Democratic Statehood in International Law. The Emergence of New States in Post-Cold War Practice* (pp. 169–201). Oxford: Hart.

Walter, C., et al. (Eds.). (2013). *Self-Determination and Secession in International Law*. Oxford: Oxford University Press.

Weller, M. (2017). Le « droit de decider » de la Catalogne selon le droit international, européen, espagnol, catalan et comparé. In D. Turp (Ed.), *Le référendum sur l'indépendance catalane: une évaluation du processus d'autodétermination* (pp. 55–72). Montreal: Institut de recherche sur l'autodétermination des peuples et les indépendances nationales.

CHAPTER 8

Exit-Related Conditionality, Federalism, and Secession

Giuseppe Martinico

1 Constitutionalising Secession

Federalism and secession are frequently seen as antithetical concepts. Moreover, from an etymological point of view, they seem to refer to opposite dynamics. While federalism comes from the Latin word *foedus* meaning 'covenant', secession comes from *sĕcēdĕre* which means to separate, to go apart, to withdraw.

However, arguing that secession has not played any role in the history of federalism would be profoundly wrong. Indeed, the federalism we know is also the outcome of secession wars (for instance the American Civil War) that have contributed to reshaping the concept, by, for instance, marginalising a particular understanding of federalism. I am of course referring to Calhoun and his Compact Theory that have been ostracised after the American Civil War.

G. Martinico (✉)
Comparative Public Law, Scuola Superiore Sant'Anna, Pisa, Italy
e-mail: giuseppe.martinico@santannapisa.it

M. Belov (ed.), *Territorial Politics and Secession*, Federalism and Internal Conflicts, https://doi.org/10.1007/978-3-030-64402-4_8

Without denying or neglecting the political side of secession, this chapter maintains that it also presents legal aspects, and indeed, courts have devised a set of techniques in order to cope with it (Martinico 2017; Castellà Andreu 2016). For many years, secession was understood as a sort of 'constitutional taboo' (Mancini 2012), at least until 1998 when the Canadian Supreme Court delivered its famous *Reference Re Secession of Quebec*.[1] When offering its view, the Supreme Court of Canada did not limit its attention to domestic law only but, agreed to take international law into account. For all these reasons, this Reference has become a turning point. Since then a new debate has started on how to constitutionalise secession (Haljan 2014; Weinstock 2001), how to tame something which had been considered for a long time as a sort of 'beast' hard to domesticate (Mancini 2012).

Before moving on it is necessary to clarify what I mean by 'constitutionalisation of secession'. By this formula I mean the effort made by the Canadian Court to treat secession as a constitutional option, which may be carried out provided that the untouchable core of the legal system is secured. In other words, by means of this decision, the Canadian Supreme Court 'rehabilitated' secession as a legal option that may be used under certain circumstances. In this sense, by 'constitutionalisation' I do not automatically mean the codification of a secession clause in a constitutional text, although as I will try to show, the inclusion of a clause like this should not be seen as an evil *per se*.

In order to tackle secession, the Canadian Supreme Court first contextualised it in a legal scenario, avoiding easy choices and facing the preliminary objections concerning the lack of legal relevance of the challenged acts or of the raised questions. This strategy was perceived as necessary in order to compensate the passivity of the relevant political actors or to try to facilitate a dialogue which had not yet started between the central and regional levels.

Also, the Canadian Court gave a complex notion of democracy which cannot be reduced to the mere majority rule. This is a very important point as we will see later which makes this Reference also a powerful tool against populism.

In that decision, it reconstructed the core of Canadian constitutional identity by recalling the untouchable principles that make the Canadian Constitution special. In so doing the Canadian Supreme Court also

[1] Canadian Supreme Court, Reference Re Secession of Quebec [1998] 2 S.C.R. 217.

presented the referendum as an instrument which needs to be mediated and which should not be considered as a source of automatic political or legal truth. This explains the deference that characterises the Reference, which is also clear in giving political actors the task 'to determine what constitutes a clear majority on a clear question'.[2] In this way the Canadian Court avoided treating the referendum as something alternative to representative democracy.

Finally, it is important to recall that the Canadian Supreme Court did not recognise a proper right to secession, rather it treated secession as an option that may be tolerated only in the presence of some important safeguards. In order to make this point the Canadian Court came up with a sort of 'exit-related conditionality' as we will see in the next section. In this way it guaranteed the respect of the constitutional identity of Canada.

This work is divided into two parts. In the first part I shall (briefly) explore the debate on how to proceduralise secession in light of the notion of 'exit-related conditionality'. In the second part, I shall highlight some reasons for prudence in the use of referendums in contexts of representative democracy. Referendums, as comparative law shows, play an essential role in the very few constitutional clauses aimed at governing secession. Minimising the populist risks of improper use of the referendum is crucial to guarantee the exit-related conditionality and to impede that a manipulation of the concept of democracy could trump the rule of law.

2 Exit-Related Conditionality and Secession

Comparative lawyers have analysed the provisions concerning the possibility of secession (Mancini 2014: 791) and also legal and political theorists have dealt with the issue of how to justify the option of secession even in legal systems whose constitutions say nothing about that, including the Canadian one (Norman 2006; Buchanan 1991). As said, the Canadian Reference has been crucial to rehabilitate-under certain circumstances-the idea of secession as a constitutional option.

This does not automatically lead the codification of a constitutional clause on that. As we know, the outcome of that decision relied on a series of unwritten principles. However, without recalling the very huge debate already mentioned, I would like to briefly mention an element that in my

[2] Canadian Supreme Court, Reference Re Secession of Quebec [1998] 2 S.C.R. 217.

view could justify the constitutionalisation of secession. This element is linked to constitutional homogeneity: federal systems tend to ensure a virtuous connection between diversity and unity with a series of mechanisms aimed at preserving loyalty and adhesion to the fundamental values of the national system (Delledonne 2017). Evidence of this can be found in Art. 28 of the German Basic Law and in Art. 51 of the Swiss Constitution which conditions, for example, the contents of the cantonal constitutions. Reasons connected with homogeneity can always suggest forms of control and monitoring and even the possibility of activating forms of centripetal intervention in case of departure from the fundamental values of the constitutional pact. Against this background, in pursuing homogeneity these legal systems develop forms of conditionality aimed at ensuring a sort of structural compatibility between their different components.

My point is the following: even the clauses on exit/withdrawal from a federal union can be read as forms of 'exit-related conditionality', by ensuring an axiological continuity between the new order and the old one. This might appear paradoxical, but it is actually a process in which the old system accepts the detachment of the seceding entity by making it conditional upon the adhesion to its fundamental values. In this way the constituent phase of the seceding legal system is partly guided and influenced by the values of the old constitution and 'exorcised' the revolutionary character of secession.

To understand what I mean by exit-related conditionality it is useful to recall the Canadian Reference according to which, in case of activation of the negotiations with Québec, 'the conduct of the parties in such negotiations would be governed by the same constitutional principles which give rise to the duty to negotiate: federalism, democracy, constitutionalism and the rule of law, and the protection of minorities'.[3]

This axiological continuity would guarantee the rights of that population residing in the territory of the new State which had not voted for the independence. By constitutionalising secession, in other words, the legal system could tame the violent side of secession and containing (which does not mean excluding, of course since legal norms may also fail) the risk of political abuses that might be produced by a contingent majority (Norman 2006: 178).

The appeal to the will of a contingent majority and the risk of 'extreme majoritarianism' is the bridge connecting secessionism and populism and

[3] Canadian Supreme Court, Reference Re Secession of Quebec [1998] 2 S.C.R. 217, par. 90.

we will see in this short chapter. A possible counter argument against the constitutionalisation secession is linked to the threat of constantly exposing a legal system to the blackmail of the exit, in a sort of game to negotiate further forms of autonomy. Actually, the Spanish scenario shows that a risk like this exists even in the absence of a secession clause. In this sense the lack of a provision like this has led to the explosion of a political crisis in the absence of constitutional paths other than the constitutional amendment. Secession has a constitutional dimension as it refers to the construction of the constitutional subject, since '[a]s much as these events appear to hinge on high-power politics, they have an important constitutional dimension' (Ginsburg and Versteeg 2019: 926).

As recently Ginsburg and Versteeg argued:

> When the constitution is ambiguous on secession, we find evidence of instability and violence. More specifically, constitutional ambiguity is associated with higher levels of secessionist violence without improving the chances of actual breakups. We also find that secessionist movements enjoy higher levels of popular support where there is constitutional ambiguity as opposed to a constitutional prohibition. Our interpretation of these findings is that when a constitution is ambiguous, secessionist movements have a plausible claim that secession might be legal and are therefore able to gather popular support. Yet, this same uncertainty regarding the legal status of the claim can also produce violence, since the central government might end up opposing the movement or the country's highest court might rule that there is no legal basis for such claims. These findings lend support to our hypothesis that, as a matter of constitutional design, it is best to confront the issue of secession head-on. (Ginsburg and Versteeg 2019: 930)

Indeed, even where there is no explicit constitutional clause, it is possible to frame secession in light of constitutional principles as the Canadian case clearly shows. In this respect, the constitutional framework matters and can help in order to avoid violence.

A very telling example is represented by the Catalan case. While many perceive the only significant difference between the Scottish and the Catalan referendums as lying in the unilateral nature of the latter, what really makes the Catalan scenario inconsistent with the local constitutional framework is the fact that there, the Autonomous Communities have no competence to call these types of referendums, as scholars have clearly pointed out in the reading of Art. 149.1.32 of the Spanish Constitution.[4]

[4] Art. 149.1.32 of the Spanish Constitution: '1. The State shall have exclusive competence over the following matters [...]: 32. Authorization of popular consultations through the holding of referendums'.

This might appear as a procedural element but it affects the substance of the issue perhaps even more than the generic content of Art. 2 of the Spanish Constitution according to which 'The Constitution is based on the indissoluble unity of the Spanish Nation'.[5]

Concerning how to design a norm relating to the exit from the federal entity examples that could be taken into account are not absent. Many of the models recalled by comparative lawyers have given referendums an important role (Mancini 2014; Ziegler et al. 2014). This makes the Canadian Reference an important message of hope, since it recognises a fundamental role to the law. Although the law cannot exclude the resolution of secessionist crises by means of violence, it has at least to procedural advantage to oblige the institutional actors to treat—*prima facie*—secession as a legal issue before resorting to extra-legal measures, by offering some binding guidelines[6] aimed at protecting minorities. This is not a detail in my view: instead of leaving this process to politics or violence, legal norms can contribute to containing the political dialectic within the rule of law. This explains why channelling referendums is important to ensure the equilibrium between federalism, constitutionalism, and the rule of law.

3 Against a 'Reductivist' Concept of Democracy

Comparative constitutional law[7] offers examples of provisions which give referendums an important role in the procedure devised to govern secession: Ethiopia,[8] Uzbekistan,[9] (former) Serbia Montenegro,[10] Liechtenstein,[11] Northern Ireland,[12] and Nevis and Saint Christopher.[13]

Scholars have traditionally pointed out the ambiguities of referendum and the risks connected with an appropriate use of the instrument. It is a

[5] Art. 2 of the Spanish Constitution.

[6] As Norman recalled 'the perceived advantages of handling secessionist politics and secessionist contests within the rule of law rather than as "political" issues that lie outside of, or are presumed (by the secessionists) to supersede, the law', Norman (2006), at 189.

[7] See also the 1947 Constitution of Burma at arts. 201–206. On this see: Gökhan Şen (2015); Qvortrup (2014); Frosina (2017).

[8] Art. 39 of the Ethiopian Constitution.

[9] Art. 74 of the Constitution of Uzbekistan.

[10] Art. 60 of the Constitution of Serbia Montenegro.

[11] Art. 4 of the Constitution of the Principality of Liechtenstein.

[12] Section 1 of the Northern Ireland Act 1998.

[13] Art. 113 of the Constitution of Saint Christopher and Nevis.

very long debate (Carré de Malberg 1931; Mirkine Guetzévitch 1931) and already Max Weber, for instance, recalled such risks and stressed that it can be used to deresponsibilise the political forces (Weber 1920, English edition).

If referendums have traditionally been understood as tricky instruments in constitutional law, the case of secession to a certain extent adds a further level of complexity. Taming the populist risks of improper use of the referendum is crucial to guarantee the exit-related conditionality described above and to impede that a manipulation of the concept of democracy can trump the rule of law.

The obsession of populist movements with the 'politics of immediacy' (Corrias 2016: 12) inevitably results in questioning many of the instruments of representative democracy and in emphasising the importance of instruments of direct and participatory democracy. Frequently, the attack on representative institutions and the emphasis on referendums are taken as two sides of the same coin, since they are both emanations of that lack of mediation that political scientists frequently portray as one of the pillars of populism (Mény and Surel 2004). As Canovan pointed out: 'New Populists often call for issues of popular concern to be decided by referendum, by-passing professional politicians and leaving decisions to the people' (Canovan 2005: 76). Referendums also galvanise that dichotomous approach frequently endorsed by populists in the constant appeal to the people understood as a monolithic entity, in the sense that they tend to represent a part of the people as the people.[14]

Against this background, the final part of this chapter revolves around three main points.

The *first one* is the idea of referendum as a graft transplanted into contexts of constitutional representative democracy. While referendums are normally seen by populist movements as a kind of 'catch all' appeal to the people, which should be used to react against the corruption or passivity of the institutions, constitutional lawyers tend to handle referendums with

[14] 'Brexiters, too, invoke the referendum as the "will of the people", a phrase understood as a singular homogeneous monolith, conveniently ignoring that 62.5% of the electorate ("remainers", and those who abstained from participating) did not vote to leave the EU but are "automatically" included in that will. That discursive populism has been voiced not only by UKIP members but by UK government ministers and governing party M.P.s; thus Priti Patel, Secretary of State for International Development, insisted in an interview on 16 October 2016 that "the British people have spoken and we will deliver for them"', Freeden (2017): 7.

care, looking upon them as a noble instrument whose compatibility with representative democracy must be guaranteed. This perspective can be justified in light of the political risks connected with excessive use of referendum, in other words referendums, if used as a full alternative to the instruments and institutions representative of democracy risk creating parallel channels of legitimation, which could destabilise and delegitimise parliaments. In order to prevent this, constitutions (even in contexts provided with partly written constitutions, for instance, the UK) come up with solutions designed to strike a balance between representative and direct/participatory (depending on how scholars understand referendums, Luciani 2008) democracy.

The *second point* I would like to make is about the artificial concept of majority.[15] It is possible to find confirmation of this in comparative law. Both the *Clarity Act* in Canada and Schedule I of the *Good Friday Agreement* give political actors an important role in detecting the existing majorities. The Clarity Act was a follow-up to the secession Reference in the part in which the Canadian Supreme Court had said: 'in this context, we refer to a "clear" majority as a qualitative evaluation. The referendum result, if it is to be taken as an expression of the democratic will, must be free of ambiguity both in terms of the question asked and in terms of the support it achieves' (Canadian Supreme Court, Reference Re Secession of Quebec [1998] 2 S.C.R. 217).

In light of this the *Clarity Act* listed some factors that should be taken into account by the House of Commons to verify *a posteriori* the existence of a majority:

> Factors for House of Commons to take into account (2) In considering whether there has been a clear expression of a will by a clear majority of the population of a province that the province cease to be part of Canada, the House of Commons shall take into account (a) the size of the majority of valid votes cast in favour of the secessionist option; (b) the percentage of eligible voters voting in the referendum; and (c) any other matters or circumstances it considers to be relevant.[16]

[15] 'A majority is not something you will find in nature. It is an artifact of law. You need legal rules to determine who counts, and in which way. You need legal safeguards of liberty, equality and diversity of opinion. You also need legal rules to determine what the majority will be able to do, which necessarily implies that the majority gets told what she is not allowed to do. In short, you need constitutional law', Steinbeis (2017).

[16] An Act to give effect to the requirement for clarity as set out in the opinion of the Supreme Court of Canada in the Quebec Secession Reference S.C. 2000, c. 26, http://laws-lois.justice.gc.ca/eng/acts/c-31.8/page-1.html

This has caused a harsh reaction in Québec as we know. A similar role, but to be played in the phase before the holding of a referendum, is granted to the Secretary of State by Schedule I of the *Good Friday Agreement*.[17] These two examples show that the majority is not a neutral or easy concept; on the contrary, it is an artificial one which can be constructed through political and legal decisions, for instance, by excluding or including particular groups of people in the right to vote. That is why procedural caveats are important, since they contribute towards ensuring the preservation of that core of untouchable values that is up to constitutionalism to defend.

Finally, the *third point* lies at the heart of the alleged tension between formal and substantive democracy or, better still, between democracy and rule of majority. This aspect has been clarified—once again—in the already mentioned Reference Re Secession of Quebec by the Canadian Supreme Court in 1998 when it said that 'democracy, however, means more than simple majority rule'. These inspirational words pronounced by the Canadian Supreme Court confirm the strong counter-majoritarian[18] nature of constitutionalism as such.

Indeed, within the principles recalled by the Canadian Court there is also the protection of minorities. Although the Canadian Court focused on linguistic minorities in that case, the language used throughout the Reference allows this Reference to be connected with a broader concept of minority as clarified by the Court itself by insisting on the distinction between democracy and majority rule (par. 63). From that and other passages we can understand that democracy cannot be used as a 'trump card' to alter the untouchable core that characterises (liberal) constitutional systems, since there are values that cannot be decided by the majority in democratic systems.

In this sense the Canadian case shows that even in the absence of explicit constitutional clauses it is possible to attempt to proceduralise this phenomenon, by contributing to its domestication and in that the Canadian Supreme Court has indeed sent a message of hope: law—especially constitutional law—can and must have a role, avoiding delegating this issue to

[17] The Northern Ireland Peace Agreement. The Agreement reached in the multi-party negotiations 10 April 1998, http://peacemaker.un.org/sites/peacemaker.un.org/files/IE%20GB_980410_Northern%20Ireland%20Agreement.pdf

[18] Here the reference is of course to Bickel (1986).

violence or politics only (Martinico 2019). Challenging a reductivist concept of democracy is functional to the preservation of federalism, constitutionalism, and above all, the rule of law. Against this background, exit-related conditionality is functional to preserving the rule of law and the sustainability of the federal system.

References

Bickel, A. (1986). *The Least Dangerous Branch*. New Haven: Yale University Press.

Buchanan, A. (1991). *Secession: The Morality of Political Divorce from Fort Sumter to Lithuania and Quebec*. Abingdon: Routledge.

Canovan, M. (2005). *The People*. Oxford: Polity.

Carré de Malberg, R. (1931). Considérations théoriques sur la question de la combinaison du referendum avec le parlementarisme. *Annuaire de l'Institut international de droit public, 2*(1), 272 ff.

Castellà Andreu, J. M. (2016). Tribunal constitucional y proceso secesionista catalán: respuestas juriídico-constitucionales a un conflicto político-constitucional. *Teoría y Realidad Constitucional, 19*(37), 561–592.

Corrias, L. (2016). Populism in a Constitutional Key: Constituent Power, Popular Sovereignty and Constitutional Identity. *European Constitutional Law Review, 12*(1), 6–26.

Delledonne, G. (2017). *L'omogeneità costituzionale negli ordinamenti composti*. Napoli: Editoriale Scientifica.

Freeden, M. (2017). After the Brexit Referendum: Revisiting Populism as an Ideology. *Journal of Political Ideologies, 22*(1), 1–11.

Frosina, L. (2017). Profili giuridici e aspetti problematici del referendum di secessione. Un'analisi comparata. *Nomos, 21*(3), 1–37.

Ginsburg, T., & Versteeg, M. (2019). From Catalonia to California: Secession in Constitutional Law. *Alabama Law Review, 70*(4), 923–985.

Haljan, D. (2014). *Constitutionalising Secession*. Oxford: Hart.

Luciani, M. (2008). Il referendum: questioni teoriche e dell'esperienza italiana. *Revista catalana de dret públic, 24*(37), 157–182.

Mancini, S. (2012). Secession and Self-Determination. In M. Rosenfeld & A. Sajó (Eds.), *The Oxford Handbook of Comparative Constitutional Law* (pp. 481–500). Oxford: Oxford University Press.

Mancini, S. (2014). Costituzionalismo, federalismo e secessione. *Istituzioni del federalismo, 18*(4), 779–806.

Martinico, G. (2017). Identity Conflicts and Secession Before Courts: Three Case Studies. *Revista General de Derecho Público Comparado, 21*(1), 1–30.

Martinico, G. (2019). A Message of Hope': A Legal Perspective on the Reference. In G. Delledonne & G. Martinico (Eds.), *The Canadian Contribution to a*

Comparative Constitutional Law of Secession: Legacies of the Quebec Secession Reference (pp. 249–263). Basingstoke: Palgrave.

Mény, Y., & Surel, Y. (2004). *Populismo e democrazia*. Bologna: Il Mulino.

Mirkine Guetzévitch, B. (1931). Le référendum et le parlementarisme dans les nouvelles constitutions européennes. *Annuaire de l'Institut international de droit public, 2*(1), 285 ff.

Norman, W. (2006). *Negotiating Nationalism: Nation-Building, Federalism, and Secession in the Multinational State*. Oxford: Oxford University Press.

Qvortrup, M. (2014). Referendums on Independence, 1860–2011. *The Political Quarterly, 85*(1), 57–64.

Şen, İ. G. (2015). *Sovereignty Referendums in International and Constitutional Law*. Berlin: Springer.

Steinbeis, M. (2017). *Majority Is a Legal Concept*. http://verfassungsblog.de/majority-is-a-legal-concept/

Weber, M. (1920). *Economy and Society*. https://archive.org/stream/MaxWeberEconomyAndSociety/MaxWeberEconomyAndSociety_djvu.txt

Weinstock, D. (2001). Constitutionalizing the Right to Secede. *Journal of Political Philosophy, 9*(2), 182.

Ziegler, R., Shaw, J., & Bauböck, R. (Eds.). (2014). *Independence Referendums: Who Should Vote and Who Should Be Offered Citizenship?* (RSCAS Working Paper 2014/90). http://cadmus.eui.eu/bitstream/handle/1814/32516/RSCAS_2014_90.pdf

PART IV

Territorial Politics Between Integration and Disintegration

CHAPTER 9

Between Two Unions: Brexit and the Secessionist Challenges in the UK

Nikos Skoutaris

1 Introduction

Brexit marks a seismic change in the constitutional and territorial politics of the UK. For one, although 52 per cent of voters that participated in the Brexit referendum voted to leave the European Union (EU), Scotland and Northern Ireland, two out of the four UK constituent nations voted to remain. As a result, members of the regional political elites and activists that have been supporting the secession of those regions from the UK have reshaped their argument. They link the constitutional future and in particular Scottish independence and Irish Unity with the EU integration prospects of those regions. As such, they are demanding the organisation of a second Scottish independence referendum and a border poll in Northern Ireland, respectively.

N. Skoutaris (✉)
EU Law, University of East Anglia, Norwich, UK
e-mail: N.Skoutaris@uea.ac.uk

M. Belov (ed.), *Territorial Politics and Secession*, Federalism and Internal Conflicts, https://doi.org/10.1007/978-3-030-64402-4_9

Unsurprisingly, the UK Government has not been amenable to the idea of consenting to the organisation of such referendums at least in the current political climate. At the time of writing of the chapter, there was a question whether the result of the pending 2021 Holyrood elections and a possible future change of political demographics in Northern Ireland would make the position of the UK Government politically untenable.

Notwithstanding the politics, purely from a legal point of view, one has to ask, first of all, whether those two regions possess the constitutional right to secede. This is a necessary but not sufficient condition for them to enjoy a closer relationship with the EU. Once, we respond to this question, we also need to assess how they can re-accede to the EU.

The present chapter aims at examining those two questions. It does so in four parts. The following section provides for a bird's eye view of the UK territorial constitution that allows us to understand the context of those secessionist challenges. Section 3 briefly explains how UK's withdrawal from the EU has created significant frictions to the system of devolution. Because of those frictions, the secessionist claims have grown during the last years. Section 4 discusses whether those regions enjoy a right to secession. It notes that although the secessionist debate dominates the Scottish politics, Scotland does not possess a self-standing constitutional right to secede. The consent of Westminster is necessary in order for such a referendum to be organised. At the same time, pursuant to Belfast/ Good Friday Agreement (GFA hereafter), Northern Ireland is one of the very few regions around the world, which enjoys an undisputable right to secede from its metropolitan State. The final section briefly sketches the various challenges that Brexit raises for the 'reincorporation' of those two nations to the European project. It highlights that the route of Northern Ireland back to the EU through the reunification of the island is more straightforward than the accession of Scotland as an independent Member State to the EU. Overall, the chapter witnesses the constitutional dilemma of those two UK constituent nations that in the aftermath of Brexit have found themselves between two unions: the UK and the European Union.

2 The UK Territorial Constitution at a Glance

The UK is a union of four nations: England, Wales, Scotland and Northern Ireland. Wales 'has been closely integrated with England for the purposes of law and administration since the late Middle Ages' (Leyland 2012,

253). Through the Law in Wales Acts 1535 and 1542, Wales was legally annexed to the Kingdom of England, the legal system of England was extended to Wales and the norms of English administration were introduced to the principality.

Scotland, on the other hand, was united with England 'into One Kingdom by the Name of Great Britain'[1] by virtue of two legislative acts: the Union with Scotland Act 1706 passed by Westminster and the Union with England Act 1707 passed by the Parliament of Scotland. Notwithstanding, the region managed to retain its own legal system and different system of education throughout this time.

Finally, the relationship between the islands of Great Britain and Ireland has been complex and often turbulent (Ferriter 2019). Following resolutions by the parliaments in Dublin and London, Ireland was united with Great Britain by the Acts of Union 1800. To accommodate deep-seated differences between unionists and nationalists in Ireland, the Government of Ireland Act 1920 'was based on partition between the six counties in the North, comprising Northern Ireland with a Parliament in Belfast, and the remainder of Ireland with a Parliament in Dublin' (Leyland 2012, 21). The Act was only implemented in Northern Ireland establishing a parliamentary system of devolved government, while the rest of the island eventually achieved its independence. Having failed to effectively address the needs of the nationalist/republican/Irish/catholic community, Westminster suspended the devolution arrangements in the North in March 1972. During an era of political violence known as 'The Troubles', Northern Ireland was directly governed by London.

While there was considerable centralisation of power with regard to Northern Ireland, during the 1970s, there was also a failed attempt to devolve power to Scotland and Wales. The original devolution legislation, however, did not attract the required popular support in the relevant referendums in 1979. Still, in 1997, the Labour party achieved a landslide electoral win with a manifesto commitment to introduce devolution for Scotland and Wales. The electorate approved the plans in the respective referendums. The Scottish Parliament and the Scottish Government in their modern form were established by the Scotland Act 1998, while the Welsh system of governance was introduced by the Government of Wales Act 1998. Both Acts have been amended a number of times. The most

[1] Treaty of Union 1706, Art I.

important changes can be found in Scotland Acts 2012 and 2016 and the Government of Wales Act 2006 and Wales Acts 2014 and 2017, respectively.

The Scottish and the Welsh systems of governance are based on a parliamentary model. The unicameral legislatures of Scotland and Wales are composed of 129 and 60 members, respectively. They are democratically elected under the additional member system. Following an election, a government is formed after the respective legislative body has nominated a First Minister. After a nomination has been accepted, the First Minister is empowered to appoint ministers from the members of the regional parliament to form the government.[2]

Unlike Scotland and Wales, the devolution in Northern Ireland was not a free-standing policy coming out of a political party's manifesto. It is one facet of the Belfast/Good Friday Agreement. At the centre of the Northern Irish system of governance lies the principle of consent. First of all, the region 'shall not cease' in its entirety to be part of the UK 'without the consent of a majority of the people of Northern Ireland voting in a poll held for the purposes'.[3] Secondly, the governance of the region is based on the consent of both ethno-religious communities. GFA provides for a 'system of compulsory power-sharing at every level of decision-making to ensure joint-participation by both communities in the process of government' (Leyland 2012, 258). 'The largest political party of the largest political designation [...] nominate[s ...] the First Minister', while 'the largest political party of the second largest political designation [...] nominate[s ...] the deputy First Minister'.[4]

At the moment and until the political demographics change, this provision means that the First Minister is from a unionist/loyalist party while the Deputy is from a nationalist/republican one. Having said that, the ministers are not chosen by this dyarchy. Instead, ministerial posts are allocated to all of those parties with significant representation in the Assembly.[5] The actual posts are chosen by the parties in the order that the seats were awarded. Finally, consent is often required when it comes to voting in the Northern Ireland Assembly. 'According to the requirement for "parallel consent", a majority from each group of [members of the

[2] Scotland Act 1998, ss. 44–47; Government of Wales Act 2006, ss. 45–48.

[3] Northern Ireland Act 1998, s. 1.

[4] Northern Ireland Act 1998, s. 16.

[5] Northern Ireland Act 1998, s. 18.

Assembly] designated as unionist and as nationalist is required to approve important legislation (e.g. on financial matters) and decisions (e.g. the appointment of the Speaker)' (Hayward and Phinnemore 2019).

Given that there is no UK codified constitution, the allocation of powers to Northern Ireland, Scotland and Wales can be found in the respective constitutive acts. In sum, sections 29 of the Scotland Act 1998, 6 of the Northern Ireland Act 1998 and 108A of the Government of Wales Act 2006 provide that the regional legislatures enjoy the residual power to legislate with regard to areas that are not reserved to Westminster. For instance, the Scottish legislature has competences over education, health, policing and modest tax-raising powers among else.

During those two decades of devolution, there has been a rather limited number of cases concerning disputes over competences between London and the devolved nations. Such dearth of litigation underlines the political nature of the UK territorial constitution and the reluctance of the judiciary to become an active umpire in the disputes between the different tiers. This does not mean that the symbiosis of those different legal and political orders in the UK is without its problems, tensions and challenges. Indeed, Brexit, as we shall see, has brought to the fore a number of them.

3 Brexit as a Challenge to Devolution

On 31 January 2020, the UK officially withdrew from the EU. Brexit marked the first time that a Member State decides to put an abrupt end to the federalist 'sonderweg' of 'an ever closer union'. Traditionally, the disentanglement of highly integrated legal orders is a very sophisticated and time-consuming exercise as every case of secession around the world would suggest. Of course, the EU is not a sovereign state. However, the EU and the UK legal orders have been in a symbiotic relationship for 47 years.

In fact, the EU legal order was providing for 'common UK-wide approaches even where those policy areas otherwise [fell] within devolved competence' (Cabinet Office 2020, 8). In that sense, the withdrawal of the UK from the EU constitutional order of States was always expected to pose a number of questions including issues related to devolution. In particular, the decision of the UK Government to withdraw from the single market and the EU customs union and the policies that it has been adopting to implement its Brexit vision consist of a significant challenge to the constituent autonomy of the devolved regions.

In order to appreciate that, this section briefly refers to three aspects of such challenge. The first relates to the fact that Brexit as a policy choice has not been endorsed by all four constituent nations. As such, two of them have withdrawn from the EU against their stated will. The second concerns the hurdles that the devolved regions face in influencing the Brexit policy and the post-Brexit future for themselves and the UK as a whole. The last one has to do with the fact that Brexit might lead to centralisation of powers rather than greater devolution.

Firstly, before the Brexit referendum took place, the Scottish First Minister argued in favour of 'an amendment, requiring that for the UK to leave the EU, each of the four constituent nations – England, Scotland, Wales and Northern Ireland – would have to vote to do so, not just the UK as a whole' (Freeman 2014). By making this argument, Nicola Sturgeon was trying to avoid a situation whereby Scotland or another constituent nation would be taken out of EU without its expressed will.

On 23 June 2016, 52 per cent of voters that participated in the Brexit referendum voted to leave the EU. Still, Scotland and Northern Ireland, two out of the four UK constituent nations, voted to remain.[6] As a result, and after more than three years of political turmoil, on 31 January 2020, those two regions found themselves out of the EU against their expressed will. From the point of view of the British political community as a whole, such development does not raise any particular concerns. The majority of the UK electorate that voted in the 2016 referendum approved the withdrawal of the UK from the European Union with an undisputed majority. Still, from the point of view of those two regional polities, it is a painful reminder of the fact that they cannot control their own political future. In fact, because of the size of the dominant constituent nation, they have to follow the decisions of the English electorate even when they clearly disagree. As such, Brexit can be viewed as a suppression of their constituent autonomy with regard to their constitutional future.

Second, in the aftermath of the Brexit referendum, the regional institutions sought to engage with the UK Government on the terms of the UK's departure from the EU. There are two main forums through which they have been trying to achieve such aim: the Joint Ministerial Committee on EU Negotiations (JMC hereafter) and the Ministerial Forum. The JMC on EU Negotiations was established to provide a means for the

[6] In Scotland, 62 per cent voted to remain in the EU, while 56 per cent in Northern Ireland. In England, 53 per cent voted to leave while 52.5 per cent in Wales.

devolved administrations to be fully engaged in determining the UK's approach to Brexit. The Ministerial Forum was created to complement engagement at the JMC, specifically in relation to UK positions for the EU-UK Future Relationship. Despite the fact that there have been around 30 meetings of those two bodies, the regional governments have often expressed their concerns over the effectiveness of those institutions and especially about whether they are suited to developing a joint position (Whitman 2017).

It is true that there is an obvious absence in the UK constitutional order when it comes to institutions that provide for robust representation of the regional interests at the central level. Regional views are represented either through informal channels like discussions and negotiations between political elites or through soft law mechanisms such as the aforementioned forums. There is neither a territorial chamber in the UK Parliament nor is there any mechanism that provides for the possibility of regional vetoes in case the devolved regions disagree with an all-UK policy. Westminster has always the power to overrule the regional institutions. Within a constitutional order that is centred around the principle of parliamentary sovereignty according to which Westminster is omnipotent with regard to its law-making power, this is hardly surprising. Still, such framework that is characterised by the absence of legally binding channels of regional participation and the dominance of England and Whitehall in the Westminster politics leaves a rather limited space to the devolved nations to participate in the shaping of the Brexit policy.

But it is not only the endemic weaknesses of the rather feeble UK intergovernmental institutions that have not allowed the regions to have a meaningful say to the shaping of the Brexit policy. The UK Government has explicitly ruled out different visions of the post-Brexit future that the devolved governments put forward. As an example we will refer to the proposal for a territorially differentiated Brexit.

In December 2016, the Scottish Government published its blueprint called *Scotland's Place in Europe* (Scottish Government 2016). There, they accepted that the UK would as a whole withdraw from the EU but argued in favour of a differentiated Brexit that would entail Scotland remaining in a much closer relationship with the EU via an European Economic Area (EEA) membership. The blueprint envisages two pathways for Scotland to achieve EEA membership. The first option entailed a UK-sponsored membership. The UK would opt for membership to the EEA but there would be a territorial exemption for England and Wales. The EEA *acquis* would fully apply only in Scotland. The precedent for that can be found in the Arctic Circle. Norway has secured a territorial exemption for the insular islands of the archipelago of Svalbard that are not part of EEA.[7] Alternatively, there should be an amendment of the European Free Trade Association (EFTA) Convention and the EEA Agreement that would allow the membership of sub-state entities. To this effect, it should be pointed out that although it is not an independent State, the Faroe Islands is currently exploring the possibility of joining EFTA (Hartmann 2019). Unsurprisingly, the UK Government rejected this proposal with regard to Scotland. In fact, the then Secretary of State for Brexit David Davis pointed out that such arrangements could lead to the creation of new barriers to trade within our union.

Notwithstanding, a territorially differentiated Brexit did take place. However, such differentiation applies to Northern Ireland but not to Scotland. In order to keep the territorial border between the Republic of Ireland and Northern Ireland frictionless, the relevant Protocol attached to the UK's Withdrawal Agreement provides that this region has a much closer relationship with the EU than the rest of the UK. The Protocol recognises that *de jure* Northern Ireland remains within the UK customs union.[8] Notwithstanding, EU customs legislation applies to the region even after the end of the transition period on 31 December 2020.[9] Similarly, a significant part of the EU *acquis* on the free movement of goods also enjoys extraterritorial application[10] with regard to Northern Ireland,[11] as is the case for EU law provisions concerning VAT and excise.[12]

The majority of political parties in Northern Ireland are in favour of such differentiation. Still, the arrangement itself is the by-product of the

[7] Protocol 40 on Svalbard of the Agreement on the European Economic Area [1994] OJ L1/208.

[8] Agreement on the Withdrawal of the United Kingdom of Great Britain and Northern Ireland from the European Union and the European Atomic Energy Community, Protocol on Ireland/Northern Ireland, [2020] OJ L29/1, Art. 4.

[9] Ibid, Art. 5(3). According to Art. 5 of Regulation (EU) 952/2013 laying down the Union Customs Code [2013] OJ L269/1, 'customs legislation' means the body of legislation made up of the following: (a) the Code and the provisions supplementing or implementing it adopted at the Union or national level, (b) the Common Customs Tariff, (c) the legislation setting up a Union system of reliefs from customs duty and (d) international agreements containing customs provisions insofar as they are applicable in the Union.

[10] Ibid, Art. 5(5).

[11] Ibid, Art. 5(4).

[12] Ibid, Art. 8.

political choices of Whitehall rather than of an approach that was inclusive and attentive towards the needs and demands of the region. Boris Johnson's administration clearly favoured a much more distant trade and economic relationship between the UK and the EU at the expense of Northern Ireland enjoying a differentiated Brexit (Skoutaris 2019). In that sense, the political machinations that led to that solution again highlight the limited say that the constituent nations enjoy with regard to their constitutional future.

At the same time, the more integrated relationship of Northern Ireland with the EU means that trade between the two sides of the Irish Sea is not frictionless any more. The extent of the friction in the intra-UK trade depends on the overall UK-EU relationship. The more distant it is, the less frictionless the trade will be between Northern Ireland and its metropolitan State. This raises again challenging questions with regard to the devolution and the resilience of the UK internal market.

As a final point with regard to Brexit and devolution, we have to refer to the issue of the repatriation of powers. At the end of the transition period, a number of competences that are currently exercised at the EU level will return to the UK. The obvious question is at which level. Which tier will 'take back control' of those repatriated powers?

According to the Devolution Acts, the devolved institutions could not legislate in breach of EU law.[13] By and large, EU law is not binding on the UK after the end of the transition period. This means that there was a significant danger that legal vacuums would be created in a number of areas such as environmental law, consumer protection and workers' rights where EU law had been the dominant regulatory authority. In order to avoid such a situation, it was of utmost importance that the UK Government and Westminster would find a way to bridge those gaps without clogging up the parliamentary timetable for years to come. This is why the European Union (Withdrawal) Act 2018 preserves and carries over into UK law the full body of EU law even after Brexit as provided in Sects. 2, 3 and 4.

Acts of Westminster that are enacted after the end of the transition period can amend such body of 'retained EU law'. In principle, the devolved institutions have a similar power. They can exercise it, however, unless a minister of the British Government freezes the devolved powers

[13] Scotland Act 1998, s. 29; Northern Ireland Act 1998, s. 6; Government of Wales Act 2006, s. 108A.

in the areas that EU law used to regulate.[14] Such power of the UK executive to issue statutory instruments curtailing the legislative autonomy of the regional legislatures will expire two years after the end of the transition period.[15] The statutory instruments themselves freezing the powers of the devolved parliaments are amendable after five years have passed.[16] Unsurprisingly, this provision met the strong disagreement of the Scottish Parliament that refused to provide consent in accordance with the Sewel Convention.[17] Notwithstanding, Westminster passed the law.

Be that as it may, such arrangement has an expiry date. Once this passes, the devolved governments will no longer be obliged to conform neither to (retained) EU law nor to statutory instruments freezing their power to legislate in those areas. That opens up the possibility for greater policy divergence that may disrupt the UK's internal trade. To guard against that possibility the UK Government proposed a Market Access commitment in a recently published White Paper (UK Government 2020). According to it, Westminster has introduced in primary legislation both a principle of mutual recognition and a principle of non-discrimination to 'guarantee the continued right of all UK companies to trade unhindered in every part of the UK'.[18] At the time of writing, the details of the new legislative framework are not yet known. However, an expansive application of such a principle threatens the constituent autonomy of the regional institutions that will not be able to differentiate even in the devolved policy areas.

4 The Right to Secede

The previous section referred to how the UK's withdrawal from the EU and the relevant implementation policies challenge the fragile balance of the UK territorial constitution. In particular, the UK Government's decision to leave both the single market and the customs union restricts the constituent autonomy of the devolved nations. This is why, in the aftermath of the Brexit referendum, a number of politicians in those

[14] The EU (Withdrawal) Act 2018, s. 12.

[15] Ibid.

[16] Ibid.

[17] According to the convention, Westminster should receive the consent of the relevant regional parliament before it legislates in devolved policy areas or in case a UK bill seeks to vary the legislative competence of the regional legislatures or the executive competence of the regional governments.

[18] Ibid, at p. 11.

regions that have been traditionally in favour of the secession of those constituent nations from the UK have reshaped their arguments. They support the secession of Scotland and Northern Ireland to achieve a much closer relationship with the EU among else.

Hours after the result of the Brexit referendum was announced, the First Minister of Scotland, Nicola Sturgeon, made clear that she intended to 'take all possible steps and explore all options to give effect to how people in Scotland voted—in other words, to secure [their] continuing place in the EU and in the single market in particular' (Sturgeon 2016). The reason being that 'Scotland faces the prospect of being taken out of the EU against [its] will' (ibid). At the same time, Sinn Féin called for a referendum for the unification of Ireland and thus for Northern Ireland to remain in the EU (Skoutaris 2017). Even in Wales, a modest debate on independence has started (Evans 2020).

Despite the fact that the UK government does not seem amenable to the idea of allowing the organisation of secession referendums, it is important to assess such possibility in UK constitutional law. A brief analysis shows that there are more constitutional hurdles to Scottish independence rather than the reunification of Ireland. According to section 1 of Northern Ireland Act 1998, Northern Ireland enjoys a right to secede to join a united Ireland if the majority of its people agree to this in a referendum.[19] On the other hand, the Scottish devolution arrangement does not include a similar clear constitutional pathway.

Scottish Independence

The Scottish Parliament has had the power to enact primary legislation from the very beginning. Its powers are defined negatively. This means that, according to section 29 of Scotland Act 1998, it may legislate in areas that are not considered as 'reserved' competences of Westminster. The latter are enlisted in Schedule 5 of Scotland Act 1998, which provides for a list of those 'reserved matters' over which the Scottish Parliament does not have legislative authority. According to Lord Hope,

> The fact that section 29 provides a mechanism for determining whether a provision of an Act of the Scottish Parliament is outside, rather than inside, competence does not create a presumption in favour of competence. But it

[19] The people of the Irish Republic should also agree to this in a separate referendum.

> helps to show that one of the purposes of the 1998 Act was to enable the Parliament to make such laws within the powers given to it by section 28 as it thought fit. It was intended, within carefully defined limits, to be a generous settlement of legislative authority.[20]

The Scottish Parliament has residual powers over the legislative competences that are not explicitly allocated to Westminster. The latter include the Constitution of which 'the Union of the Kingdoms of Scotland and England' is part. This means that '[a]s a matter of UK law, the Scottish Parliament cannot pass a declaration of independence' (Smith and Young 2017). However, referendums are not listed as a reserved matter in Schedule 5. Therefore, there is a question to be made whether Holyrood can lawfully 'hold a referendum about whether another constitutional institution should do so' (Ibid). To put it differently, it is rather unclear whether the Scottish Parliament can exercise the unreserved power to hold an advisory referendum for a reserved matter such as 'the Union of the Kingdoms of Scotland and England'.

This was precisely the topic of the constitutional debate that took place between academics and political elites in the aftermath of the landslide win of the Scottish National Party in the 2011 Scottish Parliament elections (Anderson et al. 2012; McHarg et al. 2016; Armstrong 2017). Central to that debate was the question whether an Act of the Scottish Parliament allowing the organisation of an independence referendum would relate directly to the reserved matter of the Constitution and thus it would be deemed *ultra vires* (Barber 2012; Tomkins 2012). Notwithstanding the legal arguments, the 'two governments of Scotland' decided to resolve this important constitutional question with a political agreement. The *Edinburgh Agreement* underscores the flexible nature of the UK idiosyncratic constitution (Bell 2012).[21] According to it, David Cameron and Alex Salmond agreed to amend the text of Scotland Act 1998. In accordance with section 30 of the Act,[22] an Order[23] was issued that introduced new section 29A. This new section explicitly conferred the power on

[20] *Imperial Tobacco Limited v. The Lord Advocate (Scotland)* [2012] UKSC 61, para 15.

[21] The text of the Agreement is available at http://www.number10.gov.uk/wp-content/uploads/2012/10/Agreement-final-for-signing.pdf

[22] Scotland Act 1998, s. 30(2) provides that 'Her Majesty may by Order in Council make any modifications' of the reserved matters 'which She considers necessary or expedient'.

[23] The Scotland Act 1998 (Modification of Schedule 5) Order 2013.

Holyrood to organise an independence referendum by no later than 31 December 2014.

More importantly for the purposes of the present chapter, on 28 March 2017, Holyrood passed a motion according to which there should be another independence referendum. Following that, Nicola Sturgeon asked the then UK Prime Minister Theresa May 'to begin early discussions between our governments to agree an Order under section 30 of the Scotland Act 1998 that would enable a referendum to be legislated for by the Scottish Parliament'.[24] By asking Whitehall and Westminster to allow the organisation of the referendum, the Scottish First Minister has accepted—implicitly—that a convention at a minimum or a legal obligation at a maximum has been created whereby Holyrood needs to seek the permission of the UK Government.

Overall, it seems that the constitutional right of the Scottish legislature to organise another independence referendum is at least disputed. This is why the declared aim of the Scottish Government remains to this day the same. They want to achieve a similar political arrangement to the one that led to the *Edinburgh Agreement*. In December 2019, a week after the UK Parliament elections, the Scottish Government published its case for a second independence referendum: *Scotland's Right to Choose: Putting Scotland's Future in Scotland's Hands* (Scottish Government 2019). Their case is based on three claims: first, that the Scottish people have the sovereign right to determine their own constitutional future; second, that Brexit consists of a material change of circumstances that justifies a second independence referendum; third, that the electoral wins of the Scottish National Party in the 2016 Holyrood elections and the 2017 and 2019 Westminster elections provide for a mandate to the Scottish Government to organise such referendum.

In Annex B of this blueprint, the Scottish Government goes a step further by putting forward a number of suggested amendments to the devolution act. They propose that the Scotland Act should legally recognise the right of self-determination of the Scottish people. As a result of that, the Scottish Parliament should assume the competence to organise an independence referendum permanently. And if the people in Scotland vote in favour of independence, the UK and Scottish Governments should be under a statutory duty to co-operate in securing the transition to independence.

[24] Available at https://www.snp.org/nicola_sturgeon_s_section_30_letter_to_theresa_may

Boris Johnson has already ruled out the possibility of a second independence referendum (Holehouse 2020). This is why some independentist politicians and activists are already talking about a possible Plan B. A number of them have asked Scotland's highest court to rule that Westminster's consent is unnecessary (Ibid.). Of course, even in the unlike scenario that the Court of Session agrees with them, there is nothing that prevents the UK Parliament to pass a law that makes clear that it is outwith Holyrood's competence to organise such independence referendum.

Some other supporters of independence have urged Scottish National Party's leadership to 'take the return of a pro-independence majority to Holyrood in 2021 as a mandate directly to enter into independence negotiations with the UK Government' (McCorkindale and McHarg 2020). Again, such approach is problematic and prone to failure for a number of reasons. First, legally speaking, the concept of 'mandate' is at least ambiguous. Even politically speaking, it seems somehow improper to use the result of a regional election as the legitimating factor for the abrupt rupture with the UK political order and as the foundational moment of the new independent Scotland. Secondly, Westminster has the power to overrule any laws that could be seen as a means for a transition to Scottish independence. In such a scenario, Scotland would find itself in a political and constitutional stalemate similar to the situation in Catalonia.

Irish Reunification

Unlike the case of Scotland, 'Westminster has formally conceded that Northern Ireland can secede from the United Kingdom to join a united Ireland, if its people, and the people of the Irish Republic, voting separately, agree to this' (McGarry 2010). Article 1 of the legally binding British-Irish Agreement which is part of the GFA and registered with the Secretariat of the United Nations (UN) recognises such right in no uncertain terms. In particular, the UK and the Republic of Ireland

(i) recognise the legitimacy of whatever choice is freely exercised by a majority of the people of Northern Ireland with regard to its status, whether they prefer to continue to support the Union with Great Britain or a sovereign united Ireland;

(ii) recognise that it is for the people of the island of Ireland alone, […] to exercise their right of self-determination on the basis of consent, freely and concurrently given, North and South, to bring about a united Ireland, if that is their wish, accepting that this right must be achieved and exercised with and subject to the agreement and consent of a majority of the people of Northern Ireland;

(iii) acknowledge that while a substantial section of the people in Northern Ireland share the legitimate wish of a majority of the people of the island of Ireland for a united Ireland, the present wish of a majority of the people of Northern Ireland, freely exercised and legitimate, is to maintain the Union and, accordingly, that Northern Ireland's status as part of the United Kingdom reflects and relies upon that wish; and that it would be wrong to make any change in the status of Northern Ireland save with the consent of a majority of its people;

(iv) affirm that if, in the future, the people of the island of Ireland exercise their right of self-determination on the basis set out in sections (i) and (ii) above to bring about a united Ireland, it will be a binding obligation on both Governments to introduce and support in their respective Parliaments legislation to give effect to that wish.

Those international legal obligations concerning the status of Northern Ireland have also been enshrined in UK legislation. Section 1 of the Northern Ireland Act 1998 is a rare example of a provision of a constitutional statute explicitly recognising the right of secession of a region.[25] In that sense, the organisation of such a referendum faces less constitutional hurdles—at least from a UK constitutional law point of view.

Schedule 1 of the Northern Ireland Act describes under which circumstances a referendum for the reunification of Ireland can and should be called by the UK Secretary of State. Recently, in *Re McCord*, the High

[25] Other examples of constitutional provisions that provide for a right of secession include Article 39(1) of the Ethiopian Constitution according to which 'every nation, nationality or people in Ethiopia shall have the unrestricted right to self determination up to secession' and Article 4(2) of the Constitution of the Principality of Liechtenstein according to which '[i]ndividual municipalities shall be entitled to secede from the union. The decision on whether to initiate a secession procedure shall be made by a majority of the Liechtenstein citizens eligible to vote who reside there. Secession shall be regulated by a law or, as the case may be, by an international treaty. If secession is regulated by a treaty, a second vote shall be held in the municipality after the treaty negotiations have been concluded'.

Court of Justice in Northern Ireland discussed and clarified the aforementioned Northern Ireland Act provisions.[26] It held that the Secretary of State has

> a discretionary power to order a border poll under Schedule 1 paragraph 1 even where she is not of the view that it is likely that the majority of voters would vote for Northern Ireland to cease to be part of the United Kingdom and to become part of a united Ireland.[27]

However, if it appears to her that a majority would be likely to vote for a united Ireland, then, she is under a duty to call a poll.

> If the evidence leads the Secretary of State to believe that the majority would so vote then she has no choice but to call a border poll. It is necessarily implied in this provision that the Secretary of State must honestly reflect on the evidence available to her to see whether it leads her to the conclusion that the majority would be likely to vote in favour of a united Ireland. Evidence of election results and opinion polls may form part of the evidential context in which to exercise the judgment whether it appears to the Secretary of State that there is likely to be a majority for a united Ireland.[28]

A similar statutory duty for calling a referendum on Irish unification does not exist on the other side of the Irish border. If one looks at the Irish Constitution, and especially at the text of the revised Articles 2 and 3, she would realise that there is nothing that explicitly states that the Taoiseach or any other institution and/or office holder is obliged by the Constitution, and the duties of their office, to pursue a united Ireland. The procedure for holding a referendum in the Republic of Ireland can be found in Article 46 of the constitution and the Referendum Acts. In sum, the proposal must be supported by both houses of the *Oireachtas*, submitted to and approved by the electorate and signed into law by the President. So, in purely legal terms, the decision to propose a referendum on unity lies with the parliament, while the approval or rejection of the Irish unification proposal rests with the electorate.

Overall, there is a clear and well-founded constitutional pathway for the secession of Northern Ireland from the UK and the unification of the

[26] *Re Raymond McCord* [2016] NIQB 106.
[27] Ibid., at para. 18.
[28] Ibid., at para. 20.

island of Ireland. This does not mean that such event is necessarily more politically feasible than Scottish independence. Theresa Villiers, the former Northern Ireland Secretary, has made clear that, according to her, 'there is nothing to indicate that there is majority support for a poll'.[29] To this effect, one has to bear in mind that there does not seem to be agreement among the Northern Irish political elites concerning the need to organise such a referendum and that the ethno-religious segment that would be more willing to support the reunification of Ireland, that is, the Irish/Nationalist/Republican/Catholic one, is—at the moment and until the political demographics change—in the minority.

5 Leaving the UK, Rejoining the EU

In a recent judgment, the Court of Justice of the EU acknowledged the importance of the right of self-determination within the EU constitutional order of States.

> [I]t should be noted, first of all, that the customary principle of self-determination referred to in particular in Article 1 of the Charter of the United Nations is, as the International Court of Justice stated in paragraphs 54 to 56 of its Advisory Opinion on Western Sahara, a principle of international law applicable to all non-self-governing territories and to all peoples who have not yet achieved independence. It is, moreover, a legally enforceable right *erga omnes* and one of the essential principles of international law [...].[30]

Of course, the orthodox view suggests that in metropolitan territories such as Scotland and Northern Ireland, 'peoples are expected to achieve self-determination within the framework of their existing state' (Crawford and Boyle 2013). In fact, a State that 'respects the principles of self-determination in its internal arrangements [...] is entitled to maintain its territorial integrity under international law' (Ibid). This view is in conformity with the opinion of the Canadian Supreme Court in *Reference re Secession of Quebec*.[31] There, the Court clarified 'that international law does

[29] Available at www.theguardian.com/uk-news/2016/jun/24/arlene-foster-northern-ireland-martin-mcguinness-border-poll-wont-happen

[30] Case C-104/16 P, *Council of the EU v Front Polisario* (2017) 2 CMLR 28, at paras 88–89.

[31] Reference re Secession of Quebec [1998] 1 SCR, 217.

not specifically grant component parts of sovereign states the legal right to secede unilaterally from their parent state'.[32]

Having said that, the EU has already accommodated within its legal order the results of secessions that have taken place through consensual processes. This is evident from the fact that a number of Member States such as the Czech Republic and Slovakia have become independent through such processes and this was not considered to be a hurdle to their accession. Even on the heated debate of the continuing membership of a region that has consensually seceded from a Member State as it was rehearsed mainly before the 2014 Scottish referendum the main question had to do not with whether Scotland can become an EU Member State but rather what is the appropriate process (Douglas-Scott 2014; Hillion 2014). In that sense, provided that Scotland becomes independent through a consensual and democratic process, there is a clear pathway for its accession to the EU.

An even clearer pathway exists for Northern Ireland whose re-accession to the EU may take place through the unification of the island of Ireland and thus the redefinition of the borders of a Member State. The EU legal order has recognised the occurrence of the phenomenon of moving borders. Examples include the return of the Saarland to German sovereignty in 1955; the dissolution of the Free Territory of Trieste and transfer of territory to Italy in 1954; change in the status of St. Pierre-et-Michelon from French overseas territory to overseas department; Algerian independence from France; German reunification in 1990; and a revised border agreement between Belgium and the Netherlands in 2018 (Harvey and Bassett 2019; Kochenov 2008).

Scottish EU Membership

Let us assume, for the purposes of the present chapter, that Whitehall and Holyrood reach a similar agreement to the one that led to the 2014 referendum and that the Scottish electorate votes in favour of independence in that second referendum. The next question we should address is how Scotland may become an EU Member State.

Article 49 TEU provides that '[a]ny European State which respects the values referred to in Article 2 and is committed to promoting them may apply to become a member of the Union'. After receiving such an

[32] Ibid., at para. 111.

application, the Council has to unanimously decide on opening the Accession negotiations after consulting with the Commission and receiving the consent of the majority of the component members of the European Parliament. The negotiations are compartmentalised in chapters and are driven by soft law instruments in the form of bilateral accession partnerships and progress reports.[33] Once there is an agreement that the candidate State has complied with all the relevant conditions contained in all the negotiating chapters, an Accession Treaty is drafted. The Treaty provides for all '[t]he conditions of admission and the adjustments to the Treaties on which the Union is founded, which such admission entails'.[34] The signatories are the Union Member States and the candidate State. The Member States have to ratify the Accession Treaty in accordance with their respective constitutional requirements.

Innocuous as it may sound, this might prove a cumbersome process given the stated objections of some Member States such as Spain to secessionist processes. In the long hours of the morning of 19 September 2014, former Spanish Secretary of State for the European Union, Íñigo Méndez de Vigo made clear that were Scotland to become independent, it would have had to join the queue of the other candidate States, underlining how time-consuming this might be. More importantly, his statement shed doubt on whether Spain would ever accept Scotland as a Member State, fearing that this would create a dangerous precedent especially for the secessionist movements that exist in Spain.

However, this might not be the biggest problem that independent Scotland would be facing if it joins the EU. The decision of the UK Government to withdraw from the single market and the customs union means that a Scottish EU accession would create a hard border on the island of Great Britain. Granted, Scotland may opt out of joining Schengen and may prefer to remain part of the Common Travel Area—the special free travel zone between the Republic of Ireland and the UK, Isle of Man and Channel Islands (McGuiness et al. 2019). In that scenario, the free movement of Scottish people in Great Britain and Ireland would remain unchanged. Still, some sort of controls would have to take place with

[33] For a brief analysis, see C Hillion, 'EU Enlargement' in P Craig and G de Búrca, (eds), *The Evolution of EU* Law, 2nd ed. (Oxford University Press, 2011), 187; C Hillion, 'Accession and Withdrawal in the Law of the European Union' in A Arnull and D Chalmers (eds), *The Oxford Handbook of European Union Law* (Oxford University Press 2015) 126.

[34] Art 49(2) TEU.

regard to non-British third country nationals arriving at the Scottish ports of entry. Of course, such immigration checks may be conducted in places other than borders. For instance, Ruparel has suggested that 'the enforcement of ensuring people do not over-stay' can take place 'via other mechanisms such as regulating access to social security and the job market' (Ibid, 18). Still, there will be some change in the territorial border between England and Scotland.

As the Irish border saga suggests, however, it is in the area of free movement of goods that the biggest challenges would arise. If an independent Scotland acceded to the EU, it would become part of its customs union. Following the decision of the UK Government to withdraw from the EU customs union, a customs border between Scotland and England would be created at the moment of the Scottish EU accession. There have been some suggestions about how to circumvent this problem (Skoutaris 2017) but, unless the EU somehow exempts Scotland from some EU rules concerning customs, rules of origin, VAT, sanitary and phytosanitary standards, a customs territorial border seems almost inevitable.

This is one of the reasons why some Scottish politicians including the former First Minister Alex Salmond have proposed 'that Scotland would try and join EFTA as a "transition" for an undefined period, before applying to join the EU in the longer term'.[35] Article 56 of the EFTA Convention provides that any State may accede to it on terms and conditions set out in a unanimous decision of the highest governing body: the EFTA Council. Following such decision of the four EFTA States that take part in the Council,[36] Scotland may apply to join EEA in accordance with Article 128 of the EEA Agreement. All Contracting Parties should approve the Accession Agreement.

The benefit of the 'Norway model' is that it secures the continuous membership to the EU's single market until Scotland becomes an EU Member State. Even as a permanent arrangement, however, Scotland's EFTA membership might prove quite beneficial. For instance, it could allow Scotland to remain outside the EU's and within the UK's customs union.[37] Such arrangement could absorb some of the tensions that a

[35] Available at http://www.telegraph.co.uk/news/2017/03/19/alex-salmond-independent-scotland-join-efta-get-single-market/ (last visited 28 August 2017).

[36] The EFTA Member States are Iceland, Liechtenstein, Norway and Switzerland.

[37] Art 56(3) of the EFTA Convention requires a new member of EFTA to 'apply to become a party to the free trade agreements between the Member States on the one hand and third

customs border between Scotland and the rest of Britain would create. In addition, it could allow Scotland to be outside the Common Fisheries Policy and not to adopt the Euro as its currency.

Irish Unity

Concerning Northern Ireland, the situation again seems to be simpler from an EU law point of view. The secession of Northern Ireland will not mean the creation of a new (Member) State. Instead, it will trigger the territorial expansion of an EU Member State—the Republic of Ireland—to which EU law already applies in accordance with Article 52 TEU. In a way, the reunification of Ireland could follow the precedent of the German reunification where the application of the *acquis* was extended to East Germany without an amendment of the primary legislation (Tomuschat 1990; Timmermans 1990), as agreed in a special meeting of the European Council in Dublin on 28 April 1990.[38] 'The necessary acts of secondary law were adopted on the basis of delegation of powers to the Commission, in order to avoid that the EU legislative process was overtaken by the speed of historical events' (Schiek 2017). The difference is that, in the case of Germany, the *acquis* did not apply at all in the East before the reunification.[39] In Northern Ireland, even after the expiry of the Brexit transition, a substantial part of EU law will continue to enjoy extraterritorial application.

Notwithstanding, former Taoiseach Enda Kenny asked for a special provision in any Brexit deal to allow Northern Ireland to rejoin the EU should

states, unions of states or international organisations on the other'. Despite the language, it seems that the legal framework of EFTA is flexible enough to allow Scotland not to 'sign up to those trade agreements with third countries that would be incompatible with its customs relationship with rUK' (Lock 2017).

[38] The text is available at http://aei.pitt.edu/1397/1/Dublin_april_1990.pdf

[39] The relationship of the Deutsche Demokratische Republik (German Democratic Republic) with the then Community was clarified in the judgment of the Court of Justice in Case 14/74, EU:C:1974:92. In that decision, the Court held that the relevant rules exonerating West Germany from applying the rules of European Economic Community (EEC) law to German Internal Trade 'does not have the result of making the German Democratic Republic part of the Community, but only that a special system applies to it as a territory which is not part of the Community'.

it be united with the Republic.[40] At the time of that request, the question was what would such a provision look like. There are few EU law provisions that regulate the (re)unification of (Member) States. The closest example is Article 4 of Protocol No 10 on Cyprus of the Act of Accession 2003. Protocol No 10 provides the terms for the application of EU law in Cyprus given that the island had not been unified at the moment it joined the EU. In particular, it provides for the suspension of the application of the *acquis* in northern Cyprus, a suspension which shall be lifted in the event of a solution.[41] If such solution occurs in the future, Article 4 provides for a simplified procedure that enables the Union to accommodate the terms of the reunification plan. In particular, Article 4 allows the EU, by a unanimous Council Decision at a future date and in the event of reunification, to alter the terms of Cyprus' EU accession that are contained in the Act of Accession 2003. In other words, it allows the Council to amend primary law (i.e. Act of Accession 2003) with a unanimous decision.

The example of Cyprus shows that EU law is flexible enough to accommodate the occurrence of moving borders. It could even allow for the existence of a special provision that could assist the smooth transitioning of Northern Ireland back to the EU. Notwithstanding, the UK Withdrawal Agreement does not include such arrangement. Instead, the European Council agreed the following statement in the minutes to the agreement on the Brexit negotiating guidelines on 29 April 2017:

> The European Council acknowledges that the Good Friday Agreement expressly provides for an agreed mechanism whereby a united Ireland may be brought about through peaceful and democratic means; and, in this regard, the European Council acknowledges that, in accordance with international law, the entire territory of such a united Ireland would thus be part of the European Union.[42]

So, in the absence of a specific provision, it seems that the re-accession of Northern Ireland to the EU will follow the precedent of German reunification.

[40] Available at https://www.theguardian.com/politics/2017/feb/23/irish-leader-enda-kenny-calls-for-united-ireland-provision-in-brexit-deal (last visited 28 August 2017).

[41] Art 1 of Protocol No 10 on Cyprus of the Act of Accession 2003 [2003] OJ L 236/955.

[42] European Council, *Minutes of Special meeting of the European Council (Art. 50) held on 29 April 2017* (23 June 2017).

6 Conclusion

The chapter has briefly presented how UK's withdrawal from the EU challenges the UK territorial politics. In particular, it discussed the constitutional pathways that Scotland and Northern Ireland can use and the challenges that they have to face in order to secede from the UK and rejoin the EU. In any case, it seems that there is an inherent paradox underlying the position of the ardent supporters of Brexit. The more they diverge from the EU's regulatory gravitational pull, the more they alienate two of the UK constituent nations. As a result, segments of the regional politicians and activists favour the abrupt rupture with the UK constitutional order to achieve a European future. Scotland seems to have a less clear and more challenging pathway towards re-integration with the EU. Yet, the recent polls suggest that there is a stable majority in favour of independence. Northern Ireland has a legally enshrined right to secede, while Irish reunification may secure its European future. However, the current political demographics do not seem favourable.

Ironically, the intoxicating cry of 'taking back control' seems to destabilise the Union and strengthen the European prospects of those two regions.

References

Anderson, G., Bell, C., Craig, S., McHarg, A., Mullen, T., Tierney, S., & Walker, N. (2012). The Independence Referendum, Legality and the Contested Constitution: Widening the Debate. *UK Constitutional Law Blog*. https://ukconstitutionallaw.org/2012/01/31/gavin-anderson-et-al-the-independence-referendum-legality-and-the-contested-constitution-widening-the-debate/. Accessed 1 Aug 2020.

Armstrong, K. A. (2017). The Reach and Resources of European Law in the Scottish Independence Referendum. In C. Closa (Ed.), *Secession from a Member State and Withdrawal from the European Union: Trouble Membership* (pp. 106–133). Cambridge: Cambridge University Press.

Barber, N. (2012). Scottish Independence and the Role of the United Kingdom. *UK Constitutional Law Blog*. https://ukconstitutionallaw.org/2012/01/11/nick-barber-scottish-independence-and-the-role-of-the-united-kingdom/. Accessed 1 Aug 2020.

Bell, C. (2012). *The Legal Status of the Edinburgh Agreement*. www.scottishconstitutionalfutures.org/OpinionandAnalysis/ViewBlogPost/tabid/1767/articleType/ArticleView/articleId/431/Christine-Bell-The-Legal-Status-of-the-Edinburgh-Agreement.aspx. Accessed 1 Aug 2020.

Cabinet Office. (2020). *The European Union (Withdrawal) Act and Common Frameworks.* https://assets.publishing.service.gov.uk/government/uploads/system/uploads/attachment_data/file/886372/TheEuropeanUnion-Withdrawal-ActAndCommonFrameworks.pdf. Accessed 1 Aug 2020.

Crawford, J., & Boyle, A. (2013). *Opinion: Referendum on the Independence of Scotland – International Law Aspects.* https://www.gov.uk/government/uploads/system/uploads/attachment_data/file/79408/Annex_A.pdf, 106. Accessed 1 Aug 2020.

Douglas-Scott, S. (2014). Scotland and the EU: Eleventh Hour Thoughts on a Contested Subject. *VerfassungBlog.* https://verfassungsblog.de/scotland-eu-eleventh-hour-thoughts-contested-subject-2/. Accessed 1 Aug 2012.

Evans, G. (2020). Debating Welsh Independence: The Political and Constitutional Pathways to a Referendum. *UK Constitutional Law Blog.* https://ukconstitutionallaw.org/2020/07/29/gareth-evans-debating-welsh-independence-the-political-and-constitutional-pathways-to-a-referendum/. Accessed 1 Aug 2020.

Ferriter, D. (2019). *The Border: The Legacy of a Century of Anglo-Irish Politics.* Croydon: Profile Books.

Freeman, T. (2014). *Sturgeon: Give UK Nations Veto in EU Exit Referendum.* Holyrood. https://www.holyrood.com/news/view,sturgeon-give-uk-nations-veto-in-eu-exit-referendum_13903.htm. Accessed 1 Aug 2020.

Harvey, C., & Bassett, M. (2019). *The EU and Irish Unity: Planning and Preparing for Constitutional Change in Ireland.* An Independent Legal and Academic Report Commissioned by the European Left / Nordic Green Left (GUE / NGL) Group of the European Parliament. https://www.guengl.eu/issues/publications/the-eu-irish-unity/. Accessed 1 Aug 2020.

Hayward, K., & Phinnemore, D. (2019). Breached or Protected? The 'Principle' of Consent in Northern Ireland and the UK Government's Brexit Proposals. *EUROPP.* https://blogs.lse.ac.uk/europpblog/2019/01/11/breached-or-protected-the-principle-of-consent-in-northern-ireland-and-the-uk-governments-brexit-proposals/. Accessed 1 Aug 2020.

Hillion, C. (2014). Scotland and the EU: Comment by Christophe Hillion. *VerfassungBlog.* https://verfassungsblog.de/scotland-eu-comment-christophe-hillion-2/. Accessed 1 Aug 2012.

Holehouse, M. (2020). How the Scottish National Party Risks Turning Caledonia into Catalonia. *The Economist.* https://www.economist.com/britain/2020/08/08/how-the-scottish-national-party-risks-turning-caledonia-into-catalonia. Accessed 1 Aug 2020.

Kochenov, D. (2008). Procedural Issues in the Application of European Law in the Overseas Possessions of European Union Member States. *Michigan State of International Law, 17,* 661–765.

Leyland, P. (2012). *The Constitution of the United Kingdom: A Contextual Analysis* (2nd ed.). Oxford: Hart Publishing.

Lock, T. (2017). Scotland's Place in Europe After Brexit: Between a Rock and a Hard Place? A Legal Scoping Exercise. *European Papers, 2*, 183–200.

McCorkindale, C., & McHarg, A. (2020). Constitutional Pathways to a Second Scottish Independence Referendum. *UK Constitutional Law Blog*. https://ukconstitutionallaw.org/2020/01/13/chris-mccorkindale-and-aileen-mcharg-constitutional-pathways-to-a-second-scottish-independence-referendum/. Accessed 1 Aug 2020.

McGarry, J. (2010). Asymmetrical Autonomy in the United Kingdom. In M. Weller & K. Nobbs (Eds.), *Asymmetric Autonomy and the Settlement of Ethnic Conflicts* (pp. 148–181). Philadelphia: University of Pennsylvania Press.

McGuiness, T., Gower, M., & Wilkins, H. (2019). *The Common Travel Area, and the Special Status of Irish Nationals* (House of Commons Briefing Paper Number 7661).

McHarg, A., Mullen, T., Page, A., & Walker, N. (Eds.). (2016). *The Scottish Independence Referendum: Constitutional and Political Implications*. Oxford: Oxford University Press.

Schiek. D. (2017). "Hard Brexit"-How to Address the New Conundrum for the Island of Ireland? *QUB Blog*. https://blogs.qub.ac.uk/tensionatthefringes/files/2017/02/Schiek-Brexit-and-the-UK-Ireland-relationship-CETLS-TREUP-occasional-paper-2-20171.pdf. Accessed 1 Aug 2020.

Scottish Government. (2016). *Scotland's Place in Europe*. http://www.gov.scot/Publications/2016/12/9234. Accessed 1 Aug 2020.

Scottish Government. (2019). *Scotland's Right to Choose: Putting Scotland's Future in Scotland's Hands*. https://www.gov.scot/publications/scotlands-right-choose-putting-scotlands-future-scotlands-hands/. Accessed 1 Aug 2020.

Skoutaris, N. (2017). Territorial Differentiation in EU Law: Can Scotland and Northern Ireland Remain in the EU and/or the Single Market? *Cambridge Yearbook of European Legal Studies, 19*, 287–310.

Skoutaris, N. (2019). *What's in an Irish Border? Brexit, the Backstop(s) and the Constitutional Integrity of the UK* (No. 2.2020 DCU Brexit Institute – Working Paper).

Smith, E., & Young, A. (2017). That's How It Worked in 2014, and How It Would Have to Work Again. *UK Constitutional Law Blog*. https://ukconstitutionallaw.org/2017/03/15/ewan-smith-and-alison-young-thats-how-it-worked-in-2014-and-how-it-would-have-to-work-again/. Accessed 1 Aug 2020.

Sturgeon, N. (2016). *Speech After the Referendum Result*. https://archive.news.stv.tv/politics/1358534-nicola-sturgeon-speech-in-full-after-eu-referendum-result.html. Accessed 1 Aug 2020.

Timmermans, C. W. A. (1990). German Unification and Community Law. *Common Market Law Review, 27*, 437–449.

Tomkins, A. (2012). *The Scottish Parliament and the Independence Referendum.* https://ukconstitutionallaw.org/2012/01/12/adam-tomkins-the-scottish-parliament-and-the-independence-referendum/. Accessed 1 Aug 2020.

Tomuschat, C. (1990). A United Germany Within the European Community. *Common Market Law Review, 27*, 415–435.

UK Government White Paper. (2020). *UK Internal Market.* https://assets.publishing.service.gov.uk/government/uploads/system/uploads/attachment_data/file/901225/uk-internal-market-white-paper.pdf. Accessed 1 Aug 2020.

Whitman, R. G. (2017). *Devolved External Affairs: The Impact of Brexit.* Chatham House Research Paper. https://www.debrige.de/wp-content/uploads/brexit/Richard-Whitman-Devolved-External-Affairs-paper.pdf. Accessed 1 Aug 2020.

CHAPTER 10

Territorial Politics of Regionalism in Italy Between Integration and Disintegration

Sabrina Ragone

1 Introduction

This chapter analyses the evolution of Italian regionalism, taking into account the most significant elements to clarify the current situation, with respect to the debate on "differentiated regionalism" and the recent experience of referenda on independence or increased autonomy. In order to explain the overall philosophy, main principles and frame of the Italian model, the text provides first a short and syncretic introduction to the different phases that territorial decentralisation has undergone. If the evolution of the regional system was divided into steps, the first one would be its establishment by the Constituent Assembly, followed by its actual implementation (during the 1970s for most of the Regions), culminating in its consolidation, which lasted until the 1990s (see Sect. 2).

Once the institutions were completely established and all territories had achieved substantially equal autonomy, a new phenomenon appeared, characterised by the strive for differentiation, especially with respect to "regional rights" (after the constitutional amendments passed in 1999 and 2001,

S. Ragone (✉)
University of Bologna, Bologna, Italy
e-mail: sabrina.ragone2@unibo.it

M. Belov (ed.), *Territorial Politics and Secession*, Federalism and Internal Conflicts, https://doi.org/10.1007/978-3-030-64402-4_10

which added few matters to the domain of regional statutes of autonomy) and the number and scope of the legislative domains (particularly after 2015: see Sect. 3).

The analysis of relevant constitutional amendments, legislative development and case law of the Constitutional Court provides elements to understand why and how some Regions pursued different paths with the aim of achieving a higher degree of autonomy. Of course, the chapter intersects the legal features of such claims with basic political data, particularly regarding the rise and consolidation of political parties, like the Northern League, which have made of autonomy and/or secession one of their main claims.

Overall, the Italian example proves that decentralised States—be they federal or regional—present a certain degree of instability, because the distinct representative institutions distributed all over the country are inclined to seek more autonomy. And the issue is not only cultural or political, but it can become constitutional and legal as well. The history of autonomist and secessionist claims, in fact, demonstrates that different legal instruments can be used to pursue these targets and that the resilience of the constitutional system resides in how they are managed and tackled (see Sect. 4).

2 Starting from the Beginning: The Constituent Assembly, the Establishment of a Regional Model and Its Implementation

The starting point in the development of any decentralised system consists, from a legal perspective, in the establishment of territorial entities in the Constitution or fundamental laws. In the Italian case, it was the outcome of the choice of the Constituent Assembly.[1] On the 2nd of June 1946 the Italian electorate decided to shift from Monarchy to a Republic and at the same time voted for the members of the Constituent Assembly.

The *plenum* of the Assembly selected 75 of its members who were in charge of drafting the text of the Constitution and were divided into three subcommittees (dedicated, respectively, to rights and duties; constitutional organisation of the State; and economic and social relations). The

[1] See Pedrazza Gorlero (1979) and Cerrina Feroni and Tarli Barbieri (2016).

text was approved in late 1947 and entered into force on the 1st of January 1948. Throughout the decades, it has undergone several changes (among them, a major one in 2001), but the basic features of the regional model still remain.

During the constituent phase, the process of foundation had already started for the so-called special Regions (or at least for four out of five),[2] whose identification responded to historical, cultural, geographical and linguistic issues. The total number of Regions nowadays is 20: 5 special (Friuli Venezia Giulia, Trentino Alto Adige, Sicily, Sardinia, Valle d'Aosta) and 15 ordinary (whose borders were mainly based on previous administrative-economic partitions of the Italian Kingdom; among these, some of the most industrialised and prosperous territories), and their list can be found in Art. 131 of the Constitution.

Among the fundamental principles of the Constitution, one may find the cornerstone of Italian territorial organisation: Art. 5, which states that the Republic, one and indivisible, recognises and promotes local autonomies, performing the highest administrative decentralisation in the services that depend on the State; it adapts the principles and methods of domestic legislation to the requirements of autonomy and decentralisation.[3] This general principle is further specified within the Fifth Title of the Second Part of the Constitution (Articles 114–133). The territorial arrangement constituted one of the major novelties of the 1948 Constitution and carried an element of discontinuity in the evolution of the State, due to the desire to provide a more modern arrangement and overcome the centralisation of the fascist regime.[4]

For the above-mentioned special Regions, the Constitution fixes that peculiar forms and conditions of autonomy are regulated by their statutes, which have to be adopted through constitutional laws (i.e. laws subject to a special procedure and passed by the national Parliament as well), according to Art. 116 (on their evolution: Louvin 2019). On the contrary, since 1999 the statutes of autonomy of ordinary Regions are adopted through

[2] In fact, through constitutional laws n. 2, 3, 4 and 5/1948, the statutes of autonomy of Sicily, Sardinia, Valle d'Aosta and Trentino Alto Adige were adopted. The statute of autonomy of Friuli Venezia Giulia dates back to 1963 instead, for historical and political reasons.

[3] See Berti (1975) and Bifulco (2006a).

[4] See Mortati (1947); Luciani (1997); Modugno (2014); Carnevale (2015); and Ronchetti (2018).

the sole intervention of regional parliaments,[5] as it will be explained later on.

The Constituent Assembly elaborated a type of State[6] in which, for the first time in the Italian order, two different and, to some extent, opposite concepts coexisted: unity, on the one hand, and territorial autonomy, on the other. This intrinsic contradiction laid the foundations for the future development of political decentralisation. Italy had just one potential former regional model, represented by the brief experience of the Spanish Second Republic of 1931, having to take a stand on the unitary vs. federal organisation divide as well.[7] Of course, this would lead to think that the drive towards autonomy did not arise from below in ordinary Regions and that the evolution took a distinct path. All Regions enjoy legislative, administrative, fiscal, as well as financial powers, to different extents. In fact, the asymmetry between special and ordinary Regions depends not only on the nature and scope of the respective statutes, but also on their normative domain, financial autonomy and bilateral collaborations with the State.

Due to the lack of political agreement, more than 20 years after the Constitution's entry into force had to pass before the ordinary ones were actually put in place, and so Italy had for long an unfinished regionalism which only affected a part of its territory. In fact, the regulation of the electoral system applicable to regional parliaments was adopted in 1968 and the first elections were held in 1970. From then on, regional statutes were approved, alongside the necessary laws and measures granting resources and personnel to the new regional administrations.[8]

As it was previously mentioned, I consider the following stage to be the consolidation and stabilisation of regional institutions (see Mangiameli 2014). This process covered a time-span between the decades of the 1970s and the 1990s, reaching its peak at the beginning of the new millennium,

[5] A short terminological clarification: under Italian constitutional law, the word "Parliament" is only applicable to the national legislature, as the Constitutional Court confirmed (see judgments n. 106/2002 and n. 306/2002). The English translation of the Italian term would read "legislative assembly" or "legislative council". For the sake of simplification, this chapter will employ the expression "regional parliament".

[6] On the link between the concept of "type of State" and "form of State", see Pegoraro and Rinella (2017: 282–334).

[7] See Mangiameli (2012) and D'Atena (2014).

[8] See Bassanini (1970) and Rotelli (1973).

with the constitutional amendments passed in 1999 and 2001.[9] It was a markedly dynamic period, during which decentralisation achieved its balance between central and regional bodies (Cammelli 2014).

Another feature of the "original" constitutional framework must be recalled: the division of legislative powers between the State and (ordinary) Regions was based on a closed list of legislative matters reserved for the regional level, while the rest was allotted to the national Parliament (Art. 117 prior to the 2001 amendment). Furthermore, until 2001 the exercise of regional legislative power was subject to the prior control of the so-called commissioner of the Government, who had a 30-day deadline to certify that these laws did not exceed the corresponding domain, nor affect national interests.

Two actors played a major role in the consolidation and evolution of Italian Regions, namely, the national Parliament and the Constitutional Court (Ronchetti 2014). The former was in charge of passing the relevant legislation (e.g., the above-mentioned electoral law for regional parliaments) and the distribution of administrative functions and coordination instruments for the exercise of shared powers (in particular, the so-called State-Regions Conference which was transformed into a permanent body for coordination through law n. 400/1988). The Court's role was essential to define the scope and content of the legislative matters listed in Art. 117, as well as to restrain the all-encompassing functions of the State.[10]

As the system evolved and the Regions gained stability, novel ideas about their reform arose. At the beginning of the 1990s, a bicameral Committee (*De Mita-Iotti*) elaborated a comprehensive project bringing a series of innovations which would be at the centre of the debate for long after its failure, or would even be included in the 2001 amendment, among them: (a) providing a list of legislative domains of the State, leaving the rest to Regions; (b) entrusting the State with the identification of minimum levels of benefits referring to social rights; (c) changing or eliminating the role of the commissioner providing only the possibility to challenge regional legislation before the Constitutional Court and (d) fixing financial autonomy and tax imposition as basic principles for all territorial entities. This project would have significantly expanded the potential role for regional policies in international and European relations as well.

[9] See Caravita (2002); Mangiameli (2002); and Rozo Acuña (2003).

[10] See Crisafulli (1963); Bartole and Vandelli (1980); and Bartole et al. (1988).

Few years later, a second bicameral Committee (*D'Alema*, 1997) also debated reforms of Italian decentralisation, including the distribution of legislative powers, the contents of the statutes of autonomy and financial autonomy.[11] None of these constitutional amendments succeeded, but the major changes were channelled through ordinary legislation, and in particular two of the so-called *Bassanini laws*, n. 59/1997 and n. 127/1997, many features of which were then constitutionalised two or four years later.

Of course, constitutional and legal data have to be crossed with political and social developments, especially with the spread of regionalist parties and movements.[12] The well-known *Lega Nord* (Northern League), since 2017 just *Lega*, was the result of the federation of six autonomist movements existing in Northern Italy at the end of the 1980s and the early 1990s.

In the general elections of 1994, the first ones to be held with a mixed electoral system (75% majoritarian) after four decades of proportional system, the Northern League obtained 180 deputies (out of 630), as a result of joining the centre-right coalition, which won the elections. Therefore, in the first Berlusconi Government there were five ministers from the Northern League, in charge of internal affairs, budget and economic planning, industry, European policies and institutional reforms. Nevertheless, this Government lasted just until the end of the year, as there were recurring conflicts inside the coalition. The Northern League unsuccessfully proposed a bill aiming at dividing Italy into different areas similar to the pre-unitary States. Then, a fierce fight on pensions led Berlusconi to claim there should be new elections as the pre-electoral agreement had been betrayed, while the leader of the Northern League, Bossi, said that the federal project they had agreed upon had been abandoned.

The following administration, led by Dini and defined as a "technical executive" (1995–1996), counted on the external endorsement of the Northern League as well. In the following elections (1996) the Northern League maintained a significant support, obtaining 59 deputies and 27 senators (in this case, the electoral system considerably favoured the centre-left winning coalition). These political events were essential for the independentist turn of the Northern League, whose leader, Bossi, in September 1996, voiced the wish for secession and nation-building of the

[11] See Cuocolo (1997) and Costanzo et al. (1998).

[12] At the general elections of 1983, *Liga Veneta* obtained two seats, one at the Chamber of deputies and one at the Senate; in 1987, *Lega Lombarda* got its secretary elected, Umberto Bossi, who would then become the leader of the Northern League.

northern area of the country, the so-called Padania; in January 1997, the first issue of the official newspaper of the party, entitled exactly *La Padania*, was released.

The major changes of the territorial organisation took place during the following parliamentary term, actually under a centre-left majority-based administration (constitutional amendment laws n. 1/1999; n. 2/2001 and n. 3/2001), pursuing different intertwined objectives, such as the completion of decentralisation initiated through the *Bassanini laws*, but also the enhancement of citizens' participation, which had been promoted through the above-mentioned electoral reform for the election of the members of the Parliament, and for the heads of local entities as well (Municipalities and Provinces). This last element has to be understood in the light of the social context and the transformation in Italian politics and parties occurred at the beginning of the 1990s due to the so-called *Tangentopoli*, a nationwide judicial investigation into political corruption, which determined the progressive dissolution of the party system that had been ruling the country for four decades and led to widespread mistrust towards politics.

The constitutional amendment passed in 1999 modified the nature and content of the statutes of autonomy and the direct election of the President of the Regions (affecting Articles 121, 122, 123 and 126 of the Constitution), while in 2001 the range of reforms was wider. In spite of its scope, this change was not agreed upon by the main parties, being on the contrary approved with a slight majority in the last days of the XIII legislative term (1996–2001). This political situation led to the request, for the first time under the Italian Constitution of 1948, to call for a constitutional referendum, provided for by Art. 138 of the Constitution when the 2/3 majority is not achieved. The referendum was held in October 2001 and the outcome was the popular confirmation of the amendment.

From a general viewpoint, the 2001 amendment carries a novel concept of "Republic", which according to the new phrasing of Art. 114 is composed by Municipalities, Provinces, Metropolitan Cities, Regions and the State. Municipalities, Provinces, Metropolitan Cities and Regions are autonomous entities with their own statutes, powers and functions according to the principles established in the Constitution. With this definition, the State seems to be at the same level as the other territorial entities, since they compose the Republic all together.

More specifically concerning the regional level, the approval of the statutes of autonomy of ordinary Regions (Art. 123), which was allotted to

State laws under the original constitutional regulation, was attributed to regional parliaments, now entitled to regulate significant aspects such as the form of government or political system, as well as the general principles of organisation, legislative initiative and referenda. Each regional parliament passes the statute by an absolute majority, with two votes, the second after at least two months (after that, both a new special governmental appeal to the Constitutional Court and the request of a referendum can be triggered).

Art. 117 was amended as well and since then it defines the division of legislative powers according to a federal model.[13] After 2001, in fact, it contains a list of legislative matters exclusively allotted to the State; one list of shared matters, in which the State establishes only the fundamental principles; and then all "residual" matters belong to the legislative domain of Regions. The power to approve regulations (secondary legal sources) is enjoyed by the State only with respect to its exclusive matters, as long as they are not delegated to Regions. The national interest limit for regional legislation was removed as was also the control by the governmental commissioner (the national executive can now challenge regional legislation *a posteriori*, within 60 days after publication).

Furthermore, the reform affected the distribution of administrative functions among State, Regions and local entities, as these are entrusted to the Municipalities, unless, in order to ensure their unitary exercise, they are allotted to Provinces, Metropolitan Cities, Regions and the State by virtue of the principles of subsidiarity, differentiation and adequacy (Art. 118). Financial autonomy concerning income and expenses and partial ability to establish and collect taxes were promoted, along with the presence of a compensation fund (Art. 119). The substitute powers of the State were also modified, for cases of non-compliance with international or European norms and treaties, as well as when public safety and security, or the legal/economic unity of the State, are under threat, especially if the guarantee of the basic levels of protection of civil and social rights is at stake (Art. 120). Of course, such powers have to be exercised according to the principles of subsidiarity and loyal cooperation.

Consistently with the large-scale approach of the reform, also Art. 116 concerning special Regions was affected.[14] The original phrasing provided

[13] On the tension towards federalism, see Baldini and Baldi (2014).

[14] The application of all preferential clauses, which would have led to the recognition of higher autonomy for ordinary Regions than special ones, was extended to the latter (Art. 10, constitutional amendment law n. 3/2001).

that they would enjoy particular forms and conditions of autonomy, according to statutes approved as constitutional laws; the new text is more detailed. It contains a list of special Regions and specifies that one of them (Trentino Alto Adige) is made up of two autonomous Provinces. The main novelty is included in the third paragraph, which foresees other possible differentiated forms of autonomy for ordinary Regions, in shared legislative matters or educational, environmental and cultural issues, as well as the organisation of peace justice. This mechanism will be discussed afterwards, as it has been more effectively triggered only over the past years.[15]

In fact, far from being the conclusive solution to the main issues of Italian Regionalism, the 1999–2001 reform opened up to posterior legislative implementation and completion[16] and was the object of substantial constitutional litigation before the Constitutional Court, which was (again) called to define the content of legislative matters (especially the so-called transversal clauses which allow for State intervention) and the scope of the statutes of autonomy, as it will be explained in the next section.

3 Striving for Differentiation: From Regional Rights to Increased Autonomy (or Even Independence)

After the reforms of the years 1999–2001, a novel evolutionary phase began, which is characterised by what could be called "the challenge of differentiation" (Ragone 2013) and has been shaped through two main phenomena: first, the approval of the new statutes of autonomy[17] and later, the use of Art. 116.3, which establishes that additional special forms

[15] Previous attempts to regulate this option more in depth failed, like the bill proposed during Prodi's Government, on which see Bin (2008). The budgetary law for 2014 (law n. 147/2013), Art. 1, para. 571, established a deadline of 60 days for the national Government to start engaging in the request by the corresponding Region, which must be addressed to the Prime Minister and the Minister for Regional Affairs. See Mezzanotte (2014) and on former regional initiatives, Violini (2007).

[16] For instance, through law n. 131/2003, dedicated to the adaptation of the legal system to the 2001 amendment, or law n. 11/2005, concerning the participation to European decision-making processes. See Anzon (2008) and Mangiameli (2011).

[17] See at least Olivetti (2002); Ferrara (2001); Carli et al. (2006); Bifulco (2006b) and D'Alessandro (2008).

and conditions of autonomy can be attributed to ordinary Regions through a State law. The initiative belongs to the Region concerned, after consulting local entities; an agreement between the Region and the State follows, and the Parliament passes the corresponding law by absolute majority in both Chambers.

With respect to the statutes of autonomy, two main legal issues arose, concerning the definition of the form of government[18] and the regulation of rights, which was framed as a question of legitimacy (and usefulness) of "programmatic" statutory norms.[19] Such norms were already present in some of the old statutes of autonomy, and the Constitutional Court had stated that regional legislators would be entitled to pursue some of these principles through their action, even within the mechanisms of cooperation with the State.[20] Nevertheless, the constitutional and political debate on these clauses was much fiercer after 2001, and the Constitutional Court was called again to interpret and define the constraints of regional autonomy. It confirmed that the statutes have to be "in harmony with the Constitution", without violating its text nor its spirit[21] and being consistent with its norms and principles.[22] Programmatic norms (principles and rights, mainly) were considered as a corollary of "the functions and duties of the Region", also when they indicate "priority areas of political or legislative intervention", but they were only allotted a cultural or political (not binding) value.[23]

This approach was criticised by both scholars and politicians, but the debate soon shifted towards the content of another constitutional amendment (passed by the Parliament in 2005, yet rejected in a constitutional referendum in 2006), which would have radically changed the bicameral system establishing a "federal Senate" with distinct tasks with respect to the Chamber of deputies, while differently allotting legislative matters and

[18] On this point, see judgments n. 2/2004, n. 371/2004 and n. 12/2006 of the Italian Constitutional Court and among the scholarly analyses, Fusaro (2001); Zorzi Giustiniani (2003); and Ragone (2007).

[19] See Catelani and Cheli (2008) and, from a comparative perspective, Gavara de Cara (2010).

[20] See judgments n. 40/1972, n. 829/1988 and n. 921/1988 of the Constitutional Court.

[21] See judgment n. 304/2002 of the Constitutional Court.

[22] See judgment n. 196/2003 of the Constitutional Court.

[23] See, in addition to judgment n. 2/2004, also n. 372/2004, n. 378/2004 and n. 379/2004 of the Constitutional Court.

reinserting a clause on "national interest".[24] The centre-right coalition which proposed and passed such reform included the Northern League (the fourth party of the coalition in terms of elected candidates), which had made of the so-called *devolution* one of the main points on the agenda.

The following proposed amendment, promoted and passed ten years later by a centre-left majority, also failed due to its rejection in a constitutional referendum held in December 2016.[25] This all-encompassing reform would have affected several articles of the Constitution, transforming the Senate into a chamber representing territorial entities (and composed of regional deputies and mayors), while changing again the division of legislative powers between State and Regions and including a supremacy clause similar to federal arrangements.

In between these two attempted reforms, law n. 42/2009 was passed to implement the clause on "fiscal federalism" provided for in Art. 119 of the Constitution after the 2001 amendment. In the opposite direction, the constitutional amendment passed in 2012 (during the financial crisis, as a response to European and global pressure), in order to constitutionalise the so-called balanced budget, gave the State exclusive competence on the "harmonization of public budgets", increased the financial and economic supervision by the State on Regions and established rigid economic constraints and requirements.

The overall response to the crisis shows symptoms of centralisation of powers favouring the State vis-à-vis territorial entities, which has been confirmed by constitutional case law.[26] As a consequence, the legislative decrees on fiscal federalism that had been passed in 2010 and 2011 became substantially inapplicable. During the Monti Government, in addition to this constitutional amendment, numerous legislative measures aimed to reduce the financial resources transferred from the State to Regions (and local entities) and foster austerity measures and spending cuts at all levels of government. An additional amendment bill which would have decreased regional legislative domains and autonomy did not make it to the Parliament because of the end of the legislative term.

This is the political and economic context in which the new claims for autonomy, or even independence, gained momentum over the past few

[24] See Azzariti (2006) and Pinelli (2006).

[25] See Di Giacomo Russo and Tarzia (2016); Marini and Scaccia (2016); Morelli and Moschella (2016); Lucarelli and Zammartino (2016) and Cavino et al. (2017).

[26] See Belletti (2012) and Gardini (2015).

years in two northern Regions in particular, namely, Veneto and Lombardy, two of the (supposedly) richest areas of the country.[27]

In the former, the regional parliament passed a resolution (n. 44/2012) on the "right of the people of Veneto to a complete implementation of their self-determination". In this resolution, the people of Veneto were claimed to have a specific identity based on shared language, culture and values (among them, family, nation, work, solidarity, rule of law, justice and freedom). From a historical perspective, the document asserted that the accession of Veneto to Italy in 1866 (five years after the unification) was decided through a direct consultative mechanism, but the consensus was obtained thanks to a fraud by the Kingdom of Italy and shall not be considered valid; it mentioned two precedents (from 1992 and 1998) and voiced the intention to join similar claims, such as the Scottish and the Catalan ones.

The resolution established an obligation for the President of the Region and the President of the regional parliament to engage in negotiations with the European Union (and even the United Nations), in order to effectively pursue the right to self-determination. An online vote was arranged and managed by an organisation for the independence of Veneto: *Plebiscito 2013*, which became *Plebiscito.eu*.[28] The consultation took place in March 2014 and the result gave more than 2 million "yes" (90% of the voters). A declaration of the President of the Region, Zaia (member of the Northern League), followed, stating that people's will must be respected. In spite of the potential infringement upon the Constitution, he affirmed that international law endorses self-determination and promised he would do his best to get the corresponding laws to call for the referendum passed. After these events, the regional parliament actually passed two laws: n. 15/2014 and n. 16/2014 (Serges 2015).

[27] According to the Eurostat report on the GDP *pro capite* in European Regions published in 2015, when the autonomist process (re)started (https://ec.europa.eu/eurostat/), there were no Italian regions in the first 20 slots (nor in the last 20) and this was the statistics: autonomous province of Bolzano (142%); Lombardy (134%), Valle d'Aosta (132%), autonomous province of Trento (127%); Emilia-Romagna (120%); Lazio (118%); Liguria (112%); Veneto (111%); Friuli Venezia Giulia and Tuscany (107%); Piedmont (106%); Marche (93%) and Umbria (90%). Then, among the poorest regions, after Calabria, Sicily and Puglia (61%), there were Campania (63%), Basilicata and Sardinia (69%), Molise (70%) and Abruzzo (85%). These data confirm the North/South divide which has been a constant element in Italian politics and development. On the effects of the crisis in this respect, see Lagravinese (2015).

[28] The leader of this movement is a former member of the Northern League (Gianluca Busato, expelled from the party in 1997).

Law n. 15/2014 regulated a consultative referendum on (more) autonomy, based on five different questions: (1) Do you want Veneto to be granted additional special forms and conditions of autonomy?; (2) Do you wish that at least 80% of the taxes paid every year by the citizens of Veneto to the State be used for goods and services within the regional territory?; (3) Do you want the Region to retain at least 80% of the taxes collected within the Region?; (4) Do you want the financial resources of the Region to be free from constraints of allocation fixed by the State?; (5) Do you want Veneto to become a Region with a special statute of autonomy? In case of the participation of more than 50% of the electorate and their positive vote, this law obliged the President of the Region to elaborate a negotiations programme with the State, submit it to the regional parliament and then transmit a bill to grant the Region more autonomy to the national Parliament.

Law n. 16/2014 regulated a consultative referendum on independence, with just one question: "Do you want Veneto to become an independent and sovereign Republic?". Both laws were challenged by the Government before the Constitutional Court, which decided upon them in judgement n. 118/2015.[29] It dealt with the fiscal questions invoking both the regional statute of autonomy and Art. 119 of the Constitution,[30] considering that the question concerning the transformation into a special Region would be unconstitutional as well, because Art. 116 lists them—and that is a fundamental choice of constitutional value that cannot be addressed in regional referenda. More interestingly, the referendum on independence was declared unconstitutional as it infringed upon Art. 5 of

[29] A translation into English can be found here: https://www.cortecostituzionale.it/documenti/download/doc/recent_judgments/S118_2015_en.pdf. See Tega (2015); Conte (2015) and Pastore (2019a).

[30] The legal reasoning concerning questions 2 and 3 on taxes was construed on the following steps: the statute of autonomy is the source that regulates regional referenda according to Art. 123 of the Constitution; Art. 26 and Art. 27 of the statute of autonomy of Veneto actually regulate them, explicitly excluding the possibility of holding referenda concerning taxes and budgetary issues. Therefore, the call for these questions violated the statute itself. Additionally, these questions were also contrary to Art. 119 of the Constitution, that regulates financial autonomy of revenue and expenditure, balanced with the principle of coordination of public finance, equalisation and solidarity among different territories. On question 4, the Court considered that the request to eliminate all constraints of destination for financial resources (for instance, economic development, solidarity, cohesion) would infringe upon Art. 119 of the Constitution and Articles 26 and 27 of the statute of autonomy.

the Constitution.[31] According to the Court, pluralism and autonomy do not allow Regions to define themselves as sovereign bodies.[32] The question was considered *extra ordinem*, as the unity and indivisibility of the Republic were included among those principles that cannot be touched even through a constitutional amendment.[33]

The only question that was kept in place was the first of law n. 15/2014, which inquired with respect to special forms of autonomy. The Court, in fact, stated that regional voters could be asked whether they wished Veneto to be vested with further forms and special terms of autonomy, as such question recalled the provisions of Art. 116.3 of the Constitution. According to the judgement, there is no overlap between such regional consultation and the procedure provided for by the Constitution,[34] which may thus take place normally, were it in actual fact to be activated. The consultative referendum would happen at an earlier stage that is separate from the procedure regulated by Art. 116.3. It was not obligatory, but not forbidden either.[35] The general principle confirmed in this judgement was that questions of interest for the regional community, regarding which the Region may arrange consultative referenda, can concern substantive matters that go beyond the domain and territory of the Region, therefore touching upon national issues, *as long as no fundamental choices of constitutional value are concerned*.[36]

[31] The other Articles of the Constitution allegedly violated were 114, 138 and 139. Concerning Art. 5 as a limit to the amending power, see Modugno (2014), on the interpretation of the scope of the principle of unity, and Pistorio (2015).

[32] On this point, see judgments n. 106/2002; n. 306/2002 and n. 365/2007 of the Constitutional Court.

[33] The Court stated, in fact, that "The unity of the Republic is an aspect of constitutional law that is so essential as to be protected even against the power of constitutional amendment" (see judgment n. 1146/1988 on the doctrine of the limits to the amending power beyond the explicit limit of the "republican form of state", Art. 139).

[34] That is why the referenda actually held in 2017 were consultative and represented an optional addition to the procedure. See Lauro (2017).

[35] In this respect, great relevance is given to the text of the law, because the Court refers to the wording of the question that repeats *verbatim* the expression used in Art. 116.3 of the Constitution. The Court stated that in spite of the fact that it was "the case that the question does not specify the areas in which the regional autonomy regarding which the electorate is to be consulted is planned to be expanded". This position shall be contrasted with previous case law, for instance, with judgments n. 470/1992 and n. 496/2000.

[36] See judgments n. 256/1989, n. 470/1992 and n. 496/2000 of the Constitutional Court. For such choices the electorate cannot be split and the decision has to be taken by its entirety.

The referendum which was held on the 22nd of October 2017 in Veneto (and in Lombardy, on the same date)[37] had the content allowed by the Constitutional Court. In Veneto, more than half the electorate exercised their right to vote and the quorum was met. Almost all votes were supporting the achievement of increased autonomy. The day after, the regional executive instituted the so-called *Consulta del Veneto per l'Autonomia* as a permanent body in support of the appointed negotiating team and submitted to the regional parliament a bill, which was supposed to become the basis for the future agreement with the State (bill n. 43/2017, transmitted to the Prime Minister).

In the case of Lombardy as well, the claims for increased autonomy were not a novelty. In 2000, the regional parliament had already passed a proposal for a consultative referendum aiming at obtaining from the State the transfer of functions concerning health, education and local police. In judgement n. 102/2001, the Constitutional Court had to decide whether this preliminary initiative was exceeding the regional domain, within a case of a horizontal conflict of attributions between the State and the Region concerned. The Court considered there had been no constitutional infringement, as the proposal was inspired by the pursuit of federal arrangements in administration and management, based on the principle of subsidiarity but in the framework of national unity. Furthermore, this document did not involve fundamental choices of constitutional value. The initiative was not further pursued, as meanwhile the 2001 constitutional amendment was passed, widening the legislative domain of ordinary regions.

Autonomist claims spread in different waves in Lombardy, having in mind the "model of Veneto", as it is proven, for instance, by the *Comitato Lombardo Risoluzione 44* (CoLoR44), an association which intended to enter into a similar process as the one envisaged by the above-mentioned resolution n. 44/2012. The statute of autonomy passed in 2008 (statutory law n. 1/2008, Art. 14.3 let. g) explicitly grants the regional parliament the competence to trigger the mechanism regulated by Art. 116.3 of the Constitution. In 2015, the regional parliament approved the call for a referendum and then amended the regional norms on consultative referenda in order to include the option of electronic voting (law n. 3/2015); that year was particularly important for the Region, because it hosted a World Expo. The date of the vote was then set by the President of the

[37] See Arban (2018); Violini and Dainotti (2017) and Troilo (2019).

Region, Maroni (Northern League), for the 22nd of October, the same as in Veneto.

The question in this case was more complex: "Do you want that Lombardy, in consideration of its specialty, within the framework of national unity, undertakes the institutional initiatives necessary to request the State to assign further forms and particular conditions of autonomy, alongside the corresponding resources, pursuant to and for the effects referred to in Art. 116.3 of the Constitution and with reference to all legislative matters for which this procedure is admitted by Art. 116.3?"

The explicit reference to national unity was meant as a way to keep the due distance from other attempts, like the ones undertaken by Catalonia in Spain, which infringed upon the Constitution. Regional institutions claimed there was a regional "specialty" based on several differentiating structural, social, economic and cultural factors, such as the fiscal balance (the difference between taxes paid by citizens of a Region and the quota that the State gives back to that same Region)[38]; a GDP *pro capite* higher than the European average; the extraordinary national export (1/4 of the total); an excellent health system; the lowest debt *pro capite*; the existence of an efficient public administration at the regional, provincial and municipal level. The outcome of this referendum as well was almost fully in favour of the achievement of increased autonomy, although there was a turnout of less than 40% (no quorum was required by the corresponding law).

Both Regions started negotiations with the national Government, as it is required by the Constitution, and so did Emilia-Romagna, which did not hold a prior referendum (as it is not necessary), but followed the impulse of the President of the Region, after which, on the 3rd of October 2017, the regional parliament passed a resolution.

In the Fall of 2017, the bicameral Committee for Regional Affairs concluded its investigation issuing a final document explaining to what extent the path defined by Art. 116.3 can enrich ordinary autonomy, providing a significant opportunity for the institutional system as a whole, and not only for the individual Region affected. The enhancement of identities, vocations and regional potentials can lead to a virtuous competition among territories, as long as the unity of the Republic and the principle of solidarity are respected.[39]

[38] Regional authorities claimed it was 54 billion per year. In case of a positive vote in the referendum, they would aim to keep at least half of it.

[39] See Document XVII-bis, n. 13, passed on the 6th of February 2018, on the implementation of Art. 116.3 of the Constitution with respect to the recent initiatives of Lombardy, Veneto and Emilia-Romagna.

On the 28th of February 2018, the Government signed three separate "preliminary agreements" defining the general principles, the methodology and a (first) list of legislative matters, with a duration of 10 years, which can be changed in case of factual or legal situations that justify their revision. All preliminary agreements indicate as matters of priority interest for the Regions the protection of the environment and ecosystem; health protection; education; protection of labour; international relations and relations with the European Union (see Pallante 2019).

The general elections of the 4th of March 2018 led to an executive based on a coalition between the League and the Five Star Movement (D'Alimonte 2019), the programme of which referred to differentiated regionalism (Morelli 2018). The three above-mentioned Regions informed the Government of their intention to "expand the list of matters to be transferred" and, in the meantime, other Regions (namely Piedmont, Liguria, Tuscany, Umbria, Marche and Campania) also showed interest for obtaining enhanced forms of autonomy. Further meetings between regional representatives and the corresponding Ministries took place within the framework of the Ministry for Regional Affairs.

The Council of Ministers of the 21st of December 2018 assessed the information of the Minister for Regional Affairs on the implementation of differentiated autonomy requested by Veneto, Lombardy and Emilia-Romagna. In the subsequent meeting of the Council of Ministers of the 14th of February 2019, the Minister for Regional Affairs illustrated the contents of the agreements. The procedure has gone forward also with the new Government based on the coalition between the Five Star Movement and the Democratic Party (September 2019). In fact, the document for the update of the so-called DEF (*Documento di Economia e Finanza*) 2019 confirmed the commitment of the Government for the implementation of differentiated regionalism, in the full respect of the principles of national cohesion and solidarity, and for the definition of the basic levels of protection of civil and social rights, in order to prevent a deterioration of the North/South divide. The Committee for Regional Affairs is still assessing the implementation and, exclusively as far as financial autonomy is concerned, the parliamentary Committee for Fiscal Federalism is holding hearings as well.[40]

[40] Updated information can be found here: https://www.camera.it/temiap/documentazione/temi/pdf/1104705.pdf.

4 Conclusion

The unravelling of Italian regionalism, with its periodical accelerations and sudden decelerations, as well as the emergence of autonomist or even secessionist claims, shows the feature of the aforementioned "lack of stability" connected to territorial decentralisation, which depended over time on distinct and overlapping historical, cultural, economic, political and also contextual factors (e.g., the financial crisis).

The contemporary debate on regionalism is again focused on differentiation, but in a novel meaning. Italy has always had an asymmetrical model of decentralisation, based on the dichotomy special/ordinary Regions (Palermo 2018). Nevertheless, in the past years the claim for higher autonomy has arisen within ordinary Regions, that is, independently of cultural, linguistic, geographical factors that were at the core of the dual system chosen by the founding fathers. Lombardy, Veneto and Emilia-Romagna are among the territories with a strongest economic and industrial sector and their claims are grounded on few major targets: a (potentially) better performance of decentralised regulation and public measures tailored on the specific socio-economic contexts; the reinforcement of the already excellent standards of several areas, such as technological and scientific research; the further enhancement of the (already outstanding) supply of public services.

This renewed debate on differentiated regionalism in Italy[41] poses again the question of the "sustainability" (Ragone 2013) or balance (Toniatti 2017) of such differentiation, especially in terms of social cohesion and perpetuation of the above-mentioned North/South divide. In particular, the issue of inter-territorial solidarity becomes paramount to elaborate the response to the demands of more autonomy (Guerra 2019). Art. 116.3 itself refers to the principles set in Art. 119 as guiding standards: among them, revenue and expenditure autonomy; national coordination of public finances and the tax system; the need for a compensation fund for the territories with a lower *pro capite* taxable capacity, as well as the promotion of economic development, social cohesion and solidarity and the reduction of economic and social imbalances. Of course, how these principles will

[41] On which, see at least the recent volumes by Pastore (2019b) and Villone (2019). The issue of homogeneity is addressed by Rolla (2019). Also, financial aspects and the impact of specific sectors are analysed by the contributions included in Lucarelli and Patroni Griffi (2019).

play out in practice depends on the concrete content of the agreements between the State and the interested Regions.

Additionally, Art. 116.3, as it was already mentioned, establishes that a State law regulates the differentiated forms of autonomy "on the basis" of the agreement previously reached between the Government and the affected Region. The actual margin of manoeuvre enjoyed by the Chambers when drafting the corresponding law is still debated by scholars and politicians, whose opinions span from the need for complete adherence to the text of the agreement to a discrete potential deviation. It will probably take the approval of the first laws of this kind (and a judicial intervention) to respond to the question.

A final element for reflection is the existence and, in such case, the recognition, of specific "regional identities" which would justify the access to different levels of autonomy.[42] The question of whether objective indicators (as much as they can be) could be relied upon or even whether a classification of the Regions would be desirable is on the table. The tension between disintegration and integration is still present, and only future developments will allow the observers to understand to what extent differentiating policies will lead to a better arrangement for the advancement and endurance of Italian regionalism.

References

Anzon, A. (2008). *I poteri delle Regioni. Lo sviluppo attuale del secondo regionalismo*. Turin: Giappichelli.

Arban, E. (2018). The Referenda for More Autonomy in Veneto and Lombardia: Constitutional and Comparative Perspectives. *Perspectives on Federalism, 10*(1), 242–267.

Azzariti, G. (2006). Dopo il referendum del 25–26 giugno: le prospettive del Titolo V. *Diritto pubblico, 12*(2), 585–606.

Baldini, G., & Baldi, B. (2014). Decentralization in Italy and the Troubles of Federalization. *Regional and Federal Studies, 24*(1), 87–108.

Bartole, S., & Vandelli, L. (Eds.). (1980). *Le Regioni nella giurisprudenza. Corte Costituzionale, giurisdizione ordinaria, giurisdizione speciale*. Bologna: il Mulino.

Bartole, S., et al. (Eds.). (1988). *Regioni e Corte costituzionale: l'esperienza degli ultimi 15 anni*. Milan: FrancoAngeli.

[42] From a comparative perspective, see Carboni (2019) and Blanco Valdés and Ferraro (2018).

Bassanini, F. (1970). *L'attuazione delle Regioni*. Firenze: Nuova Italia.
Belletti, M. (2012). *Percorsi di ricentralizzazione del regionalismo italiano nella giurisprudenza costituzionale. Tra tutela di valori fondamentali, esigenze strategiche e di coordinamento della finanza pubblica*. Roma: Aracne.
Berti, G. (1975). Art. 5. In G. Branca (Dir.), *Commentario della Costituzione. Principi fondamentali, Art. 1–12 Costituzione* (pp. 277–295). Bologna: Zanichelli.
Bifulco, R. (2006a). Art. 5. In Id. et al. (Ed.), *Commentario alla Costituzione*. Turin: UTET.
Bifulco, R. (Ed.). (2006b). *Gli statuti di seconda generazione*. Turin: Giappichelli.
Bin, R. (2008). "Regionalismo differenziato" e utilizzazione dell'art. 116, terzo comma, Cost. Alcune tesi per aprire il dibattito. *Istituzioni del federalismo, 29*(1), 9–20.
Blanco Valdés, R. L., & Ferraro, L. (Eds.). (2018). Europa, federalismo, diversità, asimmetrie. *Rassegna di Diritto Pubblico Europeo*, (special issue), 2.
Cammelli, M. (2014). *Regioni e regionalismo 1948–2013*. Naples: Editoriale scientifica.
Caravita, B. (2002). *La Costituzione dopo la riforma del titolo V. Stato, Regioni e autonomie fra Repubblica e Unione europea*. Turin: Giappichelli.
Carboni, G. G. (2019). *Il regionalismo identitario: recenti tendenze dello Stato regionale in Spagna, Italia e Regno Unito*. Padua: CEDAM.
Carli, M., et al. (Eds.). (2006). *I nuovi statuti delle regioni ordinarie. Problemi e prospettive*. Bologna: il Mulino.
Carnevale, P. (2015). Unità della Repubblica ed unità del diritto oggettivo. Notazioni introduttive sulla Costituzione come fattore unitario nelle dinamiche della produzione normativa. *federalismi.it, 1*, 1–11.
Catelani, E., & Cheli, E. (Eds.). (2008). *I principi negli statuti regionali*. Bologna: il Mulino.
Cavino, M., et al. (2017). *La riforma respinta (2014–2016): riflessioni sul D.D.L. costituzionale Renzi-Boschi*. Bologna: il Mulino.
Cerrina Feroni, G., & Tarli Barbieri, G. (Eds.). (2016). *Le Regioni dalla Costituente al nuovo Senato della Repubblica*. Naples: ESI.
Conte, F. (2015). *I referendum del Veneto per l'autonomia (e l'indipendenza). Non c'è due senza tre. Anche se.... Forum di Quaderni Costituzionali*. http://www.forumcostituzionale.it/. Accessed 20 December 2020.
Costanzo, P., et al. (Eds.). (1998). *La Commissione bicamerale per le riforme costituzionali. I progetti, i lavori, i testi approvati*. Padua: CEDAM.
Crisafulli, V. (1963). *Le Regioni davanti alla Corte costituzionale*. Milan: Giuffrè.
Cuocolo, F. (1997). *Bicamerale: atto primo. Il progetto di revisione costituzionale*. Milan: Giuffrè.
D'Alessandro, G. (2008). *I nuovi statuti delle regioni ordinarie*. Padua: CEDAM.

D'Alimonte, R. (2019). How the Populists Won in Italy. *Journal of Democracy, 30*(1), 114–127.

D'Atena, A. (2014). Between Spain and Germany: The Historical Models of Italian Regionalism. In S. Mangiameli (Ed.), *Italian Regionalism: Between Unitary Traditions and Federal Processes* (pp. 67–80). Cham: Springer.

Di Giacomo Russo, B., & Tarzia, A. (Eds.). (2016). *Contenuti della riforma costituzionale: luci ed ombre della revisione costituzionale Renzi-Boschi*. Naples: Editoriale scientifica.

Ferrara, A. (Ed.). (2001). *Verso una fase costituente delle Regioni?* Milan: Giuffrè.

Fusaro, C. (2001). La forma di governo regionale. In T. Groppi & M. Olivetti (Eds.), *La Repubblica delle autonomie. Regioni ed enti locali nel nuovo titolo V*. Turin: Giappichelli.

Gardini, G. (2015). Crisi e nuove forme di governo territoriale. *Istituzioni del federalismo, 3*, 533–567.

Gavara de Cara, J. C. (Ed.). (2010). *Los derechos como principios objetivos en los Estados compuestos*. Barcelona: Bosch.

Guerra, M. C. (2019). Autonomia regionale differenziata: verso la «secessione dei ricchi»? *Le Regioni, 47*(2), 413–444.

Lagravinese, R. (2015). Economic Crisis and Rising Gaps North–South: Evidence from the Italian Regions. *Cambridge Journal of Regions, Economy and Society, 8*(2), 331–342.

Lauro, A. (2017). *Tamquam non essent: riflessioni a margine dei referendum lombardo-veneti del 22 ottobre 2017. Forum di Quaderni Costituzionali*. http://www.forumcostituzionale.it/. Accessed 20 December 2020.

Louvin, R. (Ed.). (2019). *Autonomie(s) en mouvement: l'evoluzione delle autonomie regionali speciali*. Naples: ESI.

Lucarelli, A., & Patroni Griffi, A. (Eds.). (2019). Regionalismo differenziato o trasformazione della forma di Stato? *Diritto pubblico europeo – Rassegna on line*.

Lucarelli, A., & Zammartino, F. (Eds.). (2016). *La riforma costituzionale Renzi-Boschi: quali scenari?* Turin: Giappichelli.

Luciani, M. (1997). Unità nazionale e principio autonomistico alle origini della Costituzione. In C. Franceschini et al. (Eds.), *Le idee costituzionali della Resistenza*. Roma: Presidenza del Consiglio dei Ministri.

Mangiameli, S. (2002). *La riforma del regionalismo italiano*. Turin: Giappichelli.

Mangiameli, S. (2011). *Letture sul regionalismo italiano. Il titolo V tra attuazione e riforma della riforma*. Turin: Giappichelli.

Mangiameli, S. (Ed.). (2012). *Il regionalismo italiano tra tradizioni unitarie e processi di federalismo: contributo allo studio della crisi della forma di Stato in Italia*. Milan: Giuffrè.

Mangiameli, S. (2014). The Regions and the Reforms: Issues Resolved and Problems Pending. In Id. (Ed.), *Italian Regionalism: Between Unitary Traditions and Federal Processes* (pp. 1–34). Cham: Springer.

Marini, F. S., & Scaccia, G. (Eds.). (2016). *Commentario alla riforma costituzionale del 2016*. Naples: ESI.

Mezzanotte, M. (2014). *La legge di stabilità 2014 e l'art. 116, comma 3, Cost. Forum di Quaderni costituzionali*. http://www.forumcostituzionale.it/. Accessed 20 December 2020.

Modugno, F. (2014). Unità e indivisibilità della Repubblica come principio. In P. Bianchi & C. Latini (Eds.), *Costruire l'Italia. Dimensione storica e percorsi giuridici del principio di unità*. Naples: ESI.

Morelli, A. (2018). Le autonomie della Repubblica: c'è un ordine nel caos? *dirittiregionali.it, 2*, 1–11.

Morelli, A., & Moschella, G. (Eds.). (2016). *Forma di governo, bicameralismo e sistema delle autonomie nella riforma costituzionale*. Naples: Editoriale scientifica.

Mortati, C. (1947). La Regione nell'ordinamento costituzionale italiano. *Studium, 43*(10), 331–340.

Olivetti, M. (2002). *Nuovi statuti e forma di governo delle Regioni: verso le Costituzioni regionali?* Bologna: il Mulino.

Palermo, F. (2018). Lo stato delle asimmetrie regionali in chiave comparata. Miti, realtà e qualche chiave di lettura. In R. L. Blanco Valdés & L. Ferraro (Eds.), *Europa, federalismo, diversità, asimmetrie. Rassegna di Diritto Pubblico Europeo* (Vol. 2, pp. 291–316).

Pallante, F. (2019). Nel merito del regionalismo differenziato: quali «ulteriori forme e condizioni particolari di autonomia» per Veneto, Lombardia ed Emilia Romagna? *federalismi.it, 6*, 1–35.

Pastore, F. (2019a). Brevi considerazioni su unità e indivisibilità della Repubblica italiana. *Dirittifondamentali.it*, 1–21.

Pastore, F. (Ed.). (2019b). *Il regionalismo differenziato*. Padua: CEDAM.

Pedrazza Gorlero, M. (1979). *Regioni storiche e regionalismo politico nelle scelte dell'Assemblea costituente*. Padua: CEDAM.

Pegoraro, L., & Rinella, A. (2017). *Sistemi costituzionali comparati*. Turin: Giappichelli.

Pinelli, C. (2006). The 1948 Italian Constitution and the 2006 Referendum: Food for Thought. *European Constitutional Law Review, 2*(3), 329–340.

Pistorio, G. (2015). Unità ed indivisibilità nella giurisprudenza costituzionale. *federalismi.it, 1*, 1–18.

Ragone, S. (2007). Gli statuti regionali tra contenuti necessari e contenuti eventuali (con particolare riguardo alle problematiche della definizione della forma di governo e delle norme programmatiche). In E. Rossi (Ed.), *Le fonti del diritto nei nuovi statuti regionali* (pp. 63–99). Padua: CEDAM.

Ragone, S. (2013). "Sustainable Differentiation": The 21st Century Challenge to Decentralization (a Comparative Study of Italy and Spain, with Special Attention to Constitutional Case Law). In A. López Basaguren & L. Escajedo

(Eds.), *The Ways of Federalism in Western Countries and the Horizons of Territorial Autonomy in Spain* (pp. 191–199). Berlin-Heidelberg: Springer.

Rolla, G. (2019). L'evoluzione dello Stato regionale in Italia: tra crisi del regionalismo omogeneo e aspirazioni a un'autonomia asimmetrica dei territori. *Le Regioni, 47*(1), 141–184.

Ronchetti, L. (2014). The Judicial Construction of Italian Regionalism. In S. Mangiameli (Ed.), *Italian Regionalism: Between Unitary Traditions and Federal Processes* (pp. 379–404). Cham: Springer.

Ronchetti, L. (2018). *L'autonomia e le sue esigenze*. Milan: Giuffrè.

Rotelli, E. (Ed.). (1973). *Dal regionalismo alla regione*. Bologna: il Mulino.

Rozo Acuña, E. (Ed.). (2003). *Lo Stato e le autonomie. Le Regioni nel nuovo titolo V della Costituzione: l'esperienza italiana a confronto con altri paesi*. Turin: Giappichelli.

Serges, G. (2015). Autodeterminazione, diritto a decidere, indipendenza, sovranità (notazioni a margine della Legge regionale del Veneto, n. 16 del 2014). *federalismi.it, 1*, 1–16.

Tega, D. (2015). Venice Is Not Barcelona: A Less Aggressive Regional Question Gets a More Nuanced Constitutional Answer. *Iconnectblog*. http://www.iconnectblog.com/. Accessed 20 December 2020.

Toniatti, R. (2017). L'autonomia regionale ponderata: aspettative ed incognite di un incremento delle asimmetrie quale possibile premessa per una nuova stagione del regionalismo italiano. *Le Regioni, 45*(4), 635–666.

Troilo, S. (2019). Patto costituente e referendum consultivo regionale nell'ordinamento italiano. *Revista General de Derecho Constitucional, 29*, 1–18.

Villone, M. (2019). *Italia, divisa e diseguale: regionalismo differenziato o secessione occulta?* Naples: Editoriale scientifica.

Violini, L. (2007). Le proposte di attuazione dell'art. 116, III comma. *Le Regioni, 35*(2), 199–208.

Violini, L., & Dainotti, L. (2017). I referendum del 22 ottobre: una nuova tappa del percorso regionale verso un incremento dell'autonomia. *Le Regioni, 45*(4), 711–726.

Zorzi Giustiniani, A. (2003). Potestà statutaria e forma di governo regionale dopo la riforma del titolo V della Costituzione. *Studi parlamentari e di politica costituzionale, 140–141*, 45–66.

CHAPTER 11

The Catalan Secessionists' Challenge: Reconciling Their Quest for Independence and Constitutionalism

Joan Solanes Mullor

1 Introduction

The Catalan secessionist crisis represents the most serious threat to the Spanish constitutional order since Franco's dictatorship ended.[1] The crisis began in 2006 with the reform of the Catalan Statute of Autonomy—the highest ranking law in Catalonia as an Autonomous Community, second only to the Spanish Constitution—and exploded after the Spanish Constitutional Court found some parts of the above-mentioned statutory reform unconstitutional in 2010.[2] The crisis therefore involves two phases

[1] For an overview of the Catalan secession crisis, see Ferreres Comella (2017).

[2] Aversion to the reform of the Catalan Statute of Autonomy of 2006 is commonly considered the starting point of the secession crisis. The crisis intensified after the Spanish Constitutional Court invalidated parts of the reform in 2010 (see Spanish Constitutional Court judgment n° 31/2010, of 28 June).

J. Solanes Mullor (✉)
Department of Law, Pompeu Fabra University, Barcelona, Spain
e-mail: joan.solanes@upf.edu

M. Belov (ed.), *Territorial Politics and Secession*, Federalism and Internal Conflicts, https://doi.org/10.1007/978-3-030-64402-4_11

that are distinguished by the predominance of two different sentiments: uncertainty and contestation.

Indeed, the period from 2006 to 2010 was one of negotiation in which both the central Spanish and the regional Catalan governments attempted to implement the new reform at the same time that the reform itself was being challenged as unconstitutional before the Spanish Constitutional Court. The reform of the Catalan Statute of Autonomy opened the path to the implementation of new competences and principles. It was the result of a transversal transaction between the Spanish Socialist Party, which controlled the central government at the time, and a plurality of Catalan political forces led by the Socialist Party in the regional government of Catalonia.[3] Perhaps because of this conjunction, 2006–2010 saw vivid engagement between the central and the Catalan governments. However, the ongoing review of the reform by the Spanish Constitutional Court, which entered the scenario after the reform's constitutionality was challenged by the Spanish conservative party, posed a constant unknown variable regarding the final scope of the reform during its implementation.

The period from 2010 to the present started after the Constitutional Court's judgement, in which engagement between the regional and central governments and uncertainty over the final impact of the reform gave way to contention. Contestation took the form of political action from the streets—crowds of demonstrators, labour strikes and two unconstitutional "participatory processes" or "referendums" asserting Catalonia's independence from Spain[4]—in addition to unilateral institutional measures taken by the Catalan regional government that encouraged demonstrations and

[3] From the central government, former socialist President José Luis Rodriguez Zapatero (2004–2011) led efforts to pass the reform while the Catalan counterpart was led by the incumbent socialist President of the Catalan regional Government Pascual Maragall Mira in agreement with the Catalan nationalist leader Artur Mas Gavarró, who at the time headed the dominant opposition party in Catalonia.

[4] There have been also several pro-independence participatory processes, for example, the municipal consultations held in 2009–2010, yet the two most important ones, because they were directly carried out by the Catalan regional government, were (i) the so-called participatory process held on 9 November 2014 under Artur Mas Gavarro's government and (ii) the so-called referendum of 1 October 2017 under Carles Puigdemont Casemajó's government.

enacted legislation designed to upend the constitutional order.[5] The economic crisis that unfolded in parallel to the political unrest compounded the drama of these difficult years for Spain's democratic constitutional regime (González Pascual 2014, pp. 116–117).

Catalonia, then, represents one of several secessionist narratives in Western nation. While the Scots in the United Kingdom and the French-speaking regions of Canada may be the most prominent, today several States face secessionist challenges. There are the Bretons in France, the Jura in Switzerland, all of northern Italy; indeed the Catalan secessionist movement is only one among several in Spain and, compared with the Basque independence movement, is far from the most historically acute. In the context of secession articulated through constitutional norms, however, the Catalan experience becomes particularly relevant.

This chapter explores the discourse, the narrative and therefore the language and argumentation of the Catalan secessionist movement. The aim of the chapter is to distil the arguments used by the Catalan secessionists from the perspective of legal thinking and argumentation. We have in mind here Duncan Kennedy's definition of legal thought or legal consciousness, which "refers to the particular form of consciousness that characterizes the legal profession as a social group, at a particular moment. The main peculiarity of this consciousness is that it contains a vast number of legal rules, arguments, and theories, a great deal of information about the institutional workings of the legal process, and the constellation of ideal and goals current in the profession at a given moment" (Duncan Kennedy 2006, p. 27).

Constitutionalism represents, nowadays, the mainstream current in legal thought throughout contemporaneous Western societies (Ackerman 1997, pp. 771–775). Despite the complexity of the forms it takes and the deceptively rosy optimism the term connotes, it underpins the legal architecture through which Western societies currently articulate their politics.

[5] *Inter alia*, because of their importance, the enactment of (i) Law 19/2007, of 6 September, on the referendum of self-determination; (ii) Law 20/2017, of 8 September, on the legal transition and the foundation of the Republic and (iii) the Declaration of Independence of 27 October 2017, a text whose legal standing is uncertain but definitely falls below the rank of legislation, are all relevant.

It is difficult to sum up the core principles, values, arguments and theories—the constellation of ideas in Kennedy's terms—that comprise constitutionalism but, without doubt, among them is the principle of democracy as the golden rule for political decision-making. By golden rule we mean that the "people as a sovereign" makes the decisions subject to limitations by a group of principles and mechanisms that includes, *inter alia*, the rule of law, the separation of powers doctrine and fundamental rights (Bellamy and Castiglione 1997, pp. 597–603). Simply stated, constitutionalism is currently understood as limited majority-rule government, that is, a democratic government subject to limits.

This chapter analyses the discourse of Catalan secessionists under this framework because, in the end, they too are constrained, namely, by mainstream legal thought. I will argue that the Catalan secessionist movement cannot avoid constitutionalism, that it needs confront it and that doing so reveals contradictions that undermine the movement's coherence.

The chapter first deconstructs the language of the Catalan secessionist movement to show its anti-constitutionalism vein. Distilling secessionist arguments into three types—or prongs—Part II of the chapter exposes how the secessionist discourse attacks constitutionalism: the first focuses on the "sin" committed at the Spanish Constitution's origin; the second denounces the Spanish Constitution as it operates in practice. The last prong of secessionists' arguments targets constitutionalism as a doctrine.

After this analysis of the movement's discourse, the chapter explores in Part III the tools or mechanisms used by Catalan secessionists to achieve their goals. If their discourse demonstrates a clear anti-constitutionalist construction, the tools used to attain their goals are much more ambiguous. To draw out the ambiguity, I analyse in Part 4 the envisaged post-independence scenario, in which the Catalan secessionist movement seems to turn back to–and embrace—constitutionalism. Finally, I conclude by emphasising the tensions that undermine the coherence of Catalan secessionists' legal argumentation, the tools chosen to reach their goals and the centrality of constitutionalism in their projected future in order to bring out the problems that this inconsistency creates for the movement's perceived legitimacy.

2 An Analysis of Catalan Secessionist Discourse: A Three-Pronged Attack

Prong One: The Problem Goes Back to the 1978 Spanish Constitution's Origin

The Catalan secessionist movement begins with an attack on the origin of the Spanish Constitution itself, that is, the historical moment commonly referred to as the Spanish Transition.[6] This argument focuses its attention on the legitimacy of the process through which the Spanish Constitution was adopted, meaning the problem involves the historical events that combined to produce the text. Constitutionalism as a doctrine is therefore not questioned. The critique identifies an original sin that deprives the entire constitutional system and its operation of legitimacy from the outset. In fact, this critique takes two lines of argumentation, one radical and one which I describe as more moderate.

The radical attack calls into question the official historicism of the Spanish Transition as a whole.[7] The version of this period that is scientifically well-established describes a difficult passage from dictatorship to constitutional democracy.[8] In the context of stark social and political divisions, the Spanish Constitution of 1978 emerged as the expression of a minimal consensus that made it possible to put an end to the long-lasting dictatorship (Ferreres Comella 2013, pp. 12–15).

The radical attack questions this account. It calls for a revaluation to unmask this period's true nature and that of the resulting Constitution. Accordingly, the transition to democracy was not genuine. On the contrary, this account argues that the Franco dictatorship remained in place, only changing, under a false constitutional order, its outward appearance. The decisive influence of the so-called bunker (supporters of the old

[6] This period begins with the death of General Franco in 1975. However, there is debate regarding the end of the period. Some authors puts the end with the first democratic elections in 1977, others with the approval of the Constitution in 1978, still others after the attempted coup d'état in 1981 and finally some historians end the period with the general elections in 1982, which brought the Socialist Party to power. See Ortuño Anaya (2005), p. 22.

[7] For a general perspective of the radical argument in both academic circles and the media, see Pasamar (2018).

[8] For a general approach to the historical events of the Spanish Transition, see Carr and Fusi Aizpurua (1981).

regime) and the Spanish military are held up as proof of the dictatorship's continuation.[9] While the mainstream historicism has defined the Spanish Transition in terms of "negotiation" among a plurality of actors—that includes the factions of the dictatorship (Ferreres Comella 2013, pp. 8–12)—the radicals reject this account of a "negotiated path", understanding instead the new constitutional order as a continuation in power of the old regime (Gallego 2008). In conclusion, this attack calls for a review of the official historicism and is conceptualised as an effort of historical revision regarding the origins of the Spanish Constitution.

The moderate attack, however, does recognise the value of the Spanish Transition. It admits that the transition was a difficult period marked by social division, as is generally acknowledged, that the negotiation and the minimal agreement reached were carried out in good faith and that the Catalan nationalists actively participated in it.[10] In sum, the moderates argue that it produced an initial agreement to activate democracy, but not one desired by Catalans who harboured national aspirations. In other words, they see it as a circumstantial or temporal agreement open to subsequent revision. The 1978 Spanish Constitution and its treatment of Catalan aspirations represented a starting point and the calls for greater autonomy that continue to this day—which include as a cornerstone the 2006 reform of the Catalan Statute of Autonomy—are expressions of this moderate critique (Roig Molés 2006, pp. 153–161).

In any event, radicals and moderates coincide in focusing their critiques on the Spanish Constitution of 1978. They do not, at this stage, criticise constitutionalism so the attack can be understood as a specific critique of the creation, whether wholly illegitimate or simply unsatisfactory, of a concrete constitutional text. Either critique, be it calling for of the adoption of a truly European constitutional text without the legacy and illegitimate influences of the dictatorship or merely revising an initial, valid and yet insufficient original constitutional agreement, is compatible with the dictates of constitutionalism. This first attack centres on an understanding of history and the complexities of the constituent period, but not on the principles, values or constitutional imaginaries.

[9] As an example of this line of argumentation, see Casals Meseguer (2016).

[10] For a general account of the participation of the Catalan nationalism in the Spanish Transition, the elaboration of the Spanish Constitution of 1978 and the enactment of the first Catalan Statute of Autonomy of 1979, see Ysàs (1994).

Prong Two: The Problem Is the Spanish Constitution of 1978 in Practice

The second type of argument used by the Catalan secessionists relates to the practical application of the 1978 Spanish Constitution. This critique is independent of the charge of "original sin" described above. Regardless the Constitution's elaboration or its foundational context, examination of the constitutional practice would reveal, according to this critique, a failure to uphold constitutional values and institutions. This is a more powerful critique, if it is true, because it sets its sights on current shortcomings of the Spanish constitutional system.

The "original sin" argument targets past events and is much more academic, occurring mainly between historians. However, the discussion of defects of the current status of the Spanish constitutional system brings in a wide array of political actors and the media, and accordingly has larger repercussions in society. This critique points out both the breakdown of values and of institutions in the system. The values at stake are no less than the principle of democracy, fundamental rights and the separation of powers doctrine. Because it directly calls into question the role of the judiciary and the political autonomy extended to Catalonia, this critique involves respect for the very notion of self-government.

The first charge in this attack is that the practical application of the Constitution of Spain violates the principle of democracy. I will deal with this argument below when examining the dichotomy between radical democracy and constitutionalism, but for now it suffices to say that the Catalan secessionists argue that the Constitution recognises some right to self-determination or, in other words, that a referendum of self-determination is possible under the Spanish Constitution of 1978.[11] Some constitutionalists have indeed argued in favour of the constitutionality of a referendum of self-determination (De Carreras 2014; Tornos Mas 2014; Aguado Renedo 2013; Rubio Llorente 2013), but the Constitutional Court's interpretation of the Constitution has denied it.

The High Court stated that, under the current constitutional system which situates sovereignty with the Spanish population as a whole, a referendum of self-determination for one part of the territory is not

[11] See National Transition Advisory Council of the Generalitat de Catalunya, Report n°1 of 25 July 2013, *La consulta sobre el futuro politico de Cataluña*.

admissible.[12] However, the Spanish Constitutional Court has also declared that the constitutional system allows one part of the territory to pursue the independence through constitutional amendment.[13] This represents the second breakdown of the principle of democracy for the Catalan secessionists: while recourse to constitutional amendment is allowed, the rigidity of the Constitution in terms of the difficulty of amendment due to the complexity of the process makes this path unviable.[14]

Another recurrent argument in the Catalan secessionists' imaginary is that the State's conduct violates fundamental rights. This argument emphasises the right to freedom of expression of those in favour of an independent Catalonia.[15] Secessionists insist that they are victims of political and judicial persecution for their beliefs, in breach of their fundamental right of freedom of expression.[16] This claim primarily targets the judiciary and criminal procedures initiated against certain secessionist leaders. They consider both the trial itself and the final convictions as a violation of the freedoms of expression and demonstration because they punish beliefs and political ideas rather than acts (Elbal 2019). If their claims are valid, such State behaviour would reinforce their claim that Spain's democracy has broken down precisely because freedom of expression and demonstration are essential political rights for a genuine democracy.

Moreover, Catalan secessionists denounce a failure of the State to respect the separation of powers doctrine in practice, as demonstrated by a perverse politicisation of all State institutions against the pro-independence movement. The bias of the Spanish Constitutional Court

[12] Spanish Constitutional Court judgment n° 114/2017, of 17 October, para. 2.b. Previously, in relation to the Basque Country, the Constitutional Court also decided in the same line (judgment n° 103/2008, of 11 September, para. 4).

[13] Spanish Constitutional Court judgment n° 42/2014, of 25 March (paras. 3.b and 4).

[14] EFE-Barcelona. (2015). Mas ve inviable hacer una propuesta de reforma constitucional desde Cataluña. *EcoDiario.es.* https://ecodiario.eleconomista.es/politica-eD/noticias/7204202/12/15/Mas-ve-inviable-hacer-una-propuesta-de-reforma-constitucional-desde-Cataluna.html. Accessed 16 February 2020.

[15] See the preamble of Law n° 19/2017, of 6 September, on the self-determination referendum, which was declared unconstitutional by the Spanish Constitutional Court (judgment 224/2017, of 17 October). The preamble contains several references to freedom of expression as grounds for the self-determination and holding a referendum. See also Edling and Melia (2019).

[16] See, *inter alia*, the Declaration of Independence of 27 October 2017, which reports the alleged existence of a prosecution in breach of the civil and political fundamental rights of Catalan citizens. See also Jones (2019).

(Sala 2013), the lack of independence of the Public Prosecution Service,[17] the politicisation of the General Council of the Judiciary and, by consequence, the politicisation of the nomination of the judges of the Supreme and National High Courts—the courts that hear the criminal cases against the movement's leaders (Urías 2020)—are some examples drawn to support the claim. In the end, the argument asserts that the principle of democracy and fundamental rights are compromised by the failure to respect the separation of powers when the institutions charged with protecting them are controlled by political adversaries.

These violations of constitutional values stem from institutional breakdowns in the eyes of the secessionists. First, because the judiciary and the judicial proceedings involving pro-independence leaders lack impartiality (Solanes Mullor 2019, pp. 580–583). The political capture of the judiciary by the opposing faction diminishes the trust in the judiciary and leads to a conflict of interest. Not only is impartiality lacking, but the independence of the judiciary is also thrown in doubt when the Spanish Government is seen as using the judiciary and the Spanish Constitutional Court to quash the Catalan secessionist movement (Solanes Mullor 2019, pp. 580–583). In the end, the judiciary and the Constitutional Court are caught in the crossfire between one faction that sees them as the appropriate institution to solve a constitutional crisis because of their independence and impartiality and the other faction that considers the courts an inappropriate institutional solution precisely because they lack those attributes.

Lastly, the autonomy of the Catalonia's self-governing institutions is also at stake. The secessionist movement has argued that, during the constitutional crisis, the autonomy of the Catalan regional institutions has severely deteriorated, especially following the measures taken under Article 155 of the Spanish Constitution (Bernardí Gil 2019, pp. 41–43).[18] The judicial proceedings against the former President of the Generalitat de Catalunya, Joaquim Torra Pla, have also been conceived as an attack

[17] ACN (2019). Spanish president boasts of controlling public prosecutor in bid to extradite Puigdemont. *Catalannews*. https://www.catalannews.com/politics/item/spanish-president-boasts-of-controlling-public-prosecutor-in-bid-to-extradite-puigdemont. Accessed 16 February 2020.

[18] Under Article 155 of the Spanish Constitution, the central government dismissed all the members of the Catalan regional government and then took the control, until the regional elections, of the Catalan regional government and its administration.

against the Catalan institutions.[19] In sum, the secessionists argue that the current model of territorial organisation is not only insufficient, but also that it has worsened during the constitutional crisis.

Prong Three: Striking at Constitutionalism Itself

The secessionist argumentation, so far, has been local in scope, that is, its critique is against the origin and practice of constitutionalism in Spain. Constitutionalism, as a doctrine comprising certain values and principles, remains untouched. It even seems that the Catalan secessionists, in criticising the way that constitutionalism is applied in Spain, implicitly endorse constitutionalism as a set of values and principles.

There are, however, two lines of argumentation that go in a different direction and put constitutionalism as a doctrine under the spotlight. I will distinguish this type of criticism in two different arguments: the classical international law critique (invoking the right to self-determination) and a less familiar, so-called right to decide (an argument very much the Catalan secessionist's own).

The classical international law account argues that Catalonia, conceived as a nation with its own culture, language and historical roots, possesses the right to self-determination.[20] Catalan secessionists defend their right to self-determination as established by international law because the Catalan case demonstrates all the applicable criteria (Costa 2017, pp. 1–5). In the secessionist imaginary, Catalonia represents a collective national group that is subject to oppression by a State. This oppression is in breach of, in particular, the internal version of the right to self-determination; that is, while Catalonia is not an overseas colony, it is an entity within the Spanish State that is denied its right to freely express itself as a national group (Costa 2017, p. 1).

In justifying the charge of oppression by the central State that endangers Catalan national survival, the secessionists use a variation of arguments that range from unfair fiscal treatment to the persecution of the

[19] See ACN (2019). Torra to appeal ban from office, attacks Spanish justice system. *ElNacional.cat*. https://www.elnacional.cat/en/news/torra-appeal-ban-from-office-attacks-spanish-justice_453504_102.html. Accessed 16 February 2020. The President of the regional government faces an ongoing judicial proceeding for disobedience to the electoral authorities for not removing a banner in time of electoral campaign.

[20] For a general discussion about Catalonia and the self-determination right from the perspective of international law, see Blanke and Abdelrehim (2014).

Catalan language (Marinzel 2014, pp. 1–32). All such arguments conclude that Catalonia has been deprived of its right to self-expression as a nation and, above all that its right to internal self-determination is in jeopardy (Santjaume Calvet 2016, pp. 82–106).

I will not enter the debate over the veracity of these claims. What matters to me is the anti-constitutionalist nature of this line of critiques. International law and the right established in it to self-determination are deployed to trump constitutionalism. Here again there is no room for doubt that Catalan secessionists are arguing that constitutional principles are not effectively applied in Spain, denying the true expression of the Catalan demos or nation, yet there is an additional component to this line of critique. It does not ultimately question the soundness of constitutional practice in Spain, for neither unfair redistribution of wealth among territories nor the debatable quality of plurilingual education at public schools necessarily call into question the country's constitutional commitment.

The real issue is that international law offers a path to argue against constitutionalism itself along with and its corollaries in Spain. The attack is directed against the supremacy and rigidity of the Constitution. International law is invoked to circumnavigate the Constitution and its amendment mechanism. In other words, international law is used to displace established constitutional limits.

Even the Catalan secessionists realised that the classical international law critique was not truly a winning card (Tudela Aranda 2016, p. 478). They had difficulty framing this State oppression as a violation of the right to self-determination according to international law, either in its external or internal version (Ferreres Comella 2016, pp. 465–466). Thus, the so-called right to decide appeared as a new theoretical characterisation developed by Catalan political scientists.[21] The Catalan Parliament used this concept for the first time in 2012.[22] The "right to decide" has been

[21] For all, see López Hernández (2017). Also, in relation to the debate about the characterization of the "right to decide", see the contributions of the authors in Vv.A.a. (2013) and the collective book Barceló Serramalera (2015).

[22] Resolution 742/IX of the Parliament of Catalonia, on the general political orientation of the Government of Catalonia, of 27 September 2012, subsequently ratified by Resolution 5/X of the Parliament of Catalonia, adopting the Declaration of sovereignty and right to decide of the people of Catalonia, of 23 January 2013. These institutional declarations were reinforced by the so-called *Pacte Nacional pel Dret a Decidir* (National Agreement for the Right to Decide), signed on 26 June 2013 by Catalan secessionist parties and some civil and cultural pro-secessionist associations.

especially successful in political and media arenas, less so in academic debates (Tudela Aranda 2016, p. 479).

Academically, it is difficult to assert what the "right to decide" exactly means and ultimately how to differentiate it from the self-determination right under international law. Scholars have pointed out the ambiguity and the difficulties of this theoretical formulation (Ferreres Comella 2016, pp. 461–462).

Ferreres Comella has pointed out two different ways the "right to decide" might be understood. In a strong version, the right could determine the right of a collective group in a territory to secede from the State (Ferreres Comella 2016, pp. 462–466). It could be justified by democratic or national reasons regardless its basis under international law. In terms of democratic self-government, any group that seeks independence through democratic norms should enjoy the right to decide. In nationalist terms, only the groups that comply with certain national characteristics, such as a common history, culture or language, will enjoy the right. Finally, if the desire for self-governance is grounded in a "good cause", then, here, the "right to decide" converges with international law.

In a soft version, the "right to decide" only grants a right to be heard—to call and hold a referendum—not the right to secede or become independent (Ferreres Comella 2016, pp. 466–469). Again, this soft version is rooted in democratic beliefs, that is, the belief that democracy requires that collective groups have a voice in government, including those pursuing independence.

Setting aside the circumstances in which the "right to decide" coincides with international law, all the other versions approach a radical version of the democratic argument that prevails over the limits that constitutionalism sets on the democratic principle. Radical democrats argue that the principle of democracy should be limit-free or, at least, that these limits must be minimal to protect the integrity of the democratic process itself.[23] The "right to decide" construction follows this argumentation proposing, based on the principle of democracy, setting aside the limits of constitutionalism, especially the constitutional amendment process and, ultimately, the rule of law established by the Constitution. The strong version—whether rooted in democratic or nationalistic grounds—unilaterally calls

[23] For a recent debate over the relationship between democracy and constitutionalism (or between legality and rule of law) applied to the Catalan case, see Tudela Aranda (2016), pp. 478–485.

for independence regardless of the constitutional constraints, while the soft version calls for a referendum, also regardless of the constitutional constraints. In other words, the limits of constitutionalism—whether expressed through the rigid constitutional amendment process or the rule of law which requires respect for the set of rules already in place such as those establishing the competence for calling for a referendum—are invalidated by a superior right rooted in radical democracy.

The combination of the three attacks clearly qualifies the Catalan secessionist discourse as anti-constitutional. First, secessionists criticise the legitimacy of Spanish constitutionalism because of its origin and its operation in practice. Second, and more importantly, secessionists use radically democratic arguments to attack constitutionalism. The combination puts constitutionalism in the centre of the attacks. We must not forget that constitutionalism represents the mainstream legal thought. This is especially important for the popular and street debates in which it is hard for people to understand the clash between the "ought to be" of the Catalan secessionist language and the "is" of the mainstream constitutional notions.

3 The Tools of the Attack: Between Constitutionalism and Against Constitutionalism

The constitutional crisis, however, was not been set off by the language used by secessionists. Specific actions accompanying the discourse led to the clash with the Spanish constitutional structures. Behind these acts, effort was made to navigate a delicate line between changing the current constitutional order while showing respect for it and disrupting it through disobedience.

I will define the former as constitutional (pre-unilateral) actions and the latter as anti-constitutional (unilateral) actions. I use the same terminology in these definitions that is predominant in the Catalan secessionist debate, that is, the distinguishing between advocates of dialogue (who shunned unilateral, preferring independence reached through negotiation and agreement with the central institutions, hence, within the constitutional order) and calls for unilateral action (carried out in the belief that independence would be attained without the consent of the central institutions, i.e., through action that would breach the Spanish constitutional order).

Catalan secessionists have attempted, since 2006, a variation of constitutional actions to achieve their goals. The pre-unilateralism phase may be characterised as a set of measures that fall within the constitutional order, meant to achieve territorial independence gradually through incremental gains in the level of self-government. The most vivid image of a constitutional action in this phase was the invocation of fundamental rights recognised in the constitutional order. Examples are the exercise of the right to demonstration, freedom of expression and the exercise of freedom of association and political action seeking territorial independence.[24]

Secessionists went to the streets with crowed demonstrations as well as to the press and media in order to spread their ideas. Eventually they sought recourse in all the political channels—both in the autonomous regional government institutions and in central institutions—to promote their position.

The Spanish constitutional order allowed this course of action—especially the Constitutional Court, which has upheld the constitutionality of such efforts by a political party to seek the independence of the territory.[25] The Spanish constitutional order, the Court declared, is not a militant democracy and therefore opposition to the order can be legitimate when it is expressed through political rights and without violence.[26]

Such pre-unilateral action did not end with the exercise of fundamental rights within the constitutional order. Secessionists have also made other moves within the institutional system that also qualify as constitutional. The reform of the Catalan Statute of Autonomy of 2006, which followed all the relevant constitutional procedures, could be considered the first embryonic attempt.[27] During this interaction between the central-regional levels, most of the secessionist political movements participated in central elections and, therefore, have been represented or at least present in the

[24] Demonstrations have been held on Catalonia's national holiday (11 September) every year since 2010. Catalan political secessionist leaders, but also social and cultural leaders, have defended their ideas in all the media channels, from the classical press to the TV and social networks. Finally, Catalan secessionist political parties have been represented in Catalan and central institutions where they have wielded political power, especially at the local and regional levels of government.

[25] See Spanish Constitutional judgment n° 42/2014, of 25 March (para. 4.c).

[26] *Ibid.*

[27] See *supra* note n° 3.

central legislative process.[28] There, secessionists launched a range of initiatives, the most important being the request to transfer the competence to call a referendum of self-determination in Catalonia.[29] This behaviour inside central institutions was reinforced at the Catalan institutional level where Catalan institutions, especially the Parliament, have actively launched initiatives in favour of independence, albeit mostly symbolical ones.[30]

Unilateral action, however, represents the fulcrum of the constitutional crisis. This line of action began with the first "participatory process" or "referendum" supported by Artur Mas Gavarró's Catalan Government. The Catalan Parliament passed legislation allowing this participatory process and the Catalan Government issued a decree to implement it.[31] Although the "participatory process" was declared unconstitutional, it was held on 9 November 2014.[32] The Catalan members of the regional Government involved in its organisation, including the President, were found criminally responsible for these actions.[33]

However, the unilateral path increased in intensity with the approval in September 2017 of two laws by the Parliament of Catalonia, one to

[28] Since 2010, there have been five central elections and in all of them most secessionist parties participated. Only one minor faction, the *Candidatura d'Unitat Popular* (CUP), abstained from the four previous general elections. However, in the most recent election in November 2019, the CUP participated for the first time and won two representatives in the *Congreso de los Diputados.*

[29] Article 150.2 of the Spanish Constitution allows for the transfer of State competences, as long as this transfer to an Autonomous Community is made via an organic law (which requires an absolute majority of the Spanish Parliament). On 16 January 2014, the Parliament of Catalonia approved a petition of the transfer to the Spanish Parliament invoking Article 150.2. On 8 April 2014, the Spanish Parliament voted it down.

[30] There are countless initiatives, most of which are symbolic political resolutions that have been approved by the Catalan Parliament. Only as an example and because its relevance, see the Declaration of Sovereignty of 23 January 2013 in which the Parliament called for the exercise of the "right to decide" to begin.

[31] See Law 10/2014, of 26 September 2014, on popular consultation lacking the character of a referendum and other forms of citizen participation, and Decree 192/2014, of 27 September, on the call for a popular consultation about the political future of Catalonia.

[32] First, on 29 September 2014 the Spanish Constitutional Court declared the suspension of both the Law and the Decree (see the Court's decision of 30 September 2014). Despite the suspension, the Catalan Government decided to carry on with the participatory process. After the vote was held, the Spanish Constitutional Court declared some parts of the legislation in question unconstitutional (see Judgment n° 31/2015, of 25 February).

[33] See the Judgment of the Catalonia High Court of 13 March 2017 after ratified by the Spanish Supreme Court in its Judgment n° 722/2018, of 23 January.

organise a "referendum" and the other to restructure the ensuing Catalan republic.[34] That legislation was also declared unconstitutional by the Spanish Constitutional Court.[35] Notwithstanding, Carles Puigdemont Casemajó's Catalan Government held the referendum on 1 October 2017. A pseudo-declaration of independence followed the referendum.[36] For all these actions the Catalan Government's leaders were convicted on criminal charges for which they are serving prison sentences.[37] Moreover, these actions prompted the intervention of the central Government, which invoked Article 155 of the Spanish Constitution to take control of Catalan institutions.[38]

After the change from pre-unilateral to unilateral coordinated strategy, a return to the first phase would seem inviable. However, in general terms,

[34] See *supra* note n° 5.

[35] See Judgments of the Spanish Constitutional Court n° 114/2017, of 17 October, regarding the referendum of self-determination and n° 124/2017, of 8 November, regarding the on the legal transition and the foundation of the Republic.

[36] See *supra* note n° 5.

[37] See Judgment of the Spanish Supreme Court n° 459/2019, of 14 October.

[38] Article 155 reads as follows (translation of the Spanish Constitution provided by the Official Spanish Gazette): "1. If an Autonomous Community does not fulfil the obligations imposed upon it by the Constitution or other laws, or acts in a way seriously prejudicing the general interests of Spain, the Government, after lodging a complaint with the President of the Autonomous Community and failing to receive satisfaction therefore, may, following approval granted by an absolute majority of the Senate, take measures necessary in order to compel the latter forcibly to meet said obligations, or in order to protect the above-mentioned general interests. 2. With a view to implementing the measures provided in the foregoing clause, the Government may issue instructions to all the authorities of the Autonomous Communities".

To activate the measures allowed by recourse to this provision, then President of Spain, Mariano Rajoy Brey, sent a "requirement of compliance" to the President of Catalonia, Carles Puigdemont Casamajó, on 11 October 2017. The requirement of compliance is a written statement which points out the regional government's non-compliance with its constitutional obligations and the prejudice caused to the general interest of Spain. In this case, the Spanish Government asked for clarification regarding the nature and effects of the Declaration of Independence of 27 October 2017 and, specifically, whether the Declaration was legally binding, which, the requirement pointed out, would be a breach of constitutional legality requiring termination of all its effects. Following the ambiguous response of the Catalan regional government, the central government declared that the requirement had not been met because of lack of clarity in the response. Several measures intended to bring Catalan institutions back under control had been authorized on 21 October 2017, and these were subsequently approved by the Senate on 27 October 2017.

this is what happened. Beyond some minor anti-constitutional actions,[39] secessionists are again exercising constitutional actions. Examples are recourse to fundamental rights, especially the right to demonstration[40]; renewed participation in the central elections[41]; participation in regional elections even after they were called by the central Government under Article 155 of the Spanish Constitution[42]; the legal manoeuvring before Spanish judicial institutions, especially in the criminal cases[43]; the use of the international institutions to which Spain is a party such as the European Union or the Council of Europe[44] or participation in recent negotiations with the central Government.[45]

[39] See *supra* note n° 19. Joaquim Torra Pla was criminally convicted in first instance for disobedience for not removing a banner in an official building when elections were being held. See Judgment of the Catalonia High Court n° 149/2019, of 19 December 2019. The Spanish Supreme Court confirmed the conviction by its judgment n° 477/2020, of 28 September 2020.

[40] One example, *inter alia*, are the demonstrations between 14 and 18 October 2019 just after the judgment of Spanish Supreme Court convicting several pro-independence leaders was issued.

[41] See the general elections held in 28 April 2019 and 10 November 2019.

[42] See the Catalan regional elections held in 21 December 2017.

[43] In all the judicial processes closed or opened against pro-independence leaders and other citizens involved in the secessionist crisis, never have the defendants sought to delegitimize the constitutional system by abstaining from deploying any legal recourse—such as the right to defense and to appeal—available under the constitutional system.

[44] All convicted pro-independence leaders, both inside and outside the courtroom, have insisted that they will take their cases all the way to the European Court of Human Rights. See Val (2019). At the same time, the election of some of these leaders to the European Parliament, one of whom, Oriol Junqueres Vies, convicted in Spain and other three residing outside Spain but with pending European Arrest Warrants, Antoni Comín Oliveres, Clara Ponsatí Obiols, Carles Puigdemont Casemajó, have activated the intervention of the Court of Justice of the European Union. In the case of Oriol Junqueres Vies, the Spanish Supreme Court sent a preliminary reference to the Court of Justice which was decided by its judgment in Case C-502/19, of 19 December 2019, criminal proceedings against Oriol Junqueres Vies, ECLI:EU:C:2019:1115. In the case of Antoni Comín Oliveres and Carles Puigdemont Casemajó, at this stage there are pending proceedings before the General Court, which only has rejected the interim measures requested by the pro-independence leaders (Order of the President of the General Court in Case T-388/19 R, of 1 July 2019, Carles Puigdemont Casamajó and Antoni Comín Oliveres v the European Parliament, ECLI:EU:T:2019:467).

[45] Taking part in the negotiations are delegations from both the central and regional governments. See ACN (2020). Negotiation table between Spanish and Catalan government to begin Wednesday, February 26. https://www.catalannews.com/politics/item/negotiation-table-between-spanish-and-catalan-governments-to-begin-wednesday-february-26. Accessed 16 February 2020.

The shifts from a pre-unilateral stance to unilateral provocation and back reveal ambiguity in the course of action of Catalan secessionists. If their language itself mostly appears anti-constitutionalist, the behaviour fluctuated between constitutional and anti-constitutional. There could be several reasons for this ambiguity or hesitation—maybe there is lack of consensus among the movement's leaders; maybe the leaders attempted a new strategy and then abandoned it; maybe they did not expect the Spanish constitutional system to prove as strong as it has. In any case, the causes of this ambiguity are not particularly relevant for this chapter which is primarily concerned with analysing the Catalan secessionists' attitude towards constitutionalism as a legal-political doctrine.

4 The Post-Independence Scenario: A Return to Constitutionalism

The primacy of anti-constitutionalist language of Catalan secessionists and the wavering respect for constitutional principles revealed by their efforts to achieve independence contrast sharply with the strong endorsement of constitutionalism found in the image of the future (independent) Catalan state that they project. This image is primarily distilled from two key documents, the White Paper on the National Transition of Catalonia and Law 20/2017 of 8 September 2017, on the legal transition and the foundation of the Republic, along with a few documents produced during the "constituent process" that the Catalan Parliament has pursued since 2015. All these show that, in the Secessionist imaginary, constitutionalism occupies a central role in the architecture envisioned for the new state.

The White Paper on the National Transition of Catalonia was published by the Catalan Government in 2014 and included the 18 reports issued by the Catalan Advisory Council for the National Transition.[46] On the one hand, the "constituent process" described in Report n° 10 envisages a new state following a constitutional model; there is even a reference to the Spanish constituent process of 1978.[47] The starting point would be a Law enacted by the Catalan Parliament—such as the Political Reform Act of 1977—which would articulate the constituent process.[48] This Law would

[46] This was an advisory body of the Catalan Government, created by Decree 113/2013, of 12 February.

[47] Catalan Advisory Council for the National Transition, Report n° 10, 14 July 2014, p. 20.

[48] *Ibid.* at pp. 19–20.

lead to a constituent election and the elaboration of a constitution would be entrusted to the resulting parliament.[49] Finally, the constitution would be ratified by referendum.[50] The commitment to constitutionalism is easy to grasp, for the governmental advisory body calls for a new constitution and the process of elaboration is described in terms similar to the Spanish constituent process of 1978.

On the other hand, the White Paper does not address the foundations—constitutional or otherwise—of the new state in any detail. This makes sense, because the advisory body is only envisaged as a counsellor during the transition period. The new foundations of the state would be left to the constituent power. However, Report n° 16 describes the switch in legal systems, that is, the transition from the Spanish legal order to a new independent Catalan legal one. In doing so, the rule of law features as a cornerstone principle.[51] Report n° 14 is devoted to the new judicial system and the transition to it from the Spanish judicial system, and here again the commitment to an independent judicial branch in the new state is clear.[52] Therefore, while the White Paper lacks any systematic articulation or analysis of the new foundations of the Catalan state, in addressing the transition the commitment to constitutionalism stands out clearly.

More clues about the foundations of the secessionists' imagined state, however, are found in Law 20/2017 of 8 September 2017, on the legal transition and the foundation of the Republic.[53] It contains some problematic positions from the point of view of constitutionalism, including allowances for executive intervention in the governing body of the judiciary[54] and the lack of a constitutional court,[55] but in general terms the new state it describes fits well with constitutional standards.

[49] *Ibid.* at pp. 20–22.

[50] *Ibid.*

[51] Catalan Advisory Council for the National Transition, Report n° 16, 28 July 2014, pp. 10–14.

[52] Catalan Advisory Council for the National Transition, Report n° 14, 28 July 2014, pp. 6–7.

[53] This Law was declared unconstitutional by the Spanish Constitutional Court in Judgment n° 124/2017, of 8 November 2017.

[54] See Article 70 Law 20/2017. The judicial power would be governed by two bodies: the Government Section of the Supreme Court and a Mixed Commission consisting of an equal number of representatives from the Supreme Court and the Catalan Government.

[55] The idea is substituting a Constitutional Court by two institutions. First, the so-called Council for Democratic Guarantees would exercise *ex-ante* constitutional review of legislation, that is, it would examine proposed legislation before it is passed (Article 61 Law

The principle of democracy as a form of decision-making power is respected by the articulation of a typical parliamentary system in which citizens elect the parliament, without whose support the president, the leader of the executive power, cannot govern.[56] At the same time, typical constitutional limits are established, such as fundamental rights and the separation of powers principle with the judiciary serving as the primary monitoring body.[57] Finally, the Law includes a regulation of the "constituent process" in similar terms as those of the White Paper: participatory process, constituent elections, constituent parliament entrusted to elaborate a constitution and finally ratification by referendum.[58]

The last element of this analysis is the so-called constituent process, a process led by the Catalan Parliament during the XI legislature (2015–2017). It should be recalled that after the failure to launch the constituent process envisaged by first the 2014 White Paper and again by Law 20/2017, a new strategy was adopted through resolutions of the Catalan Parliament (De Miguel Bárcena 2018, pp. 144–149). The starting point was the Catalan Parliament's Resolution 1/XI of 9 November 2015.[59] That body's Resolution 263/XI of 27 July 2016 is more relevant, however, because it ratified the conclusions of the Study Commission of the Constituent Process.[60] Again, the Commission's conclusions outlined a constituent process in terms similar to those of the White Paper and served as a source of inspiration for the subsequent Law 20/2017.

20/2017). Second, a special section in the Supreme Court would be in charge of protecting the fundamental rights established by the Catalan constitution (Article 74 Law 20/2017). Thus, the new constitutional order would lack a mechanism for *ex-post* constitutional review of legislation on grounds other than fundamental rights violations.

[56] See Title IV ("Institutional system") of Law 20/2017.

[57] See Title II ("Rights and duties") and Title V ("Judicial power and its administration") of Law 20/2017.

[58] See Title VII ("Constituent process") of Law 20/2017.

[59] The Resolution was declared unconstitutional by the Spanish Constitutional Court Judgment n° 259/2015, of 2 December.

[60] The Resolution 263/XI was based on Resolution 5/XI, of 20 January 2016, of the Catalan Parliament which created the Study Commission for the Constituent Process. The Spanish Constitutional Court declared that Resolution unconstitutional, therefore the Study Commission was also held incompatible with the Constitution (see Order of the Court n° 141/2016, of 19 July). However, the Study Commission delivered its conclusions regardless, and these were approved by the Parliament in its Resolution 263/XI. The Constitutional Court found the Resolution a direct violation of its previous decisions and directly commanded the Catalan Parliament to obey (Order of the Court 124/2017, of 19 September).

Indeed, the constituent process was to include a preliminary participatory process about which the Resolution provides some details.[61] For instance, it would be led by a "Social Forum" consisting of members of political parties and civil society.[62] This forum would address specific questions about the future constitution. Its conclusions would then be discussed by the population at large, although details about the articulation of this popular discussion were not given.[63]

In any case, the Commission's conclusions clearly establish that the constituent assembly would begin its work with the results of the participatory process.[64] After this participatory process, still on condition that the "disconnection" from the Spanish State was real, the Resolution calls for constituent elections and the conformation of a constituent parliament entrusted with the elaboration of a constitution subject to final ratification by referendum.[65]

In sum, the White Paper, Law 20/2017 and the so-called constituent process launched by the Catalan Parliament all embrace constitutionalism. The constituent process articulated by all of them follows a standard constitutional model and in fact resembles the one undertaken by Spain in 1978.

Therefore, the path chosen to construct the new state—once Catalonia was effectively disconnected from the Spanish State—may be qualified as constitutional. The intention to approve a constitution is ever present and the process for doing so complies with general constitutional standards. At the same time, the foundations of the new state, especially those drawn in Law 20/2017, are in line of constitutional models. Catalan secessionists envision a state not only based on the principle of democracy as a formula for exercising public power, but also one where the democratic decision-making power is limited by fundamental rights, the separation of powers and the rule of law. That is, the new state is based on rule by a limited democratic government, which is fully in line with mainstream constitutional theory.

[61] See paras. 4–11 of Resolution 263/XI.
[62] *Ibid.* at para. 6.
[63] *Ibid.*
[64] *Ibid.*
[65] *Ibid.* at paras. 7–10.

5 Conclusions

The Catalan secessionists' discourse contains clear elements of argumentation that run counter to constitutional principles. The three-pronged attack against constitutionalism represents a cornerstone of it. The message that Spain's constitutional system is defective runs strongly through the language they use in the public discourse, whether because the system failed to truly oust the dictatorship at its outset—the original sin argument—or because it has not been effectively implemented in practice. However, the secessionists' critique is not only local; that is, it does not only pertain to constitutionalism as it operates in Spain. The argumentation also includes elements of radical democracy which clash with pillars of mainstream constitutional theory. All of these critiques put constitutionalism as a doctrine in the crossfire.

Regarding the means or tools the secessionists use in pursuit of their goals, this clear antipathy becomes ambiguous. An impartial observer would expect the anti-constitutional sentiment expressed in the secessionist discourse to be reflected in the political strategy. If secessionists truly believed there was a problem with Spain's constitutional system—or were disillusioned with constitutionalism in favour of some other political model such as radical democracy—one would not expect them to discipline the means employed according to constitutional norms.

The unilateral actions already described are embedded of this logic, that is, they reflect the anti-constitutionalism discourse. However, while unilateralism has prevailed at times, and without doubt brought about the high point of the constitutional crisis, the pre-unilateral strategy initially employed and subsequently readopted has also been operative throughout the crisis. It is not the aim of this paper to explore the causes of these fluctuations, be they genuine, strategic or based on the divisions within the secessionists, but they definitely reflect an ambiguous position towards constitutionalism.

The language used to describe intentions for the post-independence scenario, finally, embraces constitutionalism. When Catalan secessionists imagine their new state and the process to construct it, we find compliance with constitutional standards. The constituent process described in the secessionists' texts resembles the Spanish constituent process of 1978, providing for the approval of a constitution by a constituent assembly and then ratified in referendum. Moreover, the new state is modelled as a parliamentary system based on the principle of democracy and limited by fundamental rights and the rule of law. The complicated path walked by Catalan secessionists ends in a post-independence scenario fundamentally similar to the constitutional model it contests: from anti-constitutionalism discourse that is accompanied by a mix of constitutional and anti-constitutional actions to the projection of a new constitutional state.

Declaring the inconsistency of the Catalan secessionist movement may be too hasty. Its fluctuation seems contradictory with the anti-constitutionalism language, the ambiguous position between respect for and rejection of constitutional norms in the means employed to attain the movement's goals and, finally, the final return to a constitutional model when imagining the future state.

Yet more nuance is necessary. The Catalan secessionist movement is not uniform, and a local critique of constitutionalism—one that only focuses on how the model operates in Spain—is not incompatible with a post-independence scenario based on constitutionalism. The inconsistency would appear if the secessionists advanced a general critique of constitutionalism—both local and universal—and then imagined a new state in terms of a perfect constitutional order. I have identified the ambiguity in this regard when discussing the means employed by the secessionists, and here too the lack of a uniform consensus in the Catalan secessionist movement emerges. Recourse to constitutional actions, even after undertaking unilateral initiatives, is perfectly consistent with language criticising the quality or operation of constitutionalism in Spain, but only insofar constitutionalism as a doctrine is not questioned. Unilateral action, however, squares well with a completely anti-constitutionalist stance and the three-pronged attack, but clashes with the envisaged post-independence scenario in which constitutionalism is again paramount.

In any case, setting aside possible inconsistencies between language, means and results, what is clear is that this course of action brings internal disorientation. It makes it difficult for the secessionist followers to understand the fluctuations. It is even more difficult for the greater public to understand the details and nuances couched in the language, such as the difference between a critique of constitutionalism in practice in Spain and a deeper attack on the core principles and values of constitutionalism.

The political and media debates tend to simplify the language. Most of the time, the secessionist discourse has been understood as a radical attack on constitutionalism in general, especially the calls to exercise the right to self-determination or the so-called right to decide. The use of this language seems to advocate unilateral means and make respect for constitutional norms appear useless or even illegitimate. The internal disorientation increases when secessionist political leaders themselves shift position in the ambiguous terrain of means taken up, sometimes calling for respect of constitutional norms and other times calling for their disruption. Finally, erecting a new state based on constitutionalism just after carrying out a tremendous attack on the very same doctrine seems a very difficult enterprise.

Internal disorientation also causes confusion outside the Catalan secessionist movement. The anti-constitutionalist language provokes, at the least, mistrust, for constitutionalism represents the mainstream legal-political model. The three-pronged attack is difficult to understand for people outside the movement because radical democracy as a theory has little support.

At the same time, the more moderate anti-constitutional attack—the local critique—clashes with the presumption of validity of the Spanish constitutional order in the eyes of the Spanish State's neighbours. If constitutionalism is defective to a fault in Spain, Catalan secessionists bear the responsibility of proving it, because at the end of the day, Spain is party to international organisations—mainly the European Union and the Council of Europe—that monitor Spain's compliance with constitutional standards. The ambiguous stance regarding the appropriate tools to attain its objectives—sometimes relaying on constitutional mechanisms, sometimes not—signals to people outside the movement that perhaps the Catalan secessionist movement's assessment of constitutionalism in Spain is either inadequate or incomplete.

In sum, in this chapter I did not explore the substantive debate concerning the validity of the beliefs that comprise the Catalan secessionist imaginary. The aim was analysing this imaginary from the point of view of its expression and the relationship of that discourse with the precepts of constitutionalism. The analysis has brought to light inconsistencies and, in particular, internal and external disorientation caused by the language and the means employed in comparison with the envisioned result of the Catalan secession movement.

Constitutionalism is currently the mainstream political model and Catalan secessionists are struggling with it. It seems difficult to see how, using their current discourse and maintaining a similar course of action, Catalan secessionists could prevail over, to use their own words, Spanish constitutionalism.

At the very least, Catalan secessionists ought to make greater effort for clarity in their language. They should take a stand, that is, either adopt a moderate position, such as the "original sin" critique or targeting the defective operation of constitutionalism in Spain, or a radical approach—calling for radical democracy instead of constitutionalism—and then choose a course of action that is coherent with their theoretical position and with the final objective sought, for all of which a clear vision of the role of constitutionalism must be decided.

References

Ackerman, B. (1997). The Rise of World Constitutionalism. *Virginia Law Review, 83*, 771–797.

Aguado Renedo, C. (2013). Sobre un eventual referéndum consultivo en el proceso soberanista catalán. *Cuadernos de Alzate, 46–47*, 27–47.

Barceló Serramalera, M. (Ed.). (2015). *El derecho a decidir: teoría y práctica de un nuevo derecho.* Barcelona: Atelier.

Bellamy, R., & Castiglione, D. (1997). Constitutionalism and Democracy – Political Theory and the American Constitution. *British Journal of Political Science, 27*(4), 595–618.

Bernadí Gil, X. (2019). L'aplicació de l'article 155 de la Constitució española al Govern i l'Administració de la Generalitat de Catalunya. *Revista catalana de dret públic*, (special issue), 21–44.

Blanke, H., & Abdelrehim, Y. (2014). Catalonia and the Right to Self-Determination from the Perspective of International Law. *Max Planck Yearbook of United Nations Law Online, 18*(1), 532–564.

Carr, R., & Fusi Aizpurua, J. P. (1981). *Spain. Dictatorship to Democracy.* New York: HarperCollins.

Casals Meseguer, X. (2016). *La Transición Española. El voto ignorado de las armas.* Barcelona: Pasado & Presente.

Costa, J. (2017). Does Catalonia Have the Right to Self-Determination? *Catalonia Background Information, Public Diplomacy Council of Catalonia* (pp. 1–5). Series E/2017/2.1/EN.

De Carreras, F. (2014). ¿Puede celebrarse un referéndum en Cataluña? *El Cronista del Estado Social y Democrático de Derecho, 42*, 24–35.

De Miguel Bárcena, J. (2018). El proceso soberanista ante el Tribunal Constitucional. *Revista Española de Derecho Constitucional, 113*, 133–166.

Edling, A., & Melia, T. (2019). A Troubling Trend: Free Expression Under Fire in Catalonia. *Pen America.* www.pen.org/free-expression-catalonia. Accessed 16 Feb 2020.

Elbal, I. (2019). Principio de legalidad y arbitrariedad para Catalunya. *Eldiario.es*. https://www.eldiario.es/contrapoder/Principio-legalidad-arbitrariedad-Catalunya_6_955114511.html. Accessed 16 Feb 2020.

Ferreres Comella, V. (2013). *The Constitution of Spain. A Contextual Analysis*. Oxford/Portland: Hart Publishing.

Ferreres Comella, V. (2016). Cataluña y el derecho a decidir. *Teoría y Realidad Constitucional, 37*, 461–475.

Ferreres Comella, V. (2017). The Independence Vote in Catalonia – The Constitutional Crisis of October 1. *International Journal of Constitutional Law Blog*. http://www.iconnectblog.com/2017/10/i-connect-symposium-the-independence-vote-in-catalonia-constitutional-crisis/. Accessed 16 Feb2020.

Gallego, F. (2008). *El mito de la Transición. La crisis del franquismo y los orígenes de la democracia (1973–1977)*. Barcelona: Editorial Crítica.

González Pascual, M. (2014). Austerity Measures and Welfare Rights. The Spanish Constitutional System Under Stress. *European Journal of Social Law, 1*(2), 116–127.

Jones, S. (2019). Catalan Leaders' Lawyers Attacks "Vaudeville" Case as Trials Begins. *The Guardian*. www.theguardian.com/world/2019/feb/12/trial-of-catalan-separatist-leaders-begins-in-madrid. Accessed 16 Feb 2020.

Kennedy, D. (2006). *The Rise & Fall of Classical Legal Thought*. Washington, DC: Beard Books.

López Hernández, J. (2017). *El derecho a decidir. La vía catalana*. Tafalla: Txalaparta.

Marinzel, A. (2014). Catalonia: The Quest for Independence from Spain. *Senior Honors Project, 39*, 1–32.

Ortuño Anaya, P. (2005). *Los socialistas europeos y la transición española (1959–1977)*. Madrid: Marcial Pons.

Pasamar, G. (2018). Los relatos escépticos sobre la Transición española: origen y claves políticas e interpretativas. *Les Chaiers de Framespa*, 27. http://journals.openedition.org/framespa/4738. Accessed 16 Feb 2020.

Roig Molés, E. (2006). La Reforma del Estado de las Autonomías: ¿Ruptura o consolidación del modelo constitucional de 1978? Comentario al artículo del profesor Pedro Cruz Villalón. *Revista d'Estudis autonòmics i federals, 3*, 149–156.

Rubio Llorente, F. (2013). Un referéndum que nadie quiere. *El País*. https://elpais.com/elpais/2013/02/01/opinion/1359716070_365196.html. Accessed 16 Feb 2020.

Sala, G. (2013). La politización del Tribunal Constitucional: ¿Desde cuándo y hasta cuándo? *Eldiario.es*. https://www.eldiario.es/agendapublica/nueva-politica/politizacion-Tribunal-Constitucional_0_177082923.html. Accessed 16 Feb 2020.

Santjaume Calvet, M. (2016). The Morality of Secession: Secessionist and Antisecessionist Arguments in the Catalan Case. In X. Cuadras Morató (Ed.), *Catalonia: A New Independent State in Europe? A Debate on Secession Within the European Union* (pp. 82–106). London: Routledge.

Solanes Mullor, J. (2019). The Implications of the *Otegi* Case for the Legitimacy of the Spanish Judiciary. ECtHR 6 February 2019, Case Nos. 4184/15 and 4 Other Applications. *Otegi Mondragon and Others v Spain. European Constitutional Law Review, 15*(3), 574–588.

Tornos Mas, J. (2014). El problema catalán: una solución razonable. *El Cronista del Estado social y democrático de derecho, 42*, 44–53.

Tudela Aranda, J. (2016). El derecho a decidir y el principio democrático. *Teoría y Realidad Constitucional, 37*, 477–497.

Urías, J. (2020). Spain Has a Problem with Its Judiciary. *Verfassungsblog*. https://verfassungsblog.de/spain-has-a-problem-with-its-judiciary. Accessed 16 Feb 2020.

Val, E. (2019). Estrasburgo, la última palabra. *La Vanguardia*. https://www.lavanguardia.com/politica/20190210/46324222806/tedh-estrasburgo-juicio-proces-litigios.html. Accessed 16 Feb 2020.

Vv.A.a. (2013). Foro Especial: Autodeterminación. *Cuadernos de Alzate, 46–47*, 27–244.

Ysàs, P. (1994). Democracia y autonomía en la transición española. *Ayer: Revista de Historia Contemporánea, 15*, 77–107.

PART V

Territorial Politics of Sub-national Ethnocentric Constitutionalism

CHAPTER 12

Ethno-Territorial Politics and Sub-national Constitutionalism: Lessons from Bosnia and Herzegovina

Maja Sahadžić

1 Introduction

The 1995 General Framework Agreement for Peace in Bosnia and Herzegovina (the Dayton Peace Agreement) defines Bosnia and Herzegovina (B&H) as a compound of the Federation of Bosnia and Herzegovina (FB&H) and the Republic of Srpska (RS) (the Entities). The FB&H consists of ten cantons, while the RS is a unitary territorial unit. The Brčko District (BD), a small territorial unit in north-eastern Bosnia and Herzegovina, emerged in 1999 following an arbitration process. Interestingly, B&H features 13 constitutions and 1 statute. Apart from the Constitution of B&H, the Entities and cantons have their constitutions. The BD has a statute, which is similar to a constitution. Although the Constitution of B&H assigns exclusive powers to the central level these

M. Sahadžić (✉)
University of Antwerp, Antwerp, Belgium
e-mail: Maja.Sahadzic@uantwerpen.be

M. Belov (ed.), *Territorial Politics and Secession*, Federalism and Internal Conflicts, https://doi.org/10.1007/978-3-030-64402-4_12

are limited. This leaves the Entities and the BD with vast residual powers and remarkably high sub-national autonomy.

Added to this, the constitutional system of Bosnia and Herzegovina is based on the principle of parity of three ethnic groups called constituent peoples—the Bosniaks, Croats, and Serbs. The constituent peoples are the key ingredient of the constitutional system as they pierce through all levels of government. They interfere with territorial representation, influence voting procedures, and enjoy veto powers.

What is striking is that the constituent peoples have substituted the battleground for the institutions of government and their respective procedures. Repeated threats of organising independence referendums coming from the RS predominantly inhabited by the Serbs, continuous calls for organising a third territorial unit exclusively for the Croats, and ongoing unitarist demands of the Bosniaks imply highly strained relations among the constituent peoples (Perry 2015). However, failure to take concrete actions and advance the claims leaves the true nature of the claims unclear. The present state of affairs seems to be a rather complex *status quo* in which (autonomy) claims have been used simply as leverage in the political interests of status or power.

This chapter explores the effects of sub-national constitutionalism on territorial politics. By using B&H as an example, this chapter investigates the interplay between identity, territory, autonomy claims, and sub-national constitutionalism. Importantly, this gives insights about cohesive and divisive qualities of sub-national constitutionalism in B&H. Firstly, the chapter analyses the evolution of the present constitutional system of B&H. Secondly, the chapter explores whether and how wide sub-national constitutional autonomy counteracts autonomy claims in B&H.

2 A Very Basic Conceptual Structure Underlying Territoriality and Identity

One major theoretical issue that has dominated studies in territorial governance for many years concerns the link between territory and identity. However, research on this topic has remained rather oversimplified and the link is still blurred (Palermo 2016). This is even though previous research has established that variations in territory and differences in identity reflect on territorially based arrangements and institutional engineering (Leuprecht 2009; Burgess 2006). Meanwhile, the link between territory and identity is essential when discussing autonomy claims in constitutional systems burdened with internal disputes. Based on this, it is possible to identify two trends in the contemporary territorial reconfiguration of states: (1) decentralisation and (2) a change in the notion of identity.

There is a shift from unitary nation-states to various forms of heterogeneous decentralised systems (Loughlin 2007). The shift is often supported by violent territorial conflicts (Cowen and Gilbert 2008; Palermo 2016). This results in what Kolers (2009) calls a conflict resolution approach which attempts to find an agreement for each claimant's demand in a territorial conflict.

However, "[t]erritoriality alone [...] is thus a far too simple solution for a far too complex problem" (Palermo 2016). Contemporary insights prove that territorial reconfiguration is associated with the identity (Nicolini 2016). Importantly, in heterogeneous decentralised systems, the link between territory and identity is shifted from a general form of identity such as citizenry or nation to groups with specific identity markers (Palermo 2016).

In the face of autonomy claims, differences in ethnicity, language, religion, and culture put into sharper perspective changes in the original territorial demarcation. This is where the idea of ethnogeography explains the role of identity in territorial conflicts. It looks closely into conceptions of territory under the influence of identity markers and explains that ethnic groups accumulate their territorial rights through their land-use practices (Kolers 2009).

This also implies that the conceptions of territory are a societal product. They change as specific groups change their understanding of their position within a specific territory (Larkins 2010). To legitimise their understandings, territorial communities claim their shared values and therefore their collective identity (Henders 2010). This way, "the territory reflects the cultural, sociological and historical identity of the population living there" (Cristiani 2016). Territory and identity are difficult if not impossible to disconnect because of their close association (Nicolini 2016).

Ultimately, when it involves what is in contemporary literature generically called "ethnic territorial autonomous arrangements" (Osipov 2016), the goal of territorial reconfiguration is to manage diversity and preserve the cohesion of the system (Nicolini 2016). In other words, this means holding the system together.[1] However, territorial reconfiguration depends on how legal geography defines the relationship between territory and identity or, to put it differently, territorial units and groups (Nicolini 2016). Importantly, this depends on the events that preceded the reconfiguration.

3 The Development of Ethno-Territorial B&H

Pre-conflict association between territory and identity in B&H was not (strongly) emphasised. In large parts of the territory, three groups were mixed while only in some areas individual groups were the majority (Bieber 2006). In other words, the groups were geographically dispersed in a way that breaks off ethnic majority areas (Burg and Shoup 1999). The understanding of mutual interconnectedness was continually prompted through the declaration of the 1943 State Anti-fascist Council for the National Liberation of B&H. It defined B&H as neither Serbian, nor Croat, nor Muslim,[2] but Serbian, Croat, and Muslim, together with their full equality (Imamović 2006). This implied that the territorial structure of B&H was not based on identity markers (Sahadžić 2013). However, the peoples of B&H were never perceived as becoming a single (Bosnian-Herzegovinian) nation (Burg and Shoup 1999) despite B&H being a unitary system.[3]

After the Bosnian War broke out, the association between territory and identity became increasingly important. The dissolution of Yugoslavia at the beginning of the 1990s was taking place under the pressure of nationalism.[4] Not surprisingly, a similar pattern was developing in B&H. Supported by political and religious leaders, the importance of identity differences gained a crucial role in fragmenting processes in B&H (Abazović 2015;

[1] The term is borrowed from Alfred Stepan, "Towards a New Comparative Politics of Federalism, Multinationalism, and Democracy: Beyond Rikerian Federalism," in *Federalism and Democracy in Latin America*, ed. Edward L. Gibson (Baltimore, MD: Johns Hopkins University Press, 2004).

[2] The term Bosniak was officially introduced in the 1994 Washington Agreement to mark the Bosnian Muslims (Sahadžić 2012). In former Yugoslavia, the Bosnian Muslims were recognised as Muslims ("muslims with a capital M") (Bougarel 2017) to differentiate between religious and ethnic communities.

[3] Before the 1990s, B&H was never an independent state (Keil 2013).

[4] For detailed explanations see Robert M. Hayden, *From Yugoslavia to the Western Balkans: Studies of a European Disunion, 1991–2011* (Leiden: Brill, 2013).

Seizović 2014). Importantly, each group differently envisaged their position within or outside B&H.

In 1991, while the central-level authorities in B&H were struggling to put forward a proposal for international recognition and to organise an independence referendum, the Serbs in B&H organised a referendum to remain in former Yugoslavia and boycotted the 1992 independence referendum of B&H. Also, in 1992, the predominantly Serb-populated territory of B&H organised itself into the Republic of the Serb people (later renamed into the RS) and adopted its constitution.[5]

The Bosnian War gained momentum. Meanwhile, growing distrust between the Bosniaks and Croats lead to a conflict between them. The conflict flared up when the Croats established the Croatian Community of Herzeg-Bosnia and tried to break away from B&H (Vukoja and Sitarski 2016). The two sides signed the Washington Agreement in 1994, which ended the conflict and established the FB&H (based on ten cantons) in the parts of B&H populated by the Bosniaks and Croats. Five cantons were established as Bosniak majority areas, three cantons as Croat majority areas, while two cantons were granted a special regime because their population was mixed. The constitution of FB&H was adopted as a part of the Washington Agreement, while the ten cantons subsequently adopted their constitutions.[6] Finally, ethnic cleansing helped to deeply entrench the link between territory and identity in B&H. By the end of the conflict, three groups were concentrated in three ethnically homogeneous territories (Bieber 2006; Keil 2013). In support of this, a comparison between the population censuses in 1991 and 2013 indicate that the Bosniaks and Croats link to specific cantons in the FB&H while the Serbs link to the RS.

A critical analysis of the several peace plans for B&H reveals that each plan proposed a map with an established territory-identity link. However,

[5]The official documents can be consulted here: *Declaration on Proclamation of the Republic of the Serb people of B&H* (Official Gazette of the Serb people in B&H 2/92), *The Constitution of the Serb Republic* (Official Gazette of the Serb people in B&H 3/92), and *The Constitution of RS* (Official Gazette of RS 21/92, 28/94, 8/96, 13/96, 15/96, 16/96, 21/96, 21/02, 26/02, 30/02, 31/02, 69/02, 31/03, 98/03, 115/05, and 117/05).

[6]The official documents can be consulted here: *The Washington Framework Agreement* (Official Gazette of the FB&H 1/94) and *The Constitution of the Federation of B&H* (Official Gazette of the FB&H 1/94, 13/97, 16/02, 22/02, 52/02, 63/03, 9/94, 20/04, 33/04, 71/05, 72/05, and 88/08), *Agreement on the Criteria for the Definition of the Territory of the FB&H* (Official Gazette of the Federation of B&H 1/94), and *Law on Federal Units* (Official Gazette of the Federation of B&H 3/96).

territorial mapping of groups was a highly contentious issue (Touval 2002) and therefore a reason for failure. For example, the 1992 Cutileiro peace plan sought to redesign the territory of B&H into three component units based on ethnic principles and with wide power-sharing provisions at all levels of government. The 1993 Vance-Owen peace plan proposed to divide B&H into ten component units, three with a Bosnian Muslim majority, two with a Croat majority, three with a Serb majority, one unit with a mixed Bosnian Muslim-Croat majority, and Sarajevo as the tenth unit without ethnic identification. The component units would capture vast powers, while the central-level government would be weakened. The 1993 Owen-Stoltenberg peace plan intended to rearrange the territory of B&H into a (con)federal system with three component units based on ethnic principles. The 1994 Contact Group plan proposed a division of the territory between the newly established FB&H (51%) and the unrecognised RS (49%).[7] Although rejected, the Contact Group plan was a basis for the final solution.

The conflict ended with the 1995 General Framework Agreement for Peace in B&H (the Dayton Peace Agreement).[8] The Constitution of B&H (Annex 4 to the Dayton Peace Agreement) recognised the pre-constitutional existence of the FB&H and the RS. It changed the internal constitutional design by redefining it to make it a multilevel system based on variations in identity. In other words, the Constitution put the seal of approval on the territorial delineation and associated ethnic affiliation that developed during the Bosnian War.

Added to this, the Constitution generated foundations for the Brčko District (BD), a small component unit which was established only in 1999. Because the sides in conflict could not reach agreement about the multi-ethnic city of Brčko, they agreed to subsequently determine the status of the city by arbitration. In 1999, the Arbitral Tribunal for Dispute Over the Inter-Entity Boundary in Brčko (the Arbitral Tribunal) defined the BD as

[7] Detailed explanation for each plan can be found in Saadia Touval, *Mediation in the Yugoslav Wars, the Critical Years, 1990–95* (Basingstoke and New York: Palgrave Macmillan, 2002). Melanie C. Greenberg and Margaret E. McGuinness, "From Lisbon to Dayton: International Mediation and the Bosnia Crisis," in *Words over War: Mediation and Arbitration to Prevent Deadly Conflict*, ed. Melanie C. Greenberg, John H. Barton, and Margaret E. McGuinness (Lenham, Boulder, New York, and Oxford: Rowman & Littlefield Publishers, 2000).

[8] The Agreement has never been ratified in the Parliamentary Assembly of B&H. UN Doc. A/50/790 (1995) and S/1995/999 (1995) from 30/11/1995.

a single administrative unit under the sovereignty of B&H while Amendment I to the Constitution of B&H defined the BD as a territory in the joint ownership of the Entities.[9] Ultimately, the transformation meant (1) a split of the unitary state into a multilevel territorial structure (2) that overlaps with three ethnic communities of Bosniaks, Croats, and Serbs which each have a distinctive historical, national, ethnic, and religious background (Seizović 2014).

Today, the FB&H consists of ten (unitary organised) cantons which makes it multilevel, while the RS and the BD have unitary frameworks. Cantons in the FB&H are populated with the majority of either Bosniaks or Croats, while two cantons have a mixed population. The RS is populated mainly by the Serbs, while the BD is multiethnic.

4 Sub-national Constitutionalism in B&H

The Scope of Sub-national Autonomy

Apart from the Constitution of B&H, the Entities and cantons have their constitutions, while the BD has a statute. Added to this, based on the principle of parity, the constituent peoples evenly take part in the system of government at all levels (Sahadžić 2013). Also, the Entities and the BD enjoy full autonomy to revise their constitutional and statutory provisions. However, there is the obligatory involvement of the constituent peoples which determines the majorities required for the revisions.

Importantly, B&H features a weak central level and very strong component units. The Constitution of B&H assigns exclusive powers to the central level, however, these are limited. The result is that the Entities occupy extensive residual powers (Marko 2005–2006; Touquet and Vermeersch 2008; Sahadžić 2019). By the same token, after it was established, the BD assumed powers and functions comparable to those of the Entities (Kulenović 2012; Sahadžić 2019). Also, the central level is authorised to assume additional powers over the matters necessary to preserve the sovereignty, territorial integrity, political independence, and international personality of B&H respecting the distribution of powers and mutual agreement of the Entities.

However, transferring powers and competences from the lower levels to the central level has been unpopular in the RS because the Serbs fear of

[9] *Amendment I to the Constitution of B&H* (Official Gazette of B&H 25/09).

weakening the RS (Quattrocchi 2016). Ultimately, it makes mutual agreement impossible. It is important to realise that most of the powers and competences that were transferred to the central level were imposed by the Office of the High Representative for Bosnia and Herzegovina (OHR).[10]

The Entities can enter special parallel relationships with neighbouring countries. Also, the Entities and cantons can enter into international agreements with countries and international organisations provided that they have the consent of the central level (and the consent of the FB&H in the case of cantons).

The Constitution of Bosnia and Herzegovina is silent about the composition and functioning of the legislative, executive, and judicial bodies in the FB&H, the RS, and the BD. The composition and functioning are defined entirely by the Constitution of the FB&H, the Constitution of the RS, and the Statute of the BD. Interestingly, while each Entity and the BD developed complete judiciaries, the central level lacks a supreme court (Sahadžić 2011a). In 2002, the OHR imposed the law that established the Court of B&H (together with the Prosecutor's Office of B&H) at the central level. However, given the narrow powers and competences of the central level, this court has narrowly defined jurisdiction. This makes the Court a specialised court. Added to this, there is no established hierarchical relationship between the judiciary at the central level and the judiciaries of the Entities and the BD. This means that the Entities and the BD developed individual judiciaries irrespective of the central level.

Room to Reinforce Sub-national Autonomy: The Entities?

Representation and participation of the Entities, combined with the principle of parity of the constituent peoples, has a far-reaching influence in the central-level government. It must be remembered, though, that the BD is not represented and does not participate in the central-level government. This is due to its subsequent establishment. Its population chooses

[10]The OHR (together with the High Representative for B&H) was created in 1995 to supervise the implementation of the Dayton Peace Agreement. Among other, the OHR can adopt and enforce decisions when there is a deadlock in decision-making. Despite, the transferred powers and competences are not numerous. They include defense and security policy (unified Armed Forces of B&H, Intelligence-Security Agency of B&H, and the State Investigation and Protection Agency), the High Judicial and Prosecutorial Council, and Value Added Tax among few.

to vote either from the FB&H or from the RS. Therefore, it could be said that the BD is represented through the FB&H or the RS.

The territorial representation of the Entities coincides with the representation of the constituent peoples (Woelk 2012). For example, the House of Representatives of the Parliamentary Assembly of B&H consists of 42 representatives elected in the Entities. However, two-thirds of representatives are elected from the FB&H by the residents of the FB&H, and one-third is elected from the RS by the residents of the RS. This is because the Dayton Constitution envisaged the FB&H as the territory consisting of the Bosniaks and Croats and the RS as the territory consisting of the Serbs. This suggests that not only the House of Representatives represents the Entities but it also represents the constituent peoples (Pobrić 2000). Similarly, the Bosniak and Croat members of the Presidency of B&H are elected from the territory of the FB&H, while the Serb member is elected from the territory of the RS.[11]

Another example is a so-called entity voting procedure. This procedure is especially convenient for decision-making deadlocks for the fact that the number of representatives from each entity is decisive in reaching a decision. Compared to the procedure for the protection of the vital national interests of the constituent peoples, which is a true veto mechanism guaranteed as a safety net for the constituent peoples, the "entity voting" is a much faster and less intricate procedure. In the "entity voting" procedure, all decisions are adopted by a majority of those present and voting. However, all representatives need to make an effort to reach a majority that includes one-third of the votes from each entity. The perverse effect of these provisions is that the Bosniaks and Serbs use this procedure to block decision-making. This turns the "entity voting" procedure into a covert veto mechanism of the constituent peoples. Interestingly enough,

[11] In 2009, the European Court of Human Rights (ECtHR), deciding in the case of Sejdić and Finci v. BaH established that the constitutional provisions which render the applicants (in this case the persons who do not identify themselves as one of the constituent peoples) ineligible for election to the Presidency of B&H discriminatory. Later on, in 2014, in the case of Zornić v. B&H, the ECtHR reinforced the previous decision. Finally, in 2016, in the case of Pilav v. B&H, the ECtHR again looked into the provisions of the Constitution, this time from a different angle. In particular, the Presidency of B&H consists of one Bosniak and one Croat, each directly elected from the FB&H, and one Serb directly elected from the RS. The ECtHR held that the applicant (in this case a Bosniak living in the RS) is prevented from being entitled to stand for the election to the Presidency and therefore the Court found it to be a discriminatory feature of the constitutional system.

the Croats, due to their small number, cannot act in the same capacity as the Bosniaks and Serbs.

Finally, the ethno-territorial aspects prove to influence even the composition of the Constitutional Court of B&H. The Court is composed of nine judges. Three international judges are elected by the President of the European Court of Human Rights after the consultation with the Presidency of B&H. The remaining six judges are elected from the Entities, four from the FB&H and two from the RS. Although ethnic representation is not a requirement it is an established practice to elect two judges from each constituent peoples (Sahadžić 2013).

Room to Reinforce Sub-national Autonomy: Cantons?

Unlike in the case of the Entities, the ethno-territorial framework of each canton makes little if no effect in the legislative, executive, and judicial bodies of the FB&H.

5 Putting Sub-national Constitutionalism in Play

Territory and Identity as Cohesive and Divisive Features

Supported by violent conflicts, a shift from a unitary to a heterogeneous decentralised system in B&H was finalised thanks to the territorial reconfiguration of identity. The conception of the territory was based on each group's position during the conflict. As their understanding of their position was changing the peace plans were also changing or adjusting. This was until the Dayton Peace Agreement captured a fragile ethno-territorial equilibrium.

However, the present constitutional design of B&H does not fall within any of the ideal types of autonomy (territorial or non-territorial). It falls somewhere in between as these two types overlap (Marko and Constantin 2019). The constitutional design is not established based on the Palermo's (2016) territorial autonomy for group protection because the legal design puts more emphasis on the ethnic dimension over the territorial one. This is mainly because the territorial structure is interwoven with identity differences (Abazović 2010; Sahadžić 2019). However, it is not based on what Palermo (2016) calls a framework for the self-governing minority groups because of the principle of parity.

The constitutional design of B&H is based on a heterogeneous ethnic-territorial framework (see Palermo 2016). The Dayton Constitution settled territorial claims based on ethnic-national groups. Because of that, the constitutional design consists of a multiplicity of territorial units that are constituent parts of the system: the central level, two entities (the FB&H and the RS), ten cantons in the FB&H, and the BD. Meanwhile, the ethnic groups that make up the constituent peoples of the country (the Bosniaks, Croats, and Serbs) force their way through all levels of government. Given that they have acquired equal power ratio during the conflict (Keil and Kudlenko 2015) their parity is an essential ingredient of the system of government (Pobrić 2000).

The association between the territory and identity in B&H simultaneously displays cohesive and divisive features. The acknowledgment of the ethno-territorial reality resulting from the Bosnian War bonded fragmenting layers of the country together. The territorial reconfiguration certainly fulfilled its goal of managing diversity. At the same, this enabled holding the system together.

However, the ethno-territorial reconsolidation of the country is not without its deficiencies. The territorial elements that are linked to the ethnic criteria fracture the country in political, social, and economic aspects. As the most numerous, the Bosniaks insist on the model of what Henders (2010) describes as a single authority over a single citizenry or nation hoping this would secure loyalty to collective B&H identity. They often promote the patriotic narrative of a civic country (Latal 2019) which is a pre-war unitary republican model without the so-called ethnic keys.[12]

However, as specific groups gain opportunities to articulate their distinctiveness they are naturally set against a single authority and citizenry or nation (Medda-Windischer 2011; Choudhry and Hume 2011). This is displayed in further decentralising aspirations of the Croats and Serbs.

The Croats have called for revisiting the Constitution of B&H to include the third entity in the constitutional structure.[13] Despite being the constituent people, the Croats are handful compared to the Bosniaks and Serbs. Due to their small number, they are underrepresented and often unable to influence the decision-making process at the central level. Also, they find it difficult to influence the elections for the Croat member of the

[12] The term "ethnic key" is colloquially used to define the ethnic balance of constituent peoples.

[13] One of their demands used to be a separate TV channel in Croatian (see Knezevic 2017).

Presidency of B&H (Radio Free Europe, Radio Liberty 2018).[14] With this in mind, the idea of the third Croat entity is intended to balance their territorial and political autonomy within the system (Zdeb 2016).

The Serbs often threaten to organise independence referendums in the RS (Keil 2012; Surk 2018). These threats usually unfold during the discussion about transferring powers and competences to the central level (Quattrocchi 2016).[15] However, other topics include the opposition to B&H's accession to North Atlantic Treaty Organization (NATO) (Kovacevic 2019) and the ruling of the Constitutional Court of B&H that B&H, not the RS, is the owner of the land which the RS had declared it was the property of the RS (Kovacevic 2020).

Identity differences put in the perspective changes in the original demarcation finalised in the Dayton Peace Agreement. Every threat for further decentralisation coming from the Serbs and Croats is reciprocated with a push for more unitarism coming from the Bosniaks. Meanwhile, the pursuit of unitarism is met with vehement criticism from the Croat and Serb sides. Such tense relationships are depicted in somewhat aberrant behaviour of each constituent people.

For example, in 2015 the Constitutional Court of B&H was deciding on the request of the Bosniak member of the Presidency of B&H for review of constitutionality of the Law on Holidays of the RS. The claimant argued that the Day of the Republic celebrated on 9 January is a holiday that had been established by referendum in 1992 without the participation of the Bosniaks and Croats. After a public hearing, the Court decided that the disputed law was unconstitutional. In response, the representatives of the National Assembly of the RS filed applications to the Constitutional Court to review the constitutionality of the Law Declaring 1 March as Independence Day of the Republic of B&H and the Law on

[14] Željko Komšić served as a Croat member of the Presidency of B&H during two mandates from 2006 to 2014. In 2018 he was elected for a third term. However, the Croats acknowledge that he has been legally elected but his legitimacy has been highly contested. This is because, even though he declares himself a Croat, his political views coincide with the Bosniak political views. This makes him popular among the Bosniaks who vote for him. As a result, the Croats blame the constitutional design and protest against the election system for their inability to influence their choice.

[15] For example, the RS has highly disapproved of the establishment of the Court of B&H, the Prosecutor's Office of B&H, and the High Judicial and Prosecutorial Council of B&H. Because the powers and competences were imposed by the OHR, the RS and the Serbs opposed the work of these institutions to the point that the RS has threatened to organise a referendum to abolish the institutions.

Proclamation of 25 November as Statehood Day of the Republic of B&H. The applicants argued that the holiday on 1 March had been established thanks to the referendum on the independence of B&H which was supported only by the Bosniaks and Croats. The Serbs boycotted the referendum. The applicants also argued that the national holiday on 25 November was established during the conflict and is celebrated only in the FB&H which implies the intention to exclude the Serbs. In both cases, the Constitutional Court ruled that the laws are consistent with the Constitution of B&H.

Finally, one thing is rather paradoxical in B&H. The Constitutional Court of B&H intended to disable the ethno-territorial link by confirming the principle of the constituency of the peoples regardless of the Entity (The Decision of the Constitutional Court of B&H U-5/98). This way, the Constitutional Court highlighted the constitutional premise that each constituent people is associated with the entire territory of B&H (Sahadžić 2011b). However, the territorial link is still institutionalised (Seizović 2008). The observable effects of these dynamics are visible from the discussion above.

Sub-national Constitutionalism and Its Cohesive and Divisive Features

Considering the analysis above, it is apparent that fine ethno-territorial balance is maintained through the institutionalisation of conflict. However, the balance is also sustained through broad sub-national autonomy. It would appear that the spectrum of sub-national autonomy is broad enough to guarantee to hold the system together. The self-constituent capacity of the Entities, cantons, and the BD is wide and accompanied by full autonomy to revise their constitutions and the statute. They all enjoy vast powers and competences and institutional autonomy. While this layered structure is designed to guarantee cohesion, it is also sustenance for the division.

Keeping a delicate equilibrium in complex constitutional systems requires a set of specific skills of policy-makers who are designers of an appropriate constitutional structure (Benz and Broschek 2013). Not surprisingly, the party system in B&H is based on ethnic party lines (see Abazović 2015). Further devolutionary aspirations based on sub-national constitutionalism survive due to divisive political narratives. The political elites among the constituent peoples do not deviate from the usual pattern. They use rhetoric to build popular support and coerce their territorial demands. As indicated by Goddard (2010) rhetoric is not meant to initiate conflicts, however, it has unthinkable consequences as it can lead to stagnating relations caused by incompatible claims.

Sub-national constitutionalism is of the utmost importance in the RS. Unlike the FB&H, the RS is suitably designed for autonomy claims as it is organised as a single territory and populated by predominantly one constituent people—the Serbs. It certainly helps that the political establishment in the RS is unanimous about self-government. Regardless of their political affiliation, political leaders in the RS maintain mutual political narrative about the importance of sub-national constitutionalism and autonomy claims. This is passionately built around the Constitution, powers and competences, and institutions, which are considered the foundation of the RS. Also, the general populace in the RS displays a high awareness of the importance of sub-national constitutionalism. Thanks to recurring public campaigns they support broader autonomy for the RS, even separation from B&H. Ultimately, representation and participation of the RS at the central level strengthens sub-national awareness. This is because the central-level institutions become an arena for measuring power.

In stark contrast, sub-national constitutionalism has never gained importance in the FB&H. One reason for this is that the FB&H is split into cantons which makes it less compact. Equally important, the Bosniaks and Croats share the territory of the FB&H. In this kind of configuration, the Bosniaks remain attached to a centralised form of governance and pose no divisive threats. The Croats, although pursuing devolutionary aspirations, are split across several cantons. This seemingly decreases the importance of sub-national constitutionalism because there is no single force to act as a divisive factor. Despite that, the FB&H defies the argument that "[i]f a territory regardless of its ethnic composition, can autonomously decide on a number of issues [...] it is likely that decisions will be qualitatively better and that the territory will develop more harmoniously with benefits extending to all communities settled there" (Palermo 2016).

An additional layer of complexity in FB&H is that the Bosniaks and Croats have an incompatible vision about the constitutional architecture of B&H. Although the Croats pose no separatist threats, they demand internal territorial and institutional reform. This might be linked to their perception of recognition. Recognition requires autonomy and integration through individual and group rights to avoid assimilation and secession (Marko 2019). If there is no recognition, groups are not able to voice their demands which renders integration and cohesion impossible (Marko and Constantin 2019). A lack of territorial and institutional recognition of the Croats results in their inferior position within the system. Earning their sub-national constitutional autonomy is then considered a remedy for the lack of recognition. Finally, the issue of sub-national constitutionalism is rather unknown in the BD, most likely due to its small size and multiethnic composition.

6 Conclusions

This chapter attempted to explore the interplay between ethno-territorial politics, sub-national constitutionalism, and autonomy claims in B&H. The first task was to analyse the evolution of the present constitutional system. One aim of this exercise was to test the theoretical premise about the association between territory and identity in deeply divided systems. Another aim was to link the development of extensive sub-national constitutionalism to the territorial delineation and associated ethnic affiliation.

The chapter described how, during the Bosnian War, the constituent peoples in the making became aware of their collective identity. That stimulated them to change their understanding of their territorial status and entrench into ethnically determined parts of the territory. Due to three irreconcilable views on the future of the system, extensive sub-national constitutionalism was acknowledged as a way to keep the system together.

The second task of the chapter was to analyse ways in which sub-national constitutionalism interacts with autonomy claims. To do this, the chapter explored cohesive and divisive factors. Contrary to the expectations, extensive sub-national constitutionalism does not seem to counteract autonomy claims in B&H. In the case of the compact RS and the Serbs, it even triggers or accelerates paramount autonomy claims. However, the failure to put these claims into action might imply that they are used only for political gains. In the case of the FB&H, sub-national constitutionalism is not pronounced because this territorial unit is further split into cantons which adds a layer of complexity. Added to this, not only the Bosniaks and Croats share the territory of the FB&H, but are also split across cantons. As for the BD, its small size and a multiethnic format do not create foundations for autonomy claims similar to those in the rest of B&H.

References

Abazović, D. (2010). Rethinking Ethnicity, Religion, and Politics: The Case of Bosnia and Herzegovina. *European Yearbook of Minority Issues 7*, 321–330.

Abazović, D. (2015). Religious Claims During the War and Post-War Bosnia and Herzegovina. *Borderlands, 14*(1), 1–23.

Benz, A., & Broschek, J. (2013). Conclusion: Theorizing Federal Dynamics. In A. Benz & J. Broschek (Eds.), *Federal Dynamics Continuity, Change, and the Varieties of Federalism* (pp. 366–388). Oxford: Oxford University Press.

Bieber, F. (2006). *Post-War Bosnia, Ethnicity, Inequality and Public Sector Governance*. Basingstoke/New York: Palgrave Macmillan.

Bougarel, X. (2017). Islam and Nationhood in Bosnia-Herzegovina: Surviving Empires. London, Oxford, New York, New Delhi, Sydney: Bloomsbury Publishing.

Burg, S. L., & Shoup, P. (1999). *The War in Bosnia-Herzegovina: Ethnic Conflict and International Intervention*. M.E. Sharpe.

Burgess, M. (2006). *Comparative Federalism, Theory and Practice*. London: Routledge. Book.

Choudhry, S., & Hume, N. (2011). Federalism, Devolution and Secession: From Classical to Post-Conflict Federalism. In T. Ginsburg & R. Dixon (Eds.), *Comparative Constitutional Law* (pp. 356–384). Cheltenham/Northampton: Edward Elgar.

Cowen, D., & Gilbert, E. (2008). The Politics of War, Citizenship, Territory. In D. Cowen & E. Gilbert (Eds.), *War, Citizenship, Territory*. New York/London: Routledge.

Cristiani, F. (2016). International Economic Law and Conflict Resolution: The West Bank Between Dominium, Land Ownership and Land Grabbing. In M. Nicolini, F. Palermo, & E. Milano (Eds.), *Law, Territory and Conflict Resolution, Law as a Problem and Law as a Solution*. Leiden/Boston: Brill Nijhoff.

Goddard, Stacie E. (2010). Indivisible Territory and the Politics of Legitimacy, Jerusalem and Northern Ireland. New York: Cambridge University Press.

Greenberg, M. C., & McGuinness, M. E. (2000). From Lisbon to Dayton: International Mediation and the Bosnia Crisis. In M. C. Greenberg, J. H. Barton, & M. E. McGuinness (Eds.), *Words over War: Mediation and Arbitration to Prevent Deadly Conflict* (pp. 35–75). Lenham/Boulder/New York/Oxford: Rowman & Littlefield Publishers.

Hayden, R. M. (2013). *From Yugoslavia to the Western Balkans: Studies of a European Disunion, 1991–2011*. Leiden: Brill.

Henders, S. (2010). *Territoriality, Asymmetry, and Autonomy, Catalonia, Corsica, Hong Kong, and Tibet*. New York: Palgrave Macmillan.

Imamović, M. (2006). *Osnove Upravno-Političkog Razvitka I Državno-Pravnog Položaja Bosne I Hercegovine*. Sarajevo: Pravni fakultuet u Sarajevu.

Keil, S. (2012). Federalism as a Tool of Conflict-Resolution: The Case of Bosnia and Herzegovina. *L'Europe en Formation, 363*(1), 205–218.

Keil, S. (2013). *Multinational Federalism in Bosnia and Herzegovina*. Farnham/Burlington: Ashgate.

Keil, S., & Kudlenko, A. (2015). Bosnia and Herzegovina 20 Years After Dayton: Complexity Born of Paradoxes. *International Peacekeeping, 22*(5), 471–489.

Knežević, G. (2017). Public Tv Survived the War, but Can It Survive Peacetime in Bosnia? Radio Free Europe, Radio Liberty. Accessed 15/04/2020.

Kolers, A. (2009). *Land, Conflict, and Justice, a Political Theory of Territory*. Cambridge/New York: Cambridge University Press.

Kovacevic, D. (2019). Bosnian Serb Lawmakers Claim Right to Self-Determination. *Balkan Insight*. https://balkaninsight.com/2019/11/12/bosnian-serb-lawmakers-claim-right-to-self-determination/

Kovacevic, D. (2020). Bosnian Serb Leader Repeats Demand for Secession Referendum. *Balkan Insight*. https://balkaninsight.com/2020/02/15/bosnian-serb-leader-repeats-demand-for-secession-referendum/

Kulenović, N. (2012). Skupština Brčko Distrikta Bih: Parlament Ili Općinsko Vijeće? In S. Gavrić & D. Banović (Eds.), *Parlamentarizam U Bosni I Hercegovini*. Sarajevo: Sarajevski otvoreni centar/Fondacija Friedrich Ebert.

Larkins, J. (2010). *From Hierarchy to Anarchy Territory and Politics Before Westphalia*. New York: Palgrave Macmillan.

Latal, S. (2019). Bosnia Remains Hostage to Old, Obsolete Narratives. *Balkan Insight*. https://balkaninsight.com/2019/10/28/bosnia-remains-hostage-to-old-obsolete-narratives/

Leuprecht, C. (2009). Demographic Change – A Catalyst for Federal Asymmetry. In F. Palermo, C. Zwilling, & K. Kössler (Eds.), *Asymmetries in Constitutional Law, Recent Developments in Federal and Regional Systems*. Bozen/Bolzano: Europäische Akademie Bozen/Accademia Europea Bolzano.

Loughlin, J. (2007). Reconfiguring the State: Trends in Territorial Governance in European States. *Regional and Federal Studies 17*(4), 385–403.

Marko, J. (2019). The Minority Protection to Multiple Diversity Management. In J. Marko & S. Constantin (Eds.), *Human and Minorities Rights Protection by Multiple Diversity Governance, History, Law, Ideology and Politics in European Perspective* (pp. 396–429). London/New York: Routledge.

Marko, J. (2006). Problems of State-and-Nation-Building in Post-Conflict Situations: The Case of Bosnia-Herzegovina. *Vermont Law Review, 30*, 503–550.

Marko, J., & Constantin, S. (2019). Against Marginalisation, the Right to Effective Participation. In J. Marko & S. Constantin (Eds.), *Human and Minorities Rights Protection by Multiple Diversity Governance, History, Law, Ideology and Politics in European Perspective* (pp. 340–395). London/New York: Routledge.

Medda-Windischer, R. (2011). New Minorities, Old Instruments? A Common but Differentiated System of Minority Protection. *International Community Law Review, 13*(4), 361–391.

Nicolini, M. (2016). Territorial and Ethnic Divide: A New Legal Geography for Cyprus. In M. Nicolini, F. Palermo, & E. Milano (Eds.), *Law, Territory and Conflict Resolution, Law as a Problem and Law as a Solution*. Leiden/Boston: Brill Nijhoff.

Osipov, A. (2016). Studying Territorial Autonomy as a Multiplicity of Ways to Institutionalise Ethnicity. In M. Nicolini, F. Palermo, & E. Milano (Eds.), *Law, Territory and Conflict Resolution Law as a Problem and Law as a Solution*. Nijhoff: Brill.

Palermo, F. (2016). Territory and the Law of Ownership: From Misunderstanding to Opportunity. In M. Nicolini, F. Palermo, & E. Milano (Eds.), *Law, Territory and Conflict Resolution, Law as a Problem and Law as a Solution* (pp. 16–38). Leiden: Brill.

Perry, V. (2015). Constitutional Reform in Bosnia and Herzegovina: Does the Road to Confederation Go through the Eu? *International Peacekeeping, 22*(5), 490–510.

Pobrić, N. (2000). *Ustavno Pravo*. Mostar: Slovo.

Quattrocchi, G. (2016). Bosnia: Republika Srpska Referendum and the Threat of Secession. Mediterranean affairs. Accessed 14/04/2019, http://mediterraneanaffairs.com/republika-srpska-referendum-and-the-threat-of-secession-in-bosnia/

Sahadžić, M. (2012). "Skupštine Kantona." In Parlamentarizam U Bosni I Hercegovini, edited by Saša Gavrić and Damir Banović, 137–61. Sarajevo: Sarajevski otvoreni centar/Fondacija Friedrich Ebert.

Sahadžić, M. (2019). Mild Asymmetry and Ethnoterritorial Overlap in Charge of the Consequences of Multinationalism. A Country Study of Constitutional Asymmetry in Bosnia and Herzegovina. Chap. 47–76. In P. Popelier & M. Sahadžić (Eds.), *Constitutional Asymmetry in Multinational Federalism, Managing Multinationalism in Multi-Tiered Systems*. Cham: Palgrave Macmillan.

Sahadžić, M. (2011a). Priroda Političkog Sistema U Bosni I Hercegovini. In D. Banović & S. Gavrić (Eds.), *Država, Politika I Društvo U Bosni I Hercegovini – Analiza Postdejtonskog Političkog Sistema* (pp. 15–37). Sarajevo: University Press, Magistrat izdanja.

Sahadžić, M. (2011b). Uspostavljanje Vrhovnog Suda Bih, Aktualna Pravna Misao O Teoretskoj Nedosljednosti U Praksi. Sveske za javno pravo/Blätter für Öffentliches Recht, No. 4.

Sahadžić, M. (2013). In D. Mirović (Ed.), *Ustav Hercegovačko-Neretvanskog Kantona O Ljudskim Pravima I Slobodama I "Ostalim": O Postuliranju Krepke (Ne)Konstitutivne (Ne)Ravnoteže Nauštrb "Ostalih" I Ustavnopravnom*

Perverzitetu U Hercegovačko-Neretvanskom Kantonu. Edicija (Ne)Konstitutivni Centra Za Političke Studije. Sarajevo: Centar za političke studije.

Seizović, Z. (2008). *Međunarodno Javno Pravo: Zbirka Eseja*. Zenica: Univerzitet u Zenici.

Seizović, Z. (2014). Političko-Pravni Uzroci Nacionalne Mobilizacije I Dekonstitucionalizacije U Bosni I Hercegovini. In *Paradigma Bosna, Juče, Danas, Sutra*. Sarajevo: dobra knjiga.

Stepan, A. (2004). Towards a New Comparative Politics of Federalism, Multinationalism, and Democracy: Beyond Rikerian Federalism. In E. L. Gibson (Ed.), *Federalism and Democracy in Latin America*. Baltimore: Johns Hopkins University Press.

Surk, B. (2018). Milorad Dodik Wants to Carve Up Bosnia. Peacefully, If Possible. *New York Times*. https://www.nytimes.com/2018/02/16/world/europe/dodik-republika-srpska-bosnia.html

Touquet, H., & Vermeersch, P. (2008). Bosnia and Herzegovina: Thinking Beyond Institution-Building. *Nationalism and Ethnic Politics, 14*(2), 266–288.

Touval, S. (2002). *Mediation in the Yugoslav Wars, the Critical Years, 1990–95*. Basingstoke/New York: Palgrave Macmillan.

Vukoja, I., & Sitarski, M. (2016). *Bosnia and Herzegovina – Federalism, Equality, Sustainability, a Study of Bih Redesign to Secure Institutional Equality of Constituent Peoples*. Mostar: Institute for Social and Political Research (IDPI).

Woelk, J. (2012). *Bosnia-Herzegovina: Trying to Build a Federal State on Paradoxes*. http://weblaw.haifa.ac.il/he/Events/eveFile/bosnia%2D%2Dwoelk%20def%20FN.pdf

Zdeb, A. (2016). The Need to Have Something 'of Their Own': Croat Parallel Institutions in Bosnia and Herzegovina. *Swiss Political Science Review, 22*(4), 545–564.

CHAPTER 13

The Law and Politics of Internal Secession: The Ethiopian Experience in Comparative Perspective

Yonatan T. Fessha and Zemelak A. Ayele

1 Introduction

The date 20 November 2019 might go down in the history as one of the turning points for federalism in Ethiopia, a federation composed of nine ethnically defined states. After clamouring for their own state for decades, the Sidama, the fifth largest ethnic group in the country, were allowed to have their day in a referendum. On the morning of that historic day, there were already long queues of excited voters. They were voting on whether to secede from the Southern Nations Nationalities and Peoples (SNNP)

Y. T. Fessha (✉)
University of the Western Cape, Cape Town, South Africa
e-mail: yfessha@uwc.ac.za

Z. A. Ayele
Addis Ababa University, Addis Ababa, Ethiopia

M. Belov (ed.), *Territorial Politics and Secession*, Federalism and Internal Conflicts, https://doi.org/10.1007/978-3-030-64402-4_13

state, one of the nine states that make up the Ethiopian federation and home to more than 50 ethnic communities.[1] According to the results announced by the National Electoral Board (NEBE), 98.5% voted for internal secession. The Sidama are not however the only ethnic community in the country demanding for own state. In the SNNP only, the local government councils of ten ethnic communities have resolved to secede from the state and establish their own states[2]

The 1995 Constitution of Ethiopia has established what is commonly referred to as ethnic federalism, which is primarily founded based on the principle of self-determination that explicitly includes the right of every ethnic community to both external and internal self-determination.[3] The right of an ethnic community to secede from the federation and establish its own independent country represents a recognition of the right to external self-determination. The right to internal self-determination, on the other hand, has found expression with the establishment of ethnic-based state and local governments.[4] The Constitution authorises ethnic communities that do not have their own states to secede from the state wherein they found and establish their own state. It is based on this

[1] The Sidama had had a history of distinct administrative existence going back to imperial days. More recently, the ethnically defined State of Sidama was established in 1991. That was abolished when the Constitution was adopted in 1995. Since then, members of the Sidama community have been demanding to have their own state. Even in the days when raising such questions was unwelcomed, members of the community did not hesitate to petition federal authorities. Thanks to the prevailing democratic centralism in the past, which expected party members to toe the lines of the central committee of the ruling party, Sidama petitioners were forced to write another letter to withdraw their request.

[2] These are Wolayta, Kaffa, Gofa, Sheka, Bench Maji, Kembata, Gurage, Dawro, Hadiya and Gamo.

[3] Article 39(1) of the Constitution provides that every ethnic community 'has an unconditional right to self-determination, including the right to secession' referring to external secession.

[4] It should be noted that the Constitution does not seem to envisage that the right to a full measure of self-government necessarily have to find expression through the establishment of a state to each ethnic group. It seems to imply that some ethnic communities might have to exercise their right to self-government, including the right to establish institutions of government in the territory they inhabit, within the territorial boundaries of the regional state in which they are situated. In other words, they have to exercise their right to self-government in some form of local autonomy. Thus, over 20 ethnic local governments, known as special zones and special *woredas* (districts), have been established in five states (SNNP, Amhara, Afar, Gambella and Benishangul-Gumuz). For more on this see Ayele and Fessha (2012).

constitutional right that different ethnic communities are agitating for internal secession.

Although secession has been the subject of much scholarly work, the focus has largely been on the external dimension of secession, the decision of a territory to leave an existing state and establish itself as independent country (Anderson 2016; Kohen 2006). Little attention has been provided to the less radical solution of internal secession, the right of a community or territory to secede from a subnational unit and establish its own unit.[5] Using the Ethiopian experience as a case study, this chapter discusses the law governing the process of internal secession in a comparative perspective. It also touches on the politics of internal secession.

The chapter is structured in five interrelated parts. The second part provides the constitutional and political context that leads ethnic communities to demand for own states. The third part deals with the process of internal secession. It in particular deals with the issue of whether internal self-determination in the form of internal secession is constitutionally recognised as a right and whether and under what conditions it could be exercised. It discusses the grounds that may justify internal secession and the procedure that must govern a request for internal secession. It also examines the role and powers of the national government and the subnational unit from which the territory is seeking to secede. It discusses whether internal secession should be a unilateral affair or an outcome of a negotiation. The fourth part reflects on the politics of internal secession before it concludes with brief remarks.

[5] Internal secession refers to a process in federal states in which 'new states are carved out of the existing ones and given member state statuses'. It is thus 'an internal enlargement, where the number of member states grows but the territory of the union does not' (Requejo and Nagel 2017). Indeed the right to external self-determination of ethnic, linguistic or religious communities under international law has been a subject of continuous debate. Some also argue that the right to internal self-determination in the sense of a group of people being able 'to develop itself socially, economically and culturally ... and to determine its political status within [a] state' has at least implicit recognition in the UN Charter and explicit recognition in other human rights instrument (Seymour 2011). The right to internal self-determination as recognised in international law does not necessarily involve internal secession and can find expression in other forms, including democratic participation.

2 The Context: Ethnic Federalism and Internal Secession in Ethiopia

Ethiopia, country of about 80 ethnic groups, has adopted a federal system which is largely conceptualised as a 'federation of ethnic groups' in which the various ethnic communities (nations, nationalities and peoples in the parlance of the Constitution) that inhabit the country are assumed to have 'joined together in a federal union' (Herther-Spiro 2007). Under the federal dispensation, therefore, Ethiopia is seen as a state 'founded by and belongs to all ethnic groups' (Gebre-Sellasie 2003). In addition to the right to external self-determination recognised in the form of the right of an ethnic community to secede from the country, the constitution (Article 39(3)), as mentioned earlier, provides each ethnic community with the right to self-rule and establish institutions of government within the territory it inhabits. However, as can be seen in Table 13.1, only five of the nine states – Amhara, Afar, Oromia, Somali and Tigray – are home to a particular ethnic community that accounts for the overwhelming majority of their respective populations.[6] Each of these states is also named after the ethnic community which is a majority in the state. The remaining ones are markedly multi-ethnic in which no particular ethnic group accounts for the majority of their respective populations. This asymmetrical treatment of ethnic groups has unavoidably provoked a call for equal treatment from some of the ethnic groups that also want to have their own state.

The situation is complicated by the fact that some 'numerically stronger' ethnic communities in the SNNP are denied the status of a State while other 'numerically weak' ethnic communities are allowed to have 'their own' state. The State of Harari is home to the eponymous ethnic community with a population size of less than 200,000. On the other hand, there are ethnic groups, like the Sidama, Wolayita, Kaffa, Hadiya and the like that boast a population size of more than a million people and do not have a State of their own. For instance, the Sidama have a population size that exceeds the combined population of some of the subnational entities. In short, while few ethnic communities are provided a state in which they are in majority, many cannot point to a territory they inhabit that has achieved the status of a State. The good thing for ethnic communities

[6]The nine states are Amhara, Afar, Benishangul-Gumuz, Gambella, Harreri, Oromia, Somali, Southern Nations Nationalities and Peoples (SNNP) and Tigray, These are listed under Article 47(1) of the Constitution.

Table 13.1 Intra-regional ethnic diversity

State	*Ethnic groups*						
Amhara	Amhara (91%), Agew (5%), Oromo (3%), Others (2%)						
Oromia	Oromo (87%), Amhara (7%), Ghurage (1%), Somai (1%), Others (4%)						
Tigray	Tigrawi (96.55%), Kunama (0.7%), Irob/Saho (0.71%), Others (2.4%)						
SNNPR	Surma (0.17%)	Zeyise (0.10)	Gidecho (0.03%)	Arbore (0.04%)	Geleb	Kore (1.01%)	Gideo
	Gurage (7.52%)	Hamer (0.31)	Gewada (0.43%)	Basketo (0.52%)	Burji (0.37%)	Alaba (1.35%)	Bena (0.17%)
	Kambata (3.81%)	Shinasha (0.01%)	Dawro (3%)	Bumi	Dime	Tembaro (0.64)	Shekicho (0.44%)
	Kafficho (5.43%)	Wolaita (10.71%)	Gacho	Nao (0.05%)	Tsemay (0.13%)	Hadyia (8.02%)	Alaba (1.35%)
	Qebena (0.29%)	Gamo (6.96%)	Derashe (0.19%)	Bench (2.33%)	Yem (0.50%)	Konta (0.54%)	Amhara (2.79%)
	Konso (1.46%)	Sidama (19%)	Me'enite (1%)	Mareko (0.38%)	Oida (0.05%)	Ari (1.89%)	Gedeo (4.92%)
	Gofa (2.39%)	Oromo (1.57%)	Silte (5%)	Desenech (0.32%)	Surma (0.11%)		
Afar	Afar (90.3%), Amhara (5.22%), Argoba (1.5), Others (2.98%)						
Gambella	Anywaa (21.17%), Nuer (46.65%), Mejenger (4%), Amhara (8.42%), Oromo (4.33%), Others (18%)						
Benishangul-Gumuz	Berta (25.90%), Gumuz (21.11%), Shinasha (7.5%), Mao (2%), Koma (1%)						
	Agew (5%), Amhara (21.25), Oromo (13.32%), Others (2.92%)						
Hareri	Hareri (8.65%), Oromo (56%), Amhara (22%), Somali (3.87%), Guraghe (4%), Others (5.8%)						
Somali	Somali (97%), Others (3%)						

Source: FDRE Population Census Commission (2008)

without own state is that the Constitution has kept the door of statehood ajar for other ethnic groups that would advocate for the establishment of a state of their own.

The practice, however, has not been encouraging. The demands for internal secession have largely been ignored. This is largely attributable to the political stance of the Ethiopian Peoples' Revolutionary Democratic Front (EPRDF)—the party that enjoyed an exclusive political control over the country for close to three decades. EPRDF assumed power in 1991, after having ousted the *Derg*, the communist military junta that ruled the country for 17 years, in the name of bringing about a political era in which the right to self-determination of every ethnic community of the country would be recognised. Initially, especially during the transitional period (1991–1995), the party was not only willing to accommodate demands for own state and ethnic local government but also it was actively encouraging them.[7] For instance, during the transitional period, there were 14 states and some of the major ethnic communities in the SNNP, including Sidama, Hadya and Kaffa, had their own states (Vaughan 2003). Moreover, almost every ethnic community demanding for own local government received a positive response. That did not last long.

Soon the party had a change of heart about ethnic-based claims for territorial autonomy. The creation of territorial units purely based on ethnic criteria, without taking into account economic and administrative factors, was no longer encouraged. Instead of allowing the creation of new ones, the party began merging the already existing states and ethnic local governments. It was then that the Sidama, Hadya, Kaffa and other states were merged to form the state now known as the SNNP (Vaughan 2003).

Moreover, in the early 2000s, the party adopted what is known as developmental state paradigm, according to which, achieving development and making Ethiopia a middle-income country was considered as the sole political and economic agenda of the country.[8] Centralised decision-making process was regarded as the preferred vehicle to achieve the developmental goals set by the national government. The party even refused demands by ethnic communities for own local government, let

[7] 'Fieldwork suggests that between the mid-1990s and the end of that decade, there was an observable and orchestrated move by the EPRDF in the Southern Region, [SNNP], to claw back control over what some have described as the "ethnic free for-all" in political and administrative organisation, which had applied over its first few years. During the initial part of the transitional period, groups of all sizes, claims, and credibility had been encouraged by the party to organise and mobilise their populations for self-determination. After several years, however, the government started to argue that, for reasons of budgetary efficiency, it made sense to consolidate the myriad zones, regions, and political parties which had emerged in response. A precursor to this process was the amalgamation in 1992 of the series of smaller, initially federated units clustered in the south, to form the Southern Region' (Vaughan 2003).

[8] Meles Zenawi is credited with articulating the arguments in favour of the developmental state paradigm in his various writings. A developmental state would 'have to transform the political economy of patronage and rent-seeking' into one that is 'value-creating'. To achieve this, the developmental state should have a strong centre capable of mobilising the people and the country's resources to achieve economic transformation, which in turn requires 'a strong, cohesive and centralised party'. Once economic transformation is achieved, the developmental state dies a natural death and is replaced by liberal democracy (De Waal 2012; Yeibyio 2015).

alone own state, since it viewed ethnicity as detrimental to the country's development (Aalen 2008).

The right to self-rule has thus become secondary to development; various lawful demands for own state and local government were denied in the name of development and efficiency. As Aalen notes with respect to the SNNP, 'a principled decision [was made] to separate "identity issue" from "administrative issues", stating that the request for new zone or special *woreda* administrations should from now on be considered from a purely administrative perspective, which was clearly separated from the right of nationalities to self-determination'.[9]

Obviously, the political elites of the different ethnic communities have various incentives for demanding for own states. In addition to the symbolic benefits of recognition that come with having one's own state, state-owning ethnic groups enjoy powers and rights that are constitutionally guaranteed to ethnic groups and States, respectively, while ethnic groups with no State of their own are limited to enjoying rights that are given to ethnic groups. To be sure, some of those ethnic groups, like the Sidama, are given their own local government, allowing them to exercise powers that are reserved to local administrations (Ayele 2014). The powers and functions entrusted to local government are not, however, comparable to those of State governments.

More significantly, the place that an ethnic group assumes, albeit indirectly, in the administrative hierarchy of the federal arrangement determines the amount of money it receives from the federal redistribution regime. State-owning ethnic communities receive a much more substantial share of the federal transfer than those that are made to exercise their right to self-administration at the level of local government who do not have direct access to federal transfers.[10] This is irrespective of the fact that some of the ethnic communities that do not have their own State boast a population size that is far larger than some of the State-owning ethnic groups. State-owning ethnic communities are by far in a better position to

[9] 'It was decided that groups which before could argue that recognition of a separate ethnic identity should automatically give them the right to a separate administration would not be heard anymore' (Aalen 2008).

[10] The federal government does not even make direct revenue transfer to ethnic local governments since these do not have direct relationships with the former. It transfers the money to the states and the state, using their own formula, make revenue transfer to the ethnic local government (Ayele 2014).

provide their members with better economic opportunity, political power and social statuses.

Over the past 27 years, several communities have demanded for their own state. These communities include the Sidama, the Wolayita, the Gumuz and the Berta communities who have for a long time aspired to possessing their own state (Keffale 2012). In fact, the Sidama local government council had gone as far as approving a demand for a separate state—a demand which also received support from the Council of Nationalities, the second chamber of the state parliament. However, the federal government intervened and stopped the implementation of this decision (Aalen 2008). Moreover, members of the Berta community had also petitioned for secession from the Benishangul-Gumzu state and the establishment of a Berta state. The EPRDF dismissed their petition 'as an unpopular wish of the Berta political elite, not a genuine demand of the people' (Keffale 2012).

However, after almost three decades of exclusive rule, EPRDF began to face public resistance in the form of public protests. The public protests began in Oromia two years after Meles Zenawi died and soon after the 2015 elections, in which EPRDF claimed 100% victory. The protests spread throughout the country and continued until 2018 leading to the resignation of Hailemariam Desalegn as the Prime Minister of the country which in turn paved the way for Abiy Ahmed to assume the premiership.

Abiy took several measures and introduced various reforms, among other things, with a professed aim of democratising the country. He invited all political parties and organisations, including those in exile and those that had raised up arms against the government, to return to the country and take part in the political life of the country. His invitation was accepted by almost all political parties and organisations which are now negotiating political reforms with the government. Several laws, including the anti-terrorism, media and civil societies organisation (CSO) laws were revised with the declared aim of opening up the political space and making future elections competitive and representative (Tsige 2019; Fana Broadcasting Corporate 2019). Abiy rebranded the EPRDF with new name—the Ethiopian Prosperity Party (EPP)—and new ideology—abandoning the 'revolutionary democracy' ideology and the 'developmental state paradigm' (Gebreselassie 2019).

Members of the Sidama community saw an opportunity when Abiy Ahmed was elected in 2018 as the Prime Minister and introduced a series of political reforms. More importantly, there is no longer a strong ruling party that forces state governments to toe the lines of national government. The Sidama local government council felt emboldened enough to publicly declare its intention to secede from the SNNP and demanded the organisation of a referendum. To the surprise of many, the Parliament of the SNNP supported the request for a referendum to allow the people of Sidama to decide their fate. In the meantime, members of the community intensified their demand for statehood. Thousands marched in an all-women rally in support of internal secession. Reportedly, a consultation on a draft constitution for the new state is underway. Sidama activists gave the country an ultimatum. 'Declare the day of referendum before 18 July 2019 or we will proceed to declare the formation of a Sidama state' (Yokamo 2019).

The federal government tried to avoid holding a referendum to the Sidama. The Central Committee of then EPRDF later came up with a proposal, which it called was based on 'scientific study', of dividing the SNNP into two states in which the Sidama would have their own state, while the rest of the SNNP would remain intact (Addis Standard 2019). However, political parties and informal youth organisation of the Sidama community known as *Ejetto* threatened that they would unilaterally declare the Sidama state on 18 July 2019, exactly a year after the regional government approved the demand for own state before which the NEBE was supposed to organise referendum (Tronvoll et al. 2020). They even began replacing posters of Sidama local government offices with 'the Sidama Regional State'. Outside the Hawassa airport, they erected a huge billboard that reads 'Welcome to the Sidama Regional State'. They also began flying what they called the Sidama state flag instead of the state flag of the SNNP (Reuter 2019).

A few weeks before the deadline set by the Sidama parties and other political groups for the unilateral declaration of the Sidama state, the NEBE declared that it would hold the referendum in November 2019 (Tronvoll et al. 2020). However, on July 18 a massive public protest began in the Sidama local government area which involved burning of churches and attacking non-Sidama people in the area. A semblance of peace and order was restored in the area only after the Army was deployed. Many Sidamas who agitated for the unilateral declaration of the state of Sidama were arrested. Finally, as was indicated in the introduction, the referendum was held on 22 November 2019 in which 98.5% of the Sidama voted in favour of the formation of the Sidama state.

3 Internal Secession and the Formation of SNU in Federations

The Ethiopian federation is not the only federation that envisage the creation of a new subnational unit out of the existing ones.[11] Provisions permitting or envisioning the alteration of state boundaries through internal secession seem to be rather common in federal constitutions. The national constitutions of many federations, including Argentina, Australia, Brazil, Austria, Belgium, Canada, German, India, Malaysia, Mexico, Nigeria, Russia, Switzerland, South Africa and the USA, contain a provision or two referring to the alteration of subnational boundaries and the creation of new ones including through the division of an existing one.[12]

Practice also shows that several new states have been created through internal secession in different federations. For instance, in the USA, the states of Kentucky, Maine, Vermont and West Virginia were created through a process of internal secession or state partition. There are still numerous proposals for internal secession from 1 of the 50 states of the USA. In Switzerland, the Canton of Jura was created through the process of internal secession (Dominice 2006). Likewise, in India the states of Nunavut and Jharkhand, among others, were the states that were created in the latest round of state reorganisation (Gilliland 2013).

Although the Ethiopian Constitution is not the only constitution that allows for the creation of new subnational units, it departs from its

[11] According to Article 47(3) of the Constitution, the exercise of the right to internal secession has to be initiated first by the approval vote of 'a two-thirds majority of the members of the legislative council' of the community concerned and the demand is presented in writing to the state council. The state council then organizes a referendum within one year from the time it receives the relevant council's decision to form its own state. When the demand for internal secession secures the majority vote in the referendum and the State Government has transferred its powers to the newly created state, the new state that is 'created by the referendum' directly becomes a member of the federations without any need for application.

[12] S 13, Constitution of the Argentine Nation (1994); Art 73, Mexico's Constitution of 1917 with Amendments through 2015; S 121 Australia's Constitution (1906); Art 3(2) Austria: The federal constitutional law of 1920; Art 6 and 7, Belgium's Constitution of (1831); Art 18, Brazil's Constitution of 1988; Art 42(1)(f), Canada's Constitution of (1867); Art 29, Basic Law for the Federal Republic of Germany (1949); Art 2 & 3, India's Constitution of (1949); Art 2, Federal Constitution of Malaysia (1957); Art 8, Nigeria's Constitution (1999); Art 1(3), the Constitution of the Islamic Republic of Pakistan; Art 65, Russian Federation's Constitution (1993); Art 53, Federal Constitution of the Swiss Confederation; S 3, the Constitution of the United States (1776); 103, The Constitution of the Republic of South Africa (1996); Spanish Constitution (1978).

counterparts because it has elevated the demand for the creation of a new subnational unit to the status of a constitutional right. Article 47(2) of the Constitution provides for the right to internal secession and provides for a procedure according to which the right to internal secession can be exercised. More importantly, it is not a right available to any territory but to ethnic groups. According to the Constitution, it is ethnic groups that do not have their own states that have 'the right to establish, at any time, their own States'.

We are not aware of other constitutions that explicitly provide ethnic groups the right to internal secession though some of them allow a group of people to petition for own state. In many countries, the creation of new subnational units is not also necessarily meant to empower a cultural or ethnic group. New subnational units are often created as a result of political mobilisation and a political decision that is made by a reluctant national government.

What also makes the Ethiopian constitution different from the others is that those seeking their own state are not required to provide a justification. The Constitution does not outline grounds under which a demand for internal secession can be made. The right to an internal secession is an independently existing right. The claimants are not required to demonstrate a legitimate condition that warrants the exercise of this right. The Constitution, for example, does not impose any requirement in terms of population and territorial size that an ethnic community has to fulfil in order to have its own state (Bihonegn 2015). In principle, even an ethnic community of a few thousand population can demand for own state.

In many other federations, the creation of a new subnational unit is permissible only under certain legitimate causes and when certain conditions are fulfilled. In some of them, the creation of new subnational unit is allowed if it can facilitate democratic inclusion or create administrative convenience.

In Germany, for instance, the creation of a new subnational unit is possible if it is necessary to achieve efficiency. The German Basic Law (Article 29(2)) provides that the current territorial structure of the federation might be revised, including through the creation of new *Landers*, if doing so is necessary for ensuring that each *Land* is 'of a size and capacity to perform its functions effectively'. Article 29(4) of the Basic Law also provides that a new *Lander* may be formed through the merger of two or more 'clearly defined and contiguous residential and economic areas located in two or more *Lande*'. The economic and residential areas that seek to be within a single *Lander* have to have a minimum of one million inhabitants of which one-tenth are eligible to vote in national elections (Article 29). Here again the claimants request must be justified by the need to create administrative convenience and respond to demands for democratic inclusion. The Mexican constitution (Article 73(III) (1)) implicitly provides that a portion of a state may petition to be granted statehood if it has a minimum of 120,000 population and that 'it possesses enough elements to assure [its] political existence' as a state. This seems to respond to democratic demands of citizens and not to accommodate an ethno-national group.

Hence, it is clear that internal secession is not a constitutional entitlement made available to ethnic groups in most federations. New states are created in most federation often following incessant demands for own state in the name of democratic inclusion and administrative efficiency. Indeed, as is the case in Jura, an ethno-national group can demand for own state by invoking the right to self-rule. While nothing prohibits such demands, there is no general entitlement for an ethno-national group for own state. Ethiopia remains the exception by providing ethnic groups an unconditional right to internal secession.

4 The Process of Internal Secession

The Ethiopian Constitution provides for a rather simple procedure according to which the right to internal secession can be exercised. According to article 47(3) of the Constitution, the exercise of the right to internal secession has to be initiated first by the approval vote of 'a two-thirds majority of the members of the legislative council' of the community concerned, which presumably is a reference to the council of the local government area in which the petitioning community is located. The demand, once approved by the local government council, is then presented in writing to the state council. The state council then organises a referendum within one year from the time it receives the relevant council's decision to form its own state. When the demand for internal secession secures the majority vote in the referendum and the State Government has transferred its powers to the newly created state, the new state that is 'created by the referendum' directly becomes a member of the federation without any need for application.

The Use of Referendum

From the above, it is clear that what is required from the community demanding for internal secession is to show that it has proven support through a referendum.[13] The use of a referendum for the purposes of the creation of new subnational units is not uncommon. In fact, popular referendum is a requirement for the creation of a subnational unit under the constitutions of Austria,[14] Belgium Brazil, Germany, Switzerland and Nigeria. Article 53 of the Swiss Constitution, which defines the procedure for the creation a new canton, requires the holding of plebiscites at different level.[15] Section 123 of the Australian constitution provides that alteration of a state, including increasing, diminishing or in any way altering the limits of the State, needs to be approved by popular referendum. Although Section 124, which deals with the formation of a new state, is silent on the issue of popular referendum, it seems the creation of a new state needs approval of the electors in the affected state since it results in the alteration of the state.[16]

[13] The threshold is not significant as simple majority is sufficient to determine the wishes of the community.

[14] The referendum has to be requested by one-third of members of any of the two houses of the federal Parliament (Article 44(3)).

[15] This provision was inserted to fill the constitutional vacuum that emerged in relation to the Jura case. Districts in Jura with Catholic and French-speaking communities demanded to be allowed to secede from Bern. When the demand of own canton and its counter movement led to break down in law and order, the federal government, at the request of the Bern canton, established a committee which recommended that the Jura problem is as a rule the internal matter of the Bern. However, if Bern decided to resolve the issue by allowing Jura to secede, the matters would cease to be Bern's internal problem since the creation of a new state requires constitutional amendment. The committee thus recommended that secession should be a last resort. If it has to be done, a procedure that lead 'winner takes all' situation should be avoided. Hence about five plebiscites were held. First the constitution of Bern was amended to provide for procedure for secession which was approved through referendum. Then a plebiscite was held at regional level followed by others at district and municipal level. Each municipality was asked if it desires to join the new canton or remain with Bern. The idea was that 'in such crucial decisions, even small minorities belonging to a municipality must be part of the consensus-making'. Three of the seven districts (predominately catholic and French speaking) decided to join the new canton while four districts (predominantly French-speaking protestant districts) to remain with Bern (Fleiner 2002; Gilliland 2013).

[16] To the contrary, the constitutions of the USA, Argentina, India, Pakistan, Malaysia, Mexico, Russia and South Africa do not require popular referendum for the creation of a new subnational unit.

The use of referendum for the purposes of creating new subnational unit raises a number of issues. In the case of Ethiopia, there is some level of disagreement with respect to who has the right to vote in a referendum relating to internal secession. As mentioned earlier, the Ethiopian constitution provides the right to internal secession to an ethnic group.

This has raised the question whether the right to vote is limited to members of the ethnic group in question or extends to other residents of the territory that is in question. Some argue that members of the petitioning ethic community have exclusive right to vote in the referendum. This is because, goes the argument, the right to self-determination, according to the Constitution, belongs to an ethnic community not to residents of a given territorial area. Hence only members of the ethnic community demanding own state should take part in the referendum. In any case, non-Sidama residents of Hawassa and other towns, which are found within the Sidama zone, were allowed to vote in the recently held Sidama referendum.

The practice of extending the right to vote to all residents of a territory, irrespective of the ethnic group they belong to, is consistent with the practice and laws of many other countries. In Australia, for example, citizens/ residents of the affected state, who are of voting age, are entitled to vote in such referendum. In Switzerland referenda take place at different levels including at municipal, district, regional, cantonal and national levels. Thus, not only those directly affected by the creation of a new canton, the entire Swiss population has a say on whether or not a new canton should be established and be admitted into the federation.

In Germany referenda are held throughout an affected *Landers* and a separate referendum is held in the areas where the new Lander would be established (Basic Law, Art 29(3)). The majority votes in each of the referendum have to support the establishment of the new Lander. If the majority of the population of any of the affected Lander reject the proposal for the creation of a new Lander, the latter will have to be supported by two-third majority in the referendum that would be held in the areas where the new lander would be established.

The Brazilian constitution (Article 18(3)) provides that only members of the population who are 'directly interested' on the creation of or otherwise of the new state could vote in the plebiscite. In case of creating new state, this is interpreted to extend the right to vote to all those residing in the would-be new state.

In the case of Ethiopia, the fact that the referendum has returned an overwhelming majority supporting the establishment of the State of Sidama, for example, means that there is a clear and very strong majority in favour of internal secession. Unfortunately, the circumstances under which the Sidama referendum was conducted has left unnecessary stain on the results of the referendum. This was not a referendum that was preceded by a process in which the public was given the chance to reflect on the merits of a new state. Even after a decision was made to conduct a referendum and the date of the referendum was fixed, it is difficult to claim that there was a forum that allowed the 'leave' and 'remain' camps to participate in a genuine deliberative process.

The Ethiopian Human Rights Commission and a consortium of civil society organisations have also expressed their reservations that this was a referendum without a proper campaign season. To be precise, there was a lot of campaigning, but it was one-sided. It was only the voice of those that clamoured for the creation of the new state that dominated the months leading to the event. Those that belonged in the 'remain' camp did not or were not able to make their case.

The environment needed for voters to receive information and reflect on that information was simply non-existent. That may not have significantly altered the results of the referendum, but it casts doubt on whether the public was well informed on what it was asked to vote. That has reduced the referendum into a ceremonial act that is simply used to tick all the boxes of the constitutional requirement. This is unfortunate. After all, referendums are not cheap, both politically and financially.

Internal Secession as a Constitutional Amendment: Is the Consent of Others a Requirement?

What is not, however, clear is whether the expression of proven support in a referendum completes the act of internal secession. In his address to law makers, the Prime Minister of Ethiopia, in relation to the referendum for the formation of the Sidama state, maintained that a demand for statehood needs the support of the other states. A majority vote in favour of statehood might not be sufficient. This, he argued, is because the constitution only lists nine states that constitute the federation. Getting the prospective state of Sidama into that list requires a constitutional amendment. In effect, he was arguing that the formation of a new state entails the consent of the existing states, including the consent of the affected state, which in turn requires a constitutional amendment.

The practice in other federations is mixed. In countries where the constitution does not contain the list of the constituent units, the formation of a new subnational unit, it seems, does not always entail the amendment of the national constitution. This is the case, for example, in the USA, Australia, Germany, India, Brazil, Malaysia and Pakistan.[17] However, there are also a number of countries where the formation of a new subnational unit seems to require constitutional amendment. This is the case under the constitutions of Switzerland, Austria, Canada, Mexico, Nigeria, Russia and South Africa. What is common about the constitutions of these countries is that all of them contain the list of the subnational units that make up the federation.

In the case of Ethiopia, many were quick to dismiss the equation of internal secession with amendment as an act of legal gymnastics by a Prime Minister who has found himself between a rock and hard place. After all, the Constitution states that a new state joins the federation automatically without any need for application. At the same time, the Constitution contains the list of 'member states' of the federation. It is possible that the drafters of the constitution have not thought of the paradox of a federal constitution that lists the constituent units while at the same time allows for internal secession that does not depend on the approval of the other members of the federation. Perhaps one may be tempted to dismiss this as an oversight on the part of the drafters and ignore the argument that equates internal secession with a constitutional amendment.

[17] Parliament of the Common Wealth is authorised to admit a state into the Australian federation by using ordinary parliamentary act, preventing the need for constitutional amendment. The US constitution does not contain a list of all of the 51 states. Indeed, the 13 original signatories to constitution are mentioned under section 2 of the constitution in connection with the number of representatives that each state can send to Congress. The 13 states and the persons who signed on the constitution representing them are also mentioned in the constitution. The other states are not even mentioned in the constitution which clearly means the remaining 38 states were admitted into the federation without any constitutional amendment. Moreover, the constitution requires only the consent of Congress and the legislature of affected states with respect to the formation of a state resulting from the splitting of the state. In fact, Kentucky, Maine, Vermont and West Virginia each became a state and was admitted into the federation through the division of an existing state. The admission of these states into the US federation did not however result in the amendment of the constitution.

The problem, though, is that dismissing it as an oversight does not solve the dilemma. An action is still required to complete the act of internal secession. If, for example, Sidama's quest for statehood is to be completed, changes must be effected to article 47 of the Constitution that lists the member states of the federation. And this cannot be dismissed as clerical work that has to be effected by the executive or parliament. It is a constitutional amendment that requires the blessing of the joint session of the federal parliament and the legislative assemblies of two-thirds of the states.

Of course, the argument from constitutional amendment should not deny members of the Sidama community the right to vote for their own state. But it suggests that a new state cannot make it to the list of the Constitution, and hence be regarded as duly formed, without the approval of the other members of the federation.[18]

This is consistent with the practice in other federations. There is no country that allows internal secession simply based on the wishes of the territory or the community that seeks it. Almost in all federal constitutions, the consent of the relevant federal government, in particular the legislative branch, is a key requirement for the creation of a new. This is for instance the case under the constitutions of the USA, Australia, Argentina, Brazil, Nigeria and the like. In Brazil, Germany, Pakistan and India federal legislatures retain an exclusive authority to decide on whether a portion of a state should secede and become a state in its own right (Art 18, Brazil Con). The US Constitution authorises Congress to decide on such matter. In addition, in many cases the state which would be affected by the creation of a new state has to give its consent for the secession or at least it has the right to be heard on the matter. The federal constitutions of Argentina, Australia, Malaysia and Nigeria explicitly require the consent affected states. In Germany affected Landers have the right 'for an opportunity to be heard' (Basic Law, Article 29(2)) even though the final decision belongs to the federal government. The same is true in India and Pakistan where an affected state has the right to express its views on whether a portion of its territory should be allowed to secede and become

[18] What does that leave us with? A *de facto* secession? That would be a confusing state of affairs. Most of the powers and functions that a state government is expected to perform depend on a constitutional recognition as one of the member states of the federation. On what basis would such a state be able to exercise the constitutional powers allocated to state governments? On what grounds would it be able to join intergovernmental forums? On what constitutional basis would such a state be able to share from the national division of revenue?

a state (Indian Con Section 3). In Mexico the consent of an affected state is as rule not required. However, an affected state may make the process of creating a new state at least immensely onerous. Under the Mexican constitution (Article 73(III)) a draft legislation providing for the creation of a new state has to be approved by the legislatures of the majority of the states in addition to being endorsed by two-third majority in both houses of Congress. If the legislature of the affected state rejects the proposal, the new state can be created only if the proposal to this effect is approved by two-thirds of the state legislatures. In short, from Switzerland to India, national governments and other affected governments play a decisive role in the creation of new subnational units.

One may argue that a suitable referendum result should place an obligation on the federal government and other member states to effect the necessary constitutional amendment and that the democratically expressed wishes of the petitioning community should not be undermined by others. To borrow the famous lines of the Supreme Court of Canada in the Québec Secession Reference in 1998, 'a clear expression of a will by a clear majority' of the population of the petitioning community to secede from a state should create an obligation on the rest of the country to do what is constitutionally necessary.

But is it possible to coerce a state from which a territory is seceding to vote for a constitutional amendment that effectively presents a threat to its territorial integrity? After all, there is no language of obligation in Article 47 of the Ethiopian Constitution. In as much as it gives ethnic communities the right to demand internal secession, it does not impose a corresponding duty on the others to accept it. It simply outlines the procedure that must be followed in the formation of a new state without imposing an obligation on the state government to accept the wishes of the seceding community, again suggesting that negotiation is inevitable.

Even if such obligation exists, arguably, it can only be a constitutional obligation to negotiate. In the case of the Sidama, for example, this means that the concerned parties, including the federal government, the government of the SNNP and the Sidama local government, must come to the table to negotiate the possibilities and ramifications of a new state.

The point is that the Ethiopian Constitution, like many other constitutions, does not provide for unilateral internal secession. That is why, for example, it would have been unconstitutional for members of the Sidama community to unilaterally declare the formation of a new state. The Constitution may be silent on what should be done in the event a state or federal government refuses to entertain a request to secede from a state.

But it does subject internal secession to a procedure. This suggests that it does not allow for unilateral declaration of secession.

In any event, a petitioning community that is facing a recalcitrant national government is not without redress. The constitution requires appeal to be directed to the House of Federation, the second chamber of the federal parliament and the body constitutionally tasked (Article 62(1) & (2)) with deciding issues relating to the right to self-determination, including on complaints that the actions or omissions of the state and federal government have frustrated the claim for internal secession. The House of Federation is given a maximum of two years to make a decision on the matter.

5 The Politics of Internal Secession

The potential creation of the Sidama state represents the introduction of one more ethnically defined state; a state that would be explicitly associated with a particular ethnic group. This means that the ethnic basis of the Ethiopian federal system will be further strengthened. That perhaps also explains the strong support that the movement for the creation of the Sidama state enjoyed from some of the movements that claim to represent the Oromo, the largest ethnic group in the country, that basically want to strengthen subnational citizenship based on the ethnic nature of the federal arrangement. This might be a blow to those that have always considered, and perhaps correctly so, the communities that make up the State of the Southern Nations, Nationalities and Peoples', from which the Sidama have decided to break away, as one of the strongholds of pan-Ethiopian conception of citizenship.

The campaign that led to the creation of the new state and the establishment of an ethnically defined state might have dented the hope of those that were planning to use the Southern population to challenge subnational citizenship and ethnic federalism. The offshoot, it seems, is the reinforcement of the federal design that attaches importance to ethnicity as a primary political identity.

The floodgate effect of the creation of the Sidama state was evident long before a decision was made to let the Sidama have their say on a referendum. Given the relatively not-so-stringent procedure, the fear has always been that allowing a community to form its own state will create the floodgate of similar requests for statehood. That fear is no longer theoretical. It did not take long before ten other ethnic groups in the same state petitioned for the formation of their own states.

Suddenly, the authorities of the Southern State are having a second thought. Demands for new states are no longer encouraged. It is not clear on what basis the federal and state governments can reject the similar demands of the other communities after heeding to the requests of the Sidama, albeit grudgingly. But then again it is difficult to accept every request. We are not sure if the provision of territorial solution in the form of the creation of new state is a viable and, and more importantly, sustainable solution to the concerns of ethnic communities, more so in a country where there are more than 80 ethnic groups.

However, these concerns need to be balanced against the legitimate demands of other groups which should not simply be dismissed. The floodgate effect should not be a reason to outrightly dismiss the legitimate demands of ethnic communities.

Ethiopia will not be the first federation to see the breakup of existing states and the creation of new ones. Nigeria started as a federation of three states. It is now composed of 36 states. In India, 15 new states were carved out from 14 states between 1956 and 2009. Both countries continue to entertain demands for the creation of new states. Yet, neither of them is facing the imminent danger of disintegration.

It is also important to remember that Ethiopia started the road to federalism with 14 states before the current constitution reduced it to 9 states and 2 self-governing cities. So, having more states is not necessarily a bad idea. The breaking up of large states and the creation of smaller states might even be a blessing in disguise as it might have the effect of strengthening the federal government, an important asset in the context of a divided society that needs a glue to hold it together.

Importantly, what is needed is a federal government that does not believe that the fate of the country is at stake whenever it is faced with a demand for new state. The government must be flexible enough to accommodate reasonable requests for the creation of new states while at the same time nudging the demands for the creation of new states to be an outcome of negotiations that increasingly look beyond ethnic homogeneity into administrative convenience and economic viability.

6 Conclusion

As the discussion above shows the Ethiopian constitution appears to be straightforward on the issue of internal secession and the formation of new states. It entitles every ethnic community, regardless of its population and territorial size, the right to have its own state. It also provides extremely simple procedures for the establishment of a new state. The practice however has been the opposite of what the constitution provides. This was so mainly because of the political stance of the Ethiopian Peoples' Revolutionary Democratic Front (EPRDF)—the party that enjoyed an exclusive political control over the country for close to three decades.

However, the federal government seems still unprepared to allow the formation of the tenth state of the Ethiopian federation let alone positively responding to the other demands for own state. Six months after the referendum, the state of Sidama is not yet in existence. The government of the SNNP has not formally transferred power to the government of the Sidama state. At the federal level no action has been taken that signifies that the federal government recognises the Sidama as one of the states of the federation. The Constitution is not amended. Federal financial transfers are still sent to the SNNP government and, despite the protest of the authorities of the Sidama local government, the latter receives federal funds only through the SNNP government.

Moreover, over ten ethnic-based local councils in the SNNP, most notably the councils of the Wolayta, Kaffa and Hadya communities, have resolved demanding for own state. However, the state and federal government have given deaf ears for such demands. Furthermore, the Prime Minister has visited almost every ethnic local government area in the SNNP and held discussion with politicians and elders of the ethnic communities with an intention to dissuade them from demanding for own state. He had also recently held a meeting with the local leaders of the SNNP to the same effect.

As the case of Sidama has amply demonstrated, simply ignoring the concerns of those that clamour for their own state might cost the country dearly. More than two dozen of people lost their lives when the attempt of activists from the Sidama ethnic group to declare their own state did not materialise. The decision of Abiy Ahmed's government to reject the unilateral declaration of the creation of new state and force the actors to follow the constitutional path towards the creation of a new state was appropriate. Yet, a proactive negotiation with all stakeholders and a quick deployment of security forces when violence broke out would have saved the numerous lives that were lost unnecessarily in July 2019.

References

Aalen, L. (2008). *Institutionalizing the Politics of Ethnicity: Actors, Power and Mobilisation in Southern Ethiopia Under Ethnic Federalism*. Unpublished PhD thesis, University Oslo.

Addis Standard. (2019, August 9). *EPRDF [Executive Committee] Endorses "Scientific Study" Recommendation to Split SNNP into Two, Postpones Unification Talks.* http://addisstandard.com/news-eprdf-ec-endorses-scientific-study-recommendation-to-split-snnpr-into-two-postpones-unification-talks/. Accessed 30 May 2020.

Anderson, G. (2016). Unilateral Non-Colonial Secession and Internal Self-Determination: A Right of Newly Seceded Peoples to Democracy? *Arizona Journal of International & Comparative Law, 34*(1), 1–64.

Ayele, Z. A. (2014). *Local Government in Ethiopia: Advancing Development and Accommodating Ethnic Minorities.* Baden-Baden: Nomos Verlagsges.

Ayele, Z. A., & Fessha, Y. T. (2012). The Place and Status of Local Government in Federal States: The Case of Ethiopia. *Africa Today, 58*(4), 89–109.

Bihonegn, T. (2015). Federalization with a Constitutional Guarantee to Secession: Controversies, Paradoxes and Imponderables in Ethiopia. *Regional and Federal Studies, 25*(1), 45–70.

De Waal, A. (2012). Review Article: The Theory and Practice of Meles Zenawi. *African Affairs, 112*(446), 148–155.

Dominice, C. (2006). The Secession of the Canton of Jura in Switzerland. In M. G. Kohen (Ed.), *Secession: International Law Perspectives.* Cambridge: Cambridge University Press.

Fana Broadcasting Corporate. (2019, January 2). https://fanabc.com/english/2019/01/newly-amended-charities-and-societies-law-to-come-into-effect-soon/. Accessed 29 May 2019.

Fleiner, T. (2002). Recent Developments of Swiss Federalism. *The Global Review of Federalism, 32*(20), 97–123.

Gebreselassie, E. (2019, October 10). As EPRDF Bonds Loosen, Fresh Coalitions May Lie in Terra Incognita. *Ethiopian Insight.* https://www.ethiopia-insight.com/2018/10/10/as-eprdf-bonds-loosen-fresh-coalitions-may-lie-in-terra-incognita/. Accessed 29 May 2019.

Gebre-Sellasie, A. (2003). Ethnic Federalism: Its Promise and Pitfalls for Africa. *Yale Journal of International Law, 28*, 51–107.

Gilliland, A. C. (2013). *Federalism and the Creation of New States: Justifying Internal Secession*, 75. Doctoral thesis, Universitat Pompeu Fabra.

Herther-Spiro, N. B. (2007). Can Ethnic Federalism Prevent "Recourse to Rebellion?" – A Comparative Analysis of Ethiopian and Iraqi Constitutional Structures. *Emory International Law Review, 21*, 321–371.

Keffale, A. (2012). *Federalism and Ethnic Conflict in Ethiopia: A Comparative Study of the Somali and Benishangul-Gumuz Regions*. Routledge.

Kohen, M. G. (2006). *Secession: International Law Perspectives*. Cambridge: Cambridge University Press.

Requejo, F., & Nagel, K. J. (2017). *Democracy and Borders: External and Internal Secession in the EU* (EUBORDERS Working Paper 14).

Reuter. (2019, October 15). *Ethiopia Postpones Autonomy Referendum for Ethnic Sidama: Fana News Agency*. .https://www.reuters.com/article/us-ethiopia-politics/ethiopia-postpones-autonomy-referendum-for-ethnic-sidama-fana-news-agency-idUSKBN1WU2LJ. Accessed 30 May 2020.

Seymour, M. (2011). Internal Self-Determination and Secession. In Aleksandar Pavkovic, & Peter Radan (Eds.), *The Ashgete Research Companion to Secession*. Abingdon: Routledge.

Tronvoll, K., Boroje, F., & Tezera, K. (2020). *The Sidama's Quest for Self-Rule: A Study of the Referendum on Regional Statehood*. European Institute of Peace.

Tsige, T. (2019, March 2). Anti-terror Law Makes About-Turn. *Ethiopian Reporter*. https://www.thereporterethiopia.com/article/anti-terror-law-makes-about-turn. Accessed 29 May 2019; 'Newly Amended Charities and Societies Law to Come Into Effect Soon'.

Vaughan, S. (2003). *Ethnicity and Power in Ethiopia*. Unpublished Phd thesis, University of Edinburgh.

Yeibyio, A. F. (2015). Development with or Without Freedom. In E. Brems, C. Van der Beken, & S. A. Yimer (Eds.), *Human Rights Development: Legal Perspective from and for Ethiopia* (p. 101). Leiden: Brill Nijhoff.

Yokamo, Y. (2019, May 5). Sidama Declares State of Impatience. *Ethiopian Insight*. https://www.ethiopia-insight.com/2019/05/05/sidama-declares-state-of-impatience/. Accessed 30 May 2020.

Zenawi, M. *African Development: Dead Ends and New Beginnings*. Dissertation, Erasmus University.

CHAPTER 14

Paradise Lost: Impacts of Ethnic Nationalism in Sri Lanka and the Tamil Secessionist Movement

Punsara Amarasinghe

1 Introduction

"The greatest adversary of the rights of nationality is the modern theory of nationality. By making the state and the nation commensurate with each other in theory, it reduces practically to a subject condition all other nationalities that may be within the boundary" (Lang 2002, pp. 21). Perhaps, these words uttered by Lord Acton in 1862 would be an apt remark to understand the modern political history of Sri Lanka in considering the ethnic discontents sparked in post-independent Sri Lanka that eventually paved the path to a brutal civil war which lasted for 30 years. The ethnicity and the mistrust that pervaded in the territorial political domain in Sri Lanka even before the independence was a significant factor

P. Amarasinghe (✉)
Global Legal Studies Center, University of Wisconsin Madison, Madison, WI, USA

M. Belov (ed.), *Territorial Politics and Secession*, Federalism and Internal Conflicts, https://doi.org/10.1007/978-3-030-64402-4_14

which nourished the notion of secession while creating large division between Sinhalese and Tamil communities in the country.

Sri Lanka's progress compared to other post-colonial societies seemed to be a success story when British granted the independence to the island nation in 1948, especially its progress on key social indicators such as poverty, education and infant mortality put Sri Lanka ahead of its neighbours (Subramanium 2019). But, from a very realistic perspective, Sri Lanka lacked the consensus and commitment for multi-linguistic society in the post-colonial context as the Sinhalese elites of the country dominated the welfare and preferential policies for Sinhalese majority as a political strategy while alienated Tamil community and its leaders looked for a separate state (Peebles 1990, pp. 30).

In this chapter, the prime questions that I will address are rooted in unfolding how communitarian sentiments undermined the territorial politics in post-independent Sri Lanka which resulted in an inevitable conflict between Sinhalese and Tamil communities inhabiting the island. In discussing the genesis of this ethnic discontent that turned into a separatist movement which embraced violence, I would first seek to trace the constitutional trajectories that intensified the path for a separatist movement on a larger scale. Secondly, I will discuss how ethnic and religious politics played an indispensable role in post-colonial politics in Sri Lanka creating a dilemma to the new nation. In analysing the militant movement arose from the Tamil community in Sri Lanka which was adamant to obtain a separate state by military means, I would unveil the lost opportunities that Sri Lanka missed in the past that could have simply prevented a bloodiest civil war lasted for three decades. In conclusion, this chapter will assess to which extent Sri Lanka has succeeded in seeking a feasible solution for its ethnic conflict and distrust between Sinhalese and Tamil communities under the constitutional or political framework in the aftermath of the civil war context.

2 In the Beginning

The ethnic division within the political stricture in Sri Lanka was conceived during the colonial rule of Sri Lanka under the British period, and any attempt that would examine the roots of separatism will realise how ethnic identities between Sinhalese and Tamil communities were constructed in favour of British interests. Yet, it remains a fact beyond conjuncture that Sri Lanka's ethnic identity historically has been an anomalous one as both Sinhalese and Tamil ethnicities adhered to their own claims over the island.

Reminding of the Aryan theory of races, Sinhalese view holds that they are the direct descendants of Aryan settlers who arrived in Sri Lanka from Eastern India in the sixth century B.C. They spoke Indo-Aryan language later developed into Sinhalese. On the contrary Tamil narrative over their history in Sri Lanka has emphasised the claims of their own governing bodies, Hindu religious traditions, caste system in the Northern part of the island which were fundamentally different from the Sinhalese. Also, Sinhalese conversion to Buddhism in third century BC was another crucial juncture in the history of ethnic discontents in Sri Lanka due to the fact this conversion decisively created a new civilisational image for Sinhalese.

Alluded by the imperial mantra of "Divide and Rule" (*divide et impera*), British were much cautious to keep ethnic differences alive and prevented the growth of cross ethnic all island political identification. In 1833 the legislative reforms in colonial Sri Lanka, which was known as Colebrook, maiden attempt to bring the ethnic differences to the attention of the masses as the reforms included the ethnic representation at the newly formed legislative council. David Scot's celebrated work "Refashioning Futures: Criticism after Postcoloniality" (Scot 1999) has aggrandised this colonial legislative reform as a crucial break with the past, escorting Sri Lanka's modernity under British values, but the notion of representation based on ethnic identities under 1833 legislative reforms was a catalyst factor that would later continue to escalate the ethnic politics in Sri Lanka.

In analysing the Colebrook reforms and the dubious way it planted the seeds of separatism in Sri Lanka, Asanga Welikala states: "In consciously obliterating the territorial and demographic markers of the last domestic kingdom of Kandy, remnants of which had survived within the British administrative system between the cession of Kandy in 1815 and 1833, and uprooting forever the galactic model of the pre-colonial state, these reforms conformed conventionally to the 'diffusionist model' of colonial state-formation" (Welikala 2015, pp. 34).

However, reflecting the mechanism in which the modern statehood was introduced to Sri Lanka under 1833 reforms, the next stage of Sri Lanka's preparation to the self-government was completed by introducing electoral democracy in year 1931, which made Sri Lanka to become the first Asian country to be bestowed with universal suffrage. The fostering of electoral politics and the universal franchise to all the citizens in Sri Lanka was a recommendation made by the Royal commission visited the island in 1928 under Lord Donoughmore. Driven by the contemporary British liberal political values Donoughmore regarded the continuity of communal-based political representation in the colony as a negative factor which would impede the people from realising the self-government (Wickramasinghe 2006). He therefore felt that the rapid development of electoral political system along with the introduction of universal franchise could transform the colony into an ideal democracy detached from racial discontents. While later historians would criticise the intensity of introducing franchise to an oriental society in the manner of imposing modernity, Donoughmore commission had their observation regarding the situation of Sri Lanka.

In their report they particularly mentioned the growing tendency of racial disharmony among the ethnicities in Sri Lanka as a major setback for the political unity. For instance, before the departure from the Lord Donoughmore stated: "It is almost true to say that the conception of patriotism in Ceylon as much as rational as national, and that the best interests of the country are at times regarded as synonymous of the welfare with the particular section of its people" (Welikala 2014, pp. 36).

Nevertheless, the idealistic goals embedded with Donoughmore recommendations were marred as the electoral politics and political party system emerged in the aftermath of the reform in 1931 became completely engulfed by the numerical majority of Sinhalese ethnic votes which clearly swiped the Tamil representation from the political stage. The second election held under Donoughmore reforms in 1936 was a palpable reflection of the emerging Sinhalese hegemony in the territorial politics as the board of ministers at the State Council was completely consisted of Sinhalese representatives indicating a bad sign for the communal harmony (Rambukwella 2018, pp. 77).

The next constitutional recommendation under British rule in Sri Lanka set the path to gain independence and the constitution born out of the recommendations exposed the newly independent nation Sri Lanka to the British Westminster model of governance. The architect of Sri Lanka's first constitution was the English legal scholar Sir Ivor Jennings who had penchant for introducing British parliamentary traditions for South Asian colonies. However, having realised the growing tension between Sinhalese majority and ethnic minorities in the island Jennings was cautious to include provision that limited Parliament's power to enact legislation having discriminatory effects among diverse "communities" and "religions". Yet at the process of drafting the constitution that would lead Sri Lanka to a Dominion status, Jennings was not inclined to include an adequate minority representation in the constitution despite knowing the growing communal disharmony in the island. According to constitutional scholar Rehan Abeyaratne, "Jennings abiding faith in the Westminster system and the relentless focus on the inherent virtues prevented him from taking the communal representation as grave concern" (Abeyaratne 2020, pp. 1265). On the other hand, Sinhalese leader and first premier of independent Sri Lanka D.S. Senanayake had played a larger influencing role behind the drafting process of the constitution through his astute hobnobbing with Jennings which finally resulted in Jennings' reluctance to include minority representation in country's first constitution as Jennings considered "Communal representation encourages communalism: and what a self-governing country must develop is .... common loyalty" (Abeyaratne 2020, pp. 1267).

However, Jennings' draft of the constitution was subjected to the robust criticism among the ethnic minorities as a document driven by majority of Sinhalese aspirations that would make the ethnic representation of other minorities redundant in the future independent Sri Lanka. Tamil leader G.G. Ponnambalam was a strong vocal proponent who demanded a fair representation in the new parliament for all the ethnic minorities in the island. He was adamant in arguing that 50 percent of the parliamentary seats should be reserved for ethnic minorities in the country. However, his argument was rejected by the Soulburry Commission and Jennings, denying any kind of a communal representation for the newborn state (Mainuddin & Aiecher 1997, pp. 53).

Jennings' alternative for the grievances among the ethnic minorities in Sri Lanka was only confined to including Section 29 (2) in the constitution that prohibited Parliament from enacting laws infringing the free exercise of religion and laws that privilege or disadvantage one community or religious group over another. Even though Jennings included Section 29 (2) with the intention of preserving the rights of the ethnic minorities in Sri Lanka, the events took place followed by independence in 1948 denoted the rise of Sinhalese ethnic dominance in the territorial politics of the island.

The new government of premier D.S. Senanayake enacted legislation exactly one year prior to gaining independence in 1948 and this enactment called "The Citizenship Act 18 of 1948" mainly disfranchised the Indian Tamil community resided in Sri Lanka as labours and plantation workers leading to mass exile. This incident was the first systematic discriminatory act executed by Sinhalese majoritarian government in independent Sri Lanka as this controversial Act legitimised the removal of citizenship of Indian Tamil community in Sri Lanka regardless of Section 29 (2) drafted by Ivor Jennings to safeguard the rights of the minorities.

Furthermore, the Act was not abolished by the Supreme Court of Sri Lanka by referring to Section 29 (2) of the Constitution while hearing the writ petition on the ground of narrow interpretation of Section 29 (2) of Jennings' constitution and the Court admitted the Parliament's ability to alter the electoral laws of the island as it pleases. To the biggest dismay of the Tamil ethnic minority in Sri Lanka the same judgement was justified by the Privy Council in the United Kingdom when the appellants made an appeal and Privy Council's decision provided two main justifications: (1) that it is a "perfectly natural and legitimate function of the legislature of a country to determine the composition of its nationals"; and (2) that the negative effects of the two Acts on the Indian Tamil community "have nothing to do with them as a community" (Abeyaratne 2020, pp. 1278).

Indeed, the circumstances appeared after the independence of Sri Lanka mainly driven by Sinhalese majoritarian ideology were the first factors that agitated the Tamil leaders to look for alternatives in their own nationalist discourse paving the path for separatist ideology in Tamil politics. The nation-building process in the post-colonial context of Sri Lanka was marred at its very outset by virtue of the ethnic politics and political chicanery.

3 Moving Towards Greater Disharmony

As I discussed above the growing ethnic discontent between Sinhalese and Tamils in Sri Lanka was not an offshoot of any random factor. On the contrary, they were rooted in the deliberate strategies used by the British colonial rulers for the sake of their imperial mission which was culminated by the influx of Sinhalese majoritarian political movement before the independence that resulted in creating an ambivalence among Tamil politicians towards the Sinhalese leaders.

Nevertheless, it is important to note that the rise of Sinhalese nationalism which took a steeping increase in the first decade after Sri Lanka's independence accelerated Tamil's nationalist movement in the island. In ascertaining the growth of separatist ideas in Tamil political discourse in post-colonial Sri Lanka, we need to examine the significant role played by the Tamil Federal Party. Grounded on the federalist principles the party leaders advocated for a federal system in government with considerable autonomy for the Tamil regions in the North and Eastern provinces of Sri Lanka, but none of them had the explicit inspiration for a separate Tamil land in the infancy stage of Tamil Federal Party (Wilson & Delton 1982, pp. 155).

Yet, the writings dating to the early days of the inception of Sri Lanka Federal Party have shown the interest persisted among the Federalist Tamil leaders in Sri Lanka in search of a separate land to share the common language, own ethnic identity and culture of the Tamil people in Sri Lanka. The resolution adopted by Tamil Federal Party in Sri Lanka in 1951 declared:

> the Tamil speaking people in Sri Lanka constitute a nation distinct from that of the Sinhalese by every fundamental test of nationhood, firstly that of a separate historical past in the island at least as ancient as glorious as that of the Sinhalese, secondly by the fact of their being linguistic entity entirely different from that of the Sinhalese, with an unsurpassed classical heritage and a modern development of language which makes Tamil fully adequate for all present day needs, and finally by reason of their territorial habitation of definite areas which constitute over one third of the island. (Tamil Arasau Kacchai 1951)

In the backdrop of such a demand came from Tamil federalists, the political victory recorded by Sinhalese populist leader of SWRD Bandaranaike by invoking the Sinhalese nationalism and Buddhism in her political slogans in 1956 parliamentary election in Sri Lanka became another crucial milestone in island's political history. SWRD Bandaranaike's political propaganda caused a rift among the ethnicities in Sri Lanka for further deterioration as his method of involving Sinhalese nationalist ideology and Buddhist religion made an appeal to revive Sinhalese civilisation and this calling was echoed in the Sinhalese majority in 1956 election to accept SWRD Bandaranaike as the popular leader which eventually resulted in crating pure Sinhalese majoritarian rule (Rambukwella 2018, pp. 106).

The rapid growth of Sinhalese chauvinism under Bandaranaike in Sri Lanka after 1956 was an apt illustration to Anderson's thesis on nationalism from the way it arrayed in the Sinhalese ideology generating their supremacy of the island imbued with Buddhism and Sinhalese language. The proclamation of Sinhalese language was the climax of the chain of event under SWRD Bandaranaike in Sri Lanka which clearly gave sign of a political diversion between Sinhalese majority and Tamil minority. As already mentioned, the key element of separatism was agitated by a wave of Sinhalese ethnocentric majority in Sri Lanka after independence that produced a detrimental effect upon the whole pluralistic nature of Sri Lankan society and the government decision of proclaiming Sinhalese the national language in the island segregated Tamil minority paving the path for tenser political actions. By this time Sri Lankan Tamil Federal Party had appeared as the strongest political representative of the Tamil community that advocated for autonomy in Northern and Eastern provinces of Sri Lanka, yet the idea for secession dwelled under shadows albeit Tamil concerns were seriously at stake under SWRD Bandaranaike's rule consisted of Sinhalese Buddhist nationalism.

Satyagraha and civil disobedience movement in Tamil-speaking regions with no involvement in political violence were the first acts carried out by the Federal Party in showing their resentment towards language policy of SWRD Bandaranaike's government (Wriggins 1959, pp. 32). For instance, Tamil Federal Party of Sri Lanka and its prominent leaders such as J. Chelvanayakam and Kandiah conducted a mass of Satyagraha movement in Sri Lanka which was sabotaged by Sinhalese mob violence.

However, Bandaranaike could not completely stave off the reactions of Tamil Federal leaders. Thus, he reached an agreement with Tamil Federal party in 1957 known as Bandaranaike-Chelvanayakam pact which enshrined the right of Tamil people by creating a body of regional councils with a certain level of autonomy. But the ultra-nationalistic pressure arose from the same forces those who brought SWRD Bandaranaike to the power such as Buddhist clergy and Sinhalese nationalists became more rigorous as they found this pact to be a symbol of ravishing the Sinhalese ethnic pride that finally compelled Prime Minister Bandaranaike to tear up the pact with Tamil Federal party.

Thereafter, communal tension exploded into violent rioting in Sri Lanka in 1958. The state lawlessness prevailed during the riots and government's initial inability to take immediate actions to control the situation marred Sri Lanka's good name as a model dominion state that achieved the independence from the British without a military engagement. Later historians have claimed that riots of 1958 in Sri Lanka as a catalyst event in post-colonial Sri Lanka to intensify the Tamil cause of political representation to the direction of separatism (Rathnapalan 2012, pp. 45).

The constitution drafted by Sir Ivor Jennings with his staunch faith in that Westminster system would harbour the stability of Sri Lanka as an ideal dominion state proved itself to be a less effective tool before the ethnic turmoil befell Sri Lankan society after 1956. Especially, Section 29 (2) of the constitution was again tested by the Tamils as their last resort of hope when SWRD Bandaranaike's government enacted the Sinhala Language Act, which enforced a law that all government officials must reach minimum fluency in Sinhala language. In challenging the legality of this decision, a writ petition was filed by a Tamil government official in the Supreme Court, alleging that the test requirement and the Official Language Act violated Section 29 (2) of the constitution. But the Supreme Court again rejected the petition on the basis of procedural process, and this again demonstrated the futility of Jennings' Section 29 (2) in safeguarding the rights of the minorities (Attorney General Vs Kaneswaran 1967).

The political atmosphere in the aftermath of 1958 ethnic riots was less consoling for the grievances of Tamil minority under the Sinhalese language hegemony. Since the colonial period Tamils had upheld their reputation in academia, government service and armed forces, but the removal of English from working space by replacing Sinhalese cut off their chances in the government sector rapidly. From 1956 to 1970 the proportions of Tamils employed by the state fell from 60 to 10 presents in the government profession, from 30 to 5 presents in the administrative service, from 50 to 5 in the clerical service and from 40 to 1 percent in the armed forces (Kearney 1978, pp. 527). The gradual decline of the Tamils holding responsible position in Sri Lankan society further pushed Tamil aspirations away, while it persuaded Tamil politicians to change their political strategies to cope with Sinhalese dominance in national politics. But even after envisaging a severe segregation under language policy imposed by SWRD Bandaranaike's government, still Tamil federalists were unenthusiastic in moving towards a separate state in Sri Lanka for Tamil community.

Meanwhile in northern and eastern provinces of Sri Lanka which are historically considered Tamil-populated areas saw a mass Sinhalese colonisation launched by Sri Lankan government that caused an unrest among Tamil community about losing their cultural and social values at the hands of Sinhalese colonisers. American historian on South Asian studies Patrick Peebles has sharply analysed the impact made by Sri Lankan government process of forming Sinhalese colonies in the Eastern and Northern dry zones of the island to worsen the ethnic tension between Sinhalese and

Tamil ethnicities in the island. He further discussed how Sinhalese politicians made an appeal to Sinhalese rural villages to move to colonies by invoking the mythical past and it often referred to the prosperity of ancient Sinhalese culture while depicting Tamils as the foes of Sinhalese Buddhist civilisation (Peebles 1990, pp. 37).

The dawn of 1970s marked a crucial juncture in post-colonial political identity of Tamils in Sri Lanka. The growing tension between the two communities and lethargic response by Sri Lankan government to the political created a sweeping momentum for Tamil separatist ideology which came to another important milestone in the year 1972 when coalition government established by Sirimavo Bandaranaike (SWRD's widow) promulgated the first autochthonous constitution in Sri Lanka by detaching all the bonds existed with Britain.

In fact, those who were in the vanguard of constitutional change in Sri Lanka in 1972 were idealising a republican vision in their constitutional drafting and it was hoped the establishment of republic would herald a new epoch of the people. But what the pomp and glory that marked the adaption of new republican constitution concealed was that this so-called Republican Constitution had no unilateral consensus from all the political parties of the island except the ruling alliance of Mrs. Sirimavo Bandaranaike (Jayawickrama 2013, pp. 567). In particular, the Sri Lankan Tamil Federal Party had vehement opposition to the overarching new changes to the constitution such as the removal of Section 29 (2) from the constitution and inclusion of special protection for Buddhism. Tamil Federal Party boycotted the constituent assembly debates and it connoted that the constitution that represented the new republican "*Grundnorm*" itself was on the shaky ground (Jayawickrama 2013, pp. 567).

The new constitution of 1972 in Sri Lanka consolidated political power in the legislature, in such a context Tamils demanding broader power devolution to represent their ethnicity in a Sinhalese-dominated legislature found themselves less influential. Also, Tamils were gutted by the decision of the government to introduce standardisation in higher education through a legislation in 1974, which reduced the entry of Tamil students from their regions to national universities (Shastri 1990, pp. 56–77).

All these acts fostered the Tamil notion for a separate land and the anxious Tamil youth began to organise themselves in forming different militant groups in the Northern and Eastern provinces in Sri Lanka. The *Vaddukoddai* resolution passed by Tamil United Front in 1976 was the first explicit expression that Tamil political parties sought to form a separate Tamil state in the country and the resolution itself was a reflection of the depravations faced by Tamils since the independence. After illustrating the Tamil's historical claims to the Northern and Eastern regions of Sri Lanka the core of the resolution affirmed a legitimate claim for secession. It states:

> The convention resolves that restoration and reconstitution of the Free, Sovereign, Secular, Socialist State of TAMIL ELAM based on the right of self-determination inherent to every nation, has become inevitable in order to safeguard the very existence of the Tamil nation in this country. (Matthews 1986, pp. 34)

Many of the historians and scholars have univocally admitted the pledge given by Tamil leaders in Vaddukoddai in 1976 was the first and the strongest moment in the separatist movement in island's history on the ethnic discontent in post-independent period. Deprived by the higher educational opportunities as a result of the Sirimavo Bandaranaike's government's "Standardisation Act" and also less attention paid by Sinhalese majoritarian rule towards improving livelihood of Tamils in their regions, the impoverished status appeared in 1970s accelerated the Tamil youth's ardour for separatist movement.

However, the mechanism executed by Tamil youths in Northern and Eastern provinces in Sri Lanka took a complete different root from the conventional Tamil politicians as they changed the course of seeking a Tamil homeland from political strategy to a militant movement. The emergence of various Tamil youth militant groups in Northern and Eastern provinces in Sri Lanka after 1972 was rampant as a radical reaction for Sinhalese majoritarian rule, but their demands were not reciprocated and Sri Lankan government embraced another new constitution in 1978 under President J.R. Jayewardene, which also provided no remedy for ethnic dilemma in Sri Lanka.

4 Thirty Years War

The ethnic relation filled with hesitation between Sinhalese and Tamils in post-independent Sri Lanka reached its most deteriorated stage in the year 1983 when Tamil militants killed 13 Sinhalese soldiers which was followed by carnage of Tamils in Sinhalese-dominated regions in Sri Lanka. The rupture of ethnic clash in 1983 July marked the onset of civil war in Sri Lanka.

In the wake of civil war, Sri Lankan parliament passed the Sixth Amendment to the 1978 Constitution which completely banned the advocacy for secession by securing the unitary status of Sri Lanka. Under the Sixth Amendment to the Constitution all Parliament Members in Sri Lankan parliament were required to pledge their allegiance to preserve the unitary status of the Sri Lankan state, but the members of Tamil Federal Party including the leader of opposition refused to take such an oath, thus all of them lost their seats in the parliament. The anti-secessionist provision introduced by the 6th Amendment to the Constitution in its Article 157A (4) stated "Where any political party or other association or organization has as one of its aims or objectives the establishment of a separate state within the territory of Sri Lanka. Upon such a deceleration being made, the political party or organization stands proscribed and any member of such party or organization, who is a Member of Parliament vacates his seat" (Welikala 2014, pp. 271).

Given that the consolidation of power that has been embodied in Sri Lanka's constitutional history since British colonial reforms to the post-independent constitutional making, the explicit inclusion of the unitary status of the state was less surprising when current constitution of Sri Lanka was promulgated in 1978. The Section 2 Article 2 of both republican constitutions in Sri Lanka were made on the ground of Sinhalese nationalist desires stemmed from their longing to the mythical history of Sinhalese glory in Sri Lanka as preservers of "Theravada Buddhism" and regardless of the steeping growth of the uneasiness of the Tamils in the island both republican constitutions glorified the privileged status of Buddhism. The cultural appealing arose from the inclusion of Buddhism and the reiteration of the unitary status of Sri Lanka was a symbolic message conveyed by Sinhalese rule was described by Asanga Welikala as a state evolved into a Sinhalese Buddhist ethnocracy that has preferred hegemonic control over accommodation or even integration. Quoting Yiftachel, Welikala provides following explanation on how notion of ethnocracy can be applicable in fathoming the Sinhalese hegemony in state apparatus:

> Ethnocracy denotes a type of regime that facilitates and promotes the process of ethinicisation that is expansion and control. It surfaces in disputed territories, where one ethno national group is able to appropriate the state

> apparatus and mobilize its legal, economic and military resources to further its territorial, economic and cultural interests. The struggle over the process of ethnic expansion become the central axis along which social and political relations evolve. (Welikala 2014, pp. 123)

The ethnocentric superior motives in the post-independent constitutional building process in Sri Lanka primarily focused on safeguarding Sinhalese identity and the preservation of Buddhism. Reading the preambles of 1972 and 1978 constitutions provide adequate cultural symbolism to grasp the rapid changes that had been taken in Sri Lanka under the guise of Sinhalese ethnic hegemony and the special privilege to Buddhism (Wijeyarathne 1996, pp. 321).

After the outbreak of Sri Lankan civil war in 1983, the movement formed by Tamil politicians and federalists to seek solutions for their common problems under federal structure reached its ebb as Tamil cause was led by Tamil youth militant groups in Northern and Eastern regions of Sri Lanka. In an escalating tense situation of a war between Tamil militants and Sri Lankan state that India proposed devolution of power in Sri Lanka under Indo-Lanka accords in 1987. Thirteen Amendment to the Constitution was the offshoot of Indian intervention to Sri Lankan ethnic conflict in 1987 and the Indian backed devolution of power by introducing Provincial Council system received a hostile reception from the Sinhalese as they regarded it as an attempt made by India to subdue the integrity of a sovereign nation (Dixith 1998, pp. 121). Nevertheless, the 13th Amendment to Sri Lankan constitution was enforced in 1987 by Provincial Councils Act No. 42.

Even though the 13th amendment was intended to be a remedy for the ethnic conflict in Sri Lanka, the scepticism prevailed in Sri Lankan government and Sinhalese society was rather salient as it erupted a massive resistance from the Sinhalese which finally resulted in making a petition to the Supreme Court. The divided consensus on the power devolution process in Sri Lanka was embodied in the judgement from the way how judges held delivered their ruling.

As already noted, both autochthonous constitutions in post-independent Sri Lanka were imbued with the idea of preserving the unitary status of the country. Hence, the two main questions presented before the Sri Lankan Supreme Court were whether devolution in the form set out in the two impugned bills was consistent with the republic being a unitary state and also whether the devolution of executive and legislative powers to Provincial Council was an unconstitutional alienation of the sovereignty of the people (In Re 13th Amendment 1987).

The majority of the judges in the bench rejected the petition, and coming to a conclusion of their judgement, they affirmed that the proposed 13th Amendment to the Constitution was in accordance with Articles 2 and 3 of 1978 Sri Lankan constitution that deals with the notion of sovereignty. The contention brought by the majority of judges pointed out that the existence of subsidiary law-making bodies would not violate the unitary status secured by the above-mentioned two articles in the constitution, but the minority of the judges clung to the arguments raised by the petitioners.

Especially, the main dissenting opinion of Justice Wanasundara was a conspicuous reflection of Sinhalese society's uncertainty towards the 13th Amendment as a foreign mechanism to intensify Tamil aspirations for secession. As a Supreme Court judge with fervent sense of Sinhalese nationalism, justice Wanasundara was convinced that 13th Amendment to the Constitution would alter the basic unitary structure of the constitution by paving the path for a quasi-federal system in Sri Lanka.

Notwithstanding, the severe opposition arose from Sinhalese society and the attempts made by various groups to thwart the power devolutionary process, the 13th Amendment to the Constitution was passed by virtue of Indian influence. But the implementation of the objectives in power devolutionary process through Provincial Council system became another horrendous task as a result of the opposition shown by main Tamil militant group Liberation Tigers of Tamil Eelam (LTTE) and they finally firmly believed in the notion of a separate land for Tamils.

5 Interim: Between War and Peace

The influx of LTTE as the sole representative of the Tamils in Sri Lanka was a catalyst factor that entirely changed the course of the territorial political realm in Sri Lanka and the military ideology embraced by LTTE indeed caused havoc in Tamil political scope as LTTE began to kill all the Tamil politicians who criticised their military ideology. In writing an article titled "Liberation or Terrorism? The Politics of naming the LTTE" Suthaharan Nadarajah and Dhananjayan Sriskandarajah have described the irreversible damage committed by LTTE to the cause self-determination of the Tamil people in Sri Lanka (Nadaraja and Sriskandaraja 2005, pp. 92).

In particular, the LTTE's denial of the provincial council and their vehement reluctance to negotiate with Sri Lankan government while legitimising their violence as the necessity for the liberation of Tamil people were notable factors which clearly distinguished them from the Tamil politicians in the post-independent Sri Lanka. Also, the LTTE's path for secession was driven by utter military ambition and LTTE evasively avoided all the efforts made by the international community to seek a political solution which resulted in the international condemnation of LTTE as a terrorist organisation (Weerakoon 2004, pp. 34). Thus, the secessionist movement in Sri Lanka after 1983 can simply be described as a militant epoch dominated by one militant group who opted for the path of violence and it lasted till Sri Lankan government forces militarily crushed LTTE in 2009.

Nevertheless, in examining the lacuna of the Sri Lankan government aspired by Sinhalese interests, it becomes an evident factor that the devolution of power under the 13th Amendment to the Constitution was not sincerely executed by Sri Lankan government as a need to reconcile and rectify the errors of the past. Especially the government's apathy to empower provincial councils as many autonomous bodies hindered the objectives of the 13th Amendment and the third list of the power devolutionary process through the provincial councils, which was known as the concurrent list, was one of the biggest obstacles in fulfilling the devolution of powers in Sri Lanka. Continued centralisation appeared to be a weakening factor for the devolution of power as Sinhalese politicians were engulfed by the notion that granting more autonomous status for Northern and Eastern provinces is inimical for the unitary status of Sri Lanka (Ankitell 2017, pp. 32).

Even after establishing provincial council systems under the 13th Amendment to the Constitution regardless of LTTE's opposition, the Tamil aspirations for more autonomous status prevailed; it was duly manifested when the elected Chief Minister of Northern and Eastern province Mr. Vardaraja Perumal made a Unilateral Declaration of Independence (UDI) on the 1st of March in 1990 by proclaiming the "State of Eelam" in North-Eastern provinces. Indeed, Perumal's abrupt decision appeared to be a comic opera as it contained no legitimacy under any pooper framework. Neither LTTE nor any other important Tamil political party in Sri Lanka acknowledged the UDI of Vardaraja Perumal, yet Perumal converted the North and Eastern Provincial Council for a constituent assembly which was named as "National State Assembly of Free and Sovereign

Republic of Eelam" without official participation from the major Tamil political parties creating a greater absurdity in Tamil political sphere in Sri Lanka. On the other hand, the "Provincial Council Act" passed by Sri Lankan parliament in 1987 had curtailed any sort of separatist attempts which can arise within the councils by keeping the grip of central government's influence over the provincial councils. Thus, Perumal's Unilateral Declaration of Independence was a mere futile effort as then Sri Lankan President Ranasinghe Premadasa dissolved the Northern and Eastern Provincial Council under the executive power (Shastri 1992, pp. 32).

All in all, the Provincial Council System embodied a paradoxical attempt to institute something as close to a federal structure as possible within the unitary system which created an anomaly. After the UDI made by Northern and Eastern Provincial Council's chief minister, Sri Lankan Government became much cautious in its approach to the process of devolution of power as a remedy for ethnic discontent in the island. Sri Lanka's fear of secessions was a conspicuous in examining the way Sri Lanka treated the worldwide secession attempts by completely denying the legitimacy of such acts in international level. For instance, when Catalonia made Unilateral Declaration of Independence from Spain in 2014, Sri Lankan government categorically disapproved the Catalan UDI and made a strong statement insisting the importance of preserving the territorial integrity of Kingdom of Spain (Gilbert 2017).

6 Conclusion

The civil war which was lasted for three decades creating a mayhem in Sri Lanka came to its very end in 2009 after Sri Lankan government forces militarily defeated LTTE and the Sinhalese nationalists were erupted in jubilation. Yet, the Sri Lankan government's reaction for the problems of Tamils in post-conflict period has given no sign of reconciliation and the asymmetrical attitude shown by the government has been further bolstered by the steeping growth of Sinhalese nationalism which has inherently been hostile towards the notion of devolution of power. The biggest fear that has pervaded the whole Sinhala society is still rotating around their ambivalence to acknowledge Tamil's right for more dignified life and more political participation.

The lack of serious commitment to seek a satisfactory answer for the ethnic discontent under political framework appears to be the biggest problem in post-civil war Sri Lanka. The tragedy of the situation emerged after 2009 is mainly an offshoot of the Sinhalese populist political discourse in the Southern Sri Lanka and which is the exact resemblance of the political events Sri Lanka faced in the aftermath of colonialism. The sheer resentment driven by political motives or to gain more votes from the Sinhalese Buddhist voters has become prevalent in the post-war political scenario as a trend and the parties based on Sinhalese Buddhist ideology with larger support of Buddhist monks in Sri Lanka saw a massive growth during the rule of Sri Lanka's former president Mahinda Rajapaksa as he heavily relied on the support of the Sinhalese Buddhist votes rooted in the rural Sri Lanka (Waha 2018). It is a fair contention to build that his lacuna of a strong commitment to address the grievances of the Tamil community was largely attributed to the way how Sinhalese nationalist political parties manipulated his decision-making process.

Sinhalese phobia on secession and rise of Tamils whom they regarded as their historical adversary still continues to linger on and this political pessimism was rather evident when a petitioner applied to Sri Lankan Supreme Court and the petitioner wanted to seek whether Tamil Federal Party had secession as its objectives and consequently for its proscription as required by the Sixth Amendment to the Constitution, which has prohibited any political party to supporting the establishment of a separate state in Sri Lankan territory. In examining the argument of the petitioner and the respondent Tamil Federal Party, Court made an astute analysis of country's constitutional history while tracing the applicability of Right to Self-Determination in International Law (Chandrasoma Vs Senathiraja 2014).

Furthermore, Sri Lankan Supreme Court made two references to the Quebec Secession Reference and Kosovo Advisory Opinion in ICJ (2010). In doing so, for the first time in post-independent Sri Lanka, Supreme Court has admitted Tamil people's right to internal self-determination. In particular, the response of Sri Lankan Tamil Federal Party clearly denoted to which extent Tamils enjoy the international law principle law of self-determination that includes the right in the form expressed in the covenants. This judgement delivered by Sri Lankan Supreme Court in 2017 known as Chandrasoma Vs Senathiraja became a decisive one with its gravity confirming the judicial recognition of Tamil People's right for self-determination as a right, which was wrongly interpreted by the respondent as an act of secession.

In discussing the importance of Chandrasoma judgement, Sri Lankan constitutional law scholar Asanga Welikala brings an important issue arising from the judgement. He undoubtedly regards the judgement as a paramount juncture embodying the liberal turn in Sri Lankan constitutional law and judicial attitude to the ethnic discontent. Having known the rigidity of Sinhalese Buddhist society, especially the chauvinist Sinhalese political parties, Welikala reiterates: "What happens would also depend on the response of Sinhala nationalists and others opposed to devolution beyond the 13th Amendment-and indeed reformists who would prefer a much less radical foundation for a new devolution settlement – once they realize the potential implications of the judgment, which they would unequivocally regard as subversive" (Welikala 2019, pp. 141).

In this chapter, I have attempted to trace the exact historical causes that nourished the growth of separatism from the colonial period in Sri Lanka and these historical explanations given in this chapter are by no means some mere factual references as they have shown the development of the ethnic rift in Sri Lanka. The ultimate reality stems from examining the whole saga of separatism in Sri Lanka. It provides two major insights. First, it unveils how a state can reach a decadent stage by political chicanery based on ethnic politics. The examples I elucidated in this chapter while discussing the undue manners adopted by Sinhalese politicians in post-colonial Sri Lanka through Sinhalese Buddhist nationalism and how it escalated Tamil separatism as a counter reaction aptly prove the substantiality of the first insight. Second, the failure of constitutional building in Sri Lanka since 1948 stands as one pivotal factor which shows how it excluded the masses while consolidating political aspirations that eventually destabilised the society. The objectives of constitutional building were engulfed by ethnic motives as a political strategy of Sinhalese majoritarian politics and its overarching effect was repugnant to the whole nation. The mere obsession of preserving the unitary status of the Constitution under narrow interpretation has prolonged Sri Lanka's post-war constitutional development towards a pluralistic society.

References

Books

Dixith, J. N. (1998). *Colombo assignment.* New Delhi: Conrack Publishers.
Rambukwella, H. (2018). *Politics and poetics of authenticity: Cultural genealogy of Sinhala nationalism.* London: UCL Press.

Scot, D. (1999). *Refashioning futures: Criticism after Postcoloniality*. Princeton, NJ: Princeton University Press.

Weerakoon, B. (2004). *Rendering unto Caesar: Fascinating story of one man under nine prime ministers*. Colombo: Vijitha Yapa Books.

Wilson, A. J., & Delton, D. (1982). *The States of South Asia: Problems of National Integration*. Honolulu: HI Honolulu University Press.

Waha, L. T. (2018). *Religion and state formation in a transitional societies: Sri Lanka from a comparative perspective*. Oslo: Nomos Verlagsgesellschaft.

Book Chapters

Jayawickrama, N. (2013). Reflections on the making of the making and content of the 1972 Constitution. In W. Asanga (Ed.), *The Sri Lanka Republic at 40: Reflections on constitutional history, theory and practice*. Colombo: Center for Policy Alternatives.

Welikala, A. (2019). Commonwealth: The Quebec secession reference and Sri Lankan constitutional discourse. In G. Delledonne & G. Martinico (Eds.), *The Quebec secession reference and Sri Lankan constitutional Discourse*. London: Palgrave.

PhD Thesis

Welikala, Asanga. (2014). Beyond the liberal paradigm: The constitutional accommodation of national pluralism in Sri Lanka. Edinburgh University, Edinburgh.

Journal Articles

Abeyaratne, R. (2020). Uncertain sovereignty: Ceylon as a dominion 1948-1972. *Icon, 17*(14), 1256–1268.

Ankitell, N. (2017). The unitary status, parliamentary sovereignty and the sovereignty of the people. *Bar Association Law Journal, 6*(2), 20–36.

Kearney, R. (1978). Language and the rise of Tamil separatism in Sri Lanka. *Asian Survey., 18*(5), 513–530.

Lang, T. (2002). Lord Acton and the insanity of nationality. *Journal of the History of Ideas, 63*(1), 15–29.

Mainuddin, R., & Aiecher, J. (1997). Religion and self determination: A case study of Sri Lanka. *Indian Journal of International Affairs, 10*(1), 37–58.

Matthews, B. (1986). Radical conflict and the rationalization of violence in Sri Lanka. *Pacific Affairs, 59*(1), 21–35.

Nadarajah, S., & Sriskandarajah, D. (2005). Liberation struggle or terrorism? *Politics of naming the LTTE. Third World Quarterly, 26*(1), 80–99.

Peebles, P. (1990). Colonization and the ethnic conflict in the dry zones of Sri Lanka. *The Journal of Asian Studies, 49*(1), 13–39.

Rathnapalan, L. M. (2012). Memories of ethnic violence in Sri Lanka among immigrant Tamils in the UK. *Ethnic and Racial Studies, 21*(4), 22–50.

Shastri, A. (1990). The material basis for separatism: Tamil Elam movement in Sri Lanka. *The Journal of Asian Studies, 49*(1), 56–77.

Wriggins, H. (1959). Ceylon's times of troubles 1956–1958. *Far Eastern Survey, 28*(3), 19–35.

Wickramasinghe, N. (2006). Sri Lanka's conflict: Culture and linage of the past. *Journal of International Affairs, 60*(1), 103–118.

Wijeyarathne, R. d. S. (1996). Ambivalence, contingency and failure of exclusion: The ontological Schema of the 1972 constitution of republic of Sri Lanka. *Colombo Law Review, 12*(3), 89–91.

New Paper Articles

Subramanium, Aravind. (2019, November 20). Is Sri Lanka the next Argentina?. Korean Herald, 23.

Online Documents

Gilbert, Rod. (2017). Lanka Opposes Unilateral Declaration by Catalonia. https://newsin.asia/lanka-opposes-unilateral-declaration-independence-catalonia/. Accessed 26 May 2020.

Court Cases

Attorney General Vs Kodeswaran, 121, N.L.R 70 (1967).

Chandrasoma Vs Senathiraja, 81, S.C/S.P. L 3 (2017).

In Re The 13th Amendment to the Constitution, 81, S.L.R 2 (1987).

CHAPTER 15

Conclusion

Martin Belov

The contributions published in this book have demonstrated some of the 'rough edges' of contemporary territorial politics. The book's target is to challenge, reassess, and critically deconstruct some of the established concepts and paradigms of fundamental importance for constitutional and international law and related to territorial politics. Territoriality, jurisdiction, and borders are problematized in conjunction with sovereignty, self-determination, and democracy. The territorial structure of the state is explored both from within (from constitutionalist) and from outside (from international law) viewpoint.

Two main phenomena are at the centre of the discussion. These are the territorial politics and the secession. They are explored through multitude of viewpoints and analytical paradigms on the basis of both theoretical conceptualisations and comparative research. The book includes also a range of topical case studies. The book provides dissection of the problems from sub-national, national, and supranational perspective. It offers also original analysis from the viewpoint of the paradigms of transterritoriality and territorial pluralism.

M. Belov (✉)
University of Sofia 'St. Kliment Ohridski', Sofia, Bulgaria
e-mail: mbelov@uni-sofia.bg

M. Belov (ed.), *Territorial Politics and Secession*, Federalism and Internal Conflicts, https://doi.org/10.1007/978-3-030-64402-4_15

In that regard, the book offers a combination of sound theoretical research with conceptual implications, comparative constitutional law analysis, and insightful idea exchange ranging from constitutional law through public international law to the theory of international relations. Naturally, it also engages in discussions which are central to the theory of comparative federalism.

The case studies have been carefully selected providing critical assessment of current issues of territorial politics and secession in Europe, Asia, North America, and Africa. The normative and institutional research is explored within the socio-legal context. Thus, the book explores the social entrenchment of territorial politics and secession, the political factors triggering and mastering their dynamics, the socio-political outcomes they produce, but also their embeddedness in the realm of ideal, philosophical, and moral discourses.

The book tries to offer topical research of territorial politics and secession at the beginning of the twenty-first century. Nevertheless, the historical roots of territorial entrenchment of politics and the path dependency of many of the issues stemming from it are also not underestimated. The book researches territorial politics with regard to its manifestations in the past, the present, and the future. Most of the contributions explore the supranational, national, and sub-national territorial politics. Thus, the book has historical deepness, but is topical as well. It focuses on national, but also on comparative and supranational aspects. The sub-national dimension is not forgotten as well. Special chapter is devoted to sub-national constitutionalism. Sub-national issues of territorial politics and secession are explored also in other chapters focussing on particularly important cases of disintegrative territorial politics, for example, in the UK, Spain, and Italy.

The book provides for wide-ranging research of various forms of territorial politics. It offers informative account on external and internal secession, ethnocentric sub-national constitutionalism, and the role of direct democracy for self-determination. It provides novel conceptualisations of territory, territoriality, and territorial politics of devolution, regionalism, and exiting. There are also chapters devoted to international territorial dispute resolution, humanitarian intervention, and other forms of territorial politics.

Several conclusions can be drawn up from the intellectual discourses provided in this edited volume. The first one is that territory still matters. And it matters a lot. Territory is a common denominator for sub-national,

national, transnational, and supranational politics and policy-making. It is the background for staging the public law play. It is a fundamental precondition for sovereignty, self-determination, jurisdiction, and authority and is still important for legitimacy, democracy, and the rule of law.

However, the territoriality of the twenty-first century, based on human rights protection, self-determination, and global fluidity of the demos, is also a challenge to traditional territorial stereotypes entrenched in public law—constitutional and international—that has been inherited from the intellectual traditions and normative orders of the nineteenth and the twentieth centuries. Thus, we need to reconceptualise territory, territoriality, and territorial politics in order to adjust it to the socio-legal and intellectual context of the twenty-first century.

Furthermore, secession is exposed in multiple ways. It is conceptualised as both constitutional and international law phenomenon and constitutional and anti-constitutional endeavour. Secession is analysed from constitutional, comparative constitutional, and international law perspective. Not only the external but also the internal secession is researched by different contributors to this volume. Secession is explored in a range of autonomous although interrelated discourses: in the social and political practice being de facto phenomenon, in the constitutional orders, in the jurisprudence of courts, and so on. Moreover, secession is exposed as both conservative and revolutionary concept, for example, in the chapter of Margiotta, but also of Martinico.

Indeed, an original contribution of this book to the vast scientific debates on secession consists in the provision of an analysis of the integrative function of secession, which is eventually possible in certain contexts. At a first glance, such thesis seems not just contradictory, but rather absurd. Secession is typically associated with territorial disintegration and disintegrative territorial politics. However, some of the contributors to the volume, for example, Margiotta and Martinico, demonstrate how secession may serve also as conservative device at least partially and provisionally tempering more radical and revolutionary secessionist claims. The need for timely and adequate response to secessionist and disintegrative claims that could be pacified through the channels of official constitutional territorial politics is shown also by Ragone, Fessha, and Ayele. The paradox of fostering claims for integration produced by secession and exiting is clearly visible in the case of the UK where the withdrawal from the European Union (EU) is triggering both secessionist tendencies from the UK by Scotland and Northern Ireland and desires for reintegration in the

EU. Thus, secession is indeed a key tool of disintegrative territorial politics but may exceptionally serve also an integrative function in various contexts, especially if viewed from supranational or sub-national perspective.

The problems of secession lay at the core of the book. Nevertheless, many phenomena which are related to it but still possess a degree of legal and socio-political autonomy are also explored. These are the referenda for self-determination, the territorial disputes and the mechanisms for their resolution, the humanitarian intervention, and so on.

Special attention is devoted to integrative and disintegrative territorial politics. Again, disintegrative territorial politics includes secession, but is definitely not limited to it. The historical roots of territorial integration and disintegration, their constitutional foundations, implications, and reflections are demonstrated with conceptual, legal, and comparative arguments. They are exposed against the background of important case studies focusing on the UK, Canada, Italy, Spain, and many other countries experiencing challenges of territorial disintegration.

The contributors to this volume explore the path dependency, socio-legal contexts, institutional dynamics, and the political strategies of territorial politics. They devote attention to the reasoning stemming from ethnocentric, nationalist, or sovereigntist constitutionalism. The challenges to democracy and the rule of law resulting from a range of constitutional and conceptual models of territory and territoriality producing integrative and disintegrative territorial politics are critically assessed.

To sum up, the book should be conceived as an insightful reading for all who are interested in the dynamics of territorial politics and secession on the edge between constitutional and political epochs. It tries to conceptually and critically assess the impact of contemporary challenges to territorial politics in all its diversity on the fringe between Westphalian, post-Westphalian, and neo-Westphalian constitutionalism.

Index[1]

[1] Note: Page numbers followed by 'n' refer to notes.

M. Belov (ed.), *Territorial Politics and Secession*, Federalism and Internal Conflicts, https://doi.org/10.1007/978-3-030-64402-4

The manufacturer's authorised representative in the EU is Springer Nature Customer Service Centre GmbH, Europaplatz 3, 69115 Heidelberg, Germany. If you have any concerns regarding our products, please contact ProductSafety@springernature.com

Printed and bound by CPI Group (UK) Ltd, Croydon, CR0 4YY
30/09/2026
02225696-0004